GEORGE SCHÖPFLIN

Nations
Identity
Power

NEW YORK UNIVERSITY PRESS
Washington Square, New York

148298

First published in the U.S.A. in 2000 by
NEW YORK UNIVERSITY PRESS
Washington Square
New York, NY 10003

Library of Congress Cataloging-in-Publication Data
Schöpflin, George.
    Nations, identity, power / George Schöpflin.
        p.   cm.
    Includes Index.
    ISBN   0–8147–8117–9
    1. Nationalism. I. Title
JC311.S34   1999
320.54—dc21   98-24516
                                                                        CIP

Printed in Malaysia

CONTENTS

iii

ACKNOWLEDGEMENTS

Several of these chapters have been published previously, sometimes in a different form or language. My grateful thanks to all the copyright-holders for permission to republish here.

Ch. 2 appeared as 'Civil society, Ethnizität und der Staat. Eine dreiseitige Beziehung' in Emil Brix (ed.), *Civil society in Oesterreich* (Vienna: Passagen Verlag, 1998), pp. 47-63; Ch. 7 as 'A Taxonomy of Myths and their Functions' in Geoffrey Hosking and George Schöpflin (eds), *Myths and Nationhood* (London: Hurst, 1997); Ch. 9 as 'Aspects of Language and Ethnicity in Central and Eastern Europe' , *Transitions*, vol. 2, no. 24 ,(29 Nov. 1996), pp. 6-9, 64; Ch. 11 as 'Why Empires Fail' in Pál Jónás, Peter Pastor and Pál Péter Tóth (eds), *Király Béla Emlékkönyv: Háború és Társadalom, War and Society* (Budapest: private edn, 1992), pp. 255-62; Ch. 14 as 'The Rise of Anti-Democratic Movements in Post-Communist Societies' in Hugh Miall (ed.), *Redefining Europe: New Patterns of Conflict and Cooperation* (London: Frances Pinter, 1994), pp. 129-46; Ch. 15 as 'Nationhood, Communism and State Legitimation', *Nations and Nationalism*, vol. 1, pt 1 (March 1995), pp. 81-92; Ch. 16 as 'Culling Sacred Cows? State Frontiers and Stability', *Brown Journal of International Affairs*, Winter 1997; Ch. 17 is a vastly expanded version of 'Ethnische Minderheiten in Mittel-und Osteuropa: Das Verhältnis von Staat, Zivilgesellschaft und Ethnie', *Internationale Politik*, vol. 52, no. 10 (Oct. 1997), pp. 5-10; Ch. 22 as 'Jugoslavia: State Construction and State Failure' in Stefano Bianchini and George Schöpflin (eds), *State Building in the Balkans: the Dilemmas on the eve of the 21st Century* (Ravenna: Longo, 1998); Ch. 23 as 'Power, Ethnicity and Politics in Jugoslavia', *New Hungarian Quarterly*, vol. 33, no. 4, pp. 1-32; Ch. 24 'Hungary as Kin State' in Katlijn Malfliet and Ria Laenen (eds), *Minority Policy in Central and Eastern Europe: The Link between Domestic Policy, Foreign Policy and European Integration* (Louvain/Leuven: Garant, 1998), pp. 34-42; and Ch. 26 as 'Inter-Ethnic Relations in Transylvania: Rhetoric and Reality', *RFE/RL Newsline*, 8,9 September 1997.

London, May 2000   GEORGE SCHÖPFLIN

1

INTRODUCTION
THE NATURE OF THE BEAST

The study of nations, nationhood and nationalism has been one of the great growth industries of the 1980s and thereafter. Inevitably, this outpouring has produced its share of weak analysis, dubious emphases, misunderstandings, the projection of one's own agendas on to others, the failure to appreciate the complexity of culture-driven politics and just plain nonsense.

Before around 1980 – the date is notional – the field, while not exactly fallow, was hardly very inspiring. Indeed, it was almost as if academics and other communicators were united in dismissing the subject as irrelevant and marginal, as something that would disappear. 'Normal politics' were understood to be either derived from liberal individualism or class. Identity politics disturbed this happy, even tenor and introduced, to be precise reintroduced, political forces that had been thought dead and buried by the *bien pensants* or, maybe, *mal pensants*. For all practical purposes, a cognitive closure was in operation.

There was an explanation for this odd state of affairs – odd, because *prima facie*, all phenomena should be investigated. The defeat of Fascism and Nazism was widely interpreted as the defeat of nationalism as well, in other words Fascism was seen and still is in some quarters as the logical extension of nationalism, and nationalism as the logical outcome of identity politics. Better do away with it, then, was the attitude.

Paralleling this was European integration, which was driven by the terrible legacy of three Franco-German wars in barely seventy years and the determination that there should never be any repetition of them. In the process, national identities were to be reformulated in the name of a higher, European identity and the interests of the nation-state were, for a while, regarded as vaguely illicit. If nothing else, there was a kind of underlying assumption that the existing nation-states were as many as were

1

Nations, Identity, Power

needed and the idea that new ones might come into being was sternly frowned on.

The European delegitimation of identity politics was backed up by strong US pressure towards the same end. The United States tends to have great intellectual difficulty in appreciating the proposition that existing states are the product of contingent, historical events and not in any way sacrosanct, that some states are much less well founded than others. Therefore secessionist movements seldom received much sympathy, unless they could be defined as decolonialist. And decolonisation could not be applied to Europe.

The reflection of this political closure on academic enquiry was largely to ignore the entire problematic of nations, nationalism and identity politics as a relic of the past.[1] Intellectually, this marginalisation was underpinned by liberal and Marxist paradigms, neither of them well adapted to understanding the rationale of cultural reproduction. Liberalism emphasises individual imperatives, while Marxism regards economic identities as paramount. Hence the field was left untouched and the labours of individuals received scant recognition. Historians continued to chronicle the story of nationalist movements, but did not enquire too closely into the nature of nationalism itself.

For many, nationalism was a negative residual category into which everything that might vaguely be associated with the loosely defined nation could be dumped. This attitude of intellectual laziness lingers on. Here is one instance from Lee Walker:[2] 'The nation remains a highly nebulous category.' This is tantamount to saying, 'I give up, I can't define what I'm talking about.' Walker continues: 'The absence of defining characteristics [of nations] also means that the determination of who is considered to belong within the group (i.e. the definition of its boundaries) becomes largely a question of self-identification ... The existence of nation-states is similarly fictitious.' A similar instance of denial is to be found in Rogers Brubaker's *Nationalism Reframed*.[3]

[1] Walker Connor, *Ethnonationalism: the Quest for Understanding* (Princeton University Press, 1994).

[2] Leokadia Drobizheva, Rose Gottemoeller, Catherine McArdle Kelleher and Lee Walker (eds), *Ethnic Conflict in the Post-Soviet World: Case Studies and Analysis* (Armonk, NY: M.E. Sharpe, 1996), p.5.

[3] Rogers Brubaker, *Nationalism Reframed: Nationhood and the National Question*

There was, however, a sea change from the late 1970s to the early 1980s. This was the beginning of what might be called the Great Debate on nationalism. It used social science categories and duly incurred the opposition of those who resent this, and it sought to look systematically at the consistencies to be encountered in the phenomena associated with nations and nationhood.

The debate has seen basically the following divides. First, there is the one between the modernists and the perennialists. The former argue that nations, as they exist currently, are a new pheno-menon and came into being in the eighteenth century, while perennialists claim they have always existed. However, some of the modernists argue that the pre-modern roots of nations are vital in determining the shape nations assumed subsequently (this is my position).[4]

A second divide is between those who argue that the roots of the nation lie solely or overwhelmingly in ethnicity as against those who see the role of the state and citizenship as significant[5] (my position, as will emerge, is a synthesis of these views). A third divide is between those who claim that the nation was invented or imagined,[6] to which the response, roughly, is 'So what? That does not make them any the less real.' For that matter, all social phenomena are constructed, invented or imagined: class, gender, race, the lot.

A fourth disagreement is between universalists and particularists; the former tacitly or explicitly reject the particularism of national movements, while the latter insist that these should have primacy, that national identities are real and should be respected. Beyond that, a great deal has been written from the perspective of ethnic

---

in the New Europe (Cambridge University Press, 1996).

[4] Anthony Smith in his *The Ethnic Origins of Nations* (Oxford: Blackwell, 1986) and John Armstrong, *Nations before Nationalism* (Chapel Hill: University of North Carolina Press, 1982), are the best known representatives of this position.

[5] Michael Mann, *The Sources of Power: The Rise of Class and Nation-States 1760–1914* (Cambridge University Press, 1993) and his 'A Political Theory of Nationalism and its Excesses' in Sukumar Periwal (ed.), *Notions of Nationalism* (Budapest: Central European University Press, 1995), pp.44–64.

[6] Eric Hobsbawm and Terence Ranger (eds), *The Invention of Tradition* (Cambridge University Press, 1983), and Benedict Anderson, *Imagined Communities*, 2nd edn, (London: Verso, 1991). And while he might have disclaimed being in this category, Elie Kedourie's position was not too far from theirs, see his *Nationalism* (London: Hutchinson, 1960).

conflict management, of secession and irredentism, of state and sub-state nationalism, from that of identities without political consequences, boundaries and boundary markers, patterns of cohesiveness and so on. In a word, the study of nationhood and ethnicity is enjoying a boom.

In this study a variety of problems are tackled. My approach has been to pull together the different and contradictory strands of the debate and to fashion something quite new out of them. There are reflections on other problems, notably that of ethnic minorities, and, given that my area of specialisation is Central and Eastern Europe, there are attempts to look closely at the relationship between post-communism and nationhood. In particular, this study seeks to answer a number of otherwise unanswerered questions, not least:

– The problem of the relationship between nationhood and power. Much of the sociological analysis tends to underestimate the role of identity politics in the generation, legitimation and reproduction of power. Historians too often simply assume it and ignore it.

– Some of the confusion that exists could be cleared by conceptual rigour and consistent use of language. The use of 'nationalism' as a residual category is a blot on the landscape that should erased. Crucially, nationhood is an interactive set of processes involving ethnicity, the state and citizenship. All these are identity-forming. Understanding interactivity is vital; it is the only way to get at a holistic view and at the dynamism of nationhood.

– The legacy of Marxism and a kind of tacit economic determinism lingers on; this allows its protagonists to dismiss nationhood as 'irrational'. Somewhere in this corner there is a wistful feeling that if only the problem were to go away, all would be well. It won't go away. In this study, the basic, underlying assumption is that ethnically motivated behaviour is fully rational by the criterion of cultural reproduction.

– In much of the analysis there is an over-emphasis on ethnicity, which is seen as the most dangerous and destructive force in the modern world. This may be true, but doing so and omitting analysis of the presence or absence of the state and citizenship produces poor results. Further, there is a strong propensity to overlook the success stories of ethno-national conflict regulation and to look only at the pathologies. This is very misleading, though it is also much more exciting.

– Then there is a kind of residual 'Hans Kohnism', the proposition that there is a Good Western nationalism (civic, democratic, peace-loving etc.) and a Bad Eastern nationalism (nasty, brutish and anything but short). This attitude is truly lazy. It projects Western illusions and worse on to Central and Eastern Europe and, incidentally, gives rise to very poor political analysis, to the effect that if only these benighted Easterners could be shown the error of their ways, they would rapidly become Jeffersonian democrats. The reality is much deeper, more complex, more subtle and if there is an 'Eastern' nationalism, there are perfectly good reasons for this evolution, not merely the cussedness of people who speak – insist on speaking – obscure and unpronounceable languages.

– The public discussion reflects this 'Hans Kohnism' by the use of its vocabulary. The word 'tribal' is pure dismissal, given its connotations of primitive, backward collectivities that have yet to be civilised by the West. Indeed, if a writer uses the word, we can be quite secure in the knowledge that what follows is likely to be charged with a lack of understanding. 'Ethnic' is heading in the same direction. In the United Kingdom it has been reserved for non-whites, as if Scots or Irish living in England did not have an ethnic identity. By reserving it in this way, one is obscuring the proposition that the so-called large civic nations of the West, the positive examples in Hans Kohn's dichotomy, also have ethnic identities; it is just that these are framed by the state and citizenship (civil society).

– There is a paradox in the rise of identity politics all the same. Traditionally, at least in the first six or seven decades of the twentieth century, basing political demands on identity was associated with the political right. The left based its political demands on individualism or class, both ultimately derived from the universalist message of the Enlightenment, that all citizens, regardless of their origins, should enjoy the equal rights of citizenship. In the 1960s or thereabouts this began to change. Not least as a response to non-European migration into Europe and the real and perceived discrimination suffered by migrants, the left took on their cause and began to insist on identity-based rights. The problem for the left, still unresolved, was that of consistency. If migrants should be accorded rights on the basis of their identity, then why not non-migrants? In effect, the problem is papered over; autochthonous, long-established ethnic groups are increasingly recognised as political actors, but only when they are members of a minority. As members of a majority, they are the ones who should grant rights to minorities. Ironically, the far-right has in some cases adopted the cause of ethnic majorities, as in France. The left dismisses this as 'racism' and 'fascism', two terms that are increasingly emptied of meaning through over-use and inconsistency. There is a distinct possibility that the left will discover that it has been supping with the devil and that its embrace of identity politics will leave it open to capture by its enemies.

A holistic analysis allows one to theorise simultaneously about Western and Central and Eastern Europe (I claim no expertise about the rest of the world) with a degree of validity. If the analysis that follows is persuasive, then we can be several steps closer to understanding the mechanisms by which identity politics operates, and by which nations respond, the nature of collective meanings and emotions, and to being able to construct policies that will address the real problem rather than the one to which we happen to have a solution.

Therefore, what is new in this book is the following:

– There is a synthesis of the different approaches to the origins of nationhood in my argument that both ethnic origins *and* state construction played a role in the rise of the modern nation-state. In this context, the rising level of consent to be ruled demanded a deeper grounding of the exercise of power than allowed for in the civic contract. Hence to gain proper access to the functioning of the modern nation-state, we have to examine how the civic and ethnic dimensions operate on one another. Thus, without ethnicity, it is argued, it is difficult to secure democracy. Some people will probably be scandalised by this proposition.

– This has led to a radically new formulation of the nature of the modern nation-state. I argue that it should be understood as the dynamic interaction of ethnicity, citizenship and the state, all three being identity-forming processes and sources of power. The implication is that Western states, far from having 'left ethnicity behind', as it were, have in reality done something else – they have contextualised it, they have successfully hemmed it in by constructing state machineries and civil societies that ensure that ethnicity is not the sole source of political power (a state of affairs that does indeed give rise to the evils associated with ethnicity). Thus it is not ethnicity that is the problem, but the absence of other processes that dilute its impact on power.

– It follows, therefore, that the West too has ethnicity, so the question to ask is how Western democracy has contained it. Framed this way, there are lessons to be learned and transmitted to other parts of the world that are grappling with the creation of democracy, multi-ethnicity and consensual rule.

– Then, my analysis relies on a number of analytical categories and concepts taken from various of the social sciences. The first of these is that all societies place received ideas into the implicit sphere, so that certain propositions are seen as 'normal and natural' or 'common sense', ideas that are not questioned. This is Bourdieu's '*doxa*' and Mary Douglas's 'implicit meanings' applied to political power.[7]

– The second concept is sacralisation, that to ensure that these implicit meanings are not questioned, we place them beyond question by making them sacred or taboo. If they were questioned, the society would either shift its sacralised sphere somewhere else or it would fragment. The essential foundations of a society cannot be left open to investigation by Enlightenment rationality.[8]

– The third concept is cultural reproduction. I argue that the purposiveness of all institutions is that they survive, that they ensure that whatever else happens, they remain intact and retain their basic elements untouched. Applied to ethno-national communities, the concept of cultural reproduction explains why ethnicity has persisted, is persisting and is likely to persist, despite its having been repeatedly dismissed as 'irrational'.

– The fourth concept is that of thought-worlds, each giving rise to a thought-style.[9] Particular cultures generate particular ways of doing things, particular forms of expression, of resolving problems and ensuring their cultural reproduction. Communication between one thought-world and another is possible, but more difficult than Enlightenment rationality would lead us to believe. Crucially, Anglo-Saxon thought-styles are alive and well and are resisted by other cultures; this does not mean the other cultures are

---

[7] Pierre Bourdieu, *The Field of Cultural Production* (Cambridge: Polity, 1993); Mary Douglas, *Implicit Meanings* (London: Routledge, 1975).

[8] This proposition draws on Thomas Kuhn, *The Structure of Scientific Revolutions* (University of Chicago Press, 1962); Mircea Eliade, *The Myth of the Eternal Return: Cosmos and History* (London: Penguin, 1954); Elemer Hankiss, *Az emberi kaland: egy civilizació-elmélet vázlata* (Budapest: Helikon, 1997); and Mary Douglas, *Implicit Meanings* (London: Routledge, 1975).

[9] Mary Douglas, *How Institutions Think* (Syracuse University Press, 1986).

'backward' and 'obstinate', because 'progress' and 'rationality' are not – in my view – an Anglo-Saxon monopoly.

– The fifth element is the proposition that we live not only in a concrete and palpable world of institutions and procedures, but also of symbols and rituals.[10] Our sense of security in the world, our identity – both individual and collective – depend on the coherence of symbolic and concrete factors. In politics, where a group is threatened as to its cultural reproduction and lacks access to institutional power, it will seek to compensate for this by emphasising its symbolic articulation and presence. This also points towards the vital importance of creating coherence in the world, both at the individual and at the collective level. That which is seen as disturbing that coherence is either screened out or eliminated.[11] Hence it is very difficult to live with the kind of difference that disturbs coherence, whatever democratic theory may say to the contrary.

– Finally, there is the problem of 'false consciousness'. Traditionally, this concept was used by Marxists to characterise attitudes and behaviour that they regarded as 'irrational' by the criteria of economic rationality. My argument is that liberalism also has its moments of relying on 'false consciousness' and the imposition of cognitive closures, and that reliance on these makes it hard to understand the behaviour of others. I argue that Western antagonism, particularly Western of the Anglo-Saxon persuasion, towards the rationality of ethnic cultural reproduction makes a range of analysis of Central and Eastern Europe rather weak and, simultaneously, feeds a certain attitude that is best described as 'Anglo-Saxon universalist'. This is a contradiction in terms, of course, but the paradox is used to underline the proposition that universalism has its particularisms too and that cognitive closures, often very difficult to penetrate because they are encoded in *doxa*, give rise to false consciousness. I recognise that in stressing my critique of Anglo-Saxon attitudes, I am privileging my own *doxa* and making my own hidden agendas a little less hidden.

[10]   Hankiss, *op.cit.*; Geoffrey Hosking, and George Schöpflin, *Myths and Nationhood* (London: Hurst, 1997).

[11]   Bruce Kapferer, *Legends of People, Myths of State* (Washington, DC: Smithsonian Institute Press, 1987).

Part I. WHAT IS THE NATION?

2

REASON, IDENTITY AND POWER

Among the great debates in Europe since the eighteenth century has been whether to organise power on the basis of reason or of identity.[1] This debate continues, indeed, it cannot be settled. It affects us in virtually every sphere of our lives and has far-reaching consequences for bread-and-butter issues, like citizenship and the entitlement to welfare that derives from it. The evolution of European citizenship as a legal, political, economic, cultural or social concept and of a European identity are both parts of the debate and underpin this entitlement.

There are various standpoints in this debate. There are those who contest the very idea of identity politics or try to reduce it to a minimum.[2] They would prefer that rights be derived wholly from function and reason. Then, there are those who like some identities but not others. Ranged against them, as it were, are the identity politicians, who insist that all problems are derived from identity and should be solved by the criteria of identity. Then, there are yet other aspects of the debate: the nature and patterns of Western and post-communist Europe, how they differ in their responses to politics, how much weight they give identity and how much weight they think they give.

The argument to be put forward here is that ultimately the opposition between reason and identity is a false one. They are

[1] Ernest Gellner, *Reason and Culture: the Historic Role of Rationality and Rationalism* (Oxford: Blackwell, 1992).

[2] Michael Ignatieff can be taken as a representative of this line of thinking. See his *Blood and Belonging: Journeys into the New Nationalism* (London: Verso, 1994) and 'Who are we now?', *Prospect* no. 29 (April 1998), pp.18-23.

9

conceptually different, of course, and have to be distinguished. But both are authentic, and one will not triumph over the other; indeed each needs the other. What follows, therefore, is a synthesis, an attempt to see how reason and identity are in a dynamic relationship, how they sustain and energise one another and how they exist in complex interdependence.

In essence, recourse to reason provides clarity in understanding action, consistency, accountability, predictability, the ability to question motives and place them in a frame of reference. Identity, as against this, offers individuals the security of community and solidarity, of shared patterns of meanings, a bounded world in which to live and in which one can find others like oneself. Power operates in both these spheres. The exclusion of either reason or identity creates unease. Without reason, there is a real danger that power will be arbitrary, generate disorder and create fear. But relying solely on reason and denying identity leaves individuals isolated and open to the suspicion of lacking a moral dimension. Equally, when all action, all motivation, is ascribed to identity, the outcome is a massive reductionism, a denial of the individual and choice. The answer has to be in the synthesis of the two.

This perspective runs counter to much of the current debate on identity. There is a very strong tendency to see reason and identity as mutually exclusive and to blame identity for many of the ills of the world – ethnic cleansing being only one of them. Indeed, there is a particular variant of Anglo-Saxon thinking which argues that identity politics is, simply, irrational, that once people return to their 'true' interests, they will drop their identity-driven claims and recognise a universalist rationality.

The intellectual origin of this form of rationalist argument has several strands. One is clearly the Enlightenment proposition that all claims, all forms of power, all sources of privilege should be subjected to scrutiny. The world is driven by cognitive growth. Crucially, nothing is sacred, nothing can escape investigation by the paramount intellectual tool of reasoned argument. Liberalism's assertion that individuals are sovereign and responsible for their own destinies, is closely related. By stressing the sovereignty of the individual, the underlying assumption of liberalism is severely critical of the demands of collective identities. Marxism added another strand in its claim that there was a single prime cause, a single primary identity, in the form of the individual's economic interests. All legitimate collective identities were to be derived from this, and any other identity was to be dismissed as 'false consciousness'. These attitudes and approaches remain influential and function often enough as a tacit assumption.

'False consciousness'

Indeed, there is an argument to be made that 'false consciousness' was a highly damaging concept that made a material contribution to the demise of Marxism. Liberalism runs an analogous danger with its overfree use of 'irrational' and 'tribal' in characterising those identity-political demands that its proponents disapprove of, particularly in journalistic discourse. At the theoretical level, the problem with these categories is that they allow those who use them simply to side-step the issue. 'False consciousness' is not only an intellectual escape-hatch, but it also blocks any serious thinking about the subject. It helps to explain why Marxism never developed any serious, sociologically persuasive theory of nationhood: it never needed to. It had merely to label ethnicity and national sentiments as 'false consciousness' and the problem was solved. At the political level, because it was dubbed 'false', it could be dealt with by coercion. Predictably, when coercion failed with the loss of self-legitimation, communist leaders were left intellectually naked. This was undoubtedly a key aspect of the failure of the Soviet Union and played a role in Yugoslavia too. Aphoristically, the difference between Milošević and Gor-bachev was that the former understood nationalism and the latter did not.

This inherent weakness in the Marxist tradition affected all its protagonists. Lenin, who established the cultural infrastructure of many if not most of the Russian and Soviet ethnic groups, did so because he was firmly convinced that ethnic identities were epiphenomenal, that they would dissolve in the 'superiority' of economic development and, if that did not work, they would be forced to do so. The marginalisation and ultimate execution of Sultan Galiev, who sought to combine Marxism and non-Russian nationalism, illustrate this vividly: he was purged in 1923, during Lenin's lifetime, and executed under Stalin.[3] Even Austro-Marxism,

---

[3] Alexandre Bennigsen and S. Enders Wimbush, *Muslim National Communism in the Soviet Union* (University of Chicago Press, 1979).

the most open-minded strand of Marxism with respect to ethnicity, never evolved any underlying, theoretically coherent and satisfactory account of the phenomena for which Bauer and Renner offered their practical solution. It was assumed that economic identities would transcend cultural ones and that if cultural arrangements were adequate, they would not become the basis for political demands.[4]

In liberal universalism, 'irrational' is something of a functional equivalent. It constitutes a category that demands, by perfectly circular logic, no further investigation because it is irrational. In effect, this is a cognitive closure that screens out the need for further investigation – flying in the face of cognitive growth – and carries risks for policy makers, because when faced with identity politics, they will lack the preparedness to cope with its imperatives. Non-exchanges of this kind were in evidence during the negotiations that accompanied the wars of Yugoslav succession.

The hegemony of rationality

To return to the assessment of philosophical currents underlying the paramountcy to rationality: its position was strengthened by the contingent, historical events of the twentieth century. The defeat of Nazism and Fascism and the launching of European integration that followed amounted to a rigorous screening out of the claims of identities. Nazism was for many the necessary and automatic consequence of identity politics – ethnicity leads to nationalism, nationalism leads to Nazism – and its defeat was received with intense and understandable relief. The Jean Monnet paradigm, to create institutions that would transcend the identities of European nations and thereby make further war in Europe impossible, was conceived as a direct response. In the background, the Cold War ensured that Western Europe sustained a very high level of unity, while Central and Eastern Europe under Soviet occupation and communism experienced an analogous situation.

Another source for the belief that rationality was permanently in the ascendant was the role of the state, which in the West appeared to function well. The welfare-state paradigm successfully

[4] Tom Bottomore and Patrick Goode (eds), *Austro-Marxism* (Oxford University Press, 1978).

resolved problems of poverty and need that had blighted the interwar years. In a very real sense, although this was seldom argued in these terms, the role of the state had ceased to be an issue of conflict between left and right in the West, where étatism was accepted as beyond question by both. This implicitly confirmed the state as the ultimate repository of rationality, albeit not to the exclusion of society, and strengthened the belief that rationality had triumphed. The supremacy of the state went unquestioned until the 1980s, although the challenge of the 1960s culminating in 1968 hinged to some extent on the relationship between society and the state. In this very stable order, collective identities had no serious, explicit role to play.

Internationally, conflicts over identity were avoided by a shared state discourse of rationality. When conflict did take place, this could be resolved by rational discussion into which 'irrational' questions of identity did not enter. By screening out identity as a factor in politics, West European identities did come to resemble one another and this was, and remains, one of the keystones of European integration.

All this created an illusory order to the effect that identity as a source of political power and, in particular, nationalist politics were something of the past, at any rate as far as Europe was concerned. The belief was that by and large the age of reason had come and that identity, other than as a benign sense of cultural expression, was no longer important. Fukuyama's thesis of the 'end of history' was not much more than a polemical distillation of this set of assumptions. In this mindset, Northern Ireland, the Basque country or Corsica were simply temporary anomalies.

Consequently the apparently sudden rise of ethno-nationalism in various parts of Europe after 1989 was unexpected and profoundly unwelcome. Elites and public opinion alike lacked the cognitive tools to know how to respond. Various theories, mostly assumptions, prejudices and illusions, were revived to account for this seemingly inexplicable throw-back to a world that Western Europe had largely thought buried. The misuse of history, particularly when marshalled as a convenient ideological narrative absolving the West and blaming Central and Eastern Europe, was standard, for example, the proposition that Central and East Europeans were always (biologically?) 'tribal' and, by implication, always would be. This was pseudo-history with a vengeance and it cast the Western identity in a rather unfavourable light, as unable to cope with the challenges that had surfaced with the collapse of communism.

Since 1989, therefore, the West has had to face an unprecedented challenge, one without blueprints: to deal simultaneously with pressure for the reintegration of Europe from Central and Eastern Europe, and for the redistribution of power at home. The tenets of 1945-89 upon which a very stable order had been built have eroded and the existing distribution of power has come into question as the pressure to widen democracy through 'empowerment' has gathered strength. The situation demands a new balance between rationality and identity, and the 1990s have become far more fluid as a result.

The complex of issues has been further bedevilled by an unexpected consequence of the collapse of communism. While communism was evidently a system shot through with contradictions – and these eventually brought about its demise – Marxism-Leninism, in common with liberalism, claimed to be a legatee of the Enlightenment. In this sense, the contest between communism and Western democracy sustained the hegemonic claims of rationality over identity. Neither liberalism nor Marxism offered any consistent explanation for why collective identities continued to exist and to feed into politics. They preferred to dismiss the phenomenon. Correspondingly, the end of communism has weakened rationality as such, with far-reaching consequences for the West. The rise of identity politics demands a new approach to the problem of rationality, as well as of identity. The European identity has to be reconfigured.

The post-communist undertaking

In Central and Eastern Europe, the problem is analogous, though the route and antecedents are different. The hyper-étatist communist system tried to wipe out all other rationalities. It largely succeeded with civil society, but could not make serious inroads into ethnicity. But the vesting of all rationality in the state had an unexpected result: the collapse of communism also meant the collapse of the communist state.

Hence Central and Eastern Europe is at a very different starting point from the West. It has to reconstruct the state as an accountable state; it must make provision for the emergence of civil society;

and it must find some way of maintaining the necessary degree of coherence while these are happening. Inevitably, ethnicity, the preeminent available identity with access to the public sphere, has found itself pitched into the foreground and required to fulfil roles that it cannot discharge, such as providing the criteria for citizenship; hence ethnicisation. In this context, Central and Eastern Europe needs Europe and a European identity to foster coherence and stability, and to offer usable materials for the reestablishment of civic identities.

It should be clear enough from the foregoing that to make sense of the problematic of a European identity in the run-up to the millennium, identity itself must be scrutinised. The post-1989 transformation requires that this be undertaken with the maximum of care. In a very real sense, the term 'identity politics' is a misnomer, because it implies that there is such a thing as 'non-identity politics'. This is nonsense, of course, because it further implies that there are political actors without identities. We all have identities and these influence how we engage in politics. The distinction between reason and identity refers more to what (some) people regard as desirable politics.

Everyone, then, has identities, ways of responding to the communities that they create and in which they live. It is impossible to imagine politics without communities and, indeed, human beings without communities are universally recognised as not the same as those who belong. This is the drama of ostracism, of exile, of isolation, of hermitry, of marginalisation. Individuals may undergo it, suffering greater or lesser trauma, but when a community faces loss of identity, it reacts to the prospect very badly. The outcome is anomie, disruption, loss of meanings. In fact, communities will do anything to prevent disruption from coming about; on the contrary, a significant aspect of communities is that they are engaged in a continuous process of cultural reproduction. Cultural reproduction, then, establishes its own rationality. This, one might say, is where identity politics begins.

Cultural reproduction

The key aspect of cultural reproduction for our purposes is that it establishes the means by which communities seek to keep themselves in being. Here, it is important to understand that despite the claims of Enlightenment rationality that all things are subject to cognitive growth and may be scrutinised, in fact at all times collectivities try to ensure that their existence is not questioned. Certain areas of life, certain processes, certain phenomena are simply coded as 'normal and natural', as doxic in Bourdieu's language, and we do not question them. This is the everyday reality by which we make sense of the world, the common sense so beloved of Anglo-Saxon thought-styles. And this is the sense in which identity permeates all aspects of what we do, such that we can no more place ourselves outside of identity politics than we can fly under our own power.

The implications of this proposition are far-reaching, because they undermine certain favoured Western presuppositions and, equally, damage key assumptions that are current in the post-communist world. For the West, the proposition that there are 'good' and 'bad' identity politics is standard; gender, race, and the ethnic identities of migrants are good, everything else is bad or uncivilised or tribal. For Central and Eastern Europe, the proposition that ethnic identities are contextual and not essential, that they are constructed rather than inherent, is frequently unacceptable. Living as they do in a universe of fixed epistemologies, the certainties of ethnicity are seen as unassailable and unbargainable. And these certainties will remain until the state and civil society are cohesive enough to provide the necessary order to permit ethnicity to be diluted. The suggestion made here that *all* identities (gender, migrant ethnicity, race etc.) are in many ways alike flies in the face of much of current Western and democratic thinking, particularly on the left.

Identities and the left

This demands a small detour. The left has traditionally seen itself as the most salient defender of Enlightenment rationality. It has a tradition that is steeped in the universalism of class: regardless of 'nation', all those who labour are alike. Class and economic activity are somehow more universal than any other attribute, rather than being contingent on the economic history of the nineteenth century (as we tend increasingly to see it).

This was the left-wing tradition of both Social Democracy and of communism, though both would make occasional (accelerating?) concessions to non-economic identities. In reality, this was un-avoidable; in the light of this present analysis, identities and rationality live in a dynamic, reciprocal relationship. However, in the 1960s and 1970s, the Western left took a fateful turn. Instead of remaining with economic identity as the central axis of what it meant to be on the left, it accepted that some other identities were now to be considered as a part of the left-wing project: gender, feminism, race (migrant ethnicity) in the first place. Environmentalism was also integrated to some extent, though the relationship between the left and the Greens was always a somewhat uneasy one. At the outer fringes of environmentalism, animal 'rights' were far less easy to coopt, though the movement was capable of generating considerable energies.

This alliance was essentially structured around a single overriding proposition, to the effect that capitalism could not provide the social justice that continued to exclude various groups from proper access to power. It took a while for the traditional left to recognise – many have still to do so – that economic identities were bound to decline in significance once prosperity had become the norm for, say, four-fifths of the population. Further, the revolutionary shift in working patterns away from manual labour, the decline in manufacturing and the corresponding rise in services were bound to change the economic identities on which the left traditionally depended. The economic identities and political weight of the remaining poor and unskilled were too weak to serve as the basis for maintaining the traditional politics of economic identity.

This is not to suggest that economic identities are wholly uninfluential. They can and do have influence, particularly within bounded cultural communities and, more rarely, across cultural boundaries. The market, for example, does tend to homogenise lifestyles and create broadly similar leisure activities, tastes, dress codes and so on, regardless of ethnicity. Industrial working did much the same *mutatis mutandis* in Marx's time.

What economic identities seem incapable of doing, however, is to transcend the boundaries that they create. An economic boundary remains just that, an economic boundary. It is influenced by economic impulses and calculation and precisely because it is transparent, even quantifiable, it has only limited symbolic resonance. The loyalties of economic identities are too exposed to rationality to be able withstand the impact of major change. Thus it was always a complaint of the traditional left that once a proletarian had improved his economic status, he would desert his antecedents. Of course he would, he was behaving rationally.

Deeper levels of loyalty are structured by something other than supply and demand. The imperatives of the cultural community become paramount. The symbolic sphere created by that community is dominant and the imperatives of an economic identity stay restricted to economic activities. Hence looking at lifestyles, fashions or working practices and concluding that the world is becoming very similar is a mistake, made both by the traditional left and by extreme nationalists, albeit on very different grounds. In reality, economic identities are surprisingly weak in governing non-economic identities. It is only in a few special circumstances that economic identities can affect identities beyond economic activities. When prosperity is relatively evenly spread as between two or more ethnic communities living in a single state, this removes economic grievances from the range of potentially troubling issues in inter-ethnic relations. Thus economic identities are no more than a helpful condition in settling inter-ethnic friction.

As far as the new coalition was concerned, it argued that those excluded from power should be given access to it precisely because they were denied power by reason of their identities. Although this switch was hardly noticed at the time, it marked a significant moment in extending the agenda of the left from primarily economic to certain non-economic identities. In effect, this was tantamount to saying that the satisfaction of economic identities was no longer to be regarded as meeting the demands of social justice, an analysis that was perfectly correct as far as it went.

What is striking about all these 'new' identities is that they claim, implicitly or explicitly, universal applicability. The protagonists of gender and race as identities insist not only that theirs is the sole identity from which values should be derived, but that these are the values – and thus the identities – by which all societies must be organised. The proposition that they may in reality be derived from the contingent circumstances of the developed West is rejected as mischievous. This claim to universal applicability is probably explained by the origins of these new political identities. They were defined against the universalism of the seemingly hegemonic contest between socialism and capitalism, both claiming universal applicability themselves. In order to make inroads into the power of the hegemons, it was necessary to define oneself similarly as universal. Ethnicity does not do this in making its claim to power. Its claim is restricted to a particular community, but it generally does accept that all ethnic communities have legitimacy.

Whatever the rightfulness or otherwise of this move from economic to broader identities, it had the unintended consequence of returning the question of identity politics to the political agenda and doing so not from the right, where it had traditionally been, but from the left. The problem was that the left, broadly speaking, sought to delimit what were acceptable identities and what were not, but politics does not work that way and once non-economic identities were back in the political mainstream, various other claims came to be made in the name of identity that were unwelcome from the left-wing perspective. Ethnicity not only referred to the sanctioned constituency (Third World migrants in the West), but also to the ethnic identities of the long-settled Europeans. With this development, ethnicity came to acquire a saliency that it had not had since 1945.

The noteworthy feature of non-migrant ethnic politics in Western Europe was that the democratic state tolerated it grudgingly, and sought to marginalise it as far as it could. The ethnic revivals of the 1960s and 1970s (Scotland, Catalonia, South Tyrol, but also the less politically significant movements, like that of Brittany) were dealt with as 'protest' movements that could be satisfied with economic concessions and a few cultural provisions, like support for the local languages. Each case was dealt with as a single instance rather than as part of a pattern, and collective rights were firmly rejected as a solution. Underlying this approach was the assumption that with such concessions these movements would fade away.

Assimilation

There is a particular perspective through which much of identity politics in the twentieth century can be understood, that of assimilation. Before modernity, assimilation was an occasional fact without much political significance and was hardly a mass phenomenon, given low levels of migration. The assimilation of the Huguenots, a good pre-modern example, by English and Prussian society was a slow, three-generation affair; the relics are still there in the French surnames. The great bulk of the population lived in an unchanging, static condition, in which ethnic identity could

occasionally be the source of conflict, but as it was not regarded
as the primary basis of political power, it did not give rise to
deep cleavages. Rulers did not mobilise their peoples by calling
upon them as members of an ethnic nation.

This is the state of affairs to which some contemporary commentators appeal as a golden age, when members of different
ethnic groups lived peacefully side by side and their world was
not disturbed by the evils of politicised ethnicity. We can leave
the accuracy of this picture to one side and we can also pass
over the uses and abuses of history involved. Rather, we should
ask what was different, why ethnicity was not a serious political
problem before the coming of modernity and, therefore, why
assimilation was not an issue. The central change was in the
nature of the state and its growing rationalising capacity, which
then required higher inputs of consent, and consent was most
effectively generated via ethnicity. Consequently, states actively
promoted assimilation as an instrument of stabilisation.

Thus, for much of the period of nationalism, from the French
Revolution to the aftermath of the Second World War, assimilation
was widespread, accepted and regarded as praiseworthy. It was
the latent face of modernisation. It was espoused by the liberal
and socialist left alike. Assimilation meant an exchange. Broadly
speaking, it proposed that in exchange for access to citizenship,
the rural population abandon whatever its rural and thus non-
political (ethnic, social, economic) identities were and acquire
another, political identity, thereby gaining access to high culture,
a higher standard of living, and generally superior life chances.
In the majority of cases, of course, there was no serious ethnic
boundary to cross.

Urban and thus civic identities, the models for assimilation,
had already been constructed by the dominant majority, and those
who could be considered as being of the same language group
philologically moved relatively smoothly into the same political
language group.[5] The implication of this was that rural identities
were to be wholly, and largely voluntarily, abandoned in exchange
for the benefits of political and economic modernity. This applied
even when seemingly there was no ethno-philological boundary
to cross. Rural Frenchmen or Italians, for example, in reality had

<hr>

[5] John Armstrong, *Nations before Nationalism* (Chapel Hill: University of North
Carolina Press, 1982).

often to learn a new language or at any rate a fairly remote variant of their rural speech.

One of the central motifs of the trauma of modernisation is that the accumulated knowledge that is encoded in the rural way of life is not just useless in the city, but positively misleading. The peasant arrives with a set of expectations conditioned by the rural thought-world of his upbringing and has to learn an entirely new set of skills, which may include a philologically different high cultural language, and simultaneously shed what he has learned so far. It is a singularly cruel process, because it makes him doubt his human essence.

The new standard languages of high culture were far more complex and, vitally, more suited to dealing with the demands of modernity than the dialects. Without such a language, an ethnic group could not claim equal status among nations. Modernisation necessitated the elaboration and acceptance of a modern language by the population. Rural dialects had restricted political vocabularies and were not equipped to deal with the requirements of modernity. Similarly, they lacked the cognitive capacity that the command of a high cultural standard conferred. The acquisition of a new language and a new way of life added up to an assimilation through the acquisition of a new identity. In this sense, upward social mobility constituted assimilation.

The passage from rural to urban was somewhat more complex and culturally more stressful when the high cultural standard had no philological connection with the rural speech. This shift is what is usually meant when assimilation is discussed. Until the 1960s this kind of assimilation was far more common and widespread than is understood today, at a time when assimilation is increasingly severely frowned on by the proponents of multiculturalism. But such disapproval is not enough to explain the decline, though not the absolute disappearance, of assimilation. Another factor was at work, namely the rising consciousness of belonging to an ethnic group even in rural areas as the twentieth century wore on. Modernity and war, the two together sometimes, had a far-reaching impact on the entire population of Europe, and after the Second World War it was hard to find groups without some kind of an ethnic consciousness and, coupled with that, an awareness that ethnicity had a certain connection to political power. If nothing else, the twentieth century has been an era of vast deruralisation. There were rare exceptions, like some of the rural population of Ukraine and Belarus, which continued to define itself primarily by religious identification.

The implication of the foregoing is that assimilation was rejected in the 1960s because of a realisation that assimilation was finished. There was no rural population in Europe to be assimilated. And this rejection was then simply projected onto all outsiders and incomers, all 'others', to the effect that they should all keep their 'otherness' and be happy with the idea. The shift, it should be added, represented an intellectual sliding by the left from its traditional attitudes, a somewhat surprising move at first sight, but logical given the tacit abandonment of its privileging of economic identities and as a response to the new sociological reality of large-scale Third World immigration. The non-whites who migrated to Europe were invariably identified as such and their socio-economic status was ignored. They were expected to integrate as fully-fledged citizens, and the provision that was made for them was hardly adequate, given that they were peasants, that they were moving from pre-modern rural areas to ultra-modern urban ones and that they had not magically shed their rural value systems by virtue of travelling from one continent to another.

Much trouble could have been avoided had the migrants' identity not been subjected to this reductionist definition. In practice, the migrants were constrained into a Procrustean bed of assimilation, but not an ethnic one. They were required to absorb civic and etatic identities in a very short space of time and the resulting traumas and dysfunctions were simply ascribed to the racism of the majority. This racism certainly existed, but it was not the sole factor involved.

Looking more deeply at this process, it would seem that there is an unexplored relationship between the espousal of identity politics by the left and assimilation. As suggested, historically the left had regarded ethnic, not to mention civic, assimilation, as desirable and progressive. Correspondingly, it held the ethnic identities of newly modernising groups (in Europe) in low esteem, an attitude that has yet to disappear. The use of words like 'tribal' and 'Balkanisation' to characterise unapproved ethnicity is just such a relic. No one would dream of calling the ethnic identities of Third World migrants 'tribal'. Thus, after the 1960s, the view of assimilation changed and overnight it became reactionary. The shift coincided with the arrival of sizeable numbers of non-white migrants in Western Europe and the deeper question addresses the precise link between these two processes.

Certainly, as far as the left was concerned, the identities of Third World migrants in the West were to be seen as positive and the preservation of these identities as its historic task through the formula of multiculturalism, even while the agenda of assimilation became a right-wing affair. But the problem is deeper and more painful. By rejecting the possibility of assimilation as an option for non-European migrants, the left has in effect arrived at the uncomfortable position of denying that non-whites could assimilate at all. By developing the project of multiculturalism, the left has for all practical purposes ended up saying that non-whites were unassimilable and denying them that option.

In reality, as is clear from the foregoing, assimilation is a far more complex process than the project of multiculturalism appears to assume. Historically, assimilation demanded that in exchange for the benefits of citizenship, the individual abandon his or her rural identity. Currently, rural migrants from outside Europe are encouraged to sustain their ethnic identities, even while their acculturation into the civic and étatic modes of European modernity is not helped by the forms of knowledge encoded in the ethnic identities that they bring with them. The match between the two is a poor one.

The fate of intra-European migrants is subtly different, however. It should be evident that assimilation of any kind implies a journey, a real and symbolic leaving of the bonds of solidarity of the countryside. Thus the acculturation of European migrants would seem to require further analysis. For the most part, they have already acquired a political and cultural consciousness. They have already been touched or reshaped by modernity. They generally speak languages with high cultural content and these languages have recognised moral worth. Do they, then, assimilate or remain as an unassimilated body within the ethnically different majority? The answer varies according to a number of factors. First, there is the size of the migrant group; when this reaches a critical mass, their assimilation is slowed down or even blocked. Second is the question of the circumstances of departure; when they have left as emigrants, never intending to return, whether the motive be political or economic, their assimilation is faster and easier. They seem determined to shed as much of the old as they can; here the exchange principle seems preeminent. When their departure is a going into exile, they are more likely to retain an attachment to the culture they have brought with them and to transmit it to the next generation. Thirdly, much depends on the host culture, its openness to immigrants and the terms of assimilation. In some cultures, openness is high and the terms are generous; in others, this is less evident. Where the terms of assimilation are difficult, the process itself will be slower.

Currently, most West European states and societies have come to act as hosts to European migrants and have the dilemma of formulating a two-track, somewhat contradictory policy towards the identities of incomers and the majority. The dominant approach seems to be to pretend that there is no difficulty or in so far as there is, to attribute it to the xenophobia of small groups. The migrants are seen as wholly reactive in this respect and, accordingly, take no initiatives, are passive and have no views as to assimilation or non-assimilation. European migrants, however, are discouraged from claiming the status of 'ethnic group' and are assumed either to be in the process of assimilating to the majority or sustaining their own culture. Again, the tacit understanding is that they can assimilate, an option not open to non-whites.

Within this broad framework, there are many variants. At one end of the spectrum is France, which pursues a policy that looks like civic acculturation, but because the French civic identity is so thoroughgoingly Gallicised, it amounts to assimilation. France, therefore, rejects multiculturalism and claims that there is no need for it. In a very real sense, the strength of the French far-right is a response to the failure of this policy with sizeable groups of Muslim migrants who have attained a critical mass and are looking to transmit their culture to the next generation.

Britain, the Netherlands and Scandinavia follow various types of multicultural policies, with varying success. One of the unstated conditions of success, it would seem, is that new immigration should be slowed down to a trickle.[6] Bad relations with migrants are made worse when the majority fears that the process is open-ended. It may be too soon to assess the full story of multiculturalism, but there are some indications that in Britain a process of accul-turation is taking place that will come to be seen as the preliminary stage to assimilation, that the second generation of migrants is

[6] Ignatieff, 'Who Are We Now', *op. cit.*

fully assimilated in speech and habits and only difference in physiognomy keeps them separate, and not all that separate, from the majority. The implication of this proposition, if accurate, is that in a relatively short time the concepts of race and multiculturalism will actually impede further integration.

Germany receives a good deal of negative publicity about its inter-ethnic strategy. There is explicit dislike of its policy of giving automatic German citizenship to – as it is put – all ethnic Germans. Correspondingly, there is a widespread view that (all?) non-German immigrants are subjected to racial discrimination, because of Germany's adherence to *ius sanguinis* as the basis for citizenship.[7] This view is simplistic and misleading. In the first place, it is not correct that everyone of German descent is automatically entitled to German citizenship. Those who migrated to states that came to be ruled by communism are so entitled; those who migrated elsewhere are not. Thus Germans from, say, Brazil, who left Germany at much the same time as the Volga Germans, are not covered by *ius sanguinis*, which means, of course, that it is not 'blood' pure and simple but descent plus politics, a very different proposition. Austrians, who if they are anything are ethnic Germans by descent, are likewise excluded.

In reality, Germany pursued a strategy dictated by the sociology of the post-war years. After 1945 West Germany was faced with having to integrate approximately 13 million Germans. Given German traditions – Germany was an assimilating country before 1914 and even afterwards – it was logical that Germany would seek to assimilate them to West German étatic and civic modes, for these Germans from the East may have been German by descent, but they were not very German in any other respect. West Germany, therefore, became very skilled at assimilating Germans. Predictably, while attention was concentrated on this process, Germany tended to neglect the integration of non-Germans. Here again, the situation is more complex than it appears. It has indeed proved difficult to integrate and acculturate Turks, but this has not been the case with Yugoslavs, which implies that it was the religious boundary that posed such serious problems for the Turks, both in terms of their own thought-worlds and those of the

---

[7] Rogers Brubaker, *Citizenship and Nationhood in France and Germany* (Cambridge, MA: Harvard University Press, 1992) is representative of this approach.

majority, something that has been far less salient with the South
Slavs.

In Central and Eastern Europe, on the other hand, assimilation
during the communist period had a different history. In theory,
Marxism-Leninism took the view that ethnic identities were of
no great consequence, hence the assimilation of minority groups
would happen anyway (being a matter of 'historical inevitability'),
so that the dominant ethno-national group in the state filled most
of the ethnic space. After 1989, however, these dominant groups
woke up to the unwelcome realisation that they lived after all
in multi-ethnic states. Since then, there has been a slow and
occasionally uneven coming to terms with the relationship between
multi-ethnicity and democracy. The proposition that democracy
in the 1990s is not the democracy of the 1890s and that assimilation
of minorities is neither feasible nor praiseworthy has proved hard
to swallow at times.

It is not feasible because settled populations do not assimilate
if they remain in their villages and if they are a part of ethnic
communities that have already moved towards establishing a high
cultural norm. Equally, the possible moment of opportunity for
assimilating members of minority ethnic groups during the symbolic
journey from country to town has been missed. Communist urbanisation was so crude that it could not provide the exchange
that democratic societies could and did offer, entrance to citizenship.
The communist identity lacked the attractiveness to do this, because
that was not what it was designed to do. The *homo communisticus*
was never intended to be a citizen. Hence the great population
movement under communism, which might have offered such
an opportunity – the average proportion of the rural population
fell from around half to a quarter under communism – did not
serve as the occasion for acculturation, but for little more than
the adoption of a simple communist-proletarian identity, with
minimal ethnic content. In this sense, Marxism-Leninism did ethnic
minorities an unintended favour.

However, the memory of the various tribulations undergone
by ethnic minority groups during the communist period has created
patterns of inter-ethnic distrust, fear of assimilation on the part
of the minority and frustration in the majority. The far greater
openness of the democratic structures now in place, coupled with
pressure from the West, are gradually leading towards a state of

affairs in which the traditional visceral fear for group survival can be eased, albeit there is and will be repeated backsliding.

The conclusion to be drawn from this assessment of assimilation is that in the West multiculturalism is likely to be a time-bound phase of about a generation, after which the postponed decision of what to do with the non-white groups whose identities are increasingly close to those of the majority will return to the political and cultural agenda. In this sense, multiculturalism may turn out to have been a strategy for delaying the formulation of a fully integrative response to the presence of sizeable numbers of non-whites in white majority populations. In Central and Eastern Europe, inter-ethnic relations have entered a wholly new era in which the assimilation of ethnic minorities is over (because they are non-migrant groups) and the complexity of continued inter-ethnic negotiation will be the normal feature of these systems.

The movement of power

In order to have a better insight into the nature of the political context in the 1990s, when reason and identity are much more overtly involved in the generation of political power, it is important to understand the movement of power. This requires an analysis that looks not only at the concrete, institutional aspects of power, at the explicit procedures and instruments of politics, but also at its symbolic, implicit dimensions. In essence, the visible dimension of power is susceptible to reason and can be analysed in terms of function and efficiency, but this does not exhaust the way in which politics operates. At all times and in all human communities some of what we do to establish order, to 'make cosmos out of chaos' (to quote Mircea Eliade[8]) is encoded in symbolic form and acted out through ritual. The fundamental need is for coherence; identities create and express coherence. The survival of this coherence cannot be left to chance. In order that the bases of community be secure, these processes are sacralised, made immune to scrutiny and proof against cognitive growth.

Cultural reproduction is so important for communities that it must be protected from everyday cognition. Its rules cannot become a part of the political contest, for if that should happen there

[8] Mircea Eliade, *The Myth of the Eternal Return: Cosmos and History* (London: Penguin, 1954).

would be no second order regulation, no regularity to govern the formal, overt rules or procedures that ensure the movement of power. The framework of informal, implicit rules, the terms of solidarity and of understandings would all be in danger. And a community where all forms of power are continuously open to contest is on the road to chaos and anarchy, a potential war of all against all. Hence the role of the symbolic sphere is essential to safeguard the stability of the community and to establish the boundaries within which the politics of identities is played out. Roughly, this is where reason and identity meet, at the point where institutions encounter symbols, where the visible parts of society touch the invisible.

The proposition that power be made accountable also means that it can be encompassed by individual experience. Hence power has to permit the sense that it will be responsive to the individual and at the same time that it will not be used capriciously against him. The personal has to be balanced by the impersonal. This implies that the individual must feel that the neutral, impersonal procedures and mechanisms of power are a part of one's real personal experience and equally that the personal power of others has been neutralised by the procedures in question. This is a really difficult move to bring off and cannot be done without some kind of an active relationship between reason and identity. One provides the neutral reassurance, the other provides the familiarity of experience. The two acting together can create the sense of order and coherence that allows the individual to feel that power is used justly and that the use of power is not a source of fear.

The great bulk of political analysis, including analysis of identity politics, tends either to ignore the symbolic dimension or to dismiss it. Yet without an understanding of the role of symbols the analysis is imperfect and limited in its insight into causation and motivation. It is by looking at the role of symbols, myths and rituals and taking on board the implicit processes in which human societies are involved that the full rationality of cultural reproduction becomes clear and the apparent contradiction between reason and identity is resolved.

Crucially, if we accept the idea that human beings in groups are engaged in constructing communities from which they draw meanings, moral regulation, communication and forms of knowledge, one can find persuasive explanations for behaviour that is otherwise seen as meaningless or irrational. A whole range of collective human action acquires a patterning, an ordering by which one can assess action at the concrete, institutional level if one includes the symbolic dimension in the analysis.

The nature of the modern nation

It follows from the foregoing that identities are created at both the institutional and symbolic levels and the two should be seen as functioning reciprocally. An institution creates its symbolic dimension and is reproduced in part by reference to those symbols. Thus the use of symbols – flags, monuments, ceremonies and so on – is not a superfluous extravagance, a throw-back to a pre-rational age, but a central component of identity creation and maintenance. They are neglected at one's peril.

Identities are formed by every type of collective human activity. In the political realm, four processes of identity formation are most significant; they function together in a web of mutual dependence. First, there are the identities structured by the state.[9] People who live within the ambit of a particular state evolve shared habits and practices in their response to it. Those who are taxed and policed in the same way share these experiences. The modern state is one of growing complexity and intensity; the identities formed by multifarious state regulation bind people living in one state together. But without the consent of its citizens or when it has been invested with too great a role, the state has a tendency to become rigid and bureaucratic. Just as monocultures become vulnerable to disease, so heavily étatised countries tend to grow top-heavy and frail. The state needs civil society to remain open to change, to variety, to challenges, to living with difference.

Second, there are the activities of civil society, of the web of associations, NGOs, lobbies, corporations through which individuals and groups formulate their aspirations and make choices. But without the protection of a reliable, consistent legal framework, as well as the protection of different groups in society from one another, civil society rapidly becomes uncivil and anarchic. Only the state can provide such a framework.

The third such process is ethnicity. This is the most controversial

---

[9] See *inter alia* Csaba Gombár *et al.* (eds), *És mi lesz, ha nem lesz? Tanulmányok az államról a 20. század végén* (Budapest: Helikon for Korridor, 1997).

identity and attracts any amount of negative comment when the ethnicity of Europeans in a majority community is discussed; minority ethnicity is something else again. This is too simple. Ethnicity does not exist in a vacuum, but is constrained by the state and by civil society. Equally, the state has an unacknowledged debt to ethnicity because it is through ethnicity that the bonds of solidarity that underlie consent are established. Civil society too depends on ethnicity to furnish it with modes of communication and tacit understandings; these of course can be attained across ethnic boundaries, but that is invariably more difficult than within an ethnic collectivity. The existence of a state that is seen as neutral is a vital element in this process.

Fourth and finally is the relatively new and growing importance of the international dimension. As Europe has integrated, a new supra-national, supra-state set of identities has come into being. The European Union, above all because it has the power to take initiatives autonomously of its member states, has become a focus for political, economic, social and cultural action, and whether that action is supportive or hostile, it has come to generate attachments that function as an identity. In this connection, the role of the *acquis communautaire* is vital, in that a part of the European identity consists, willingly or otherwise, of the *acquis*, of living with it or objecting to it. In this sense, the European Union is already functioning somewhat like a state. It lacks the extraordinary regulatory capacity of the modern state, of course, but the analogue holds. But there is more to the international identity than the EU. There exists a nascent international civil society, the network of NGOs and lobbies that play a role across frontiers and, correspondingly, there is an economic dimension provided by multinationals and cross-frontier economic activities. The attempts to supervise these activities constitute another strand in the growing international identity. To the above may be added globalisation. This is not merely globalisation in the economic realm, but also in communications, taste, leisure and the general interdependence of decisions that is such a marked feature of the 1990s. This process is unlikely to abate.

All these four identity-forming processes should be seen as acting on one another, although the intensity of the action may vary. When one of the processes is weak, the others will gain in strength and then the identities derived from those processes will be in disequilibrium. This is what underlies the perceived excesses of ethnicisation in Central and Eastern Europe. It is not the case that in the post-communist world, people are obdurate in their attachment to 'outdated' ethnic identities, but rather that the institutions of the state and civil society are weak and not trusted, whereas ethnicity has authenticity. This further implies that once the historic task of reconstructing the state as a neutral body is achieved, the preeminence of ethnicity will diminish and citizenship can be de-ethnicised.

The gap between West and East

The West has had a very different experience from Central and Eastern Europe. This is a truism worth restating because neither the West nor the Central and East Europeans have made much progress towards understanding each other. Indeed, their relationship since the end of communism has been a tale of incomprehension or at best half-understanding. There are deep differences in style and substance, profound gaps in unrelated discourses. Journalists and politicians, practitioners and academics use a vocabulary that has very restricted currency. Indeed, the very word 'ethnic', which academics may continue to use relatively neutrally, has acquired very negative overtones when applied to Central and Eastern Europe, though paradoxically, it has positive resonance in the context of the ethnic identities of Third World migrants in the West.

This gap has very real practical consequences. Westerners go to Central and Eastern Europe with agendas of their own, sometimes idealistic, sometimes exploitative, sometimes selfless, sometimes self-aggrandising. What they very seldom do is to understand the very different meanings attached to life experiences in Central and Eastern Europe. What they hear is translated into their own thought-styles and own experience. The outcome is not always conducive to the creation of positive images. The Westerners can come away with a sense of the unreliability and obstinacy of the Central and East Europeans, whereas the latter are inclined see the Westerners as patronising and insensitive.

Western thought- and speech-styles are described (by Westerners) as pragmatic, professional, future-orientated and not structured by explicit value judgements, as 'rational'. Post-communists, on the other hand, are seen as relying heavily on history, on pathos, on a sense of resentment and injustice. The pattern of 'Eastern' and 'Western' nationalism, so regularly encountered in conventional accounts of the history of Europe, seems to be repeating itself. It should be clear that these distinctions are no more than symptoms and no more than partial symptoms at that. They are not evidence of some kind of inherent Central and East European deficiency, but are the product of specific historical, cultural and sociological circumstances that have given rise to these responses as the most appropriate and rational available. The Central and East Europeans respond in this way because for them fear for the cultural reproduction and survival of their communities is a real and authentic experience. Westerners may scoff, but it is a reality that they have not had to experience.

The next step in the integration of Europe – eastward enlargement – will give rise to problems as yet barely formulated, let alone clearly understood. Currently, the European Union acts as a surrogate state, i.e. has the power to regulate and rationalise, albeit only over a relatively small area of life, yet even this restricted power has begun to impinge on the areas traditionally reserved to the state. Notionally this extension of EU power is consensual, but in reality it derives from agreements among elites and generates two sets of problems. The extension is simultaneously contested and welcomed. At the core of the EU is the process that once its member states have ceded power to it, the EU applies them autonomously without further reference to the member states. The inference to be drawn is that the EU is currently operating as an identity-forming process. It is seeking to create an order and a coherence of its own; societies respond to this rationalisation and to that extent become more alike: the outcome is a European identity.

In essence, where the state is a high-capacity state, able to implement its will, and has been successful in integrating the diverse identities of the population into a single state-ethnicity complex, ceding more power to Europe is done reluctantly. It must, by definition, affect not merely the power of the states concerned, but impinge on the underlying ethnicity-driven consensus. Thus it affects not just sovereignty, the terms in which it is argued, but ethnicity, which is infinitely more sensitive to issues of this kind. In such conditions further integration tends to provoke an ethnic response, though often enough this is argued in the language of tradition (the United Kingdom, France, Sweden and to some extent Germany are most obviously in this category).

Where the existing states have high capacity and have been successful in integrating diverse populations into a single, fairly cohesive identity that relies on both étatic (state-driven) identities and ethnicity, further extension of the EU is seen as threatening because it is perceived as affecting not the sovereignty of the state but the ethnicity of society. In such situations, further integration provokes a response with ethnic overtones, though it is only occasionally argued explicitly in ethnic terms. More often, the anti-integration position is expressed in terms of tradition and symbolism, as in the United Kingdom or France.

Elsewhere, where state capacity is lower, the relationship between the state and ethnicity may be less intense, hence transfer of power to Brussels generates less heat. Indeed, if the state is not trusted to be effective or neutral, Brussels may be actively welcomed as superior to the state, because its modes of ordering and regulation are more trusted. The post-communist state falls into this latter category. Here the European Union is needed to substitute for the failed communist state. Simultaneously, however, because the capacity of the post-communist state is relatively low, the implementation of the *acquis* will be correspondingly more difficult, implying that the EU-driven identity will be less intense, less pervasive.

Thus the problem has yet more ramifications. High-capacity states do implement the *acquis* thoroughly and effectly. Low-capacity states do not. This accelerates integration but creates unevenness in its intensity. And that unevenness can give rise to resentment, as the identification with Europe increases. It gives one nation a certain legal, moral and political right to criticise the patterns of another; this may very well have been the intention of the founding fathers, but that does not make it easier to swallow. Nation-states retain a certain sacrosanct quality and non-intervention is still time-hallowed, even in an age of accelerating interdependence.

Then, crucially, as the intensity of ordering by the EU intensifies, opposition to that ordering is likely to increase. At the end of the day, there is a threshold to be crossed, one that is not at all easy to discern. The state, as has been argued, is a very effective source of the order that dispels fear. It is tried and trusted. It has constructed an interactive, consensual relationship with society. The European Union is nowhere near this and it has to acquire that intensity of relationship before its regulation is seen as autonomous of the states that make it up. Currently, although legally and functionally the EU does operate autonomously of its member states, culturally and symbolically, by virtue of its identity, it does not create the same consensus, or only to a very small extent.

Crossing the threshold will demand a massive increase in trust in the EU, especially in the high-capacity states, where state ordering is so effective. This crossing will undoubtedly become one of the key issues in the next phase of integration. The EU is close to the threshold, yet there are understandable hesitations about crossing it.

The key question for Europe, for European integration, for the European Union is how to cross the threshold. It follows from the analysis above that institutional and legal measures are unlikely to be enough. There will have to be a shift into the implicit, symbolic dimension of generating consent. Europe's symbolic power will have to grow markedly if the enterprise is to work. Consent at the symbolic level is the major coming challenge for Europe. The question is whether the existing member states accede to this process and whether they accept it reluctantly or enthusiastically. It is very rare for a successful institution to abandon what it is good at in the hope of an as yet abstract aspiration, though this is what European integration postulates.

It is an extraordinarily far-reaching undertaking, one that is every bit as audacious as the original launching and relaunching of Europe in the 1950s. The task is made far more difficult because a significant part of it will take place in the areas of politics and power that are screened out in order to ensure the security of cultural reproduction. Eastward enlargement will complicate the task at the institutional level by posing challenges to the organisation of the EU, but the post-communist states will also be in a position to make a contribution to the crossing of the threshold by having a singular experience, that of using symbolic politics to a much greater extent than the West. The synthesis between reason and identity may actually be enhanced by the skills that Central and Eastern Europe can bring to European integration. If Europe has been structured around one idea that idea is diversity and coping with diversity. The whole of Europe is a part of that legacy.

3

CIVIL SOCIETY, ETHNICITY AND THE STATE
A THREEFOLD RELATIONSHIP

The connection between democracy and nationhood is far from being universally accepted. For most people the two are incompatible, though there has always been a body of opinion that sees civic nationhood as either a component or a necessary condition of democracy. The analysis that follows takes this argument a stage further, in proposing that modern democratic nationhood relies not only on citizenship and civil society (the civic dimension of nations), but that ethnicity, equally, has a role to play in the equation, and that crucially, within the process of forming identity, the nation subsumes the state itself. In effect, the argument that follows proposes that the concept of the nation must be wholly reformulated if its functioning is to be properly understood. Ethnicity, far from being an exaggerated or pathological condition is essential to certain aspects of nationhood and thus to democracy.

In brief, the argument to be put forward here is that democratic nationhood is composed of three key, interdependent elements: civil society, the state and ethnicity. These three are in a continuous, interactive relationship. They have different functions and roles, create different, at times overlapping, at times contradictory attitudes and aspirations, and through their continuous interaction all three are reshaped and reformulated dynamically. Hence civil society is not a static entity, a state of affairs that has been reached and is then established for good, but is fluid, shifting, conflictual, responsive to changes in politics and vulnerable to hostile pressures.

It follows from the above that none of the three processes should be analysed outside its context of interdependence. Their modes of operation are certainly autonomous and conceptually distinct from one another, but are simultaneously influenced by the interactivity sketched above. Furthermore, the contours, contents and processes of each are equally affected by its own actions,

35

aspirations, successes and failures, not to mention its traditions and rituals. The cognitive and operational range of each process, then, is far from unlimited, but is bounded by the other actors on the stage and by the way in which it understands its own history.

This approach to disentangling the nature of democratic nationhood is restricted to the three main dimensions already noted: civil society, the state and ethnicity. However, it should be noted that increasingly in Europe in the 1990s, a fourth, international, dimension is gaining in influence. European citizenship, other international organisations and the activities of NGOs are impacting on how a civil society shapes its ideas and purposiveness. The functioning of European institutions and the response to European integration have clearly begun to reshape attitudes and values and thus form identities. In this sense, Europe is a part of the normal political landscape of identity formation, even if it is only the negative pole of identification. This international dimension will only be touched on fleetingly in this analysis, but its significance should not be underestimated. What is vital to recognise is that the relationships generated by these four dimensions are causal, reciprocal and conditioning; and that they impact at both the explicit, overt level and at the unconscious, implicit one.

State and civil society

To start requires a brief look at the much-discussed relationship of state and civil society. In some analyses, this relationship is depicted as a zero-sum game, so that the stronger the state, it is suggested, the weaker civil society is. Indeed, in some libertarian arguments, the state seeks actively to oppress civil society. This assessment is too restrictive and will not be adopted here. Rather, given the emphasis on the reciprocal relationship between state and civil society, it is their mutual impact that is deemed significant. In effect, it is hard to conceive of civil society actually functioning successfully without the state. The citizen, the agent and subject of politics, is simultaneously constrained by the state and protected by it. The state plays an important role in providing the integrative framework within which civil society operates and the latter cannot function properly without that. That framework, which must include a solemnised set of rules by which the political contest is played out, must be accepted as valid by all and must be administered in as neutral a fashion as is consistent with the shared culture of the society in question. This would clearly include the rule of law and the ability of the state to create a degree of coherence without which civil society would rapidly become uncivil and potentially decline into chaos or anomie. But equally, civil society must be free to challenge the state in order to preclude the bureaucratic rationality of state action from attaining the kind of paramountcy that would generate rigidity.

Historically, modern citizenship – the package of legal, political, social, cultural and economic rights and duties that regulate the relationship between rulers and ruled – is the outcome of the rationalising activity of the rising modern state, accelerating from the seventeenth century onwards.[1] This activity sought to extend and to intensify the power of the state over the population under its rule. This was the key moment of change. The rise of the modern, rationalising, classifying, interventionist state, with a much increased capacity to implement its will, meant that a whole variety of previously diverse practices within a given territory, but under the same ruler, were coming under pressure to be made more coherent, unified, more easily ruled. Administrative, coercive and extractive (i.e. taxation) procedures were homogenised in the name of greater efficiency. State capacity was considerably improved.

This transformation of the state brought about changes in the attitudes and responses of society: broadly towards acceptance of the rationalisation but with a demand for greater control over the state's claimed monopoly of taxation and coercion. The new modes of exercising power required new modes of legitimation. Crucially, universal consent to be ruled became a factor of politics. This was a radical, even revolutionary, shift with far-reaching implications. Popular sovereignty was the necessary response to the intensification of state power; the functioning of the ever growing regulation by the state needed ever higher inputs of consent if the regulation was to be efficient. Without consent, the mounting complexity of the state would make its operation weaker; instead of coherence there would be confusion as society resisted actively or passively. The state, if it was not to be undermined by repeated challenges from countervailing forces, had

---

[1] W.H. McNeill, *The Pursuit of Power* (Oxford: Blackwell, 1983).

to pay heed to the aspirations of its subjects, which were only partly shaped by it. Without this consent, the state was obliged to impose and validate its own rationality in the exercise of power; this inevitably tended towards a one-sidedness, an absence of feedback, a reductionism and bureaucratic rigidity that were hostile to innovation, found technological change hard to cope with, prefered the pursuit of bureaucratic interests and were ultimately self-defeating in terms of the exercise of power. The more or less reluctant recognition that reciprocity of rights and powers[2] existed for all – as distinct from those who had this right as a privilege of birth – gave the state its modern form.

Legitimacy was now likewise a two-way process, rather than dynastic or religious, and the ruler had to accept that this legitimacy would have to be renewed regularly through transparent procedures. Consent had to extend to competing rationalities, aspirations and visions of the future. In states ruled by ideological monopoly, customarily a vision of harmony, the evolution of contest and alternatives were relatively easily marginalised. Such a state of affairs tended to favour the development of a bureaucratic mindset protected by overt rules of its own devising, a closed corporate culture and identity to be imposed on the ruled, and consequent cognitive closures that left the state incapacitated when obliged to respond to the shock of the new.

The transformation had another, usually undiagnosed consequence. If the system needed ever higher inputs of consent to make it efficient, if not viable in the long term, this necessarily implied that all members of society were now given power, potentially and symbolically and often in concrete terms. This inevitably brought changes to the nature of identity politics. Whereas in pre-modern polities, ethnicity was not a very significant factor because very few people were actively involved and they could arrange political power around other criteria, the mass politics of citizenship utterly changed this. Rigid elite politics had to give way to negotiations of enormous complexity to take collective opinions into account. If everyone was politically empowered, popular prejudices would find a role in the scheme of things. Access to power for all meant a new contest for power, with

---

[2] Jenö Szücs, *Vázlat Európa három történeti régiójáról* (Budapest: Magvetö, 1983), partly translated as 'Three Historical Regions of Europe' in John Keane (ed.), *Civil Society and the State* (London: Verso, 1988), pp.291-332.

new rules and new threats to order and coherence. Trust had to be renegotiated across ethnic boundaries, which required new skills. In the new mass order, symbols were bound to acquire a greater significance in sustaining a uniform system; public contests for power grew more contorted with the ever greater number of actors, so the role of symbols and rituals was intensified, in order to establish clarity and coherence. Thus the cultural pluralism of the pre-modern past in which different groups could readily coexist had simply become irrelevant. Indeed, multi-ethnicity could now act as a source of friction, when different ethnic groups were seen as having or demanding access to power, to real and symbolic resources. Hence occupationally differentiated ethnicity, a source of stability in pre-modern polities, grew to be a serious burden as newly enfranchised groups questioned why people who defined themselves differently but lived side by side with them and whose solidarities they could not rely on should be politically or economically or culturally favoured.

Rule by consent permits a continuous and dynamic interaction between rulers and ruled. The problem, then, was how to achieve consent under the new conditions.[3] And logically the problem of consent raises the problem of dissent – what is to be done if a section of the population withdraws its consent to be ruled over a period of time, if it repeatedly demonstrates that it wishes to be ruled differently but cannot change the system? Equally, the problem of consent raises the question of trust, for if there is no trust, then the rulers will be extremely reluctant to share power with the ruled, for fear that they will be swept away and liquidated.[4]

A good deal of theoretical analysis emphasises the civic contract as the key instrument for regulating the new relationship between rulers and ruled. But the civic contract is only a metaphor and does not provide answers for the dilemmas sketched above. Hence the answers have to be sought elsewhere, at a deeper, less self-evident level. In this context, it is important to understand that certain social and political processes are implicit rather than explicit, that every community encodes its regulation in tacit as well as

---

[3] A.W. Orridge, 'Varieties of Nationalism' in Leonard Tivey (ed.), *The Nation-State: The Formation of Modern Politics* (Oxford: Martin Robertson, 1981), pp.39-58.

[4] John Hall, *Coercion and Consent* (Cambridge: Polity, 1994).

overt codes of behaviour, which then come to constitute a part
of its cultural reproduction.[5]

Consent to be ruled

The proposition here is that the deep foundations for the consent
to be governed are generated by and vested in the bonds of
solidarity that are encoded in ethnicity. Where a set of values
and identity are broadly shared between different social strata,
where they regard one another as sharing certain commonalities
and respond to the same symbols, where they take the view that,
whatever may divide them, they do share certain key moral aims
and obligations, the basis for a redistribution of power becomes
a less hazardous enterprise. A society and polity must not only
rely on solidarity, but it must organise itself in such a way as to
reproduce it. There must be a strong publicly shared and privately
internalised classification of norms and values.[6] Under pre-modern
conditions, the level of consent was lower and affected fewer
people, so that ethnic identities were less of a factor in the relationship between state and society, but the growth of state power
and capacity generated the need for a new basis of trust. Why
this trust should have been argued in the language of nationhood
is explained by the particular phenomenon of European political
language. The right to participate in politics was accorded the
members of the *natio*, the body politic (*corpus politicum*); the demand
corresponding to the expanded power of the modern state was
that all the subjects of the ruler should be considered members
of the *natio*.[7] Initially, this was a civic concept, but the pressure
for the radical redistribution of power required that nationhood
be given an ethnic content. Where this ethnic content was absent,
the redistribution of power could not take place or the state was
divided. The failure of Royal Prussia – German-speaking but subject to the Polish crown – as a state, illustrates this process vividly.

By the same token, the trust that is engendered in this way
makes it possible for those affected by the ever-expanding activities
of the modern state to accept it as being a necessary part of being

[5] Mary Douglas, *Implicit Meanings* (London: Routledge, 1975).

[6] Mary Douglas *How Institutions Think* (Syracuse University Press, 1986), p.96.

[7] John Keane, 'Nations, Nationalism and the European Citizen', *Filosovski Vestnik/Acta Philosophica* (Ljubljana), vol.14, no.2 (1993), pp.35-56.

ruled. It comes to be seen as the 'normal and natural' political order and provides the fundamental legitimacy of the state which, crucially, is not questioned. Once this tacit acceptability of the state is attained, the question of consent is removed from the agenda, because it is made automatic, indeed axiomatic. This process is, therefore, the most effective way of creating consent; in reality it preempts dissent. The attainment of this consent does not, however, mean that it will stay off the agenda for ever. In certain circumstances, a consensual state may come to be questioned by a minority which, for whatever reason, rediscovers its own, separate identity and withdraws its previously given consent. The outcome of such a division may be state failure, which – as will be argued – is far more common in Europe than is generally recognised.

It follows that the modern state has an interest in promoting a degree of ethnic homogeneity, notably by using the state educational system.[8] The reciprocal relationship between the state and ethnicity is a real one. It is not contended in this assessment that the state is actually capable of creating an ethnic identity out of nothing, but where it establishes what might be termed a working relationship with an ethnic identity, the state can shape, enhance, promote and protect it. The difficulty arises when the state finds that it is unable to impose its ethnicised codes on a group which has acquired a separate ethnic consciousness sufficient to generate its own cultural reproduction. In such circumstances, which are common enough, either some kind of a compromise is reached and the rulers of the state are prepared to share the state with other groups or, if the competing ethnic group has the territorial cohesion, it can opt for secession. The dynamic of state action sustains and develops ethnic consciousness; usually the one dominant ethnic group imposes its ethnic vision on the state to create an étatic identity and this is then imposed in turn on all the ethnic groups in that territory. That, in essence, is the building of the modern nation state.

The overall outcome of this somewhat obscure relationship between ethnicity and the state is, as implied, the acquisition of a degree of ethnic colouring by the state. When two actors are in continuous contact, each becomes marked by some of the

---

[8] Ernest Gellner, *Nations and Nationalism* (Oxford: Blackwell, 1983).

features of the other. This gives rise to a momentous conclusion: the universalism of the state and of the citizenship that depends upon it is more apparent than real. Both will be lightly, or less lightly, ethnicised. French citizenship is permeated by French ways of doing things, French codes, French points of reference and a French perception of what is 'normal and natural'.[9] This proposition can be applied elsewhere, to other states, including some of the most deeply civic and democratic polities. Ethnicity does not, then, vanish in the civic states of Western Europe; it merely slips out of sight. Nor is ethnicity necessarily destructive of democracy. But it can undermine democracy when either the state or civil society, or both, is too weak to contain it, and hence ethnic criteria are used for state and civic purposes.

Citizenship

What then happens to citizenship demands further attention. Citizenship is defined in this analysis as the package of overt legal, political, institutional, economic and other analogous relationships that bind society and the individual to the state and which govern political relationships within society. For the most part, citizenship is explicit, open to questioning directly and subject to continuous political engagement. It is through the rules of citizenship – informal as well as formal – that civil society finds expression. In this realm, there are the procedures, the mechanisms, the provisions that make power transparent and predictable. In monoethnic states or states which perceive themselves as monoethnic (i.e. where the existence of minorities is screened out) arbitrary power will not be so threatening, as the basic constitution of solidarity is not significantly open to competition. Societies in this position can live with a fair degree of chaos, like Russia in the 1990s. The rules are vital, therefore, for without the stabilising element of citizenship, the exercise of power becomes arbitrary and generates insecurity; this insecurity then reacts on ethnicity and can give rise to a sense that one's ethnic identity is threatened. That in turn can trigger off a radical narrowing of perspectives, an ideo-logisation, a deep-seated intolerance born of the fear that one's ethnic identity is in danger. This phenomenon is found when

[9] Eugen Weber, *Peasants into Frenchmen: The Modernization of Rural France, 1870-1914* (London: Chatto and Windus, 1977).

the state is too weak to protect civil society or sees no interest in doing so. The combination of state and ethnicity when used against civil society is what usually underlies nationalist excesses – the shift towards ethnicisation of politics – when all or virtually all power is exercised by ethnic criteria.

Hence, those aspects of citizenship that impinge upon the ethnic underpinning of the state are evidently difficult to deal with through civic codes. The language of the state is manifestly one of these, for language has at least two functions: it is the medium of communication through which the individual relates to the state; but is also one of the pivotal instruments of ethnic reproduction, part of the process by which an ethnic identity is articulated and sustained. The interaction between the civic and ethnic dimensions of language is one of the most frequent sources of conflict in the modern state.[10] Members of ethno-linguistic minorities will claim access to the rights of citizenship in both dimensions and thereby challenge the ethnic codes of the majority. Often, majorities will try to delegitimate these demands by reference only to the civic or state dimension, that the language of a particular state is, say, Ruritanian and that all citizens, as citizens, must learn the language of the state; this disingenuously ignores the problem of minority cultural reproduction. The solution to this admittedly difficult problem is to include all the ethnic communities within the area of the state in the codes of citizenship and to accept that citizenship will be coloured by more than one ethnicity. In practice, this is extremely difficult to achieve, precisely because much of this activity takes place at the implicit, indirect level, rather than the overt one where the codes of citizenship rule.

Without citizenship, then, cultural reproduction is endangered, because of the unpredictability of power, even while without ethnicity consent to be ruled is hard to establish. And without the state, the framework for citizenship cannot operate. Hence the key proposition in this analysis is that citizenship, ethnicity and the state exist in mutual interdependence. The ideal situation occurs when a threefold equilibrium has come into being. This is a necessary condition of democracy. Thus in situations where only two of the three elements are present, the use of democratic instruments like elections, even if free and fair, will not produce

[10] George Schöpflin, 'Aspects of Language and Ethnicity in Central and Eastern Europe', *Transition*, vol.2, no.24 (November 1996), pp.6-10.

democracy, but some hybrid like consensual semi-authoritarianism. Croatia in the first half of the 1990s exemplified this instance.[11] Where state, citizenship and ethnicity are all weak, as in Belarus, the existence of independent statehood is strongly questioned by its inhabitants. Generally, where both civil society and the state are weak, ethnicity flourishes and democracy will not be easy to sustain, as is the case with post-communism generally.[12]

It should be understood, however, that as the triad of relationships (state-citizenship, state-ethnicity, citizenship-ethnicity) is dynamic, the equilibrium does not have to be perfect. A wide variety of solutions is possible. In Europe today, there is a highly fluid state of affairs, a questioning of received wisdom. After 1945 political systems were significantly étatisé through the establishment of the welfare state and this is now under challenge. This can give rise to different models of democracy, with different forms of equilibrium. France can be said to have a strong state, strong ethnicity and a civil society that is weaker than the state, with the result that French civic consciousness is markedly ethnicised. In Italy, there is an inefficient state, a well articulated civil society and a strong ethnicity, with the result that much social action is citizenship-driven but without the equilibrating function of the state. England (not Britain) has a high-capacity state (which is growing stronger), a weakening civil society and a strong but implicit ethnicity; the outcome has been the growing étatisation of identities.

Challenges to the state, however, bring the danger of state failure in their wake. There are various roads to state failure, but the collapse of a multiethnic state has been the commonest in Europe (Austria-Hungary, Yugoslavia, Czechoslovakia). In a sense it can be argued that the period 1945-89 was unique in European history in that it was free of state failure, but otherwise virtually every European state has experienced it. The criteria of state failure used in this analysis are: complete disappearance (Montenegro); the loss or addition of territory; major upheaval or discontinuity, like foreign occupation, the aftermath of war or civil war; and possibly decolonisation, the loss of empire. In each case,

---

[11] Vesna Pusic, 'Dictatorship with Democratic Legitimation: Democracy versus Nation', *East European Politics and Societies*, vol.8 no.3 (Fall 1994), pp.383-401.

[12] Leslie Holmes, *Post-Communism: An Introduction* (Cambridge: Polity, 1997).

the state is to some extent incapacitated or loses consent and is unable to provide the security that its citizens expect of it.

The incorporation of new territories within the boundaries of the state is a complex and difficult operation for the modern state. It adds new citizens with different aspirations and ways of life (even when there is no ethnic difference), thereby disrupting established bureaucratic patterns and weakening state capacity. This can dilute the bonds of citizenship and intensify ethnic allegiances. In practice, though few people recognise it in this way, the addition of territory is much more of a burden than it appears at first sight. The belief that territorial expansion is a source of greater power is a misconception left over from early modern or pre-modern times, when the switching of territory from ruler to ruler was much easier and more common. Currently, the values, attitudes and identities that come into being in response to a particular state are long lasting,[13] making the integration of new territory complex and painful. Indeed, the identity created by experience of a previous state persists and integration is seldom fully achieved. Ethnicity is self-evidently insufficient for this purpose as the case of German reunification shows. Romania and Poland both show traces of their previous state experience to this day; even Alsace has retained some of the features that it acquired as a part of the Reich before 1918.

In fact, by accepting that the state is much more contingent than it seems and, therefore, a part of the normal pattern of political change, it becomes possible to see a very large number of state failures in twentieth century Europe and to deduce from this that in Europe, the problem of dissent or withdrawal of consent is regularly solved by secession, rather than the acceptance of high levels of instability through the presence of unintegrated minorities. This idea may only occasionally be conceptualised in this way, but secession is legitimated overwhelmingly by reference to ethnicity, which strengthens the argument that ethnicity plays a vital role in state stabilisation and stability. In the United States, on the other hand, the idea of secession is anathema (as the Civil War demonstrates), presumably because the integrity of the US is guaranteed by a civic contract – the Constitution – which can

---

[13] Michael Mann, 'A Political Theory of Nationalism and its Excesses' in Sukumar Periwal (ed.), *Notions of Nationalism* (Budapest: Central European University Press, 1995), pp.44-64.

only work if territorial integrity is not open to question. To this may be added that in certain circumstances, generally before polarisation is far advanced, confederal solutions or cantonisation or other forms of deconcentrating power can produce success, if success is measured by holding a particular state together, and provide space for civil society and ethnic reproduction (this, in essence, is the story of Belgium).[14]

Multi-ethnicity

Multi-ethnicity creates a whole set of problems that exacerbate the difficulties of generating consent. If ethnicity really does play the crucial role in underpinning consent as argued above, then in a multi-ethnic state, this consent ought logically to be impossible to attain. But while there are very real difficulties in this area of political management, they are not insuperable.[15] In essence, the answers are to be found in various forms of power sharing and the application of the principle of self-limitation to ethnicity, admittedly neither popular nor straightforward given that cultural reproduction can be seen to be threatened. The fact is that virtually every European state is multi-ethnic in some respects, even if the many differences among them require that a variety of solutions be considered. These must all begin from citizenship: that in a democratic state all citizens have equal right to cultural reproduction and to share in the material and symbolic goods of the state if they are to be perceived as citizens and if they are to identify fully with the state in question. This identification is vital if multi-ethnic relations are not to be troubled by unmanageable suspicion and distrust.

The heart of the problem is that the codes of solidarity and cohesiveness, the nature of reciprocal loyalties and bonds, implicit communication, the construction of what is regarded as 'normal and natural' are all located in ethnic identity and, obviously, these will vary in their expression from one ethnic group to another. Here one finds fertile ground for suspicion and distrust. Is it, in

---

[14] Geert van Istendael, *A belga labirintus avagy a formátlanság bája* (Budapest: Gondolat, 1994), a translation of *Het Belgisch labyrint of de schoonheid der wanstaltigheid* (The Belgian labyrinth or the charms of formlessness).

[15] John McGarry and Brendan O'Leary (eds), *The Politics of Ethnic Conflict Regulation* (London: Routledge, 1992).

fact, possible for one ethnic group to trust another sufficiently to share power with it within one state? The answer, if all parties are sensitive to the imperative of cultural reproduction and accept that the rights that they demand for themselves must be extended to others, is yes. This implies that the political and institutional systems and citizenship must be set up in such a way as to cope with the extra burden of the continuous renegotiation of power across an ethnic boundary. The distribution and legitimation of power must take account of this imperative for majorities and minorities in order to provide for the security of both. Note, too, that cultural reproduction is sensitised by multi-ethnicity; the question of identity is raised on an everyday basis and one's understanding of 'normal and natural' is challenged daily. Without formal and informal regulation there is a real danger that small issues can grow very rapidly into major ones as ethnic ranks are closed and perspectives are narrowed. Symbolic conflicts are readily perceived as an onslaught on one's cultural integrity and security. This last proposition is nicely illustrated by the differences between Hungarians in Hungary and Hungarians in Rumania. For the former, their Hungarian identity is taken for granted as 'normal and natural'; for the latter, especially those outside the largely ethnic Hungarian Székely counties, being Hungarian means continuous engagement with the Romanian quality of the state and with the Rumanian majority which results in a much more accentuated awareness of being Hungarian.

Yet, having sketched the undoubted difficulties in this area, there are some very real success stories and it is a common mistake to place excessive emphasis on the pathologies. In summary, where multi-ethnicity has been effectively regulated, the groups in question have agreed to differ on some aspects of what constitutes loyalty to the state and they do not take these differences as vital to their existence. All the groups must have an overt and accepted loyalty to the integrity of the state; secession cannot be an issue. The state lives with lower levels of integration and rationalisation than it might prefer, it lives with different – and therefore unequal – solutions to certain issues (e.g. education). Nor is there an insistence that the different groups actually like one another, enjoy living together or feel that they must share ethnic bonds. The difference is there but is dealt with in a non-universalist fashion. (Switzerland, Finland and Spain are instances.)

To the foregoing should be added the contingent problems of the 1990s. There are three significant trends acting on the democratic systems of the West.

The collapse of communism. This has meant the end of the discipline which constituted one of the parameters of power. Whereas before 1989 pressure from civil society for greater empowerment could be resisted by offstage reference to the communist threat, this is no longer accepted as legitimate. Hence the relationship between civil society and the state, which seemed to have been quiescent since the upheavals of 1968, is back on the agenda. At the same time, the end of communism has forced Western Europe to look more closely at what it means to be European, where Europe ends, who is European and who is not. The Jean Monnet paradigm for the construction of Europe has clearly run out of steam and new instruments are being debated. Equally, while there is near universal agreement that the states of Central and Eastern Europe are, indeed, a part of Europe, what this means in practice is hotly contested. What are the obligations that Western Europe owes Central and Eastern Europe? Is Russia in Europe or not? And what should Europe do to ensure stability and democracy? And finally, the collapse of communism has also brought with it the collapse of the communist state which claimed to be the supreme embodiment of rationality. This has inevitably tainted by association the widely held belief in the state in the West. Etatism, whether associated with the left or the right, has become increasingly doubted. These are all new questions which have arrived with quite some urgency on the agenda and demand a far-reaching reappraisal.

Welfare and empowerment. The problem of the welfare state and the simultaneous pressure for the greater empowerment of society have raised a different set of issues. As the welfare state paradigm has lost its effectiveness, as state capacity has declined with overload, as dependency has grown, as the cost of welfare provision has risen and the labour force has stagnated, coupled with the causal link between the high cost of labour and high unemployment, questioning has correspondingly intensified. Crucially, there has been a certain loss of trust in the ability of the state to deliver, and with no widely accepted alternative, the prestige of the state has declined. This last proposition is all the more serious, because the modern state has in many respects become the unacknowledged repository of ultimate rationality, so that the loss of faith in the state has much deeper implications than might appear at first sight.

Globalisation. The impact of global processes erodes the tradition-driven belief systems by which groups and individuals structure their lives and this loss of the past, in turn, creates an insecurity about the present and the future. The state is losing control over information, money, consumption, leisure, technological change and other forms of innovation. This has not made the state impotent, but it has changed many of its traditional tasks, especially in the provision of material and cultural security. As time-hallowed structures have been weakened, the state, as well as civil society have to find a new role and new relationship, even as the parameters of action are shifting with great speed.[16]

Finally, there is the new issue of European citizenship. In the last decade, the evolution of a network of transnational associations centred on the European Union has generated new forms and hierarchies of power, of social knowledge and information, and of political capital. Importantly, these side-step the traditionally conceived nation state and establish connections directly among non-state actors and with Brussels. This process of development is still at a relative early stage, but it is nonetheless real and will become more intensive as European integration proceeds. The significance of these processes is that existing hierarchies of power that have their location within the state are threatened in a way that cannot be easily delegitimated by those affected (e.g. decisions of the European Court of Justice). The new instruments of empowerment that result can then be used to reform or reshape domestic structures. European citizenship provides new resources and creates new identities that can transform long-standing patterns (e.g. the far-reaching reshaping of Irish identity as a European one). Civil society will certainly benefit from European citizenship by having a new centre of power to which to appeal when it comes to dealing with the state, but it is an open question as to whether the European Union can provide the stabilising functions that were traditionally the task of the state.

---

[16] Anthony Giddens, *The Consequences of Modernity* (Cambridge: Polity, 1990).

The whole question of consent reappears in a new guise: what is the nature of the consent to be ruled in the relationship between civil society and the European Union? What are the implications of the democratic deficit in this context? And how will eastward enlargement effect further changes? What is beyond doubt is that European citizenship is also recasting ethnic identities as ethnic actors engage directly with Brussels and can use European resources in the contest for power at home. Overall, in this area the outlook is one of fluidity and innovation, which will gradually or sharply reconstitute the state, civil society and ethnicity in the Europe of the 1990s and beyond.

4

CITIZENSHIP, ETHNICITY AND
CULTURAL REPRODUCTION

In democratic politics today, the paradigm has shifted. The focus is on citizenship, ethnicity and cultural reproduction, whereas in the very dim distant past, the 1980s, it was class and participation. Like all paradigm shifts, this is as much apparent as real, but the end of the Cold War has sharpened the focus and has brought different aspects of our world-view into relief. Problems of identity and the nature of identity politics were present throughout the period 1945-89, but they were not seen as salient. Indeed, the dominant modes of seeing the world – liberalism and Marxism – were both rather dismissive of identity politics, identifying it as a regrettable leftover from the past.

All this has changed and we now accept that identity does have a key role to play in the structuring of a democratic order. This shift has posed a particular problem, I would suggest, for the Anglo-Saxon world-view – the United States, United Kingdom and other states of the English-speaking world – because in these systems, the problem of identity really had been successfully marginalised. One needs only to recall the collective sigh of relief when the referendum on a Scottish parliament was lost in the 1970s – after the rules had been rewritten to help that objective – and how no one would listen seriously to the argument that the problem had just been swept under the carpet, not solved. Hence the revival – real, apparent – of identity politics in the 1990s has been unwelcome to polities that had made a single, rather cohesive conception of citizenship the pivot of their identities. What I shall argue is that citizenship too is a part of identity politics, that it is nothing like as universal as its proponents like to think, but that without citizenship, democracy becomes very difficult to sustain.

The key to the analysis that I am proposing is that the relatively homogeneous – and homogenising – definition of citizenship which I have taken as my starting point is misleading because societies are becoming more complex and that complexity will ultimately find expression in the political realm. Class dealignment, the rise of education, the impact of globalisation and the quest for different sources of identity have all played a role here. Evidently, one can cite a wide variety of identities in this context, but I would like to deal with ethnicity, not least because I regard it as the central (though not the sole) constitutive matrix within which individuals and societies live their lives. And secondly, in this connection, no society is mono-ethnic. Throughout the world, both as individuals and as members of groups we are coming into contact, and conflict, with members of other groups. It is worth signalling at this point, that the rules for individual contact and those governing group contact vary, something that can give rise to considerable conflict.

My major theme is multi-ethnic polities, my primary area of interest is Central and Eastern Europe, and I would like to suggest that some of the lessons of post-communism are of wider applicability. Indeed, we can learn something about our own societies by making comparisons with those that are in the process – at an early stage – of building democratic systems. The shortcomings and successes, the functions and dysfunctions of our own systems gain greater clarity by comparisons of this kind.

No one has ever said that constructing democratic systems in multi-ethnic polities is easy. The seductive side of Anglo-Saxon citizenship is that there really are fewer problems with a notionally universal citizenship than with multi-ethnicity. Ethnicity is troublesome, it gets in the way, it forces politicians to adopt positions that seem unreasonable and, crucially, makes compromise, bargaining, dealing – the exercise of power – that much less tractable. The standard charge is that ethnicity, arguing from a reference to ethnic belonging, is irrational. This is the unthinking war-cry of the universalists, who decry difference and tacitly seek to impose their own agendas on others.

The shortcomings of universalism

I am not persuaded by this admittedly simplified and caricatured variant of universalism. If nothing else, had the universalists been correct in their strategic analysis, then ethnicity really would have faded away. Neither Marxism, which has largely faded away, nor liberalism has offered an adequate answer to the question of why ethnicity persists. Without an understanding of the impulses which keep ethnicity in being, we cannot even begin to construct systems which will allow democracy to function in any recognisable form; the universalists are to that extent, I believe, correct in their argument that democracy and ethnicity are *prima facie* incompatible in a world where ethnicity is made the sole source of meanings. Democracy must take account of ethnicity and ethnicity must come to terms with democracy.

So, why ethnicity? Why does it persist? What is it for, to put it at its simplest? I would like to offer an explanation from the methodology of cultural reproduction. My starting point is the proposition made by Mircea Eliade,[1] the Romanian sociologist of religion: what societies do is make cosmos out of chaos. They seek to impose order on a world of conflicting, chaotic, contradictory impressions and experiences. They create a world. And individuals have to belong to a world, otherwise they lose their humanity, their lives become – to quote someone light-years away from Eliade, namely Hobbes – 'solitary, poore, nasty, brutish and short' (not, as has been unkindly suggested, 'nasty, British and short'). The essence of creating cosmos is that groups cohere around different ways of world-making. And these different groups will therefore understand the world differently.

The communities that are so constituted will go through a number of processes that are broadly similar both in terms of methods and aims. They will seek to ensure that the basic constitution of the group is unchallenged, whether from within or by outsiders. They will seek recognition for themselves as human communities. In modern terms, they will expect to be accepted as communities of moral worth, as coequal with other such groups. And the members of the group will regulate their identity and all that flows from it by the definitions that they give to their collective existence. The community, then, is there to provide meaning – particularly answers to fundamental questions of morality – to ensure coherence, predictability, stability, consistency. Correspondingly, exclusion from the community is dire. Nothing could be worse. Exile or banishment strip the individual of his identity and thus of a part of his humanity.

[1] Mircea Eliade, *The Myth of the Eternal Return: Cosmos and History* (London: Penguin, 1954).

By moral regulation I mean the tacit set of prohibitions and commands by which we, as members of a community, live our lives. What is right, what is wrong; what pattern of behaviour will bring punishment and what will bring reward; and importantly it is through this regulation that we accept and justify our successes and failures. In parentheses, I have a suspicion that provision of rules to account for failure is central to stability, but that is a proposition which still requires some thought. Our culture of change is derived from this set of rules — stable societies can deal with very extensive change, even the kind of rapid disembedding that is transforming the world, as long as there is some way of accounting for it. At its heart, moral regulation makes certain patterns, forms of action, responses, attitudes the norm. They make up what is 'normal and natural' in a community, the things that we can take for granted and do not have constantly to re-negotiate with fellow members of the community.

In this sense, the 'normal and natural' to which I've just referred may be contingent and relative in a universal perspective, but to any community in the world, it is fixed and unchanging. Indeed, communities will go a long way towards ensuring that certain basic norms may not be questioned. There will be tacit regulation for screening out certain questions, for making certain issues invisible. Our cognitive worlds are limited and one of the limitations is that our cognitions are bounded by our culture.

Indeed, one of the difficulties with the argument put forward with such cogency by Ernest Gellner, who spoke so eloquently of 'cognitive growth' as being at the heart of the Enlightenment[2] and thus at the heart of our own world, is that certain things do not yield readily to cognitive growth; because of the implicit processes by which we make sense of the world, when we subject them to rational analysis, the constitution of our world seems to slide from our grasp. We think we understand, allowing rationality to rule, then some new, opaque, seemingly irrational set of actions disturbs the picture. When some things become visible, others become invisible.

Let me offer a tentative example. Anyone who has spent the last thirty or more years in England — and I mean England, not Britain — cannot but be aware of the role of class and of the constant

[2] Ernest Gellner, *Plough, Sword and Book: The Structure of Human History* (London: Collins Harvill, 1988).

reiteration of the desirability of a 'classless society'. Yet there is absolutely no sign of one at all. England is every bit as much a class society as it was a generation ago, albeit, class is now structured differently. I think that I first began to smell a rat when I heard the phrase 'classless society' used favourably by a Conservative prime minister. It implied that classlessness had either been redefined out of existence or had lost any meaning or had some entirely different significance. I now take the view that for the English class has a central constitutive force, that Englishness is vitally about having a place in a class hierarchy, that without such a place one loses the stability that comes from a class identity, and that the dynamics of Englishness make these processes invisible. For the English, class has many of the functions that are performed elsewhere by ethnicity. An insider-outsider like myself can argue these propositions, although the answers I get are generally dismissive, as might by predicted. But the conventional rational analysis of class (made in terms of 'interests') or of the English identity (made in terms of customs) will not produce these insights because the nature of English cognitions screens them out. The key, I would suggest, is that the class nature of Englishness is about stability and predictability, about status, the influence derived from status and the consequent access to power that certain social strata are able to claim – cultural reproduction in other words.

My point in this context, therefore, is that communities govern their affairs and the lives of their members by both explicit and implicit codes of moral regulation. This brings me to my next proposition, that communities will do all they can to ensure that their set of codes is not threatened with elimination, that whatever happens, the community will persist. No community will abandon its own existence readily. Indeed, the stories of persistence through the most extraordinary privations are so frequent that, if nothing else, they should give those who would decry ethnicity pause for second thought.

Let me offer you one example. A couple of years ago I attended a conference in Finland on the eastern Baltic. In the closing session, a man came on to the podium and, in very halting English, expressed his gratitide that he had been able to take part. He then said, 'Now I would like to speak another language' and proceeded to do just that. I recognised it as a Finno-Ugrian language, neither Finnish nor Estonian, but no more than that. He then said, 'I have been speaking Livonian.' He paused, 'Please stand up Mr X and Mr Y.' They did so. He then continued, 'We are 10 per cent of all the Livonian speakers in the world.' A language group with thirty speakers must have very poor prospects, yet it was hard not to feel a sense of the poignancy of the determination of this tiny group to keep themselves in being as a separate cultural entity. This was the rationality of cultural reproduction in its rawest, purest sense in front of my very eyes.

The persistence of identity

But there is more to all this than just persistence. Communities are engaged, as I suggested earlier, in renewing themselves through various means of cultural reproduction. They construct boundaries, they employ a variety of instruments of reproduction.[3] Anything can be a boundary, from dress and dietary codes to language and history. Symbols, rituals, celebrations, festivals, liturgies, monuments, statues all have this role, whether people are prepared to accept this or not. The 16 February is Independence Day in Lithuania and I happened then to be in Vilnius. Now that Lithuania has its independence again, the celebrations were rather muted: flags on most buildings and a firework display above the castle of the great mediaeval ruler, Gediminas. It was all very good-natured. But until the Lithuanians gained their independence from the Soviet Union, things were nothing like so relaxed. The flags are now not a protest but a reaffirmation.

There are, clearly, various ways of reaffirming the community. What is important to note is that where one instrument is weak, something else will be found to take its place. Take the case of a community that speaks a language which is philologically the same as that spoken by another, neighbouring community with which it is in dispute. This is potentially dangerous, because there are not enough boundary markers to distinguish community A from community B. The one that feels threatened can, at that moment, decide to embark on a bit of linguistic engineering and make its language as different as it can. This in brief is what the Croats are doing *vis-à-vis* the Serbs. They are creating a language

---

[3] Fredrik Barth (ed.) *Ethnic Groups and Boundaries: The Social Organisation of Culture Difference* (Bergen/Oslo: Universitetsforlaget, 1969).

with a new vocabulary which they are trying to make as different as they can from that used by the Serbs.

The key elements of community go well beyond what I have sketched so far. Moral regulation may be the foundation, but membership of the community has other, related dimensions. Central to this connection is the set of implicit and explicit obligations that one member of a community owes another, the bonds of solidarity. These cannot be made the subject of legislation; solidarity is a voluntary act, or at any rate so it seems. All communities are communities of solidarity. This factor becomes vital in moments of crisis, when the community feels itself under stress.

Then, there is communication. We all know that we communicate better with fellow members of our community than with outsiders. We do not have to explain in such detail, we can leave certain things unsaid. In politics, in culture, in everyday life this evolves into matters of style, into form and processes that are natural to us and strike others as strange. Communication, then, eases, reinforces and reaffirms the sense of community, the sense of being a member of a group and it does so, not least, because it simultaneously excludes others.

The persistence of community, which I have been suggesting is the basis of ethnicity, as well as the functions of community should now be clearer. The universalist position has little or nothing to say on this point, yet the relationship between culture and politics seems to me to be one of the central features of our era. Indeed, in its essence ethnicity is the proposition that a cultural community has certain rights to political power, even while paradoxically the regulation of power cannot take place by the norms of ethnicity alone.

There are various factors to explain this development. Central among them is the rise of the modern state and the demand, heard increasingly from the eighteenth century, that the subjects of the modern state should have clear rights of control over the modern state. This is the demand for political participation, for the extension of access to political power to all. The modern state is far more intrusive than its predecessors ever could be: in its ability to rationalise and organise, to tax and to raise armies, to police society and to extend its legislative powers over areas previously untouched by the state administration it was something new. Because its range of power was new, that generated a corresponding demand for access to power among those affected.

Why nation? Because under the classical doctrines governing access to power, only the members of the nation – the medieval '*natio*', little or nothing to do with the modern nation – had this right. Initially, the demand that supreme political power should be vested in the nation was a legitimating discourse.

This was where the radical quality of the demand impacted. Power was now to be in the hands of all the inhabitants of the polity. From having been subjects, they would become citizens. But if power was to be exercised by consent and thus to be devolved onto the entire population, then the existing holders of power would have to be reasonably confident that the new rulers would not string the old from the nearest tree. And furthermore, the old rulers – *the ancien régime* – also had to be confident that a particular part of the state would not use its new-found power to secede. This is the central dilemma of consent. What happens when a particular group of people does not consent? By the principles of democracy, of consensual rule, they should be accorded the full right to determine their future. That solution, which has been employed of course, cannot be pushed too far. If it were, then the nature of the existing state would become completely contingent and thus unstable, thereby undermining democracy. Stalemate.

Not quite. The *de facto* solution, though it is seldom argued this way, is to implicitly base democracy on ethnicity as well as on citizenship explicitly. Indeed, the norms of citizenship are to an extent permeated by the norms of ethnicity. Modern citizenship is generally presented as being universal. In reality, the citizenship of each country differs – French citizenship is informed by Frenchness, Dutch by Dutchness and so on. The two dimensions of the nation – citizenship and ethnicity – do in fact form an interactive whole, thereby solving the problem of consent, since the devolution of power onto all the members of the ethnic group is far less risky than an ostensibly consensual, contractual solution, seeing that there are powerful elements of cohesiveness and unity built into ethnicity.

This instantly raises the problem of what one does with those sections of the territorial population who are of a different ethnicity: this is where multi-ethnic politics begins. Since the rise of modern nationhood, from the French revolution on, say, various devices have been deployed to balance the conflicting and contradictory pulls of ethnicity and citizenship. Ethnicity encodes a powerful imperative for the cultural community to run itself. Citizenship is universalistic and claims to deal with all on an equal basis. It provides for order and predictability in the exercise of power. In short, without citizenship, the bases of democracy are very weak; but without ethnicity, the devolution of power to all cannot take place. Some kind of equilibrium between the two is essential if states are not to be torn apart by inter-ethnic conflict. Some, of course, have been. Multi-ethnic politics is, as we know only too well, a difficult genre.

There are some success stories. Switzerland is the one that comes instantly to mind, but the Swiss solution is not for export, not least because no other state is willing to countenance the degree and extent of devolution of power that has been the core of the Swiss solution. Ethnically differentiated cantons are supreme bodies, vested with sovereignty. The centre exercises power only where this has been devolved up to it from below. Finland has approached the problem of its Swedish minority somewhat differently: it has given the Finland Swedes very extensive rights and powers, as well as access to the symbolic goods of the state, with positive results. Finland's Swedish minority regards itself as fully coequal to the Finns. Belgium has inched its way towards full federation, linguistic separation and division of the Francophone and Dutch-speaking (Flemish) communities. It may seem awkward and at times silly, but it has worked. Spain has done quite well in giving the Catalans extensive rights, but the full solution to the Basque question has eluded it, largely because a minority of Basques, with the support of a much wider penumbra of sympathisers, will not consent to the Spanish state, presumably because they are fearful for their future as a community, given that the great majority of Basques are Spanish-speaking, so that the possibility of losing their identity to a greater Spanish whole is always present.

Are there any lessons to be drawn from these best-case scenarios, any common threads? Is there anything more here than the application of democratic principles? Clearly, democracy and respect for the rules of democracy are a necessary condition for the regulation of a multi-ethnic state, but they are not enough on their own. After all, simple majoritarianism, as in the Anglo-Saxon states, is certainly democratic, but these states find ethnicity very difficult to deal with. The problem of Quebec illustrates this proposition vividly.

The analysis has to be deeper. In the first place, there has to be a readiness to acknowledge that all the ethnic groups in the polity have a right to cultural reproduction. The actual provisions to be made for this vary according to time and place, but they should include access to what I have called the symbolic goods of the state. Majorities should understand that citizenship, having as it does an ethnic component, should be widened to include the ethnic aspirations of all citizens. This may sound like the proverbial making of a silk purse of a sow's ear, but it can be done. Finland offers some good examples of such practice. The official name of the country is in both the languages of the state – Finnish and Swedish; Helsinki is bilingual, although the number of Suedophones who live there is tiny. Paradoxically, the state of affairs in Wales approaches this. The Principality is completely bilingual and even in areas where the number of Welsh speakers is zero, the language is, or may be, used. This conveys a symbolic message.

Let me move next to the problem of the state and its impact on identity. Any community, regardless of its ethnicity, will be affected by the nature of the state that it lives in. This is the reverse of the proposition that citizenship is somewhat ethnicised. The transforming, rationalising, organising quality of the modern state leaves a lasting impress on those who live within its ambit. This means that groups, however diverse their patterns of ethnic reproduction, will share certain procedures, certain ways of being administered, certain ways of being taxed and represented politically. Each state constructs its own particular means of creating loyalty and vertical dependency. There comes into being a semi-monopolistic relationship between the individual and the state – one particular state and as a rule the jealous sovereign nation state. So-called 'state building' is homogenising, in that variety and diversity are evened out for the convenience of the state and its bureaucracy. This is not a one-way process. It involves an exchange in which society gains equality of administrative outcomes (up to a point) and certain shared patterns of upward mobility.

States and identities

But all this has long-term consequences. There comes into being a 'state-driven' identity, with qualities all its own. This is not necessarily 'civic', because civic implies democratic accountability; these identities are better termed 'étatic' since they are common to all states. Thus the interactive, reciprocal relationship between ethnicity and the étatic identity produces a new hybrid, with its own dynamic, generating a culturally reproductive capacity of its own. All this in turn has implications for the unification or reunification of populations on the basis of ethnicity into a single state. Those who have acquired a particular étatic identity different from those of their fellow ethnics have thereby been made different and their integration into another state is generally more complex, more troubled than is widely assumed. Sharing ethnicity is not the same as sharing nationhood. The example of reunified Germany should make this clear. In 1989-90 there seemed to be no alternative to integrating East Germany into West Germany on the basis of shared ethnicity. The very different East German identity was not understood and its repercussions will continue to affect Germany for many years to come. Although Poland was reunified in 1918, a perceptive observer can still tell the difference between former Russian, Prussian and Austrian regions. And in Romania too, the difference between Transylvania and the Regat, the Old Kingdom, is fairly evident. In the 1996 elections, it was expressed in very different voting patterns between the two regions.

When a state is weakened, is severely threatened or collapses, the étatic and civic codes evaporate because there is nothing to support them. Communities then look to their ethnicity to provide them with security and regulation of power, even while this works only very poorly and impels these communities towards a belief that their collective futures are threatened. This can produce various outcomes. East Germany collapsed into West Germany; there was never any serious chance that a separate East German state could remain in being. The Serbs of Bosnia saw their protective Yugoslav identity vanishing as Yugoslavia disintegrated and, even worse, they were fearful that they would be locked into a permanent minority status in a Muslim-dominated state, thereby falling prey to myths of their own extinction. At that point, with their cognition severely reduced, they sought to preempt and destroy the Muslims and so ended up in the midst of a self-fulfilling prophecy, creating the very Muslim hostility of which they were so afraid. Russians, having moved from imperial Tsarist and imperialist Soviet identities, suddenly had to construct a Russian political nation at the same time as having to come to terms with the loss of empire, of prestige and of *c.*25 million fellow Russians who became citizens of the successor states of the Near Abroad, each of them busy creating étatic identities of their own.

Multi-ethnic politics works best if the communities in question are secure in their future, if they sense their full acceptance. The communities do not have to like one another, but they should be ready to say that the presence of the other is not an affront to their own ethnic aspirations. Italians certainly do not particularly like the Germans of the South Tyrol, but they have come to terms with the fact that that area is partly German. This was not an easy process.

Crucially, majorities and minorities should be sensitive to the other and should avoid questioning the other's moral worth. Loss of power or loss of some other benefit from the civic dimension of nationhood can be tolerated much more readily than an injury to one's sense of collective moral worth. In this context, it is really not necessary that majorities and minorities should actually live side by side or be integrated. On the contrary, this can actually intensify friction and potentially trigger off incidents inadvertently. The way in which the Dayton Agreement had an underlying aim of making Muslims live with Serbs, so recently after the ethnic cleansing of the Bosnian war, seems to me to be crying for the moon. It is preferable to keep the two parties separate, though obviously the elites should talk to one another, at any rate behind the scenes.

This brings me to the related theme of ethnic cleansing. There is a belief in some circles – not untouched by a certain kind of pragmatism – that while ethnic cleansing is dreadful, it is over now, after all: nothing that money and time cannot solve. This is plain bad sociology. The evidence is overwhelming that ethnic groups subjected to ethnic cleansing or genocide do not forget such a traumatic experience. On the contrary, the experience then becomes a constitutive part of their identities, thereby encoding antagonism and enmity against the ethnic cleansers for generations. Nor do the perpetrators of ethnic cleansing escape the consequences of this act. Their attitudes to their former victims will variously be tinged with guilt, resentment, anger and frustration that ethnic cleansing has not 'solved' the problem. The evidence is very strong for these propositions. The troubled relationship between Czechs and Germans illustrates this clearly. The expulsion of 3 million Germans after 1945 has left scars on both, and whereas one might have expected that the expelled Germans would be absorbed by German society, this has not happened. On the contrary, they have retained a separate identity. The problem will not go away, despite the expulsion of the Germans having happened some fifty years ago.

This brings into focus the very difficult question of what happens when majorities and minorities define their own existence against the existence of the other and when that process polarises inter-ethnic relations. This is the situation here in Northern Ireland, but also in a number of other deeply divided polities: Latvia, Estonia, Macedonia, to some extent Romania and Bulgaria, or for that matter Sri Lanka.

This is certainly the most intractable of all the problems in this field. I go back to first principles. What makes inter-ethnic relations intractable is not the fact of inter-ethnicity itself, but the fear, the insecurity for the future of the ethnic group, its fear of extinction. This is the level at which the solution should be sought. This proposition implies that all the actors have a responsibility for ensuring the security of the other, because that contributes to the ensuring of one's own security. Easier said than done, but nevertheless possible.

As will be clear from my analysis, I place considerable emphasis on the importance and effectiveness of symbolic politics. Elites are more easily persuaded than societies, but societies are not as immune to reasoning of this kind as some might suppose. Collective acts of reassurance, expiation for past humiliations, respect for the sacred ground of others all help, together with transparency, in placing the rules of democratic order beyond the political contest and all can be derived from democratic self-limitation. Crucially, external actors, kin states, diasporas should all be drawn into this process. That, maybe, is the hardest part of all: to make the apparent outsiders aware of their responsibility for the security of people who live thousands of miles away and for whom they feel no responsibility at all. There are patterns of interdependence that are far from self-evident.

Ethnicisation

Sometimes the balance between the ethnic and the civic or étatic modes will swing radically towards the ethnic and the codes of ethnicity are then used to determine the distribution of power. In these conditions, democracy collapses even if it is maintained in form. Ethnicisation usually has its origins in fear: of collective survival, of humiliation, of denial of moral worth, of having one's deepest concerns set aside or despised. The cognitive codes of the other by which we measure ourselves make it impossible to be recognised. We are simply ignored. This is more or less the state of affairs between Slovakia and Hungary. While relations on the ground between Slovaks and Hungarians may be fairly tranquil, when it comes to collective stereotypes it is intolerable for many Slovaks that their existence is irrelevant for Hungarians, which it very largely is, rather more in Hungary than among the ethnic Hungarians of Slovakia. Something along these lines exists between Estonians and Russians in Estonia. The two communities live entirely separated lives and the Estonians regard their Russian minority as somewhere between a nuisance and a threat, the threat being reinforced by regular growlings from Russia itself, which has, in turn, demonised Estonia as a major enemy.

Ethnicisation results in a severe shrinking of citizenship. It quickly transforms a political system into something non-democratic, where the non-members of the ethnic group are marginalised, excluded or silenced in a vain attempt to create a surface ethnic uniformity. In Serbia this was imposed on the Albanians of Kosovo, who took the next logical step and opted out of the Serbian state – with consequences that are likely to remain unresolved for a long time to come.

In these circumstances, choice is reduced, there is no neutral ground, communities are highly homogenised, a highly charged emotional-affective language fills the air, all processes are seen in terms of advantage or disadvantage to the community and all other alternatives are excluded. A legitimating discourse, that of ethnicity, then takes over with highly effective power of penetration into the deepest recesses of society. In worst-case scenarios, ideological thinking takes over.[4] In this situation there is a chain of unassailable logic deriving from the single idea of the survival of the ethnic group; a form of consistency is imposed on everything and all negative phenomena are explained in terms of the logic which identifies an enemy conspiracy as being a total explanation.

What actually constitutes a minority? The answer seems obvious, but it is not so. The definition of a minority depends on the

---

[4] Hannah Arendt, *The Origins of Totalitarianism* (London: George Allen and Unwin, 1958), esp. pp.461-75.

definition of the territory of the state, but this can ignore the international dimension of the problem. A state can make very extensive provision for the minority but still find that it remains uneasy, fearful for its collective existence. This is the case of Quebec. The Canadian approach was to start from the proposition that the Francophone Quebecois should have the right to use their language and have equal access to the material and symbolic goods of the state. Modernisation and prosperity would solve the rest. Whey has this system of regulation not worked? In essence because Canada cannot provide the full security that the Quebecois feel they need for their cultural reproduction. Indeed modernisation has made the problem more acute because their modernisation has been a North American one, it could hardly be anything else in the circumstances, and is dominated by the Anglophones, in Canada itself and in the United States. The more Quebec looks like the rest of North America, the more the Quebecois are persuaded that they must do everything they can to protect the one cultural marker that makes them different, their language. Hence their near obsessive determination to protect French, even to the extent of making serious inroads into the rights of Quebec's own non-Francophone minorities. Full state independence is, I am fairly certain, the long-term prospect. Here citizenship is not sufficient to give full protection to cultural reproduction.

5

LEFT AND RIGHT: EUROPE IN THE 1990s

The left

Was communism socialism? In the sense that it legitimated itself as such, it was. The question of content can be argued forever, but communism drew for a part of its legitimation both in Central and Eastern Europe and in the West on being a part of the socialist tradition. It was presented as the best possible – or sole – outcome of the socialist vision.

In one respect, it clearly was within the socialist tradition: it claimed to be the application – the supreme application – of rationality, of human reason to life. At the level of theory, it argued that its right to absolute power derived from this supreme rationality. This provided communism with its legitimation to destroy civil society and to eliminate feedback and self- limitation, i.e. popular participation and democratic institutions.

Hence the collapse of communism utterly discredited socialism (in whatever variant) as an ideology, as a discourse, as a utopia, as revolution and as an emancipatory aspiration. One of the relics of socialism is a certain faith in the state as an agent of rationality. Crucially, whereas under communism, the state was regarded as the sole agent of rationality and society was seen as irrational and an obstacle to progress, in the current situation, the state has lost its preeminence, but nothing else has fully taken its place. There is no civil society to do this, and civil society cannot be created out of nothing. The outcome is a political fragmentation of its own particular kind.

Possibly the single most important aspect of post-communism (the preferred term) is that the failure of communism also meant the failure of the communist state. The post-communist state, therefore, has to struggle with the very complex legacy of the remnants of overdetermined state structures of communism even while lacking the legitimacy to fulfil its obligations. Crucially, the state finds it very difficult to discharge one of its most important functions: the establishment and maintenance of coherence. (Russia is the extreme case, appropriately enough as the origin of the communist impulse, where the state has all but completely disintegrated and been replaced by various forms of private action, including private law enforcement.)

The failure of the state is a profoundly serious problem, because modernity requires a state to discharge a number of vital tasks which no other agent can (though notionally, other states and/or international organisations could in part). The supervision of infrastructure, and the relevant investment decisions are examples. In politics, the state is essential to enforce the law evenhandedly; civil society is virtually impossible without this. The role of the state is to provide order, stability and the absence of arbitrariness in the use of power. External supervision is essentially what happened to East Germany. Bosnia is similarly under an external regime and the same applies at least partly to Albania. However, while the West will intervene to prevent total breakdown, it is most reluctant to substitute for a failed state.

One of the implications of the failure of the communist state, together with that of Marxism-Leninism, is that Enlightenment rationality has also suffered in the West if not to quite the same degree as in Central and Eastern Europe. Marxism-Leninism was a legatee of the Enlightenment and while it was engaged in its epic contest with liberalism, other discourses were screened out. This is now far more difficult, which helps to explain the unexpected (for many, unwelcome) rise in identity politics.

At the centre of the dilemma facing the post-communist state is that democratisation demands that the state should preside over its own dismantling. The communist state essentially sought to control everything and virtually the entire system was in the ownership of the state (as the embodiment of supreme rationality, it was the obvious entity to play this role), but the post-communist state is busy trying to shed some of this. This instantly raises a whole panoply of questions. How much should be privatised? What is anything worth (a difficult question, as under communism nothing had a true market price)? In what order should the state be sold off? Who has the money and how did they acquire it? And by what criteria should the dismantling take place, by some abstract notion of equal access to all (which can block the most efficient use of resources) or by auction?

Closely related is the problem of citizenship. Citizenship has two aspects: those constructed by civil society, and those rights and duties (entitlements) which the individual acquires by virtue of being involved in a legal, political and economic relationship with the state. Paying taxes should mean getting something back. The trouble with the post-communist state is that, because it has failed, it lacks the legitimacy to create a relatively neutral space within which individuals can function on a more or less equal basis. This becomes a self-fulfilling prophecy: as individuals distrust the state – they ignore procedures, for example, because they are certain that they can only be disadvantaged by doing so – this attitude acquires a widespread, universal value. Those who are then able to control parts of the state, do it for their personal enrichment or for that of their patronage system (like a political party).

The post-communist state

The post-communist state is a low-capacity state. It has difficulties in enforcing its policies; the bureaucracies operate in an over-regulated environment (partly inherited from communism); there is a complex and contradictory hierarchy of rules and bodies, and a poor culture of enforcement (like the plague of stamps). Underlying this is a confusion of values and boundaries, of what is acceptable and what is unacceptable behaviour.

The functioning of the post-communist state is complicated by the expectations held of it. There is a long tradition of étatism, of the state as primary actor, initiator and goal-setter, particularly as primary moderniser; communism in this context was a kind of hyper-étatism. Even before the coming of communism, civil society and liberalism were weak. But given low capacity and the collapse of any agreed underlying system of values, any idea of redistribution is flawed and unworkable. Paradoxically, redistribution by the market is equally impossible in the absence of a base line from which to begin the redistribution. In a way, what we are seeing currently is the construction of that market, and the early years are harsh and unfair.

To the above should be added the unrealistic expectations of the population. It is a low-capacity society that has limited experience of the public sphere and it corresponds to the low-capacity state (this is what makes post-communism different from, say, Italy). The legacy of Marxism-Leninism is relevant here. It may be that societies that have lived with failed utopias need considerable time to readjust. In essence, large numbers of people have no clear idea of what politics is about, what can be achieved through politics and what cannot. They expect immediate results and are resentful when this does not happen. The outcome may be passivity, simply waiting for an external agency to act as salvation, at any rate as far as the public sphere is concerned. In addition the public sphere is deeply fragmented, and there is very little agreement on what constitutes reciprocity, mutuality or solidarity, other than what can be derived from the bonds of ethnicity.

The private sphere is something else. Just as the elites indulge in salvaging what they can from the previous system (*nomenklatura* privatisation, mafias, the accumulation of power, the reconstruction of political parties as organisations to protect a *Weltanschauung*), so individuals do something similar. Where the elites seek to restablish their symbolic capital, gained in the previous system and thus no longer legitimate under the new conditions, people look to analogous low-level strategies. The state is there as a resource to be exploited.

Under these conditions it is futile to expect anything resembling discourses of empowerment and emancipation, from whatever the left is at any rate. There are, indeed, such discourses but they are either populist or nationalist or both. Nor is community in significantly better shape. The bases of community are difficult to define in states that have just emerged from a system that was determined to impose pseudo-collective ideals on everyone. The sharing of ideals and the goal of equal access to life chances are difficult to validate. The best basis for collective action is personal; one trusts whom one knows.

Communist successor parties at first sight appear to be legatees of the socialist tradition, but in reality they are obliged to pursue the same strategy of dismantling the state and promoting the market as neo-liberals. Their appeal in the mid-1990s, which has begun to fade (communist successor parties lost elections in Poland, Lithuania and Bulgaria), was based on a claim to efficiency rather than the correcting of injustice.

There is, however, one partial exception to this picture of gloom, although that too is flawed. Very high and unrealistic hopes are attached to the EU's eastward enlargement. To some extent, eastward enlargement has been assimilated to the age-old expectation of change coming from the West. There is very little knowledge, even among the elites, of what the EU actually entails, but now, during the run-up, the prospect of membership is sufficient to sustain a future, a belief that there is an aspiration. And, though some might want to argue about this, some of the aims of the EU do correspond to the goals of socialism, though they derive from a different origin, social protectionism. But then the left never has had a monopoly of caring and fairness, whatever it may have claimed.

The right

Definitions are important in trying to understand the phenomenon that we label 'right-extremism'. In general, we mean a number of processes that may or may not have common features. There are certain distinctions between right-extremism in Western Europe and in Central and Eastern Europe. And these are significant, because if we misunderstand the nature of a political movement, the chances are good that we will apply the wrong remedies in trying to resolve the problems in causes.

In Western Europe, we define right-extremism as marked by racism, xenophobia and violence. On the whole – and there are some exceptions to this – these movements are not populist. By 'populist' I mean a movement that rejects institutional structures, that is radical in attacking all existing regime attainments and promises deliverance and salvation to its followers. Crucially, populists invariably offer more than they can deliver. This is a part of the attraction, that they do not start from the status quo, but from a mythicised or falsified view of reality.

Right-extremism almost invariably operates by postulating that somewhere there is a conspiracy that has brought into being whatever it is trying to change. Indeed, these movements are a classic example of ideological thinking, a pattern of thought in which every effect has a cause, in which something happens because someone has caused it to happen, yet the process of causation is hidden, veiled by sinister manipulators. In this mindset, there is no room for accident, for chance, for coincidence. It constitutes a thoroughgoing closure of the cognitive space. It is a way of blocking out structural analysis.

Hence right-extremism invariably needs a target, a group to which sinister powers are attributed and which is held responsible for whatever is happening. In general, this target is whichever alien minority currently most salient in the eyes of the movement concerned. Actually, the identity of the group is virtually irrelevant, so long as it is both easily identifiable and has some resonance in the eyes of the followers (e.g. the anti-Semitism, anti-Gypsy sentiment, anti-Europe sentiment, anti-Hungarianism and anti-liberalism conjoined into a single seamless whole in the propaganda of Romanian extremists in Transylvania).

A distinction should be made between the parliamentary extreme-right and extra-parliamentary extremists. The latter reject all structures and will certainly consider terrorism. The parliamentary extreme-right will be sucked into political activity by its gradual recognition that to attain power, it must gain votes and to do that, it must come to terms with the existing institutional framework. This readiness to deal with the democratic system does not necessarily make these people more palatable, but it tends to moderate their extremism over time.

Right-extremism

In part, the rise of right-extremism in the 1990s is related to the end of the Cold War and the sudden, unexpected saliency of identity politics in the mature Western democracies. To some extent this is more apparent than real – identity politics were present in the West throughout the post-1945 years – but the decline of class alignments and the loss of credibility of Marxism have given identities a much greater legitimacy than before. Equally contingent, the recession of the early 1990s contributed to the tension between long settled populations and relatively recent migrants via competition in a fast changing labour market. The impact of new information technology was highly significant in this respect.

How a population responds to immigration is to some extent a function of its own sense of security with respect to its identity. Identity politics may be decried as 'irrational', but that will not make it go away. The key to understanding this issue is to accept that cultural reproduction has a rationality of its own, which at times supersedes all other rationalities, individualism and economics included. In circumstances when a collectivity feels insecure about its identity, it will be vulnerable to agitation about alien others, or any group that can be presented in such terms.

Over and above this point, each and every collectivity has its own particular foundation and constitution (in a metaphorical sense). The core of such ethnic group foundations is that ethnicity, while an authentic experience, will not on its own provide security in the context of power. It is the stability and predictability of the state and the existence of space for civil society, together with civil social groups, that will provide the security necessary for ethnicity to be constrained. Ethnicisation is not the necessary consequence of ethnic consciousness. Hence it is perfectly possible to run multi-ethnic and multicultural political systems, as long as all the political actors accept and respect the cultural reproduction of all other ethnic groups. The same conclusion can be reached from the perspective of democratic self-limitation, which enjoins political actors to respect the right of others. There is also a prudential case to be made for multiculturalism: minorities will be a source of stability if they feel secure in the polity of which they are citizens.

The lesson to be drawn from this proposition is that there are, in fact, ways of dealing with ethnic or xenophobic agitation. It requires the state and the political elite to ensure the security (social, economic, cultural) of the groups that are responding to agitation. Note that a small proportion of the population – of any population – will always respond positively to xenophobia and racism. This will only exceed, say, 10 per cent in exceptional circumstances and that is the threshold of danger. The best strategy at that moment is to target the next vulnerable segment, those who have most to lose by change.

It is extremely important to understand that Europe today is united politically and culturally to a far greater extent than was the case before 1989. This means that events in Central and Eastern Europe can have a direct influence on right-extremism in the West. There is little doubt that the supine way in which the West simply accepted ethnic cleansing first in Croatia, then in Bosnia, then in Krajina gave encouragement to right-extremism elsewhere in Europe. The weakness of Western governments over Yugoslavia has had its revenge.

Under post-communism, right-extremism has a different political and sociological origin. Politically, all post-communist systems are struggling with the question of how to establish a moderate, democratic conservatism. The problem remains: what is a conservative actually to conserve? The past is a communist past and, therefore, anathema for the right. This inherently pushes the right in a radical direction, making the left (the communist successor parties) the home of conservatism. From a Western perspective, this is quite bizarre. But it does have the consequence that moderate conservatism in Central and Eastern Europe is largely without a cogent ideology, making it vulnerable to capture by radical nationalism. In fact, the story from Central and Eastern Europe has been quite positive. Radical nationalists gain about 10 per cent of the vote, although in certain circumstances, this may be enough to give them a disproportionate influence thanks to the vagaries of electoral arithmetic (Slovakia and the Slovak National Party (SNS), Romania under Iliescu and the Greater Romania Party). The sociological roots of post-communist right-extremism lie in the stratum of the population which rejects modernity because it has been traumatised by the alien, unequal modernisation imposed by communism.

Generally, in our analysis of right-extremism, we should be careful not to exaggerate its significance. There is a general propensity on the part of the media to concentrate on pathology and ignore health. Thus before 1994, vastly inflated attention was paid to the populist anti-Semite Istvan Csurka, in Hungary. He gained 1.25 per cent of the vote. Excessive focus on marginal right-wing groups creates anxiety in the majority and encourages extremists. A sense of balance is therefore, highly desirable.

Finally, the most effective means of marginalising right- extremism is to make democracy operate in the best sense. It should be responsive, transparent and open, provide the best balance between change and stability, and capable of making judicious judgement between the needs of short term expediency and long term predictability. No one pretends that this is simple, but all extremism, whether of the right or of the left, is the result of the shortcomings of democracy.

6

COMMEMORATION: WHY REMEMBER?

In its simplest form, a commemoration is a way of marking out a space in the public sphere. This may be physical space or space in time, usually both. It is a way of saying: 'Pay attention, this is a bit of our past that deserves our respect.' It demands respect, because celebrations of this kind embody a moral value, generally something that those who celebrate think desirable. It is perhaps possible to celebrate something that we do not like, but that seems perverse. But different communities do celebrate different values and occasionally these are values that others regard as an evil, an abomination.

Here we shall concentrate on what the concelebrants regard as positive. This term is used deliberately because every commemoration has a religious dimension – not necessarily one recognised by organised religion, but religion in the widest sense, of creating an order in the minds of people in which good and evil have their place, in which chaos has been transformed into cosmos, to quote the Romanian philosopher of religion, Mircea Eliade. And this brings us one step closer to the enigma of why we commemorate.

The explanation is not to be found in some morbid obsession with the past, an inability to put the past behind one (as Anglo-Saxons are sometimes prone to suggest). Rather, the recalling of memory in an ordered and ritualised way, regularly enough for the celebration to become a part of the way of life of those involved, reaffirms what we feel is morally proper. It reaffirms, first of all, the crucial significance of memory itself. A society without memory is blind to its own present and future, because it lacks a moral framework into which to place its experiences. It very easily becomes rootless and free-floating. This does not make such a society evil, just banal.

This is the terrible threat of eternal return, Nietzsche's prophetic foreshadowing, the constant recurrence of the same set of experiences without any understanding of their significance, without their having any significance – the state of affairs that Milan Kundera explored in *The Unbearable Lightness of Being*. This book, when given a deeper reading than is customary, is a dire warning of what happens when a society neglects the past, therefore cannot confront the future, and is the prisoner of an iron cage of the perpetual present. Kundera had the communist system in mind, but some of what he had to say applies to all modern societies, which because they must seek to satisfy all, often enough end up by satisfying none. They impose the same procedures, the same impersonal norms on all. The world becomes neutral, grey, and the individual *qua* individual has no resonance.

Bureaucracies do this, the leisure industries do this, the media do this, even (perish the thought) education does this. The result is a homogenisation of tastes, of lives, of hopes, of aspirations and – dangerously – of moral judgements, the moral judgements that are encoded in memory. This is the danger to which Guillaume Apollinaire pointed:

> *Les souvenirs sont cors de chasse*
> *dont meurt le bruit parmi le vent.*[1]

I need hardly add that I quote Apollinaire because he was, in part anyway, a Central European. His mother came from Wilno – Vilnius in Lithuanian – and was Polish.

This danger of allowing the past to be eroded in the name of a uniform present is all the greater in large, confident cultural communities, which seem to assume that the past can take care of itself, because Enlightenment rationality is sufficient to provide for all their needs. Technology will see to the rest, the satisfaction of people's primary wants is all, and the never-ending debate over moral values is superfluous. This leads one straight into the cul-de-sac of pragmatism, and a pragmatist has been defined as someone who does not know why he is doing what he is doing. At a more elevated level, pragmatism says, 'If it works, it's good.' No, it's not. There are things that work and they are manifestly evil, like ethnic cleansing, say. No, there have to be explicit or more often implicit moral values in our world, in any world, and some of these derive from commemoration. In this sense,

---

[1] 'For memories are hunting horns whose noise dies among the wind.'

the past and how we think about it is a vital part of ourselves and must not be neglected.

No Central European would ever make this mistake, that of neglecting the past. Small nations, small in population not in prestige or renown or achievement, cannot afford the kind of complacency that large ones make their own. They are driven by a particular imperative, the imperative of cultural reproduction, of recognition, of gaining the approbation of the world for their existence as communities of moral worth, that their culture must survive precisely because it is a repository of moral values, one that is unique, a way of narrating how people should live, when they should laugh and cry, when they should shudder and rejoice, and how in the widest sense they should know good from evil, clean from polluted.

The demands of this imperative cannot be ignored and sometimes, to the acid or condescending amusement of large collectivities, small ones will indulge in a near ceaseless, and to the outsider, seemingly senseless commemoration. Let me offer a personal example, in which the community in question is not even all that small. Many years ago I first went to Strasbourg, in Alsace (where incidentally some of my ancestors are from), and there I was perplexed to find a Rue du Vingt-deux Novembre (22 November Street). To this day I have not discovered what the date commemorates, though I imagine that it is the date of liberation in 1944; but I know that it is there to recall an event that was central to the experience of the city and those who live there.

Commemoration can be about the highest values, about the questioning of our very existence, about asking why we do what we do and whether it matters if it is not remembered. This is hard, very hard. Which of us is comfortable with the thought that once they are dead, they will be utterly forgotten? Or that the community in which we live will disappear? Here is 'Byzantium 7' by the late Ivan Lalić, the Serbian poet (d. 1997), whom I regard as one of the great poets of the twentieth century:

> *Under the wise escort of our ghosts someone will walk, perhaps,*
> *One day, along the contour of these battlements, where*
> *We watched the sun, a copper weight tilting into the scale of night;*
> *The sea will leach silver and flotsam on to the pebbles*
> *Rounded with future gentleness; the air will be blue*

With the smoke of our names;
but who will understand us?

(Translated by Francis Jones)

Lalić asks hard questions, ones that we in the West – well, most of those in the West – do not know even how to formulate. How are we to compose our testimony from these scattered syllables? Who will understand us? Yet these questions are real enough, they are essential to the survival of community as community and not as a group of disparate individuals, living in suspicion and distrust of one another. For community, there has to be a community of morality, of shared moral values. Shared morality does not mean a perfect conformity of views, ideas and hopes. But this is where commemoration is vital. It creates solidarity, but does not impose consensus, or even compliance. It leaves us our individuality and thus our dignity as individual bearers of moral values. We can all celebrate the same event but in subtly different ways and those subtle differences are essential to our humanity. Otherwise we might just as well be politely programmed robots (another import from Central Europe, by the way).

So commemoration is about ensuring that people retain their individuality even while they are members of the same community of values. But what if there is dispute, what if a minority and majority in a country are in disagreement and the customary modes of settling the disagreement have broken down?

When disagreement is deep and unbridgeable, when two groups both believe that their way of life is valid, moral and driven by the imperative of reproduction, then conflict seems inevitable. It is very difficult for one community to look with nothing worse than indifference at the commemoration pursued by another. Yet if we are all to survive in the European tradition that I believe is our heritage, living with diversity is a *sine qua non*.

There are moments when this appears to be difficult, because the celebrations of other communities appear to be directed against ourselves. I would like to suggest that a degree of robustness is the least undesirable way forward here. If we have the confidence in ourselves, in our values, then the commemorations of others need not be seen as offensive. We can live with them and respect them to an extent that is well within our tradition. But there is no particular need to compromise our own aspirations in the

process of accepting other traditions, in the name of a multiculturalism that seeks to impose particular restrictions of majorities.
Majorities have the same rights to cultural reproduction as minorities
and those rights should be respected.

One final thought about commemorations and why they are
important. I have spoken of the need to reaffirm the moral aspirations of communities and of individuals as members of communities.
But there is another dimension to it all – the legacy of the Enlightenment is that somewhere, somehow, we have to be rational
at all times. Now I have nothing against this principle, nothing
at all. There is a problem with it, though. For rationality to be
completely effective, it has to take everything into account, it
has to have totality, for at the moment we select, we are importing
criteria of selection and these obviously imply moral values
congenial to ourselves.

This is where commemorations, celebrations, rituals, symbols,
liturgies have their role. They are a way of saying we have made
a mark, already made a selection, and that selection cannot be
questioned head on. If it is questioned, the integrity of the community may be in danger. That is why the sense of celebrations
cannot be examined too closely, why a particular celebration may
appear sacred to some and ridiculous to others, why we need
commemoration at all – to ensure that chaos does not return to
the cosmos that we have so carefully made and that we go on
making so carefully.

Part II. ETHNICITY AND CULTURAL REPRODUCTION

7

A TAXONOMY OF MYTHS AND THEIR FUNCTIONS

This analysis begins from the proposition that there are certain aspects of our world that cannot be encompassed by conventional rationality. Various processes, ideas, values, mechanisms and so on remain hidden from customary modes of scrutiny and yet have significant implications for the way in which individuals and collectivities live. As Mary Douglas puts it, 'A good part of the human predicament is always to be unaware of the mind's own generative powers and to be limited by concepts of the mind's own fashioning.'[1]

The difficulty is that at some level Enlightenment rationality presupposes that all actions can be understood by the cognitive instruments that its practitioners fashioned.[2] The problem, however, was and is that personal idiosyncrasy is imported into this process by selection. No one can have total knowledge, hence selection is inevitable, but the criteria of selection are immediately open to question. Myth, and the analysis of myth, is one of the ways of looking at the criteria of selection, at the covert part of thinking and the biases, slants and prejudices that are, as will be argued, a necessary part of the way in which collectivities define their universe.

---

[1] Mary Douglas, *Implicit Meanings* (London: Routledge, 1975) p.xiv.

[2] Ernest Gellner, *Plough, Sword and Book: The Structure of Human History* (London: Collins Harvill, 1988).

Myth is one of the ways in which collectivities – in this context especially nations – establish and determine the foundations of their own being, their own systems of morality and values. In this sense, therefore, myth is a set of beliefs, usually put forth as a narrative, held by a community about itself. Centrally, myth is about perceptions and not historically validated truths (in so far as these exist at all), about the ways in which communities regard certain propositions as normal and natural and others as perverse and alien. Myth creates an intellectual and cognitive monopoly in that it seeks to establish the sole way of making the world and defining world-views. For the community to exist as a community, this monopoly is vital and the individual members of that community must broadly accept the myth. Note here that myth is not identical with falsehood or deception. Members of a community may be aware that the myth they accept is not strictly accurate, but because myth is not history, this does not matter. It is the content of the myth that is important, not its accuracy as a historical account.

Myth, therefore, is one of a number of crucial instruments in cultural reproduction.[3] It acts as a means of standardisation and of storage of information.[4] It provides the means for the members of a community to recognise that broadly they share a mindset, they are in much the same thought-world. Through myth, boundaries are established within the community and also with respect to other communities. Those who do not share in the myth are by definition excluded. All communities recognise a boundary of this kind. Myth is, then, a key element in the creation of closures and in the constitution of collectivities. At the heart of this argument is the proposition that myth is vital in the establishment of coherence, in the making of thought-worlds that appear clear and logical, in the maintenance of discourses and generally in making cosmos out of chaos.[5]

Myth and ritual

It is important at this juncture to define the relationship between

---

[3] Pierre Bourdieu, *The Field of Cultural Production* (Cambridge: Polity, 1993).

[4] Norbert Elias, *The Symbol Theory* (London: Sage, 1991).

[5] The reference is to Mircea Eliade, *The Myth of the Eternal Return: Cosmos and History* (London: Penguin, 1954).

myth and ritual and myth and symbol. In simple terms, myth is the narrative, the set of ideas, whereas ritual is the acting out, the articulation of myth; symbols are the building blocks of myth and the acceptance or veneration of symbols is a significant aspect of ritual. A ritual generally observes the procedures with which a symbol is invested, which a symbol compels. Thus myths are encoded in rituals, liturgies and symbols, and reference to a symbol can be sufficient to recall the myth for members of the community without need to return to the ritual.

It follows that what is not symbolised is either very difficult to communicate or cannot be communicated at all, because it is not a part of the fund of knowledge of the community. The language of symbols, rituals, myths and so on are, consequently, a part of the web of communication shared by any community and are, incidentally, more significant than language itself. Members of a community of shared symbols can continue to recognise one another and maintain communication even after they have abandoned their language (in the philological sense). The relationship between grammatical language and symbolic language is a continuous one; each can sustain the other. In cases where a particular community shares its language with another, the symbolic differentiation can be vital in marking out the distinction. Thus the web of myth-carrying symbols shapes and reshapes language and includes the techniques by which comprehension is sustained – the methods of standardisation through which the functions, processes and exchanges in the community are understood.[6]

Acceptance of and participation in ritual, one of the instruments of standardisation, is vital, if not indeed obligatory, if the system is to be sustained, but belief in the ritual and the set of explanations attached to ritual are less important.[7] Indeed, the belief may be vague and understood differently by those who come into contact with it. In this sense, ritual is more a stylised statement of belief than a fully-fledged internalisation of what the ritual supposedly expresses. But this does not imply that participation is purely formal. Ritual is important even when the participants interpret the rites differently because it is an emotional participation, an

[6] Elias, *op.cit.*

[7] David I. Kertzer, *Ritual, Politics and Power* (New Haven, CT: Yale University Press, 1988).

involvement at the non-conscious level, the terms of which condition the nature of beliefs and establish the parameters of the credible.[8]

Ritual is the means of establishing patterns of social dependence, of ensuring that the participants recognise one another and that they are in a mutual interdependence. The sharing in the ritual is the moment of anchoring the institutions concerned; the specific rationalisation of the ritual is entirely secondary.[9] So, what is crucial here is that ritual persists even while the nature of the belief and, thus, of the actual content of myth, shifts. Ritual ensures that the myth persists too, though fairly clearly in a continuously changing form.

The outcome of participation in ritual and, therefore, of accepting that one's relationship to the community is structured by myth is the strengthening of both the collectivity and the individual's role in it. The individual is linked by this action to all others who do likewise and, centrally, precisely because ritual does not impose uniformity of belief, each participant can retain his or her individuality, personal orientations and values within the parameters acceptable to the community. It is in this sense that ritual produces bonds of solidarity without demanding uniformity of belief. People can act together without consensus. Myth as the content of ritual, then, is an essential aspect of community maintenance. Thus consistency is created through communication and action, even while the participants have different beliefs or, indeed, conflicting beliefs.[10] In the political realm, this is significant because it creates potential means of allegiance on the basis of social identification. Social in this context clearly includes ethnicity and nationhood.

The notion of standardisation is again useful. Language in the broad sense, including both symbolic and grammatical codes, exposes a community to a particular experience, to particular ways of constructing the world. Those who control the standardisation process derive power from so doing. Those who can invoke myth and establish resonance can mobilise people, exclude others,

---

[8] Ernest Gellner, *Anthropology and Politics: Revolutions in the Sacred Grove* (Oxford: Blackwell, 1995).

[9] Kertzer, *op.cit.*

[10] *Idem*, p.8

screen out certain memories, establish solidarity or, indeed, reinforce the hierarchy of status and values.

So far it has been tacitly assumed in this analysis that all communities share roughly the same level of density and intensity of myth. This is not necessarily the case. Evidently some communities will have evolved a much more complex, much richer mythology than others. This allows the community in question to withstand much greater stress and turbulence (political, economic, social etc.) than those with only a relatively poor set of myths. Thus it is difficult to integrate a rural population when the integrating community has no strong myths of urban experience. When two such communities are engaged in a contest, the weaker one may find that some of its members shift their allegiance via assimilation.

Myth can, therefore, be seen as having a variety of roles, functions and purposes. It is an instrument of self-definition, in that those who accept the beliefs encoded in myth accept above all the particular world-view it reflects as well as membership and the rules that go with membership. Myth attributes special qualities to the group, extends its distinctiveness and creates a boundary. It gives content, at the same time, to the self-apperception of the community.

Equally, myth can be an instrument of identity transfer.[11] It enables a new identity to be superimposed on an older one, so that the collectivity sustains itself by creating an identity homogeneous enough to let it live with, say, major social upheaval. Modernisation, the shift of the peasantry from the countryside to the towns, is an illustration of this. By the same token, through myth the assimilation of ethnically different groups is accelerated, as the myth-poor community accepts that upward social mobility demands the abandonment of its culture, language and myth-world in exchange for something superior: for a better world. In the terms of this analysis this was essentially the aim of communism in Central and Eastern Europe.

Another aspect of myth relates to communication. As already argued, through myth and ritual, solidarity is established without consensus, but this does little to resolve the basic ambiguity that is present in all exchanges and communications. This dilemma is all the more acute when the society in question is moving towards

[11] John Armstrong, *Nations before Nationalism* (Chapel Hill: University of North Carolina Press, 1982), p. 130.

greater diversity of individuals and experience, especially owing to the influx of outsiders, with whom secure modes of communication are lacking. Thought, emotion and grammatical language can never be congruent, hence myth is a means of transcending the gap by establishing an illusion of community.[12] Cognitive processes cannot grasp the entirety of reality, so that in order to construct some kind of meaningful collective existence, aspects of experience have to be represented in a mythical and symbolic fashion. From this perspective, symbolic forms are not mimetic but constitutive of reality: the agency by which is created an object for intellectual apprehension, which is thus made visible to the community. Thus myth is a kind of simplified representation, an ordering of the world in such a way as to make sense of it for collectivities and thus make them binding on them.[13]

Yet again, myth is also a way of delimiting the cognitive field and thus simplifies complexity to make a collective response possible. The standardisation of cognitions generates coherence, but there is a danger when the coherence so created is not congruent with reality, when the perceptions of a community are at variance with the logic of other processes, like technological change. The loss of reality-congruent knowledge is likely to be highly damaging. In these conditions, standardisation can be imposed on the community – to resist the external influence that is seen as dangerous – despite the gap, possibly widening, between empirical data and its interpretation. Awareness of the gap triggers negative reactions because it amounts to an acknowledgement of the community's inability to influence events.[14] In this serious crisis of meaning, loss of coherence and cognitive anarchy the community feels its own existence to be in danger. In these circumstances, until coherence is restored, perhaps by the redefinition of myths, the members of the community may well indulge in highly destructive behaviour and be at the mercy of political charlatanry. The Serbs of Bosnia are a case in point. Communities will go to great lengths to prevent these gaps from becoming exposed.

A negative outcome is not certain when myth is employed to cope with the crisis of reality-incongruent knowledge. Myth can

[12] Ernst Cassirer, *Language and Myth* (New York: Dover, 1946), p.5.

[13] *Ibid.* p.9

[14] Elias, *op.cit.*, p.72.

be employed as a device for weathering a crisis, for securing the cohesiveness of the community while measures are taken to effect the metamorphoses needed to deal with the structural changes in question. It can be argued, for instance, that the strong emphasis on tradition in Britain during the 1950s and 1960s was a way of dealing with the shock of the aftermath of winning a war and losing the peace. Eventually, the discourses permeated with tradition gave way to others more in tune with current realities.

In politics, the role of myth is central, though it is hardly ever articulated in this way; indeed, practitioners will actively resist any suggestion that in 'modern', 'rational' polities myth and ritual have any role at all.[15] In a broader analysis, it will be clear that myth is, in fact, a significant factor in conditioning the limits of the possible, in establishing the cognitive field and in underpinning the consent to ground rules which makes politics work. Through myth, as already argued, communication within the community is intensified, making it far simpler to transmit the messages from the ruler to the ruled and enhancing the solidarity, and thus the trust, between the two parties. The way in which Slobodan Milošević used the various myths of the Serbian past in the late 1980s to amass power was an exemplary illustration. In neighbouring Hungary, József Antall was able to mobilise only a part of Hungarian opinion by his reliance on myth (like that of there being '15 million Hungarians'); he had obviously picked the wrong myth.

In ethnically divided societies, the use of myths almost invariably enhances the division, unless there are myths that unite the groups across the divide. It is possible to conceptualise myths of citizenship that transcend ethnicity – the Swiss identity is an excellent example – but these are rare. It is far easier to use ethnicity as the identifier and to exclude ethnic aliens, or, indeed, use them as the negative 'other', the object against which mobilisation is needed. The outcome of this state of affairs is that myths of collective existence within the ethnic group are emphasised and a sharper boundary is drawn against outsiders.

This process is usually dynamic and to some extent imitative. If one group feels that it has to rely more and more heavily on myths of collective existence, its demonised other – its *Doppelgänger*

---

[15] Simon Jenkins in *The Times, passim,* is an excellent example of intellectual resistance of this kind.

– will generally do likewise. Thus once the Romanian state relaunched its commitment to the myth of Daco-Roman continuity in the 1970s,[16] a section of the Hungarian minority began to use a myth of Sumerian descent as a counter. A process of this kind tends to be dynamic, polarising, and, once launched, hard to break. On both sides of the divide, mythopoeia and the fashioning of symbols permeate political discourses, with the consequence that communication across the boundary becomes extremely difficult, given that mythicised language functions for intra-community communication, not across boundaries. In trans- boundary communication, myths distort perspectives and confuse participants, because their role is to strengthen collective solidarity and not to clarify exchanges with another community.

Myth is equally a way of offering explanations for the fate of a community, for accounting for failure, for the negative outcomes of particular strategies. It can be used to make sense of otherwise inexplicable phenomena – to be precise, phenomena which are inexplicable at the collective level. Myth can be used to solidify the group in adversity by attributing a prime cause, an explanation that satisfies the community or, for that matter, individual members of the community, by offering an answer that can be probed no further. At the simplest level: 'the flood was caused because the river god was angry'; or in more sophisticated terms, 'our misfortunes are caused by evil aliens beyond our control'. Argumentation of this kind is the first step towards the construction of conspiracy theories.

The difficulty with processes of this kind is at what point does the reference to myth, the deployment of myth, reach the stage where it is an instrument for the rejection of responsibility, for the refusal to admit error, for the unwillingness to acknowledge that a particular event or set of events is likely to cause a breach in the community's hard-won coherence? As long as political elites or leaders seek to address their constituencies, they will invariably refer to myth, but there are many situations where the society in question lacks the cognitive instruments to see the message that is hidden behind the myth and will accept the causation that it is being offered as a proper explanation for its fate. The use of xenophobic narratives and scapegoating is an easy next step.

[16] Katherine Verdery, *National Ideology under Socialism: Identity and Cultural Politics in Ceausescu's Romania* (Berkeley, CA: University of California Press, 1991).

Controlling the Myth

This immediately raises the question of exactly who does control myth, and which myth. The evident answer is the political and intellectual elites in the community, those who are able to gain the ear of society, those who control the language of public communication: politicians, the monarch, the bureaucracy, maybe the priesthood, writers and so on. Usually such communication is the work of a series of intersecting elites, rather than a single one. The impact of the electronic media should be noted in this context, because television not only reaches a very large number of people and thus penetrates into areas of society not easily reached otherwise, but also because the visual image is excellent in creating a sense of mythic reality and verisimilitude which is then very hard to check against other experiences.

For a myth to be effective in organising and mobilising opinion, it must, however, resonate. A myth that fails to elicit a response is either alien to the community or it is inappropriate at the time when it is used or conceivably it evokes a response only in a small number of those addressed. This proposition is significant because of the popularity of analyses that stress the 'invented' and 'imagined' nature of national sentiment.[17] It seems that there are clear and unavoidable limits to invention and imagination and these are set by resonance. This is significant because it underpins the proposition that myth cannot be constructed purely out of false material; it has to have some relationship with the memory of the collectivity that has fashioned it. There has to be some factor, some event, some incident in the collective memory to which the myth makes an appeal; it is only at that point that the reinterpretation can vary radically from a closer, historical assessment. In effect, it is hard to see how the Czechs or Slovaks, say, could define their mythopoeias by inventing a strong seafaring tradition.

In this connection, myth plays a role in the maintenance of memory and the possibilities of forgetting; which part of memory is made salient, how it is understood and how its resonance is to be controlled are all a part of regulation by myth. The exclusion

---

[17] E.g. Eric Hobsbawm and Terence Ranger (eds), *The Invention of Tradition* (Cambridge University Press, 1983), and Benedict Anderson, *Imagined Communities,* 2nd edn (London: Verso, 1991).

of certain events from public consciousness, the consequent refusal to acknowledge that these events took place, which makes memory morally suspect, can all be derived from myth. The difference between mythic exclusion and Orwellian thought-control is that myth is harder to engineer from above; it must go with the grain of the collectivity's memories and start from a position that seems 'normal' and 'natural'.[18]

The cognitive delimiting created by myth can have a very negative result in blocking rational enquiry and the comprehension of change. By using myth to elicit a largely emotional response, political leaders can seek to block reform or soften the impact of change in circumstances discussed above. But there is a stage beyond this, where a political elite deploys myth in order to preserve its power by erecting barriers to comprehension, by stressing myth to ensure that its actions cannot be challenged because the means of making that challenge are not there. The very language of contest is made to seem unavailable, as words acquire the very particular, constricted meanings with which myth invests them.

This process will frequently go together with the construction of mythic enemies who are attempting to destroy the collectivity in a demonic conspiracy. In a worst-case scenario, a mechanism of this kind can end up a self-fulfilling prophecy. The danger the myth confronts does not actually exist, but it is painted in order to deflect attention from something else. But after repeated reference to the danger, those stigmatised as hostile begin to accept the demonic role assigned to them and behave in accordance with it. The relationship between Serbs and Croats and Serbs and Muslims in the first half of the 1990s conforms fairly closely to this model. Of course, this pattern of abuse of myth cannot last for ever, reality will break through, but the way in which it breaks through and how it is then decoded will certainly be conditioned by the mythicised experience.

Myth may reside in the political realm, but, particularly where nationhood is involved, it is intimately bound to culture. Culture embodies a variety of myths – this is what makes cultural determinism so dubious a predictor – giving a collectivity a choice of which myth to engage in different circumstances. Culture may

---

[18] On Orwellian dystopias, see Erika Gottlieb, *The Orwell Conundrum* (Ottawa: Carleton University Press, 1992).

be defined as a system of collectively held notions, beliefs, premises, ideas, dispositions and understandings to which myth gives a structure. This system is not locked in people's heads, but is embodied in shared myths and symbols which are the main vehicles through which people communicate their worldview, value orientations and ethos to others.[19]

Politics is not as a rule studied as part of a cultural system. Often it is conceptualised as being governed by strictly rational and transparent considerations of a purely utilitarian kind, of which costs and benefits are the classical model. Politics is examined as give and take in which people follow their interests as consumers of benefits, rights, duties and privileges; it is about interest groups, economic forces and power relations. However, what the analysis of myth suggests is that politics is an aspect of the overall cultural system. Every political action is embedded in a wider cultural context. Cultural presuppositions and values may not be seen as narrowly political and as having an influence upon political action and, similarly, symbolic action is not perceived as a central means of interaction between political elites and public opinion, yet they do have this role. In this sense, myth creates a field in which interests are conveyed in a symbolic fashion or with considerable symbolic baggage.[20]

Mythic and symbolic discourses can thus be employed to assert legitimacy and strengthen authority. They mobilise emotions and enthusiasm. They are a primary means by which people make sense of the political process, which is understood in a symbolic form. Attitudes are, therefore, formed more by symbolic forms than utilitarian calculation, and the potency of symbols in the political process derives from the fact that they are vehicles for conceptualisation.

At the same time, the shared cultural notions underlying and giving meaning to events and discourses are invoked in symbolic form as either explicit or implicit assumptions which underlie their logic or are their explicit subject. Discourse in this sense is socially constituted communication which leads to the production of texts and narratives, which can embody and locate myth. Myth

[19] Ladislav Holy, *The Little Czech Nation and the Great Czech Nation: National Identity and the Post-communist Social Transformation* (Cambridge University Press, 1996).

[20] *Ibid.*

as time-honoured tradition and deep-rooted cultural notion is reproduced and thus perpetually recreated in the present. These discourses are the locus of a 'management of meanings' by which culture is generated and maintained, transmitted and received, applied, exhibited, remembered, scrutinised and experimented with. Each culture constructs its discourses in opposition to another and this allows the culture to see itself as enduring, as unique, as a bearer of moral worth.[21] The element of comparison is vital here. Collectivities will monitor themselves against others, so that ethnicity is neither exclusively internally generated nor solely defined by its external boundaries. It is a perpetual interaction between the two. Further, it is an ongoing process, a continuous recreation in contemporary discourses, a work in progress without final form, though the participants will see it as stable, possibly static.

A taxonomy of myths

A great variety of myths can be identified. Indeed, there is no limit to myth, that is its Protean strength. However, a number of fairly standard myths can be found, notably in Central and Eastern Europe, and what follows is an account of some of these. There is no attempt to be exhaustive and, it should be stressed, the categories are not exclusive. Several myths can overlap, feed on one another or contradict each other. Myths may need to be relatively coherent internally, but a culture with a repertoire of many myths can live comfortably with considerable mythopoeic diversity.

To start with myths of *territory*, these are fairly common and claim that there is a particular territory where the nation first discovered itself, assumed the form it aspires to or expressed its finest self. Often, this was a land where its purity was safeguarded and where its virtues were best preserved before contact with aliens. Thus myths of territory can tie up with myths of Golden Age, like the legendary Tir nan Og of Celtic mythology, a land of harmony and plenty. These myths are extended to the current political boundaries of the state. In essence, these myths are bound up with the sacralisation of territory, a particularly powerful imperative, whereby a community will defend its frontiers to the

---

[21] Donald Horowitz, *Ethnic Groups in Conflict* (Berkeley: University of California Press, 1985).

last and is incapable of seeing it as 'real estate', as a possible bargaining counter. This makes secession or cession one of the hardest of political actions because territory is sacred space, where the existence of the community is preserved from pollution and thus its means of cultural reproduction is kept safe from outsiders.

Everything that symbolises that territory – flags, maps, anniversaries – serves to reinforce the myth and exclude alternative rationalities, like financial calculation. This has extensive implications for political action and behaviour. It suggests that states, when faced with what looks like a territorial claim, even when it is not argued in territorial terms, will readily reinterpret it that way, with the result that political negotiation becomes virtually impossible. The major reorderings of state frontiers in Europe are almost always associated with a major upheaval, like defeat in war or the collapse of communism, and new frontiers are either imposed from above (generating new myths) or affect territories that already have a separate existence, so that the loss can be integrated into a new mythic structure. The separation of Norway from Sweden or Slovakia from the Czech Republic illustrate the latter proposition; the disintegration of Austria-Hungary is an example of the former.

Myths of *redemption and suffering* claim that the nation, by reason of its particularly sorrowful history, is undergoing or has undergone a process of expiating its sins and will be redeemed or, indeed, may itself redeem the world. The prevalence of this myth in Central and Eastern Europe can be explained by the legacy of Christianity in conjunction with a sense of geographical, political and cultural marginalisation with respect to Europe. Because most, if not all, of these cultures regarded themselves as on the edge of Europe,[22] coupled with loss of power to external conquerors, these myths have had an explanatory function for survival and purposiveness. Indeed, in their form of being the 'last bastion of Europe' against the Barbarian hordes of the East, they are linked to *antemurale* myths,[23] that the nation in question nearly bled to death precisely so that Europe could flourish.

[22] Czeslaw Milosz, *The Witness of Poetry* (Cambridge, MA: Harvard University Press, 1983).

[23] Armstrong, *op.cit. Antemurale* myths claim that a particular nation fought to save Europe, defending it while acting on behalf of the defensive forces beyond the walls.

These myths, therefore, should be understood as myths of power-lessness and compensation for that powerlessness. They make a virtue of fatalism and passivity, claim a special moral superiority for having suffered – a key aspect of Christian doctrine in any case – and thereby demand recognition for certain claims in the present. These myths have implications for the individual's role with respect to the community, in that they weaken individual responsibility, by suggesting that history or malign forces have caused the suffering, that it was 'the will of God'. In effect, this myth is saying something significant about the way in which cause and effect are decoded and about how much control the individual or society has and may have over power.

There are countless examples of this type of myth. The Serbian myth of Kosovo essentially begins with the redemptive element, in that the defeat of Kosovo Polje is explained by the choice of heavenly glory over earthly power. Self-evidently, this is an *ex post facto* rationalisation of the military defeat of the Serbian forces by the Ottoman armies in 1389 and the subsequent conquest of Serbia. In the Serbian case, the myth gains added strength by incorporating divine intervention, in the narrative figure of the two falcons that are sent by God as messengers to the Serbian leader. In the modern context this myth has very powerful im-plications for Serbian-Albanian relations and, for that matter, for the way in which Serbs perceive their relations with the rest of the world. At the mythic level, the Albanians are reconfigured as Turks, the ancient enemy, who are polluting the sacred land of Serbian suffering. This myth clearly made it easier to give credence to the concept of a suffering Serbia in Yugoslavia, an idea that began to gain ground in the 1960s, and to legitimate the demand for Serbian separatism well before the collapse of the state.

The Romanian myth of the magical lamb, the *miorita*, is an analogue, as are its functions. Here the story is of a magical lamb warning its owner of his fellow shepherds' plan to kill him, but instead of taking action, he contemplates the beauties of nature and accepts the inevitable.[24] The moral is clear. There is nothing to be done, power will always be exercised without the individual

---

[24] Michael Shafir, *Political Culture, Intellectual Dissent and Intellectual Consent: The Case of Rumania* (Jerusalem: Soviet and East European Research Centre, Hebrew University, 1978).

having much control over it and it is morally superior to acquiesce. This proposition then legitimates inactivity and passivity, the acceptance of hierarchy and authoritarianism, the irrationality of power and distrust of others.

Myths of *unjust treatment* are closely related to the above. Here the argument is that history is a malign actor that has singled out the community for special, negative treatment. The group has been badly treated by history; it has had a particularly unpleasant destiny, but that remains its destiny nonetheless. Here the motif of helplessness tends to be strong.

The use of the mythic narrative of the deportations of Latvians by the Soviet authorities after the Second World War is one illustration. Here the function of the myth seems to be that the Latvians underwent terrible suffering, yet their Calvary could only make sense if in some way it could be seen as having a collective purpose – they were, after all, deported because they were Latvians. Their suffering was not in vain because eventually Latvia regained its independence, but the land that they regained was not the one they had left, in that it was now heavily populated by others – the very Russians who had caused their suffering.

Implicit in this myth, as well as in those of redemption, is that the world, in this instance Europe, owes those who have suffered a special debt, that the victims of the suffering are helpless because they suffered for the wider world and the wider world should recognise this, thereby legitimating the group's very special moral worth.

The growing use of 'holocaust' to describe any particularly terrible collective experience should also be seen in this context. This pattern appears to be on the increase in the United States, where it is becoming a way of legitimating one's collective ethnic claims to recognition in the cultural contest of American life. Used first, evidently, by Jews, the idea was then taken up by Blacks, significantly so in the term 'the Time on the Cross', and more recently an attempt was made to redefine the Irish famine as 'holocaust'. It is as if an ethnic community in the United States can only claim fully-fledged legitimacy in the world of ethnic competition if it can claim that it underwent some special redemptive experience that would give it the necessarily moral worth in the eyes of society. It is noteworthy that this appropriation of the word 'holocaust' has led some Jewish commentators to drop it and to use the Hebrew term 'Shoah' (desolation) in order, presumably, to mark the unique nature of the mass murder of Jews in Europe. It is an open question what will be the response to this bid, which has affinities with a myth of election.

Myths of *election and civilising mission* are, again, fairly common in the region. These state that the nation in question has been entrusted with a special mission, by God or by History, to perform some special mission, some particular function, because it is in endowed with unique virtues. The Christian origins of this are very evident. In the modern world, the religious motif has been transmuted into secular form, like the particular virtue of civility or literacy or capacity for modernity or simply being more 'European' than anyone else. This myth then legitimates an assumption of moral and cultural superiority to all competitors and rivals and requires them to recognise one's unique moral worth.

The Czechs claim this uniqueness in terms of democracy: that they are simply by virtue of being Czech capable of being democratic, indeed more democratic than all others. The Hungarians sustained their multinational state before 1918 by claiming that their civilising mission over the non-Magyar minorities legitimated their policies of assimilation, a motif that still surfaces occasionally in their dealings with Slovakia and Romania. The Poles claim to be European by a set of criteria abstracted from a mythic definition of Europe to which the Poles conform by virtue of their Polishness.[25] This, on the basis of the myth, entitles to them to the special favour of Europe, whether by means of early integration into the European Union or NATO or simply being accepted as a European state like any Western state. Sometimes, this myth can be closely linked to a myth of civic virtue, of being exempt from ethnic intolerance and discrimination against others. Traces of this can be found among the Czechs and, for that matter, among the French.

Myths of *military valour, of resistance and aristocracy* are tied to the foregoing, but have a few features all their own. These myths give saliency to the special regard in which a collectivity holds itself because it has performed deeds of military valour. This valour can be attributed either to an aristocracy or to the people. In some instances, it is tied closely to the idea of insurrection or revolution: the group finds the truest expression of its essence by

[25] Witold Wirpsza, *Pole, wer bist du?* (Luzern: C.J. Bucher Verlag, 1971).

rising against intolerable tyranny. This is potentially a homogenising myth, in which taking part in the collective diminishes the role of the individual but enhances the group, because of the very particular demands and qualities of group violence. These myths can be used to legitimate force as an instrument of change, to characterise a particular regime as tyrannical and, therefore, to justify mass violence against it, to downgrade incremental change as useless ('cowardly') and to deride compromise and negotiation as something that the community despises ('dishonourable').

This myth is clearly present throughout the Balkans, but also in Hungarian and Polish mythopoesis; post-war Lithuanian guerrilla activity against the Soviet authorities should likewise find a place in this category. The myth obviously sustained and fuelled armed resistance by giving it the force of precedent, by screening out suggestions for negotiation and by emphasising collective heroism. It is noteworthy that since the collapse of communism these myths have tended to play a rather restricted role, as the post-communist states continue with their experiment in democracy, which places violence beyond the boundaries of the legitimate.

Myths of *rebirth and renewal* are linked to revolutions. Ultimately they are related to the Christian themes of rebirth (palingenesis) and the Second Coming (parousia), but are also present in ancient mythical motifs like the phoenix. Here the idea is that the present is tainted and must be cleansed and through that purgation a better world can be created. They look both forwards and backwards, in that the past is unacceptable and, therefore, the group must distance itself from it, but at the same time, there is hope for a better world if renewal takes place. It is significant that both concepts are present. If a group has committed some particular act of violence towards another group, like ethnic cleansing or the analogus purge of class enemies – and these portentous words have gained wide currency – then by claiming that a renewal or rebirth has taken place, the perpetrators can argue that they have shed their sins. To be fully effective, though, the victims must in some symbolic way accept this and, ideally, be included in the cleansing ritual. Equally, as far as the future is concerned, rebirth can create a sense of a clean slate, a new start, in which the awfulness of the past can be forgotten. This type of myth is a way of legitimating change, of understanding far-reaching transformation, of creating mythic order in the chaos of a major political shift.

Examples of myths of renewal are widespread in contemporary Europe. Arguably, 1945 and the end of the Second World War have some of these functions, containing the proposition that in the new post-war world, only democracy would rule – a demand of particular weight with respect to Germany and Italy. It was present explicitly during the Solidarity period in Poland, which was actually termed *odnowa*, renewal. The slogan of a New World Order propagated during the early 1990s should also be noted here, even if it had next to no resonance.

Mention should also be made here of the closely related myths of *foundation*. Every group, every political system, virtually every area of human endeavour has to make a start, and seeks to mark that by some special act which is accorded mythic qualities. In this connection, one is dealing with a moment of innovation which is not necessarily as drastic and radical as a revolution, but which, it is felt by the participants, deserves special note in order to point to the future. The implicit, sometimes explicit message is that afterwards everything will be different ('better') and that the newly founded system has dispensed with whatever made the old reprehensible.

Some general elections have this function, like the 1945 election in the United Kingdom. A new constitution obviously acts as a marker of this kind; both the German Basic Law and the constitution of the French Fifth Republic do this. In fact, it is noteworthy that the French state is customarily referred to as the Fifth Republic, thereby symbolically delimiting it from its predecessors, but equally claiming the continuity of republican virtue that is at the heart of French politics, the legacy of the French Revolution. And all the first post-communist general elections functioned in a similar way, to mark the end of communism and create something new, different and superior: democracy.

Myths of *ethnogenesis and antiquity* answer the question of where we originate from in our collective existence. However, these myths can become more than just self-legitimation when used to try and establish primacy over all other ethnic groups in a given territory. The argument is that because one group was there first, it has a superior right to that territory over all others, meaning that, say, the rights of citizenship must take second place to those of ethnicity and that those who have primacy also have the right to define (and maybe circumscribe) the rights of citizen ship. Reference has already made to the Romanian-Hungarian mythic dispute over Transylvania and the use of the Daco-Roman continuity myth and that of Sumerian descent to counter this, respectively.

Myths of *kinship and shared descent* are linked to the idea of the organic nature of the ethnic group, to the concept of the nation as family and thus work to exclude ethnic aliens. The myth implies that there is a certain genetic transmission of the specificity of the group from which others are automatically excluded. In some circumstances, this is transmuted into racism and myths of racial superiority and inferiority. Among the functions of this myth is to impose a well-defined set of moral propositions on a group, usually a group speaking the same language, that is in the process of being welded into a nation. The model of the family, customarily the patriarchal family, is employed to make sense of the very different wider world of modernity for those who make the symbolic journey from country to town and discover that an entirely new set of cognitions is necessary in the new environment and that they may encounter ethnic aliens. The proposition that they and the fellow members of their language community share special characteristics because they are biologically related can provide the coherence that conditions demand.

However, it should be noted that myths of shared descent are not employed in anything like an equal fashion and that some groups, those which have launched a strategy of assimilation, cannot logically do so. Here the assimilands must accept the cultural codes of the group into which they are assimilating, but kinship will be loosely defined. Thus in Europe, Austrians, Germans, Hungarians, French and others have been assimilating nations and while they may have myths of kinship – in French colonies, African children were taught that their ancestors were the Gauls – these cannot be insisted on with any vehemence. By contrast, where a group feels itself at risk with respect to its future, possibly because it feels 'swamped' by aliens, it may emphasise or reemphasise its ethnic purity by referring to racial or genetic uniqueness. The concept of 'purity of blood' (*limpieza de sangre*) in Spanish myths, is a good illustration, in that it served to protect a self-image after the *reconquista*, that the Moors and Jews of reconquered Andalucia had disappeared, leaving only pure Spaniards. There are analogous though less explicit elements in both Romanian and Serbian patterns of exclusion.[26]

As will be seen from the taxonomy, myths may be closely interconnected, methodologically they are sometimes difficult to delineate from one another and they may both overlap and be contradictory. But this last factor is immaterial. Precisely because one of myths' functions is to construct coherence, different myths receive emphasis at different times to cope with different challenges. Their underlying function is the same, though: to ensure that the integrity of group is safeguarded, that cultural reproduction is not prejudiced and that the collective world made simple by myth remains for individuals to construct their identities as individuals and simultaneously as members of a community.

---

[26] Milorad Pavic, *The Dictionary of the Khazars* (London: Hamish Hamilton, 1989).

8

IDEOLOGICAL THINKING AND POST-COMMUNISM

When Western observers take a superficial look at the post-communist world, they are frequently puzzled by what appears to them as a paradox. Democracy has been introduced, elections are held regularly, there is a free press and so on, goes the argument, yet the working of these systems is in so many ways different from that of the established Western states. The salience of ethnicity causes particular concern. The tendency is to dismiss these dysfunctions of post-communism as legacies either of the communist past or of the pre-communist antecedents of the area. In this analysis it will be argued that this assessment of post-communism is flawed and that the post-communist systems have become, broadly, self-reproducing with their own special characteristics.

One of the key explanations for the divergence between Western and post-communist political systems is cultural: the impact of inherited patterns of cognition and types of reasoning, and the structure of expectations and self-definitions. In this connection, ideological thinking plays a crucial role. Ideological thinking is not, of course, the sole explanatory factor, but it does leave its mark on many other processes. In its essence, ideological thinking is the proposition that every effect must have a proximate cause because it is a part of a logical chain, that whatever happens does so because someone has caused it to happen. The causator can then be identified, usually as an alien antagonist, by whatever criteria seem appropriate.

The central difficulty that results from this approach to explaining events is that it marginalises accident, coincidence, chance and spontaneity. It endows actors with enormous, near superhuman powers and readily defaults into conspiracy theories: that 'out there', in a location defined by the logic, there are malign individuals and groups capable of damaging whatever is being assessed. It impels people to make untenable assumptions about the nature

99

of causation, to leave these assumptions unexamined and then to build a pseudo-theory that produces a closed, pre-determined outcome.

Arendt and ideological thinking

The classical exposition of ideological thinking comes from Hannah Arendt.[1] In brief, her argument is that ideological thinking begins from the identification of a transcendental 'law', which by a verbal sleight-of-hand is applied to the situation in question; this law operates independently of any consent because it is transcendental. Processes are then 'law-governed', introducing the element of motion into the argument. This signifies that something so described cannot be flouted, that it is futile to oppose it, thereby weakening individual responsibility. The 'idea' embodied in the law acquires an autonomous life of its own and an ideology implies that an idea can become the subject matter of science and is itself 'the logic of an idea'.[2] Ideologies claim to be able to explain the world, to be the basis for a complete cognitive world and to exclude everything that is false. Thus inconsistencies are simply eliminated, not reasoned. 'The movement of history and the logical process of this notion are supposed to correspond to each other, so that whatever happens, happens according to the logic of one "ideal".'[3] Ideologies take as their premise, therefore, that one idea is sufficient to explain everything. Crucially, experience can teach us nothing, because everything is already comprehended in the 'idea' and the consistent process of logical deduction. They thus offer the seeming security of a sole chain of causation, because the movement of history is by definition obliged to pass from A to B to C in a predetermined way.

Ideological thinking thus becomes 'emancipated', detached from the reality of experience, a proposition on which Arendt places particular emphasis, for it can learn nothing from it, in as much as there exists a 'truer' reality concealed behind the world of perceptions. There is instead a secret meaning and purposiveness in events, importantly a secret intent behind every act, particularly

[1] Hannah Arendt, *The Origins of Totalitarianism* (London: George Allen and Unwin, 1958), especially pp.461-75.

[2] *Ibid.*, p.468.

[3] *Ibid.*, p.469.

in the public sphere. It is an easy step from here to constructing conspiracy theories. In this attitude, reality – real enmity or friendship – is no longer experienced and understood on its own terms, but is assumed to mean something else. It is interpreted as a malign purposiveness and all perceptions are integrated according to the categories provided by the 'idea'. Reality, however, is not transformed by ideology, and to subordinate reality to its purposes, ideological thinking uses a different device. It 'orders facts into an absolutely logical procedure which starts from an axiomatically accepted premise, deducing everything from it. That is, it proceeds with a consistency that exists nowhere in the realm of reality.'[4]

In essence, ideological thinking rests on the two key methods of movement (active transformation) and emancipation from reality, for which is substituted thought. Thus it proceeds from thought to thought, rather than from object to thought or vice versa. It imposes metaphor on experience. The starting point does have a link to reality, but thereafter this is no longer the case and experience does not interfere with ideological thinking. It cannot be taught by experience. In such thought-worlds, the logic is what drives the idea forward, 'the irresistible force of logic'.[5] In this respect, it is the aim of the idea that is vital. Arendt does not consider this, but this proposition offers an excellent insight into the construction of the other. It is automatically assumed that the other is motivated by an ideology – non-ideological thinking is inconceivable to those who live within its confines – which has its aims and objectives, which may be concealed but which can be unmasked and understood by uncovering its logic. The purposiveness of the alien ideology may be hidden, but it can be dealt with by ideological thinking, because of the assumption that it functions in the same way by a process of logic that is incontrovertible. The other's ideology is all the more dangerous because it is covert, because it seeks to lull us into a sense of false security by concealing its malign purposes. This further implies that there can be only one possible logic, because ideology has to have a monopoly. Then, by a process of feedback, our own ideology and our ideological convictions are strengthened and

---

[4] *Ibid.*, p.471.

[5] *Ibid.*, p.472.

legitimated by the existence of the other. Our ideologically determined world-view is justified because we have successfully decoded the other's. Alternative explanations are simply dismissed as unrealistic or 'naive'. Thus overall, in the application of the logic its original starting point may be lost; it is devoured by the logic, because of the apparent obligation to follow the logic through all its steps. This is 'the coercive force of logicality'.[6]

The intellectual origins of ideological thinking

Ideological thinking, therefore, can be defined for our purposes as a flawed way of world-making, a faulty cognitive process, which takes a narrow slice of reality as its premise, or converts a normative proposition into analysis, and then imposes it on all who are a part of the collectivity in which it operates. If the first principle of collective life is that people gather in groups in order to make cosmos from chaos,[7] then ideological thinking is one of the distortions illicitly applied either by a collectivity to itself or by those who control the cognitive world of the collectivity.

No community comes innocent into the world. By the time it can be called community, it has acquired a quantity of cognitive baggage which will allow it to see certain processes and to screen out others. Regardless of Enlightenment rationality, selection means that some ideas, thoughts, perceptions, even experiences of reality are downgraded in an implicit hierarchy of norms that varies from collectivity to collectivity. This makes the entire history and lived past or memory significant.

In the context of post-communism, various processes have contributed to the composition of the thought-worlds that structure political values and attitudes. Some of these are grasped as a part of the historical legacy, others as derived from an examination of the sociology of the post-communist world. The first of these, to which indirect reference has already been made through Arendt, is the experience of Marxism-Leninism. While Arendt was sketching an ideal-type totalitarian model when she wrote her book, the reality of communist rule by the 1980s was different. The totalisation remained and at the level of legitimating ideology

[6] *Ibid.*

[7] Mircea Eliade, *The Myth of the Eternal Return: Cosmos and History* (London: Penguin, 1954).

played a significant role; at the level of practice, however, the communist system was shot through with gaps and contradictions, the interstices that Kolakowski analysed.[8]

While at first sight this degeneration of the rigidity of the communist system was welcome, it also had unwelcome consequences. Crucially, it added new elements of unpredictability to an already contradictory system. The central difficulty was the *de facto* acceptance by the party that power was not monolithic, but there lacked any instrument, any criteria for the resolution of conflicts or the exercise of that power. The outcome was arbitrary and discretionary wielding of power, even if the consequences of error were no longer as drastic as they had been in Stalin's time. This meant that society was involved in an unending series of negotiations without ground-rules. The absence of rules recognised as binding by all the contestants is one of the key negative aspects of post-communism. In the absence of these rules, individuals are forced to establish some form of regularity in their lives – cosmos in a world of chaos – and as this cannot apparently be achieved from everyday experience which is bewildering and confusing, attempts are continuously made to extract rules from ideology, whatever the dominant ideology may be. Currently, this is ethnic nationalism.

The experience of discretionary power is particularly damaging because it undermines faith in the rationality of politics. Depoliticisation, the obverse of discretionary power, has left behind societies that have only a hazy idea of what can and cannot be achieved through politics and that are confused or angered when hopes are dashed. In these circumstances, it is easy to fall prey to populist discourses, which offer simplistic solutions to complex problems and explain failure by reference to the machinations of 'enemies'. Indeed, the long-term residue of discretionary power is that it provides no readily intelligible explanation for success and failure. When these are not available, understood and accepted, the sudden, inexplicable rise of some and the fall of others demands an accounting, which can then be given in the language of conspiracy.

Furthermore, Marxism-Leninism insisted that its was a scientific world-view. This too had its long term consequences, in the expectation that the world really was intelligible scientifically, that

[8] Leszek Kolakowski, 'Theses on Hope and Hopelessness', *Survey* (summer 1971), pp.37-52.

if only an extra effort were made, these scientific rules could be grasped. When the world failed to conform to these notional scientific rules, the reaction was radical rejection, apathy or the belief prompted by ideological thinking that someone somewhere was blocking the scientific path, i.e. the first steps on the road to a conspiracy theory.

Then, there is the legacy of peasant mind-sets. As Jowitt has argued, Leninism reinforced the 'limited good' attitudes of peasant life. In 'limited good' cultures broad areas of peasant behaviour are patterned in such a way that peasants view their social, economic and natural universes, their total environment including friendship, status, influence, security, and safety as something that exists in a finite quantity and always in short supply. Hence individual and family improvement is always at the expense of someone else. These zero-sum concepts and values are rigid and there is no real concept of growth. There is a congruence between this and aspects of Marxism-Leninism, for example in the relationship between party and society, with its either/or, them/us attitudes.[9] This is antagonistic to differences of opinion, to compromise, to diversity. In this sense traditional attitudes were reinforced by the experience of communism, not least because the industrial revolution and the flight of the peasantry from the land were both rapid and imposed by alien criteria. The net result has been the ruralisation of the city and the conservation of rural attitudes, as the cities, overwhelmed by incomers from the land, were unable to integrate the peasantry.

Religion has also played a role in the conservation of ideological thinking, though not in the most obvious way, through dogma. Rather, secularisation has been incomplete; indeed because the communist revolution was alien it acted as a force for desecularisation in as much as religion was a form of resistance. But just as relevant were the attitudes structured by religion, the particular patterns of thought with respect to the meaning of the universe. In this connection, it is important to understand the mediated nature of the legacy of religion. When faith and dogma decline in their effectiveness, people persist in using some of the now empty belief system to give meaning to their lives without

---

[9] Ken Jowitt, *New World Disorder: The Leninist Extinction* (Berkeley: University of California Press, 1992).

necesarilyseeing this as having anything to do with religion as faith.[10]

Thus it is important to understand the particular patterns that the residue of religion has created. In Central Europe we are essentially talking of the legacy of Counter-Reformation Catholicism, which stresses hierarchy, obedience to authority, display, form over content, complexity over simplicity, the attempt to include all phenomena even if they are left unexplained and to gloss over inconsistencies. Put in an oversimplified way, this has produced a culture in which individual comprehension of the world is downplayed, in which Weberian instrumental rationality is balanced by other imperatives and in which ideologies are counted a significant means of making the world. Globally, the Orthodox analogue is formalised and static, emphasises externalisation rather than belief, gives saliency to the futility of action and downgrades structural analysis; it stresses distrust of individual initiative, conformity and passivity (with occasional outbursts of sudden activity) and unquestioning compliance with authority and its dominant ideology. To make matters clear, it is not suggested that the residue of religion will invariably determine the pattern of belief in ideologies, but it will have played a role in the constitution of the grain of a culture. This can be resisted and even modified, but only with difficulty.[11]

Because the communist revolution arrived in semi-traditional societies, the slow transformation of religion that Western Europe experienced was halted in Central and Eastern Europe and, as suggested, some of the attitudes informed by religion persisted. All this has strengthened the preeminent role of ideologies and thus left these societies somewhat more vulnerable to the patterns sketched in the foregoing. Crucially, the Enlightenment with its emphasis on instrumental rationality was only partially integrated into the dominant political cultural currents. Cognitive growth based on scepticism, enquiry and the rejection of all sacralisation[12]

---

[10] Bruce Kapferer, *Legends of People, Myths of State* (Washington, DC: Smithsonian Institute Press, 1987).

[11] On Orthodoxy, see Michael Shafir, *Political Culture, Intellectual Dissent and Intellectual Consent: The Case of Rumania* (Jerusalem: Soviet and East European Research Centre, Hebrew University, 1978).

[12] Ernest Gellner, *Plough, Sword and Book: The Structure of Human History* (London: Collins Harvill, 1988).

– the hallmark of so much Western enquiry – was always weaker and the communist period impeded its full emergence. This necessarily made it that much more difficult to question received orthodoxies and created a more favourable matrix for the survival of ideological thinking.

To the foregoing may be added an underanalysed aspect of Central and East European thought patterns – the preference for sacralising the word, for treating the word as an end in itself and downplaying the relationship between word and the object to which it refers.[13] There is, in consequence, a propensity to favour abstraction over practicality, to interpret reality in the light of this abstracted, often mythicised cognitive instrument. Representation is verbal and detached from the concrete reality and any pattern of causation may be understood as linking words rather than actual real experience.

The potential implication of this phenomenon is far-reaching. The system of signs by which reality is made concrete, by which it is comprehended remains stuck at a level of abstraction that makes real processes that much more difficult to interpret, which then leaves society open to implied processes of causation that may be relatively harmless while abstracted but can be very destructive when put into practice. The proposition that abstraction could and should be tested against actual realities is ignored or dismissed as superfluous, since inner meaning is encapsulated in the word itself. Here the process of logicality described by Arendt, ideological thinking, has its true impact. If cause and effect are widely abstracted from reality and, indeed, if concrete reality is to some extent despised as crude or primitive, then inevitably misunderstandings – to put it at its best – will flourish and counter-arguments based on that ignored reality will have little or no purchase, but will be dismissed as a distraction.

One of the central features of Western thinking is its relative openness and acceptance of alternative, conflicting ways of world-making. In this context, we are dealing with one of the foundations of stable democracy: the acceptance of contingency as the dominant mode of thought, of the constant, fluid, fluctuating nature of democratic ideas and practice. To achieve this, absolute categories must be diluted and made relative. Effectively this signals the end

---

13 Witold Wirpsza, *Pole, wer bist du?* (Luzern: C.J. Bucher Verlag, 1971).

of fixed epistemologies. As cultures become aware of their own existence relative to other cultures, they are forced to reformulate their self-definitions.[14] This is not an untroubled process. In some cases it gives rise to acute, negative responses of rejection and aggressiveness towards the outside world. Barriers are raised against foreign influence, great emphasis is placed on the authenticity of native roots, the genuineness of the people etc. Closures of this kind can only be effective in the short term. The intense disembedding quality of modernity cannot be excluded for long. Predictably some sections of society react by accepting the apparent security of ideological discourses and defend them vehemently.

The sociological origins of ideological thinking

The sociological well-springs of ideological thinking derive more directly from the experience of communism, its sudden collapse and the erosion of hopes vested in democracy. The event was for more dislocating than anyone had expected, principally because communism had kept societies in a cocoon of ignorance about the rest of the world and thereby deprived them of acquiring the cognitive equipment for dealing with rapid change. Indeed, as Kundera so acutely described, communism sought to stop time itself,[15] with far-reaching implications for the moment when time was restarted. Perhaps it is appropriate that one of the monuments in Prague marking the end of communism is the great public time-piece overlooking the Vltava.

Communism may have been non-consensual, but it was a functioning moral order with all the security and certainty that moral orders offer. Despite its discretionary quality, as noted above, it did provide short-term predictability. The end of this is serious, because it means that the world is much more difficult to predict than before and the threat of chaos to the cosmos is ever present. When all authority disappears, the outcome is breakdown, as was the case in Bosnia. In this connection, it is worth nothing that one of the factors assisting continuity was ethnicity, for all its drawbacks as a stabilising system. But ethnicity cannot account for everything – that, indeed, is its greatest shortcoming as a basis

[14] Anthony Giddens, *The Consequences of Modernity* (Cambridge: Polity, 1990).

[15] Milan Kundera, *The Unbearable Lightness of Being* (London: Faber and Faber, 1984).

for a political order – hence the grasping at straws like ideological thinking.

The confusion that has emerged since the disappearance of communism has its roots in the weakening or erosion of the old moral criteria without the universal acceptance of new ones, a state of affairs that Zygmunt Bauman has called 'liminality'.[16] The rapid changes, the loss of a sense of direction, the failure of any supposed universal meanings to live up to their promise have led to what may be called 'moral inflation'. Different groups in society are engaged in a deep-level contest for the past, present and future of the community. The contest is not bounded by rules, hence self-limitation appears futile and the only instrument for regulation is an appeal to morality.

However, because morality is itself the target of the contest, further fluidity is the outcome, with correspondingly greater insecurity. Even while the language of morality expands, the problems it is supposed to resolve are not resolved. Thus new winners and new losers rise and fall or not as the case may be. There are no criteria for assessing just and unjust enrichment. The law is supported on paper and ignored in practice. The communists who were supposedly ejected from power are back again under another name. Individuals shift their party allegiances without any rhyme or reason other than personal advantage. There is no sense of a regulated public sphere or a universally accepted public good. And so on. The simplistic answer to this threatening chaos is a call for order, stability and predictability, of the kind that ideological thinking promises.

The manifestations of these processes are to be found in the widespread evidence of mythopoeia. This is a clear indication of the confusion and inability to understand complex patterns of causation and, where there is non-comprehension, of deep suspicion, unrealistic expectations, anger and impatience. Virtually every post-communist state has suffered some kind of banking and finance scandal. An extreme case was the pyramid selling scandal in Albania, where a sizeable number of people, having no idea of the relationship between investment and return, lost their savings. Profit was understood both by the financiers and

---

[16] Zygmunt Bauman, 'After the Patronage State: A Model in Search of Class Interests' in Christopher Bryant and Edmund Mokrzycki (eds), *The New Great Transformation* (Routledge, 1994).

investors as ultra rapid, speculative gain, but there was obviously no clarity as to the high risk nature of this kind of financial activity. The consequent losses were greeted with great anger, a sense of injustice and demands for compensation. Also noteworthy was the inability and refusal of the Albanian authorities to recognise the dangers of the course they were pursuing. In other words, as captives of a pattern of ideological thinking, they screened out all contrary information as outside the logical process; they had become detached from reality and they lacked the experience to tell them when this was happening.[17]

In the political realm, the functional equivalent is the profound suspicion of and hostility to ethnic aliens, usually a local ethnic minority. No amount of sociological evidence will convince people that ethnic others are generally differentiated, that they do not respond as a homogeneous group, that like themselves ethnically different groups have various interests and attitudes. Instead, they are constrained into the narrow cage of a logical narrative which justifies, in the mind of the narrator, the harsh measures to be taken against the enemy.

Here is an anecdotal example. Gheorghe Funar, the ultra-nationalist mayor of Cluj in Romania, is notorious for his anti-Hungarian attitudes. He explained why Romania was failing to attract much foreign investment by the following argumentation. The discrimination against Romania, according to Funar, is the work of 'the Hungarians', who have trained up a cadre of attractive young women and sent them to the West in order to seduce Western leaders and influence them against Romania. The proof of this assertion is that Romania receives very little Western investment. The circularity of the chain of reasoning is quite clear in this instance and it excludes alternative explanations, like the poor state of Romania's investment legislation and a generally hostile climate towards foreign investors.

All this has important implications for democracy, both at the level of theory and of practice. Ideological thinking makes it difficult to establish and enroot a culture of toleration of the other, because it impels one to see all others as antagonists, as motivated by profoundly destructive aims. The proposition that one's *de facto* intuition of the other is 'proved' by the logical

[17] Some details are in the *Times* leader 'Curse of the Pyramids: Albanians learn that there is no such thing as a free lunch', 27 January 1997.

process is, in reality, a subtly different process. The action of the other will never be viewed with goodwill – this is the first step. The second step is to extract from the other's standpoint a reading that will justify the worst judgement. The third step is to regard this judgement as a legitimation of one's own antagonism. The circle is then complete. Each protagonist will legitimate the other in a mechanism that is so set as to produce solely negative outcomes. The conflict-generating attitude then strengthens one's position with respect to one's own supporters by demonising one's opponent as an enemy. Polarisation and extreme attitudes are then accepted as legitimate. This mechanism can be seen clearly in a variety of situations, in the relationship between Milošević and Tudjman, for instance. Each needed the other as a way of justifying their own policies at home.

Intimately related to the above is the problem of rules. In order for a political system to function with clarity and predictability and for institutions to be accepted as genuine, for civil society to operate with a degree of autonomy, for self-limitation to be possible, it is essential that the rules governing the exercise of power are not themselves a part of the political contest.[18] Under post-communism this has only happened very partially. Rules are changed by the criteria of those in power and it is expected by their opponents that the rules will be adjusted to the benefit of power holders. The result is short-termism and insecurity, so that actions are explained in ideological terms and the political actors are captured, if not actually devoured, by the logic with which they attack the situation.

The fluidity and contingency of institutions and procedures not only impede a stabilisation of the political system, but give rise to the instruments of its destabilisation. The mechanism in this context is that where the rules are contested, neutral space is not created, for neither the political actors nor society has the perspective to see processes in an even remotely detached way. Hence they are engaged with them and by them with an immediacy that prevents calculation in an instrumental way, because politics and the results of politics are interpreted as directly impacting on one's deepest existential imperatives.

[18] Claus Offe, 'Agenda, Agency and Aims of Central East European Transitions' in Stefano Bianchini and George Schöpflin (eds), *Europe and the Balkans: How They View Each Other*, vol.1 (Ravenna: Longo, 1998).

Reactions are permeated by passion,[19] distrust and fear, and the most coherent explanation, the one that comes closest to satisfying the demands raised by those passions, is to rely on ideological explanations, because these sustain the belief that others are like oneself. If the universal assumption is that everyone is motivated by fear and distrust and, therefore, uses ideological legitimation, there is a continuous reproduction of ideological thinking. Neutral space cannot, therefore, come into being; there is no ambivalence, only a false certainty.

Cosmos then comes to resemble chaos as any wider view of the regularities is lost. Explanations are transparent only over a rather narrow range of action, and the unpredictability of the motives of others and the impenetrability of the language in which those motives are set out generate patterns of identity and behaviour which can be termed pre-political, in the sense that for the polis to function as a public sphere, the individuals making it up must have a set of shared values and a shared language. The absence of this state of affairs does not imply that there is no politics at all, only that the conduct of politics cannot easily be made the object of instrumental rationality.

The problem of ethnicity requires some discussion in this connection. Why, the question might be put, does ethnicity not provide the necessary cement by which the polis can be brought into being? In essence, the explanation is that this is not what ethnicity is about. The role and function of ethnicity are aimed at regulating a different set of problems, those of the uncodified rules of the game, the implicit conditions of society, of the tacit internalisation of right and wrong and of the bonds of solidarity.[20] The significance of this should not be underestimated. Without these implicit rules and the bonds of solidarity, society would find it extremely difficult to sustain itself. On the other hand, the rules of ethnicity have little to say about the nature of institutionalisation and distribution of power. These processes, broadly speaking, are regulated by citizenship, not formal legal citizenship provision, but the general set of expectations, habits, shared attitudes

---

[19] Zygmunt Bauman, *Modernity and Ambivalence* (Oxford: Blackwell, 1990).

[20] David I. Kertzer, *Ritual, Politics and Power* (New Haven, CT: Yale University Press, 1988).

that govern politics.[21] Consequently, reliance on ethnicity to determine the conduct of politics, a fairly widespread phenomenon when institutionalisation is weak, turns out to be counterproductive, in as much as contrary to expectations, the security of the ethnic group is not guaranteed by ever greater emphasis on its reproduction. Here again, we can see that the potential response to collective insecurity is to have recourse to ideology and to revert to the forms of circular reasoning sketched above. This is all the more serious because fear as to the existence of the ethnic collectivity generates profoundly negative reactions.

Prospects

Despite the fairly pessimistic tone and emphasis of this analysis, the picture is not wholly occluded. There are patterns that can genuinely be seen as positive. For example, one can discern some forms of self-limitation, like the fact that to date every change of government in the post-communist world has taken place as a result of an election and that constitutional courts are playing an important and accepted role in regulating the public sphere.

At the same time, there are also processes from below that hold out the promise of a slow transformation of attitudes. It is crucial to understand here that cultural analysis is not deterministic. There are always choices, though those choices will generally be made by the mainstream cultural imperatives. But, as Arendt pointed out, people have the capacity for innovation which then becomes 'the moment of freedom'[22] and, it might be added, they have a capacity for acquiring experience that can lead to a questioning of an ideologically determined universe. The prospects for this pattern are all the stronger now that the ideology is not sustained by coercion or the threat of coercion, but 'only' cultural reproduction.

Besides, cultures are not homogeneous. All cultures contain a variety of traditions and strands and different ones can be used in different situations to act as legitimation and guidance for action. It is within this wider context that ideological thinking should be understood. It is an important, and from the perspective of democracy highly destructive, cultural current, but there are other

---

[21] David Miller, *On Nationality* (Oxford University Press, 1995).

[22] *Op.cit.*, p.473.

cognitive processes. Sometimes these latter will be too weak to challenge the ideologised mainstream; at other times it will be the reverse and ideology will be discounted. The experience of reality, especially of grassroots, street-level interaction, whether in politics or in the market, forms a vital part of the transformation. It should be understood, however, that this will be slow and that it holds the seeds of another potential misunderstanding, maybe a negative myth, that of betrayal by 'Europe'. If integration into Europe is perceived as the necessary condition for democracy and stability, the outcome will be disappointment. Europe will not as such ensure peace, democracy, prosperity or any of the other utopias current in the post-communist world; nor will it eradicate ideological thinking, not least because Europe is not immune to it either. But the presence of an alternative, even a mythicised alternative, can be positive in making it easier to analyse, dissect, delegitimate and rebut ideological thinking and, the off-spring of ideologies, conspiracy theories. But no one should make the mistake of thinking that this will be rapid. It will not.

APPENDIX
SOVIET ARMY IQ STUDIES REVEAL
RUSSIAN SUPERIORITY

24 January 1997
From usenet.alt.current-events.russia

smirnov@lpd.moscow.ru (Nikolai Sergeyevich Smirnov) wrote:

A book called *Russkaya umnost'—sud'ba i budushchnost' nashevo naroda* ['Russian Intelligence – Fate and Future of our Nation'] by illustrious Russian psychometricians B. E. Kolokovsky and L. L. Krutinskaya, sponsored by the Liberal Democratic Party, will appear in a few weeks.

I have been given privilege to read and review pre-publication version of this book, and I want to present some of the issues here.

The two military psychologists, specialists in psychometry, Kolokovsky and Krutinskaya, have been able to study results of intelligence tests (=IQ) and other standardized tests given to test intelligence of soldiers administered by Soviet Army between years 1970 and 1990. The basic findings, which are summarized in chapter one are the following. No matter what tests are given, no matter what circumstances, main nationalities of former Soviet Union seem to follow consistent pattern. If intelligence measure is normalized for 100 points = normal then we find:

Russians	120
Jews	115
Belarussians	110
Latvians, Lithuanians	105
Armenians	103
Estonians, Moldavians	98
Ukrainians	93
Georgians, Azeris, Uzbeks, Kazakhs	90
Turkmenians	86
Tajiks	82
Kyrghiz	72

This pattern, the figures, and the standard deviations show an unexpected consistency year after year and test after test.

In the remaining chapters the authors try to explain the reason that the figures are so consistent. Nobody is surprised that Russians and Jews are the smartest main peoples of ex-USSR, or that Tajiks and Kyrghyzis are stupidest. Surprising is that European Ukrainians have IQ scores more similar to central Asian peoples than to European peoples.

One possibility that the authors consider is the Ukrainian language. This language is inferior to Russian in many ways, and perhaps being forced to interact with the world using its unsystematic grammar and restricted expressive means contributes to 'preadolescent underdevelopment of frontal lobes syndrome' which is handed down to next generation. The authors of the book have teamed up with a group of physical anthropologists working at the Russian Academy of Sciences under Professor L.O. Lobachevsky and developed an 'index of forehead slope'. Their thesis is that the larger are the frontal lobes of an adult, the closer will be the value of the index to 90 degrees. Applying this to identification photos of Soviet Army recruits and doing tens of thousands of calculations, the research team was able conclude a 'significant correlation of forehead slope to mean I.Q. score' for Soviet soldiers. The sloping forehead which, as everyone who has seen a picture of Russified Ukrainian Khrushchev knows, is such a prominent feature of the Ukrainian-type face, thus is 'a visible and evident for all the world to see index of congenital cognitive disability'. The implications of the findings of this book are very important for Russia and the world. Here for the first time we have objective evidence that the Russians are the master race.

Russkaya umnost'—sud'ba i budushchnost' nashevo naroda will appear in two weeks in Moscow. I think that it will be standard reading for people who have doubts about if Russia should reunite with ex-Soviet republics and take over Western Europe, California, Alyaska, and other ancient ex-Russian lands.

SMIRNOV

9

LANGUAGE AND ETHNICITY IN
CENTRAL AND EASTERN EUROPE
SOME THEORETICAL ASPECTS

There is hardly a more high profile political problem in Central and Eastern Europe than that of ethnicity; and language is universally interpreted as the innermost sanctum of ethnicity. Much ethnic conflict evidently centres on language. An outsider might conclude that if only language issues could be settled – and they seem so obvious and trivial – the ethnic tensions that plague the region could be eased. After all, reasonable people should not really care about low-level difficulties like whether a village has monolingual or bilingual street signs. And by the same token, does it really matter if an ethno-linguistic minority is obliged to learn the language of the majority – everybody has to learn the language of the state, do they not?

The argument to be put forward here is that this level of analysis misses the underlying dynamics of language, ethnicity and power and that while it is possible to find solutions for inter-ethnic tension, the true causes of it have first to be identified. This requires a close look at the exact nature of ethnicity and why language plays such a salient role in ethnic self-definitions, particularly in Central and Eastern Europe.

Much of the conventional analysis begins from the assumption that ethnicity is only made political by 'artificial' means and that people belonging to different ethnic groups have lived together in peace for centuries, implying that were it not for these 'artificial' interventions, they would continue to do so. This approach misses several points. Indeed, it implies a kind of moral disapproval and says nothing about the dynamics of ethnicity, which might actually help in understanding inter-ethnic relations.

The clue to a sharper insight into the phenomenon is that ethnicity operates simultaneously on several planes, only one of which is political. But while in pre-modern societies the political

6

116

system did not impinge too directly on cultures, with the coming of modernity it began to do so. This had far-reaching consequences for the way in which cultures now had to define themselves politically and to respond to the imperatives of political power. Culture, politics, society and the way in which they interact have to be clarified before some sense can be made of what ethnicity does and why.

The starting assumption in this argument is that ethnicity is about cultural reproduction.[1] Those who are members of a cultural community will spend much of their lives in sustaining it, nurturing it and gaining the approbation of others for their collective attainments. There is a persuasive explanation for this. A culture is a system of moral regulation in the deepest sense. It seeks to establish a coherent world,[2] about which a community can organise itself and draw meanings for and about its own existence.

How people live, the individual's relationship with the wider world, other people included, is structured by their membership of the community. The way in which a community is constituted, the precise nature of the relationship between the individual and the community – this inevitably comes to involve questions of political power – varies from community to community. These variations then come to constitute the raw material for ethnic conflict, because each community is axiomatically convinced of the rightness of its morality and its superiority to all others. In short, each and every ethnic community is looking to validate its 'moral worth', its standing in the world, in its own eyes and in the eyes of others.[3]

Ethnic groups are, therefore, structured around systems of moral regulation. They define themselves by a wide range of possible means, both internally and towards the outside world. Anything can play this role of marker[4] to delimit the external boundary of

---

[1] Pierre Bourdieu, *The Field of Cultural Production* (Cambridge: Polity, 1993).

[2] On the psychology of coherence see Csaba Pleh, 'A narrativumok mint a pszichológiai koherenciateremtés eszközei' (Narratives as instruments for creating psychological coherence), *Holmi*, vol.8. no.2 (February 1996), pp. 265-82.

[3] Donald Horowitz, *Ethnic Groups in Conflict* (Berkeley: University of California Press, 1985).

[4] On boundaries and markers, see Fredrik Barth (ed.), *Ethnic Groups and Boundaries: The Social Organisation of Culture Difference* (Bergen/Oslo: Universitetsforlaget, 1969).

the community: language, religion, territory, history – to be precise, memory, i.e. history as recalled – and seemingly banal instruments of cultural reproduction, like dress codes and foodstuffs. Crucial to this process is that both explicit and implicit markers are involved. People will adhere to certain ways of doing things without having any idea of why – they are then involved in the process of cultural reproduction.[5] By definition, no one can fully comprehend all the social and cultural processes of which they are a part; no one has perfect rationality.

Language is widely regarded as the central if not indeed sole boundary marker. There is a widespread assumption that a nation, in order that it can call itself a nation, should have its own language. This proposition is a misperception, though one that is understandable, given that most of the obvious transactions within a collectivity take place through the medium of language and the members of the group come to regard that medium as theirs alone and as the 'natural' means of expressing their own existence.

Language and ethnic markers

The role of language as an ethnic marker has been particularly salient in Central and Eastern Europe and cultural communities in the region use language in this way with great emphasis. There are good reasons for this, to be found in the history and social structure of the area. Nationalism came to Western Europe first in the eighteenth century and it was constructed around the then existing framework of states and institutions. Essentially this meant that the pre-existing system of states, which used loyalty to the monarch as the principal cement, received a new legitimation, that of nationhood. Nationhood was the medium through which political power, the monopoly of the aristocracy until then, could be devolved to other social strata, because it offered a set of loyalties cohesive enough to ensure that the newly empowered groups would not secede. In this sense, the coming of nationalism was expressly democratic.

In Central and Eastern Europe the new doctrine was received with enthusiasm as a way of challenging the power of the ruling empires and to launch the process of modernisation. This was

---

[5] Michael Billig, *Banal Nationalism* (London: Sage, 1995).

understood as meaning reaching the standards of power, economic well-being and above all moral worth (power of cultural attraction)[6] that was seen in the West. The reception of nationalism, the newly developed doctrine of popular enfranchisement and empowerment, was particularly welcome to a newly arisen social stratum – the secular intellectuals. The Enlightenment brought into being a sizeable group of individuals who saw as their *raison d'être* the generation of new ideas, of new means of interpretation and the shaping of social and cultural values, independently of church and monarch.

In the West, the activities of the intellectuals took place in a relatively confined arena, against the competition of other groups, like the rising entrepreneurial classes, the remnants of the aristocracy, the new bureaucracies and the industrial working classes as the nineteenth century wore on. In Central and Eastern Europe, however, these strata were weak to non-existent, so that the intellectuals had the field largely to themselves. The encounter between the new intellectuals and the equally new doctrine of nationalism was a key moment. It turned out to be highly successful and the intellectuals have never looked back.[7]

The central activity of intellectuals is their use and control of language and in Central and Eastern Europe they acquired a near-monopoly. They were directly involved not merely in interpretation and evaluation, but through their formulation of the new national languages and the reformulation of the national community, they gained access to authority and prestige without parallel. No longer involved in the supervised legitimation of dynastic or ecclesiastical power, they were largely unconstrained and could pursue moral legislation, in the definitions of past and future and in elaboration of the lifeworld, thanks to their control of the language.

From the outset, Central and East European intellectuals found themselves having to define cultural communities from rather limited raw materials and having to argue their case in political as well as cultural terms, given that the ruling empires were looking

---

[6] Isaiah Berlin's 'bent twig' argument is directly relevant in this context. See his 'The Bent Twig: On the Rise of Nationalism' in *The Crooked Timber of Humanity* (London: John Murray, 1990).

[7] Zygmunt Bauman, 'Intellectuals in East-Central Europe: Continuity and Change', *East European Politics and Societies*, vol.1, no.2 (spring 1987), pp. 162-86.

to homogenise their populations in the name of greater efficiency and imperial loyalty. Thus from the outset, questions of language and literacy acquired a political dimension in Central and Eastern Europe that they did not have in the West.[8]

The arguments used to legitimate the bid for power began as a mixture of legal, historical and political claims, but it was soon evident that these propositions would not provide the popular base needed to mount a challenge serious enough to induce the ruling dynasties to cede power. In this connection, the example of the French Revolution was infectious. To mobilise the people, the people had first to be defined. Given the emphasis on language that was the stock-in-trade of the intellectuals, coupled with the weakness of other means of mobilisation, 'the people' were those who spoke the same language. This was perfectly logical, for conditions were unlike revolutionary France, where all the subjects of the Kings of France were simply 'citizens'.

There were, as a matter of fact, some attempts to construct political nations on a geographical rather than a cultural-linguistic base – Bohemianism, the idea that all the inhabitants of Bohemia, regardless of their culture and language, constituted a nation, being a case in point. It failed, because it lacked the dynamism that derives from an authentically felt sense of community. Language was the factor that worked.

The implication is that where the state has not carried out the process of civic homogenisation, as it had in the West, culture as embodied in language was a much more effective basis for political power than contiguity. The devolving of power on all could only take place if those with power could be secure that the newly empowered would use it responsibly. Thus in Central and Eastern Europe, the use of language as a primary instrument of mobilisation and thus of differentiation has left an indelible mark on politics, on the cultural community and on relations with other cultures.

The pre-modern traditions of political discourse should also be considered in this context. It should be evident that politics was not invented with the coming of nationalism and that the previous forms of political expression left their mark in the way they were subsumed by nationalism. Broadly, there were two

[8] Miroslav Hroch, *Social Preconditions of National Revival in Europe* (Cambridge University Press, 1985).

major, overlapping streams of political legitimation: the imperial, and the religious (Baroque and Orthodox). All of these placed great emphasis on external form, on language as a means of drama and appearance, of establishing hierarchy, of conveying meanings that are imposed rather than argued. Hence the secular intellectuals of Central and Eastern Europe were always different from those of the West, whom they sought to emulate.

The role of language in the region assumed a saliency, therefore, because it was the most effective political resource and because the gap between the existing distribution of political power and culture was too great. The integration of culture and power had not taken place, as it had in the West, nor indeed had the integration of political power and language. This made the task of the mobilisers that much more complex. Furthermore, not only did people have to be mobilised to become conscious of their cultural community, but the principal marker of the community – language – had still to be defined.

Hence language became both instrument and aim. Those who spoke or could be made to speak a particular language – a national, hence a politically legitimate language – were the usable material of the nation, its members in whose name power could be demanded. Because they spoke the language, they could be deemed a cultural community with moral worth. In this way, the circle was completed. The outcome of this process was to endow intellectuals with a particular role in the maintenance of language which they have never relinquished and language has acquired a very special quality as symbolic of the moral right to exist.

In other polities where political identities are less directly focused on language, institutions assume a larger role in the construction and maintenance of identities. The civic dimension of nationhood – that which reflects the values of citizenship – is then easier to sustain, as in Western Europe, despite the existence of ethnicity there too. But in Central and Eastern Europe, language has primacy. In local perceptions, the axiom is language; as the Hungarian writer Gyula Illyés once put it, 'The nation lives in its language.' If there is a language, then its speakers constitute a community; if a community has its own language, it must be a nation; and as a nation, it has the right to constitute its own state and become a subject of history. Needless to say, all the above is not much more than a legitimating formula, albeit one with extensive resonance and recognition in the region.

The legacy of this can be seen today in the determined efforts of the Croatian authorities to make the Croatian language as different from Serbian as possible. The creation of new vocabularies is not merely the artificial crafting of new markers but is symbolic of the proposition that the Croatian nation has its own language and, therefore, has the moral right to constitute a state.

Language, however, is nothing like as straightforward a category as linguistic nationalists, and for that matter conventional opinion, assume. Language has to be identified, codified and imposed; diverse dialects have to be forged into a single standard. This is not necessarily destructive, as some have suggested, for there is a trade-off in terms of wider comprehensibility and access to a high cultural medium on the part of those whose linguistic competence was restricted to others speaking the same dialect. Thus a degree of linguistic centralisation seems the inevitable price for mutual comprehension and the interchangeability of skills that modernity demands.[9]

At the same time, though, this process of centralisation in Central and Eastern Europe endowéd language with a symbolic as well as a functional role. The acquisition of the newly defined high cultural langauge[10] is simultaneously a way of reproducing the moral community and the legitimation of its moral worth. Hence to speak Ruritanian is effectively a duty, not just an everyday activity. Once a group has called its language into being and that move has generated a degree of resonance, the community can be said to have come into existence. Other political, cultural and economic claims and assumptions follow on from there. Note the contingent nature of language. It cannot be called into existence from nothing, there has to be some socio-cultural basis for it, but whether a group defines itself as having or not having its own language is in no way predetermined.

There are quite a few dialect groups in the region that could have formed the core of a high cultural language, but for contingent reasons its speakers would not or could not take this step (Kashub is an example). Thus in Central and Eastern Europe defining a language is not as simple as it looks with hindsight. With the

---

[9] Ernest Gellner, *Nations and Nationalism* (Oxford: Blackwell, 1983).

[10] John Armstrong, *Nations before Nationalism* (Chapel Hill: University of North Carolina Press, 1982).

exception of Polish, no language has a continuous high cultural tradition. There are discontinuities in the use of languages as effective instruments of communication matching the demands of modernity; hence their ability to claim the status of being a national language (with moral worth) was not self-evident. This was the background to the language renewals or language creations of the eighteenth and nineteenth centuries.

A high cultural language is vital both instrumentally and as legitimation. It ensures recognition for its speakers, thereby notionally placing the language community beyond assimilation. It implies control over one's destiny, over the morality and cultural codes peculiar to the language-speaking group, it demarcates the group from others, and acts as a warning sign saying 'keep off'. Equally, it is a guarantee of access to modernity and it can energise a somnolent peasant community by promising the rewards of wealth, status and power implicit in entry into the modern world. Having one's own language means that political, social, cultural and civic institutions can operate without interference from outside.

Hence the rationality of the switch by the Hungarian elite from Latin to Hungarian in the nineteenth century. On the face of it, Latin, a neutral language under the control of the Hungarian elite, would have served the rulers of multi-lingual Hungary better than insisting on Magyarisation; the switch to Hungarian was essential to legitimate the claim to a high cultural presence and modernity. Not least, Latin could not have competed with German, the language of Vienna. Having one's own language was understood as offering access to Europe, the summit of moral worth, and a further guarantee of cultural survival. Members of language groups who have never had their collective existence questioned find it extremely difficult to empathise with the fear of extinction; it is real enough as a phenomenon in Central and Eastern Europe, where genocide or attempted genocide is not unknown either.

The confluence of these process has left its mark on language in Central and Eastern Europe. There is, for a start, a very high level of linguistic intolerance in the polity, at the political level. Civic virtue is collapsed into cultural virtue and identified with monolingualism. Multi-lingualism is understood as a weakness that potentially threatens the future of the community. Hence the near-desperate contests for the symbolic continuity of the language, the insistence that the national language has always been the dominant high culture medium; in practice this is expressed as supremacy. One state must equal one language. This bears very hard on ethno-linguistic minorities.

It is worth looking briefly at the real, as distinct from the perceived state of affairs in this context. A clear-sighted sociological look at ethnic minorities will show that while they may retain an attachment to their cultures and moral regulation, where political codes are concerned, they have very largely accepted the patterns of the majority (which dominate the state). In essence, the modern, all-intrusive state has effected a very successful integration of minorities in virtually all the areas that fall under the heading of citizenship. Their loyalty to the state is high and while that loyalty can be alienated, minorities are not inherently secessionist. Indeed, their attitudes towards the kin state, where other members of the same ethnic group live, can vary from indifference to hostility.

Failure of assimilation

At the same time, the modern state – and that includes the highly coercive communist state – has proved unable to assimilate ethnic minorities once they have become conscious of their identity. Again, this proposition has far-reaching implications. Further attempts at linguistic assimilation are futile or counterproductive. Policies pursued by majorities aimed at driving minority languages out of existence will fail. Even when the minority is stripped of its intellectuals and it has no prospects for upward social mobility within the ethnic group, it will not abandon its identity. From this perspective, majorities would do better to abandon their useless attempts to weaken or eliminate ethno-linguistic minorities and to concentrate on securing their loyalty as citizens.

There are countless examples to support these arguments. The Hungarians of Romania, despite very severe repression under Ceauşescu, have not given up their Hungarian identity. The Roma, at the bottom of the social ladder and universally despised throughout the area, are currently looking to construct a new, more politicised identity – even without a shared language. The Poles of Lithuania may have virtually no intellectuals and share a religion with the Lithuanian majority, yet there is no indication that they will abandon their Polishness. The Macedonian Slavophones of Greece, despite being effectively denied the most basic rights needed for cultural reproduction, have not disappeared.

All the futility of linguistic oppression demands an explanation.

Again, it should be sought in the rationality of cultural reproduction and the perception that it is gravely threatened. Each and every nation in Central and Eastern Europe is beset by a deep fear about its survival. They see threats to their existence from their neighbours and, for that matter, in global trends. The past – memory – is seen as malign and the future is potentially dark, hence defence of the language, the 'keystone of the nation', is understood as a transcendental duty imposed on all members of the cultural community. This duty is superior to human rights, to collective rights, to individual rights, to democracy, to constitutional provisions, to international covenants or whatever, and it is insisted on with an obstinacy that only makes sense if the fear of extinction is recognised. What may appear to be reasonable concepts of compromise, that language groups can readily share the same territory and can live together, are simply pushed aside as meaningless (at best) or as aggression (more commonly).

Broadly, these factors constitute the explanatory framework for why linguistic coexistence at the high cultural level is so extraordinarily difficult to establish in Central and Eastern Europe and why seemingly simple problems acquire an apparently inexplicable and deep-rooted insolubility. What may seem 'silly' or 'tribal' to the outsider, not least the West European outsider, has profound meaning and resonance to the contestants, which no amount of mockery will wipe out or weaken.

The Western perspective is in any case less universalistic than it pretends. Attempts to introduce multiculturalism in states like France or Germany, not least when multi-lingualism is involved, tend to falter. Elsewhere, where workable solutions have been attempted, as in Belgium,[11] there is a certain tendency to smile somewhat patronisingly, as if to say that in the more 'civilised' states these complex linguistic arrangements are superfluous. In reality, of course, they have their function in providing for cultural reproduction and securing the position of all the languages used in that particular territory.

---

[11] Geert van Istendael, *A belga labirintus avagy a formàtlansag bàja* (Budapest: Gondolat, 1994), a translation of *Het Belgisch labyrint of De schoonheid der wanstaltigheid* (The Belgian labyrinth or the attractions of formlessness). It was not by chance that this book was translated into Hungarian. It was meant to serve as an example of how two communities living in the same state could arrange their dispositions in such a way as to ensure the cultural reproduction of both.

The significance of these arguments is that the interaction between politics and culture produces a set of dynamics that have to be interpreted together for the processes to make sense. The contests for language go way beyond the immediate issues of, say, bilingual administration as a technical convenience for the minority; rather, a wide range of issues at first sight having little or nothing to do with language as such are affected, bringing one community into conflict with another.

Take the example of minority language universities. On the face of it, this should be a straightforward matter of educational resources. Essentially, any language community over a certain size can support higher education and, therefore, goes the technocratic argument, the state ought to make provision for it. Politico-culturally things are not as simple. It is not a matter of technical education policies, but of a symbolic issue that the majority simply cannot accept, that the minority has intellectual aspirations that might make its members fit for high office and compete in the world of moral values where the majority insists on exclusivity. Crucially, if the moral worth of the minority is accepted, its claim to participate in the shaping of the state is very hard to deny. All this is not helped by the preponderance of intellectuals in national movements, for they tend to stress the significance of the university as a centre of national culture and moral values, thereby challenging the majority. The university, therefore, acquires a symbolic, moral value that takes it right out of the politics of education.

Given the value attached to high culture, a university becomes the symbol of moral worth that a majority will do anything to deny minorities, because – goes the argument – in one territory only one system of moral regulation can exist. Besides, a group which has its separate system of moral-cultural regulation and moral worth will gain recognition universally and that, in turn, can be understood as a weakening of the integrity of the state. Thus it is not just education but the nature of identity that is at issue – the reproduction of the minority's culture and thus of its moral substance, as well as the people to bear it through to the next generation. This analysis helps to explain the obdurate refusal of, say, the Macedonian and the Romanian authorities to allow the establishment of minority language university provision for ethnic Albanians and Hungarians respectively.

The above analysis may sound excessively pessimistic. This

need not be the case. It is not impossible for two or more ethno-linguistic communities to live together and share power in the same state. But that happy state of affairs requires a high degree of sensitivity towards the moral worth of all ethnic communities and before that comes about, they must all be made secure in their own future and their own unimpeded cultural reproduction.

Part III. THE STATE, COMMUNISM AND POST-COMMUNISM

10

CULTURAL DIVERSITY AND GOOD GOVERNANCE
SOME GENERAL CONSIDERATIONS

The purposiveness of government

Few aspects of the relationship between state and society, between government and people, are tested quite as severely as it is by cultural diversity. In essence, the central tension is that government and, indeed, governance, seek to produce evenhanded outcomes in a reasonably transparent and accountable fashion. Cultural diversity, on the other hand, is about the ongoing definition and redefinition of change, of the criteria of change, of individual and group identities, even while the demands of those constituting the cultural group – the community – on the state are rising and changing. In this sense, the state is engaged in a permanent race to keep pace with the faster or slower transformation of society, which in itself creates unevenness, untidiness and, for that matter, continuously changing problems of accountability, legal-rationality, transparency and all the other desirable features of good governance. In effect, good governance will always be an aspiration rather than something actually achieved.

This poses a central challenge to the purposiveness of government, a problem exacerbated by the end of the Cold War and of the discipline that went with it. In the 1990s, the state – all states, East and West – confronts a complex series of demands which are ultimately irreconcilable, because they simultaneously seek stability, equality, autonomy and rationality. Given that these aspirations are to some extent culturally determined, the task of good governance is to effect a balance between the different sets of demands flowing from these imperatives, even while the balance can always be only temporary.

This does not mean, however, that the traditional function of government has been superseded. Government of all kinds is about establishing stability by making power predictable. Good governance is about adding accountability and accessibility – the essence of democracy – to the formula. In Western Europe, though not in other parts of the world, the sense of how far-reaching this proposal is has been lost. The idea that, in theory, each individual should have equal access to power, and that those exercising power should be responsible for how they spend the individual's tax contribution and enforce the law, is deeply radical. Its radicalism arises because there is an assumption of continuous transformation, coupled with a commensurate degree of stability and predictability, over which individuals have a degree of control. When cultural diversity is added to the mix, society and the state have to live with the diversity of criteria and values that challenge the cohesiveness of all aspects of life.

Governments and cultural diversity

The bearers of cultural diversity are various, but in the political realm, ethnicity and ethnic groups are the key players. Essentially, the argument here is that ethnic groups are a central source of values and identity, significantly more so than class, so much so that the modern state has been unable to absorb them. What the modern state has done, however, is to carry through a far-reaching integration of ethnic groups, so that those living in the same state share a range of features, attitudes and values when it comes to politics. This set of shared values is the foundation of citizenship, which makes the democratic distribution of power possible. Without the integration of different ethnic groups into these shared values, there would be a perpetual fear on the part of the majority that the minority was looking for secession or was seeking to aggrandise itself excessively. Where the bases of citizenship are weak, therefore, majority-minority relations are constantly troubled. This is the state of affairs in several, though not all, of the post-communist states.

There is no single successful recipe for the stabilisation of majority-minority relations, but there are various principles which, when observed scrupulously, can defuse the potential for conflict.

In essence, the multi-ethnic state should recognise that democratic principles demand that all groups accept that the maintenance of the state is the highest value, but once accepted all should enjoy full citizenship rights. Secession is not a political option, though when a majority finds that its own agendas are seriously compromised by those of the minority, it should not exclude cession as a possible device to stabilise the situation.

Stability of the territory of the state permits all actors to begin the slow process of building mutual self-confidence on which democratic self-limitation can be built. The key in this context is that all groups must recognise the right of all others to unimpeded cultural reproduction.

The movement of politics, of political power, should be seen as operating at three levels: the institutional, the symbolic and what links the two, the atmospheric. The institutional level is clear enough. Here one is dealing with formally established bodies, with their own overt codes and procedures. No institution will ever work precisely in the way prescribed in its formal terms of reference and legal position; nevertheless, one can identify institutions that do work broadly speaking in the way they are supposed to and which are capable of finding the means to overcome serious deviations from the prescribed norm. In such cases, the political system can be said to be stable and predictable.

The symbolic level includes the myths, rituals and liturgies that all collectivities use to ensure their cultural reproduction. Memory – perceived history, the continuous reinterpretation of the past – is an essential aspect of the symbolic level. This level sees the construction and maintenance of boundaries and the corresponding boundary markers, which may take any form – from language to diet. Note that long established institutions and attachment to them can also acquire symbolic functions.

The intermediate atmospheric level is more complex. Collectivities are remarkably sensitive to changes in the political atmosphere, above all where an ethnic minority is concerned. If the atmosphere improves, the community in question can abandon some of its fears, its sense of being threatened as to its existence and cultural reproduction. Correspondingly, when there is deterioration in the atmosphere, these fears will intensify and, consequently, boundaries will be strengthened, the 'other' will be demonised, and ethnic polarisation will lead to ethnicisation, when all processes, every event, will be understood in ethnic terms.

What creates this disturbance in the atmospheric level is a situation when collective aspirations, as articulated at the symbolic level, are not reflected in the institutional arrangements. When a group feels itself excluded from power – at the institutional level – it will look for compensation at the symbolic level. The other party will, in turn, reinforce its own symbolic guardians of the boundaries. Once this process begins, collectivities will place growing emphasis on symbolic rather than institutional power, which comes to be distrusted. Informal rather than formal mechanisms will acquire saliency in the exercise of power, thereby further exacerbating the insecurity of both communities. All this bears severely on minorities because, by definition, their access to institutional power will be more restricted than that of majorities.

The central difficulty, then, is that institutions provide the stability, predictability and transparency in the exercise of power that allows a reasonably secure cultural reproduction to take place. Excessive reliance on symbols, however understandable in the circumstances is, therefore, no substitute for stable institutions, both of the state and civil society.

Minorities, if they are to enjoy full citizenship rights not merely in the legal, cultural or economic sense, but also in the sense of being full participants in the political process must have the sense that their claims to the symbolic aspects of power are fully respected. This area of political provision is unquestionably the most difficult. Majorities may accept the economic or cultural participation of minorities, but they prefer to see them, consciously or otherwise, as ghettoised, as engaged in a form of separate development which does not affect the agendas of the majority. Multicultural citizenship, as well as the imperatives of political stability, demand more than that. A minority, to enjoy full rights of citizenship, must have access to exactly the same amount of power as the majority.

To the foregoing should be added the effects of globalisation. Traditional ways of doing things are continuously transformed by forces that are not under the control of either governments or societies. The rise of an international communications system, the impact of the world media, the effect of the single money market, the spread of world-wide leisure and entertainment patterns all modify received values and thereby undermine what is considered stable, unchanging and comforting. For all practical purposes, it is becoming more and more difficult to legitimate ideas and actions by reference to tradition alone. These transformations are difficult enough to integrate into the life of Western societies, which have a relatively open culture of change. They are far more painful for the post-communist states to absorb, given their four decades of insulation from global patterns.

Western patterns

There are a number of key differences currently between the treatment of majority-minority relations in the West and in Central and Eastern Europe. Although the actual practice varies considerably from state to state, in the West it is generally accepted that ethnic minorities have certain political rights in order to ensure their cultural reproduction. This can include access to the symbolic goods of the state, as well as to the material ones.

In some cases, the majority accepts territorial provisions (e.g. internal sovereignty for the Åland Islands, the special regimes in Wales or the South Tyrol), with unfettered use of the minority language, access to education and local administration. The far-reaching bi-cultural federation established in Belgium has accomodated the frequently conflicting demands of the two language groups within a single citizenship regime. The solution adopted in Switzerland effectively creates a superordinate Swiss identity for certain purposes, while fully recognising the right of the different language groups to develop on a separate basis. Spain has moved towards extensive devolution for the Basque country and Catalonia within a broadly federal framework.

What all these instances show is that popular sovereignty and democracy can readily accommodate multiculturalism and that territorial solutions can be mixed with non-territorial ones without in any way endangering the coherence and integrity of the state. The concept of the state has changed and the structure of citizenship with it. To these factors may be added the complex web of international obligations and conventions, together with access to power, influence and resources at the level of the European Union.

Central to these achievements is the acceptance, at times the reluctant acceptance, by majorities of the minority presence as political and cultural reality and the readiness on the part of both to employ the rules, both explicit and implicit, of democratic self-limitation. The absolutely pivotal issue in this connection, however, is the nature of rules. A functioning democracy demands that the rules of the political game be respected as sacrosanct, that they should be amended only by special procedures and that the winners of the political contest will not seek to profit at the expense of the losers. Without this respect for the rules of the game, the trust that underlies mutual confidence will not come into being. The outcome will be a deep-seated fear that loss of power will bring potential or actual disruption, potentially including fragmentation and disintegration of the state. This makes good governance impossible to institute.

The post-communist pattern

Under the pattern as it has evolved in the post- communist states, many of these gains are a long way from having been accepted or, indeed, recognised as necessary. The broad attitude towards minorities – social minorities as well as ethnic ones – is that as contestants for power, they are hostile and antagonistic and, there-fore, they should be excluded from all aspects of power for fear of disruption.

This attitude is particularly marked when it comes to dealing with ethnic minorities. The explanation is roughly along the following lines. The communist system was especially destructive when it came to civic values and institutions. It sought, and succeeded, in homogenising society and socialising it into de-pendence on a hierarchical structure of power. It invested the state with the hegemonial function of being the supreme bearer of rationality and, therefore, made dissent from state power a particularly heinous activity. Yet at the same time, because the communist state lacked the capacity to enforce its extraordinarily high demands and regulations, it gave rise to various forms of informalism, corruption and deviation from the rules, and made the circumventing of the law legitimate. In effect, the post-com-munist state has a legacy that makes legal-rationality difficult to administer and thus weakens the state that is intended to be the primary agency of change, strategy, power and status. The state is both desirable and undesirable. Rules are cited and ignored. The political contest functions by a very high degree of informality and, often enough, norms are ignored.

Taking all these factors together, it will be seen that ethnic minorities have a particularly difficult time in fitting into this system. Whereas the contest between members of ethnic majorities is often unregulated, it is nevertheless operating on the tacit agreement that the state as such is sacrosanct, so that the added insecurity of fear of disintegration does not come into play. In relations with ethnic minorities, this is not so. There is far-reaching fear, a fear that is readily exploited by ethnic entrepreneurs, that the true – hidden – goal of ethnic minorities is secession. Hence, argue the ethnic nationalists, all measures are legitimate to prevent this outcome, because the territory of the state is sacred. The result may be harsh measures against the minority, which can, ironically, have the opposite effect, of becoming a self-fulfilling prophecy, as a minority concludes that its legitimate rights of self-reproduction are being overridden, so that it has to escalate its demands. The difficulty of establishing rules that are beyond the political contest has serious and far-reaching consequences in majority-minority relations.

The foregoing is not to suggest that Central and Eastern Europe is the scene only of failures in ethnic issues. There are, in fact, instances where the relationship is working and where majorities accept, maybe reluctantly, that minorities can pursue their cultural reproduction with relatively few restrictions. This does not mean that there may not be difficulties in the future, for it is in the nature of ethnic issues, as with all politics, that demands for power change over time.

In practical terms, there are reasonably good settlements of the ethnic issue in Poland, Hungary and to some extent the Czech Republic, though in the latter two the question of the status of the Roma remains open. There is no serious difficulty in Lithuania and Slovenia. The issue is sub-acute in Romania, where the new government is taking a far more positive approach than its predecessor, but much has still to be achieved in practice. In Bulgaria, where the general political situation has deteriorated alarmingly, the question of the Turkish minority is not on the overt agenda, but could potentially reappear there. Following ethnic cleansing, the proportion of ethnic minorities in Croatia is small. The situation in Albania, where ethnic minorities comprise only a small part of the population, is tense because the government has lost all its legitimacy. Majority-minority relations are, however, fraught in Slovakia and in what may be called the states with large ethnic minorities: Estonia, Latvia, Macedonia, Bosnia and Serbia.

It will be evident that the spectrum of majority-minority relations in Central and Eastern Europe shows great variation. Where politics is to some extent de-ethnicised, where issues of cultural reproduction are not high on the agenda, some kind of a tolerable arrangement is feasible. However, even where the situation is relatively relaxed, there is no guarantee that matters will remain this way, because of the problem sketched above: the difficulty of creating rules beyond the political contest. In these circumstances, it always open to an ethnic entrepreneur to bring the issue of minorities into political debate and to seek political gains by so doing.

Then, even in the states where the situation may be regarded as reasonably open, local practice in the treatment of minorities can vary and formal legal provision may be ignored. To these factors may be added the attitudes of the minorities themselves. Having only recently gained the political space for action, they may be reluctant to live with the opportunities available in order to avoid exacerbating the situation.

Broadly, where a minority is small – say, below 5 per cent of the population – some kind of minority provision will not as a rule pose problems for the majority. These problems begin where the minority is large enough to affect the distribution of political power and to make the majority feel that it has to make genuine compromises to attain a settlement.

Where the problem is acute or sub-acute, the presence of the minority evidently impedes the construction of citizenship as defined above. Democracy may operate only fitfully, or not at all (e.g. Kosovo) and both parties tend to see their futures in overwhelmingly ethnic terms. This will impact on all areas of life, not just politics – economy, culture, religion, social welfare (e.g. the Roma).

Furthermore, mention should be made of a very particular development of the post-communist period. For the first time for two generations, ethnic minorities in Central and Eastern Europe have the opportunity to pursue a semi-independent foreign policy. They can make their cases heard in a variety of European forums, use international opinion to bring pressure to bear on the majority and, indeed, act in such a way as to use the West as a counterweight to the local majority, something that local majorities greatly dislike. Not least, this development raises questions about the nature of state sovereignty in the 1990s. Equally, this development creates new responsibilities for the West, whether as governments looking for stability in Central and Eastern Europe or as articulated through the web of international organisations and covenants.

The 1990s are incomparably more fluid than the forty-odd years that have preceded. This raises new challenges for both West and East, whether at the level of states or of societies. The West is proceeding on the assumption that international stability is best achieved through good governance and that good governance should encompass relations between ethnic majorities and minorities.

The problem of ethnicity should not be seen as something that can find a permanent solution. More or less stable modes of regulation are however an attainable target. This state of affairs poses difficulties for the mature democracies of the West, many of which will discover – are already discovering – ethnic problems of which they were barely conscious. Clearly, new forms of power distribution will be formulated. In this connection, it is generally helpful if majorities proceed from the assumption that generosity towards a minority is more likely to preempt trouble in time to come than niggardliness.

In Central and Eastern Europe, the problem arises at a stage earlier than in the West. Although the post-communist system is a functioning one, it has serious shortcomings by the accepted criteria of democracy, particularly with respect to the boundedness of rules. Hence democratic stabilisation is much more difficult to establish than otherwise. In this context, ethnic minorities fare especially badly, because in a ruleless contest, their access to power will be poor and their intentions will always be suspect.

The necessary stabilisation of rules, however, cannot be imposed from outside, except at a very high cost (this, in effect, is the solution adopted in the former GDR). The Central and East European states will have to adapt at their own pace to the needs of democratic practice in general and that of ethnic minority regulation in particular. What the West can do, on the other hand, is to provide the moral, practical and symbolic support that will enhance rather than retard these processes.

11

WHY EMPIRES FAIL

The twentieth century may eventually come to be seen as the era when empires declined and then collapsed, almost as if they were stricken by a contagious disease. The First World War saw the demise of the Austro-Hungarian, Ottoman and German empires; the Russian empire survived in a revitalised form. Shortly after the Second World War, an exhausted British empire abandoned its imperial title in India and made life easier for itself by the symbolic pretence that it had become the British Commonwealth. The dissolution of Britain's colonial empire, apart from one or two hiccups like Cyprus and Aden, then proceeded with unparalleled smoothness.

Matters were harder with the French empire and it required a major constitutional collapse to encompass withdrawal from Algeria. The Belgian empire was never much more than a joke, the Dutch – defeated in war – did not stay long in their East Indian imperial garb and in Portugal, as earlier in France, constitutional crisis brought about a rapid abandonment of empire.

What seems to be shared is that, with the partial exception of the British and Dutch, the empires expired in conjunction with or as a direct result of constitutional crises in the mother country. It took a substantial reformulation of the framework and strategies of power to end the empires, which generally meant breaking the resistance of a particular social-political group that had used the imperial idea as its own legitimation.

Imperial legitimation

This proposition brings us closer to an understanding of what constitutes an empire. As a working model, the following factors should be considered as key elements. The first of these factors concerns self-legitimation: an empire should to some extent be legitimated by itself, as if to say, 'We are an empire because we are an empire', an assertion originating from the concept of 'divine reflection' – empires are of celestial origin and their purpose may not be further questioned. In the Chinese case, the doctrine of 'the Mandate of Heaven' was expressly formulated in this way. In medieval Europe, the relationship between the Papacy and the Empire – the Holy Roman Empire – likewise involved elements of divine legitimation.

In its modern version, especially after the Enlightenment, 'divine reflection' waned, though it never disappeared completely at a deeper, affective level, for both rulers and ruled. In effect, empires were sustained by a variant of Max Weber's traditional legitimation, which has generally lent the ruler self-confidence to sustain himself in the face of various challenges. The decline of traditional legitimation, a concomitant of the rise of modern mass politics and democracy in the mother country, spelt the end of empires as well.

The collapse of the Ottoman and Austro-Hungarian empires fits this model after a moment's thought. The legitimacy of the Sultan's rule over Christian subjects was already in question by the mid-nineteenth century; the growing questioning of the Ottoman nature of the state by the Young Turks and the emergence of a self-consciously Turkish national solidarity, coupled with military defeat, fatally eroded the Islamic component of Ottoman legitimacy, which would otherwise have pointed towards keeping at least a variant of the Caliphate in being. Nor did it help that the Entente powers were anxious to enlist the burgeoning Arab nationalism of the Middle East, which finally grew tired of Ottoman sloth and incompetence. Thus although mass democracy was remote from the Ottoman empire, secularism had arisen and, coupled with the loss of prestige through defeat, was sufficient to end it.

In the Austro-Hungarian case, the pivot of *Kaisertreue* provided traditional legitimation: the unimaginability of any alternative to rule by the emperor. Its collapse can be traced to the coincidence of several crises, which the empire might have been able to weather had they occurred singly. The death of Franz Joseph in 1916 robbed the system of his enormous personal prestige and authority and in itself conjured up the passing of an era. His successor, the hapless Karl, did not have the time to build up this authority for himself, because Austria-Hungary faced defeat in war, and the civilian authorities could not by the end hold together the very disparate national groups.

The national principle had triumphed, especially as the imperium had neglected to develop much of an ideology of its own to counter nationalism, and the two genuine imperial institutions – the military and the civil service – were demoralised by defeat and failure. As in the Ottoman case, it was more the *threat* of secular modernity than the practice that brought the empire to its end.

In essence, then, traditional legitimacy should be regarded as the repository of traces of the 'celestial' origins of empire, and its slow diminution, though not disappearance, in 'modern' political legitimation had a greater impact on empires than on political systems that were capable of effecting a transformation within their existing parameters because they had alternative resources at their disposal.

The imperial mission

The second factor that appears to be shared by empires is their 'civilising mission', the proposition that the imperial centre is bringing 'superior' values to 'benighted savages'. This could take the form of the 'White Man's Burden' in Africa, the activities of Christian missionaries, the spread of Islam or the more humble integration of peripheral territories into the Habsburg realms, like Bosnia-Hercegovina in 1878. Count Pahlen's memoirs testify to something analogous in the case of Tsarist Russia in Central Asia.[1] There can be little doubt that the significance of mission, whatever its content may have been, was strongly endorsed by the empire-builders of the nineteenth century, particularly where non-European cultures were involved, and this gave their activities a purposiveness, a moral certitude, as well as having energised them very effectively. In this respect, 'mission' is connected with, though separate from, legitimation. Thus 'mission' can be regarded as the expression of the imperial ideology and like other ideologies it involved a measure of belief for it to have worked in sustaining its objective. The waning of belief or the inability of those professing the ideology to adapt it to changing conditions had fatal consequences sooner or later.

The third factor shared by empires is their multinational character. In pre-modern empires this was unimportant, indeed in some cases ethnicity was directly associated with functional position,

---

[1]   Count K.K. Pahlen, *Mission to Turkestan, 1908-1909* (London: Oxford University Press, 1964).

for example the role of the Ibos in Nigeria as traders and administrators and the Hausas as warriors or the Sikhs in India similarly
as warriors. As long as nationhood had no major political role
or consequences, this multinational character may actually have
been a stabilising force, in as much as it provided clearly defined
ethnic roles in relatively static societies, which in turn could min-
imise ethnic friction or preclude a politically effective multinational
combination together against the imperium.

All this changed once nationalism emerged as the dominant
legitimating principle. From the French Revolution onwards, the
status of multinational or a-national or seemingly supra-national
empires grew increasingly difficult, as the rulers had to contend
with political forces far more dynamic than themselves. Again,
Austria-Hungary is a good illustration of this, but others can be
found in post-Shah Iran, where for a while there were serious
attempts to establish Azeri and Kurdish political communities and,
for that matter, Ethiopia, where the end of Haile Selassie's decrepit
regime was followed by fissiparous national movements looking
to ground themselves on a new basis. Nationalism has fragmented
the imperial state in the case of the independence of Eritrea,
while in Iran, the dynamism of Shi'a Islam, coupled with the
violence of Khomeini's theocracy and the cementing effect of
the war with Iraq, proved sufficient to keep sub-state nationalism
suppressed.

It follows from the above argument that empires cannot be
democratic. Once the national principle is accepted and nations
opt for some form of independence, they can no longer be considered as parts of an empire. One proposition excludes the other.
The British Commonwealth is an interesting though not particularly
convincing attempt to square the circle. Its role and function for
Britain is diminishing now that the worst traumas of 'the end of
empire' have been left behind and the Commonwealth is primarily
an inter-state organisation without power, with limited authority
but with some influence. It could conceivably also have a model
function for collapsing empires which are geographically con-
tiguous.

Empires and multinationality

Disparate, often very disparate cultures, which live side by side
without having been politically mobilised, are held together by

imperial authority. It is crucial that the cultures are so different that they can never be merged into a single political-cultural community, because for that to happen, the members of the cultural community would have to abandon too much of their cultural identity. This does not, however, prevent individuals from doing so. The proposition is clearer when there are racial or religious cleavages defining the boundary lines between the communities. It is this cultural factor which excludes Yugoslavia from the model, discounting Kosovo, which is not directly relevant or vital to the existence of Yugoslavia. The Illyrian ideology was never a complete fiction and a relatively cohesive South Slav culture, becoming the foundation of a Yugoslav political nationhood, could have been conceptualised. This was always inconceivable with the British and French empires, though it has to be said that the Portuguese made valiant efforts to overcome these cleavages, albeit they too failed.

An empire is also held together by the attractiveness of its imperial culture. It must offer the subject peoples the possibility of gaining status, power, wealth and the like through loyalty to the empire. This has a twofold impact. It offers the safety valve of a set of legitimate aspirations and creams off the potential leaders of would-be deviant groups. The many thousands of assimilated Africans who played a significant and visible role in French life or the Indian regiments which fought in Europe against the Axis powers in the Second World War – a conflict in which they had no earthly interest at all – provide clear illustrations of success.

The problems arise when this imperial culture begins to lose its attractiveness; when the subject cultures conclude that they less and less to gain from loyalty and begin to define their own anti-imperial alternatives. In Austria-Hungary the process was well advanced by the period before 1914; in India by the 1930s. It should be understood that centripetal and centrifugal processes can persist side by side for a considerable period of time and the existence of one does not cancel out the other, though there comes a time when loyalty to the nation will be regarded as the 'rational' form of behaviour by the majority. At that point, the imperium is at the threshold of dissolution and only force can hold it together. The Portuguese empire was in this state by the time of the revolution of 1974 and it duly fell apart.

The next question to be raised is what brings about the collapse of empires. In a way, the answer is already implied in the foregoing – it should be sought primarily in a legitimation crisis, an erosion of self-confidence of the ruling elite, its growing and manifest inability to cope, its widening self-questioning and its consequent loss of morale. The trigger for this process, however, is not necessarily the same in all instances. War and defeat or war and exhaustion have been the most common, but other forms of exhaustion are also possible. In particular, a growing perception that the system as such is no longer capable of self-reproduction, that it can no longer deliver the goods not just in economic and political terms, but above all in moral and cultural terms, can similarly bring about a slide into collapse. In all these cases what is involved is a recognition by an influential section of the elite that the costs of empire are too high, that too many urgent tasks at home have been left unsolved, that any benefits of status deriving from empire are smaller than they seemed and, indeed, they can be dispensed with. In these circumstances, the doubts and self-questioning of the elite, if well grounded, could spread into the ruling strata and provide a legitimation for withdrawal from empire. Unless there is some renewal of the imperial idea, the empire will disintegrate.

The Soviet case

Considering all these factors in the context of the Soviet Union the model sketched in the foregoing is broadly applicable, though there are important divergences as well. The Soviet experiment should be seen, whatever its ruling ideology may have claimed about the construction of a secular utopia, as an attempt to establish an alternative civilisation, with its own laws, patterns, regularities, goals and moral universe. In other words, the Soviet idea was aimed at satisfying all the non-material as well as material aspirations of the population. Indeed, unlike other empires, it actively sought to satisfy those needs exclusively by its own criteria and to reject all others as deviant. The scope of the Soviet experiment, therefore, was far wider than any of the other European empires.

The Soviet project self-evidently had its own legitimating ideology, its civilising mission, it was multinational, it was non-democratic, it sought to integrate very different cultures and it attempted to offer a genuinely attractive set of cultural values. Strictly, the Soviet project did not rely on any notion of 'reflection of divinity', but the promise of the secular utopia inherent in Marxism-Leninism should be seen as a functional equivalent, in as much as it offered an eschatology untestable and unfalsifiable by conventional intellectual means.

One by one, all these categories disintegrated and it is instructive to examine how and why this took place. The conventional answer only considers economic factors and explains the failure of the Soviet project by its inability to match the West in technological change and material progress. This is not entirely satisfactory, and while there is no question that economic failure played a major role in bringing about the foundering of the Soviet experiment, it does not fully explain it. Why, for example, was the Soviet Union unable to match the West in technological innovation? Why, in fact, did the planning system break down? Above all, why was the Soviet Union in a political as well as economic crisis, which were causally interlocked?

The answers to these questions go well beyond the manifest inability of the Soviet economy to function in an effective way. They concern issues of legitimation and thus of the political system as a whole, and at a deeper level, of the bankruptcy of the Soviet experiment as an alternative civilisation. The assumptions on which that experiment had been based were false and while the Soviet Union might have been able to match its competitors in military technology and the space programme, this had been at the cost of the rest of the system. Eventually the facts themselves rebelled and the ruling Soviet elite was forced to accept that radical changes were essential for the survival of any kind of a Soviet, or even Russian, polity. At this deepest level, it was the moral values which are essential for sustaining any kind of an organised community that had failed and with this failure went the Soviet community as such.

Nowhere was this more vividly shown than in the field of nationalities policy. The original Soviet assumption had been that ethno-national identities could be and would be subordinated to a higher 'Soviet' identity, that the Soviet man would be so attractive a point of reference that the numerous national groups in the Soviet Union would abandon their ethno-national loyalties and submerge themselves in a 'higher' Soviet identity.

This was not an inherently unworthy enterprise when judged by its intentions. The proposition, that all the various ethnic groups in the Tsarist empire could be given access to a new and more dynamic culture, in, say, education, health or transport, and become a part of a much wider society, thereby greatly expanding individual choice and enhancing life chances, was not at all unattractive. In the early years of the Soviet Union, many people, non-Russians as well as Russians, took the slogans of internationalism seriously and believed in the genuineness of the experiment and were committed to it, although it is doubtful if they ever constituted a majority and, of course, the experiment was imposed in the teeth of the opposition of a sizeable minority.

What happened thereafter was that the leadership was captivated by its own ideology and became its prisoner – it forgot or ignored the broader purpose of the experiment and inexorably the Soviet project grew into the exercise of power for its own sake. This naturally enough undermined the new ideology and over time the slogans of internationalism and equality became empty of meaning. The imperium lost its ability to attract as it grew more and more repressive and its purposes turned towards the construction of a military-industrial complex under Stalin and his successors. While a genuine Soviet 'civilising mission' might have been worthy of the sacrifices that it called for, the aim of making the Soviet Union a Russian superpower was not. In this context, the dismal record of the Soviet empire in actually civilising human relations is particularly noteworthy. The Soviet experiment actually gave rise to very poor relations between individuals, largely because the overt and unwritten rules of conduct were in constant conflict, thus requiring high levels of repression to keep the empire in being. This brutalised behaviour rather than civilising it.

The failure of the Soviet empire

The expansion of this system into Central and Eastern Europe after 1945 merely highlighted its shortcomings. Whereas the Soviet 'mission' might have had some authenticity in the former Tsarist lands, it was entirely alien in the territories newly attached to the empire. In this respect, the expansion of Soviet power into Central and Eastern Europe proved to be a major error, in that it illuminated the fact that the project was ultimately a local one, that it could not integrate the different cultures further to the West and it was forced to rely on heavy repression or the threat of force to maintain itself.

Possibly there might have been a chance to salvage something from the experiment after Stalin's death, partly because expectations were so low and partly because some of the original Marxian vision was still alive in the 1950s. This opportunity was thrown away by Stalin's successors, who could not bring themselves to accept the need for wider choice, but insisted on rigidly adhering to predetermined dogma. With this, especially with the Brezhnev years, the Soviet project degenerated and grew static, exchanging verbal dynamism for the real thing.

On each and every occasion when the opportunity for introducing dynamism reached the agenda it was vetoed by a Soviet leadership fearful of its own position, power and legitimacy – they were, indeed, prisoners of their ideological preconceptions. The thought-world in which they lived prevented them from seeing the real political, economic, social and other processes that were taking place, above all because of the black-and-white Manichean view promoted by the ideology. The leadership and the bureaucratic elite that was the beneficiary of the system was caught in a trap of its own devising and could no longer escape, even while a growing number of people throughout the empire were actively looking for alternatives.

The combination of internal inanity, of international failure, of constant and insoluble political stress, and of an economic bankruptcy made increasingly evident by comparisons with the West exhausted all the resources of the Soviet empire. The reflection of divinity in its secular form, the Marxist utopia promised by the party had lost its allure and its power as a moral undertaking; the 'civilising mission' had proved completely unsuccessful and was challenged on all sides; the demand for genuine democratic choice similarly served to underline the weakness of the experiment; the multinational character of the empire was now expressed as the striving for autonomy; and the leadership was lost in its own uncertainties.

The empire abandoned its Central and Eastern European colonies because it recognised that these were too costly, and in the heartland, in Russia, the sense of mission, the idea that Russianness could be and should be spread among the non-Russians, was given up in favour of a recognition that the Russians' own national agendas had suffered as a result of the imperial dream. For the first time ever, Russian separatism began to acquire serious support. Both the Tsarist and the Marxist-Leninist projects had failed. Nationhood and the aspiration for democracy had triumphed over the idea of empire.

All of this points strongly towards one of the determinants of the 1990s – the strength of the nation-state and the role played by nationhood in undermining empires. Empires were never concerned with the consent of their subjects, indeed the classic colonial empires began to erode at the point when consent reached the political agenda. The consent to nationhood, on the other hand, remains more powerful than ever. From this point of view, nationhood becomes important precisely because it undermines empires and, as is evident from the argument put forward here, empires are much less suited to achieve the satisfaction of their subjects than polities based on consent. And in the current climate of opinion, the nation-state, whatever its shortcomings, remains the most effective instrument for this.

12

THE COMMUNIST EXPERIENCE
AND NATIONHOOD

National identity was the original mass political identity of Central and Eastern Europe. When the first waves of modernisation began to impact on the region in the nineteenth century, the local sub-elites turned to the newly emerging idea of nationhood as the instrument to accomplish several tasks. Independence would be won from the ruling empires; new states based on citizenship would usher in an era of universal equality and freedom, coupled with a prosperity and modernity based on the model of the developed West; and in order to achieve this project, the sub-elites would seek to legitimate the existence of the nation by a mobilisation of its potential members.

In reality, as experience demonstrated, it proved to be extremely difficult to construct citizenship on the basis of ethnic mobilisation, but that is a separate issue in this context. Once the newly mobilised nation was actually in existence, it was argued, the empires could not deny them their freedom. This project achieved its aims with the outcome of the Balkan wars and at the Paris Peace Settlement with the creation of a belt of nation-states between Germany and Russia which in the interim had become the Soviet Union.

From this perspective, therefore, nationhood was a success and established its credentials in the eyes of the bulk of the population, which understood its relationship to the state, the nature of citizenship, in national terms. Once a particular ethnic group had been brought into national awareness, it would defend its existence to the utmost and, given the contorted history and power relationship of the area, would also see that existence as constantly under threat.

Yet even while national identities attained a primacy in mediating the relationship between the individual and state, other identities were also being constructed under the impact of political, economic and social change. Among these were class and the political identities founded on its basis, viz. socialism in its various aspects. This is not the place to rehearse the complex strategic and intellectual attempts made by socialists to deal with the phenomenon of nationalism, but the fundamental and irreconcilable contradiction at the level of theory between the two should be stressed. In essence, the nationalist position was that an individual's basic identity derived from culture, while a socialist's was that it derived from class.[1]

The Marxian legacy

Consequently, when the intellectual descendants of Marx found themselves in power, they were faced with the problem of dealing with the national question at the level of policy. Lenin, having seized control of the Russian empire, had to devise a policy that would contain the national communities that had reached various stages of maturity in the new state without their in any way endangering the power of the ruling communist party and the integrity of the state. In essence, Lenin's strategy rested on a number of assumptions and propositions.[2]

As a Marxist, he began from the general principle that class would invariably transcend all other considerations, including nationhood, but that this might take time. If national consciousness was a false consciousness, as the Marxists always maintained, then conditions would have to be constructed where false consciousness would wane sooner rather than later. Furthermore, at the practical level, the non-Russians had been helpful to the Bolsheviks during the civil war and expected that the new state would reward them. To this end, Lenin decided that nations would be permitted to exercise a once-and-for-all choice to secede from the new state, something that was actually accepted in the case of the Finns, the Balts and the Poles (though the Polish–Soviet war could well have reversed this decision). In the case of the Georgians, their choice for independence was initially accepted by Moscow, but

---

[1] Roman Szporluk, *Communism and Nationalism: Karl Marx versus Friedrich List* (New York: Oxford University Press, 1988).

[2] Richard Pipes, *The Formation of the Soviet Union: Communism and Nationalism, 1917-1923*, 2nd edn (Cambridge, MA: Harvard University Press, 1964). See also Horace B. Davis, *Nationalism and Socialism: Marxist and Labour Theories of Nationalism to 1917* (New York: Monthly Review Press, 1967).

was then rescinded when the Georgian state was invaded and annexed by the Soviet Union.

As far as the other non-Russians were concerned, Lenin formulated the policy of 'national in form, socialist in content', the essence of which was that the language and culture of a particular community were less significant than the class content of its life. This proved in many ways to be a pradoxical step. The Soviet state embarked on a major effort of social engineering aimed at creating the cultural infrastructure of national communities that were at a very early stage of development. New nations were established, given languages, alphabets, cultures and so on, but under the strict control of the communist party. During the 1920s, these national communities became stronger in their national qualities than before and recognised the Soviet state as having been responsible for this development. To this extent, an overlap and even integration took place between local national identities and the Soviet identity.

Under Stalin, much of this was reversed. He saw these national communities as challenges to his concept of hypercentralised power, which he assumed to launch a highly idiosyncratic type of modernisation. As a result the newly built national cultures were severely battered during the purges. It is noteworthy that Stalin, despite using the most extreme measures in some instances, like mass deportation, was unable to extinguish these newly conscious groups. Once mobilisation into national consciousness had taken place, this could not be reversed.

Stalin, however, took his strategy further. Not only did he downgrade the role and status of the non-Russians, but he elevated the Russians to be 'the Elder Brother' within the Soviet Union. During the Second World War he came close to giving the Soviet legitimating ideology an overwhelmingly Russian national content. Khrushchev added his own innovation to the formula. Like Stalin, he had little patience for national differences and he looked forward to the time when they would disappear entirely. Khrushchev proposed a three-stage pattern of development. Through industrialisation, nations would 'flourish' and their socialist content and aspirations would intensify, making them ready for the second stage of rapprochement (*sblizhenie*). After a period of time, whatever national differences still existed would disappear and the merger (*sliyanie*) of the nations would take place into a single Soviet identity.[3] Khrushchev's project was visionary and misplaced and, even worse, it was perceived not as the enhancement of a Soviet identity, but as Russification, not least because it appeared that the 'new Soviet man' would, curiously, be Russian-speaking. There was only limited modification of this under Brezhnev; he deemphasised 'merger', implying that the stage of 'rapprochement' would last a very long time.

This, in brief, was the Soviet project that was to be imposed on the newly integrated Central and Eastern Europe after 1945. While the Khrushchevian and Brezhnevian turns were relatively marginal, off-stage points of reference to East European policy-makers, the Soviet doctrine did remain in the background and could be called on to justify policy changes.

The project in Eastern Europe

The new rulers of Eastern Europe understood that they were engaged in a major enterprise of having to resocialise the societies they ruled in order to eliminate the 'false consciousness' of nationhood and to develop the 'proper' proletarian ethos. Buoyed up by their own revolutionary beliefs and using what they regarded as the appropriate revolutionary methods, the communist parties pursued a strategy of penetration, of seeking to impose the power of the party-state, which they understood as the repository of perfect rationality, to enforce their own utopian vision on a recalcitrant society. Essentially, the views, values and beliefs of the masses were seen as reactionary and backward in as much as they did not serve whatever goals the party insisted on at the time. In broad historical terms, this was extraordinary in two respects. It reversed the broad assumption of European history that society was creative and the state was reactive. And in its attempt to construct a wholly homogeneous social entity, the party tried to eliminate feedback from all spheres.

For party ideologues, whose thinking was crude and simplistic, categories like national consciousness were relics of the past which could be rapidly liquidated. There was little problem with this approach at the level of words. Nationhood was termed 'reactionary' and bourgeois' and anything that the party did not like was simply

---

[3] Elliot R. Goodman, *The Soviet Design for a World State* (New York: Columbia University Press, 1960).

tarred with this brush, which meant that it could have criminal sanctions visited upon it. Numerous victims of Stalinism suffered as 'bourgeois nationalists'. But the party believed that agitprop, repression and the threat of force would be sufficient to achieve its aims. With a minority, this effort was successful, but the majority complied with rather than internalising the new system of values.

There were several reasons for this apart from the inherent implausibility of trying to construct a perfect system. The actual content of the new proletarian consciousness was very much at variance with what the majority understood to be authentic. Bonds of loyalty, the set of meanings through which the world was understood, cognitive categories and social identities were all coloured by the experience of nationhood. Indeed, it could be argued that even at the height of Stalinism, the existence of states with national pasts and loyalties gave the new communist systems an unacknowledged foundation – communism in this sense was parasitical on nationhood. Post-war reconstruction, the overrapid industrialisation, the massive demographic dislocation and overall social turmoil of the Stalinist period were made feasible because a sense of community with its roots in nationhood was already in place. Communism may have tried very hard to create a new identity, but it could not have undertaken its project without the prior work done by nationalism.

Yet the communists then set out to destroy these bonds of cohesion in the expectation that their own project would raise society to a 'higher' level of consciousness and thus establish a stronger community, because it would be rooted in equality and progress (as defined by the party). To this end a twofold a strategy was launched. Local histories were rewritten and the Soviet Union was made the acme of all achievement, the pinnacle of all that mankind had ever sought to create, with the aim of erecting a new focus of loyalty. Quite apart from the absurd reductionism of this proposition as an ideal, its practical implementation was bound to fall far short of the high ideals. For what it is worth, that is usually the problem with utopias, that they have to be run by real people, not the theoretically defined constructs of Marxism.[4]

---

[4] Isaiah Berlin, 'The Decline of Utopian Ideas in the West' in *The Crooked Timber of Humanity* (London: John Murray, 1990), pp. 20-48.

The rewriting of history had the objective of making it a-national, of doing away with the panoply of national heroes and other features that underpinned a sense of nationhood and replacing them with the 'people', an idealised and homogenised conception, that proposed that the true actors of history were not kings and princes ('reactionary'), but ordinary people ('progressive'). In this sense, the party was retroactively rewriting the past as the history of class struggle and claiming to be the true inheritor of whatever revolutionary activity could be scavenged by a careful, or possibly more accurately careless, scissors-and-paste job on the local national tradition. It escaped these protagonists of agitprop history that their methodology was not unlike the working methods of the 'bourgeois historians' that they affected to despise – they took the bits of history that they liked and ignored the rest. In a word, they wrote propaganda.

The other leg of this project was the glorification of the Soviet Union and, of course, its living embodiment, Stalin. This frequently descended into what would have been farce, had it not been backed up by terror. The Soviet Union, incorporating Russia, became the source of all the knowledge that mankind had accumulated, it was the source of all 'progress', technological invention, the ultimate exemplar of everything, because in effect it was perfect. The rationale of this enterprise was that communism was in the process of constructing a perfect society and this proposition was collapsed into the political decision that it already was a perfect system.[5] The Sovietisation of Central and Eastern Europe was accompanied by Russification. Not only was Russian made a compulsory language in schools, but Soviet (Russian) cultural and scientific output was imposed on the local traditions, in an attempt to dilute and transform them and thereby 'perfect' them or, to use the tautologous expression favoured then and later, 'further perfect' them. The entire undertaking was accompanied by a far-reaching restructuring of symbols and rituals, in the expectation that as a result the population would transform its system of values into one that corresponded to the desires of the new rulers.

---

[5] Argued at much greater length in George Schöpflin the present author's *Politics in Eastern Europe, 1945-1992* (Oxford: Blackwell, 1993), chap. 4.

The results of the communist experiment

So much for the aims of the communist project – the outcome was more than a little different. It did have consequences, but many of these were unintended and counterproductive from the standpoint of party goals. In fact, something approaching a communist identity was created, but it proved to be an animal considerably at variance with the aims of the party propagandists and strategists.

The communists' task was to bring into being the industrial proletariat in the name of which they had seized power (the Czech lands and East Germany excepted). This required a vast undertaking in terms of social engineering. Large numbers of people were constrained to abandon a rural existence and to adopt urban ways of life. This demographic shift was bound to be painful and the new urban masses had to be offered compensation for their travails. In material terms, this meant giving the ex-peasants a degree of existential security that they had lacked in the countryside. In ontological and symbolic terms, however, their loyalty to the system was to be cemented by the promise of an egalitarian utopia. They were to be integrated into 'socialism', a promised world of boundless plenty and the realisation of their dreams of peasant salvation through a single act of transformation.

The difficulty with this endeavour was that the socialism on offer was highly reductionist. Instead of looking to replicate the complex variety of roles, identities, values and interests of modernity, it imposed a single, simplified idea of what the ideal socialist should be like. In essence, this personage, the mythical 'communist man', was to be a figure taken from the nineteenth-century romantic if not indeed sentimentalised image of the 'worker'. The ideal was a male, manual worker, using relatively simple technology, working collectively with others. The image of Stakhanov, the Donbass miner who was to be an ideal-type figure of 'socialist emulation', illustrates this proposition quite clearly.[6]

There was more to the new identity than that, of course. The communist modernisation project impacted on every area of life, but it was an illusion, born presumably of the ideological assurance derived from Marxism-Leninism, that all previous identities would simply be wiped out by the inherent 'superiority' of the new

[6] Csaba Gombár, *A politika parttalan világa* (Budapest: Kozmosz, 1986).

system. In reality, there arose a highly complex, multi-layered interaction between what the communists wanted and the way in which different strata of the population responded. One of the key consequences of the reductionism of Marxism-Leninism was that the response to it was equally oversimplified and homogenised. The new system may have succeeded in wiping away most of the weak civil society that preceded it, but it failed in instilling a proper Marxist consciousness in society.

What the newly urbanised strata took from what was on offer was not the whole package, but what their cognitive categories enabled them to accept. This set of categories was informed by two older currents: the messianism and radicalism of the peasant mind-set and the sense of nationhood; and a newer one, fear and confusion.[7] In no way were these masses prepared for the trauma of urbanisation, let alone for the uniquely harsh and over-rapid implementation of the strategy insisted on by the communists. What came into being was a markedly particular type of identity, one born as much despite the new ruling values as in conformity with them. The essential features of this new identity were a collectivism, a dependence on the state coupled with a distrust of it and a mythicisation of nationhood, which was interpreted as the repository of the elements that the communist system denied society – freedom, prosperity, success and so on, adding up to a myth of social harmony.

The disoriented populations sought to assimilate their new experiences to their cognitive categories and to reproduce in the new context whatever they could salvage from the old. A particular role was played in this process by the socialist enterprise, the enormous factories constructed in the endeavour to build a new nineteenth century industry in the twentieth. At the very time when in the West giant workshops were being scaled down as less productive, communism glorified these factories as 'citadels of socialism'. In practice, they had a somewhat different role to play. They became a source of collective identities that strengthened the vertical bonds in the hierarchical relationships established under the system.

The individual depended on the state not only through the provision of collective consumption, but also through the employ-

---

[7] During the Stalinist period, large numbers of peasants and workers were arrested, interned, harassed etc. on trumped up charges of 'sabotage'.

ment process in a system where the state was effectively the sole employer. With this structure in place, it is understandable that the threat to dismantle these economic mastodons in the 1990s was decoded as something far worse than the restructuring and deskilling that Western heavy industry underwent in the 1970s and 1980s. It affected not only people's livelihood, but also their status, their self-esteem and their identity in a situation where there was no alternative source of employment (unlike the West) and no culture of unemployment. It is hardly surprising in these conditions that the temptation of ethnicity should be strong.

An alternative way of interpreting these processes is to see them as the immune reactions of society against the depredations of the overmighty state. Because these were societies which had traditions of a degree of autonomy and had in any case reached certain low levels of modernity, while they might have accepted the idea of a rational state, they resisted the imposition of the perfect state that accorded them a purely passive role. Their response was to develop autonomies where they could, using the system to enhance and expand their power and where appropriate to lean on nationhood as one of the props.[8]

Furthermore, dependence on the state tends to strengthen vertical relationships and thus undermines the horizontal links of community and solidarity. The hyperétatism of communism predictably produced equally pronounced forms of dependence and individuation, in which interpersonal connections and interactions, other than those within the family and with very close friends, were laden with suspicion, distrust and a zero-sum game mentality, to create an atomised society. In this context, the warm bath of emotion of ethnic nationhood appeared as a *deus ex machina*, a means of overcoming atomisation at a stroke. But this was illusory, because ethnicity could only offer a momentary cohesion and was an empty vessel when it came to deal with the problems of resolving conflicts of interest.

The most striking characteristic of the new identity was that it effectively excluded any idea of citizenship. Logically, given that communism should be seen as an attempt to construct an alternative civilisation, it rejected the received heritage of European political praxis, that the relationship between the individual and

---

[8] László Bogár discusses immune reactions in *A fejlödés ára* (Budapest: Közgazdasági és Jogi, 1983).

the state should be regulated by a series of institutions and recognised rules. Instead the new order was based on the proposition that no distinction should be made between the public sphere and the private world of individual action, that the public sphere as represented by the party-state should encompass and penetrate all aspects of society, including its system of values.

The idea of popular participation through citizenship, that the individual citizen be accorded some access to power, which has been one of the central features of European development at least since the Enlightenment, was changed by a form of words – backed up by the full coercive apparatus of terror – into participation in the communist utopia. This exacerbated an already uneasy relationship between the individual and political power. The pre-communist systems had been characterised by an over-strong state, the *Obrigkeitsstaat*, legitimated by tradition and charisma, in which power and privilege had been very unevenly distributed. This bred a certain suspicion of the state, of politics and, indeed, of 'the city' where these mysterious activities were practised. There was resentment too that the state should take away the hard-earned gains of society through taxation.[9]

The communist construct was the apotheosis of the étatist tradition. it erected an impenetrable and capricious public sphere above society, over which the individual had no control, but which he regarded as exercising unlimited power over him and which claimed to have the right to do so in the name of a perfect ideology. All this was made worse by the sense that this experience was doubly alien. It was alien in that it had its roots in 'the city' but equally so because it was seen as having its origins in Soviet Russia. The proof of this particular proposition could be seen during the Hungarian revolution of 1956, where the street fighters were overwhelmingly made up of workers motivated by anti-Russian sentiments, as well as a rather vaguer commitment to freedom and democracy.

The weakness of the public sphere

The nature of the relationship between the individual and the public sphere, one of the key constitutive elements of the newly

[9] Daniel Chirot (ed.), *The Origins of Backwardness in Eastern Europe* (Berkeley: University of California Press, 1989).

forged communist identity, was marked by several features that have tended to endure in one form or another into the post-communist period. As Jowitt has persuasively argued, there was no shared public identity between society and power.[10] The public world and the private sphere were not only rigidly separated in popular perceptions, but different moral codes applied to one's behaviour in them and traffic between the two was governed by dissimulation, the avoidance of party directives and by fear. Likewise, there was no shared medium of public discourse by which communication could be understood on the same terms by those who were sending and those who were receiving. Instead, there came into being communication by rumour, credulousness, the belief in conspiracy theories where every effect must have been caused deliberately and the attribution of mysterious power to one's opponents. This has been characterised as 'a chronic mode of semi-hysterical (pre)political speech',[11] which frightens, divides and angers those who share in it and whose insular, atomised, privatised worlds are strengthened in consequence. Correspondingly, anything resembling civil society, in which the relationship between the public sphere and the private is clearly regulated, relatively transparent and where the individual does not, on the whole, take the view that the world is moved by mysterious, malign forces, is feeble.

When a society has been compressed into this unwanted and alien identity, it inevitably takes on some of its features, even while it rejects others. The difficulty for the societies of Central and Eastern Europe was that they had, indeed, sought modernity as understood in the West, but while they were unsure about the best route; apart from a minority, they clearly did not want the Marxist-Leninist road of communist modernisation that they were given.

To this complex should be added the impact of constant shortage. The cultures of Central and Eastern Europe were in any case heavily influenced by the 'limited good' value system that regards both material and symbolic goods as existing in a given, unchanging quantity, so that one person's gain is another's loss in absolute

---

[10] Ken Jowitt, *New World Disorder: the Leninist Extinction* (Berkeley: University of California Press, 1992).

[11] *Ibid.*, p. 289.

terms. It should be stressed that this proposition applies not merely to concrete items, but also to relationships, status, connections and so on. The economic system that came into being under communism, Kornai's shortage driven economies, perpetuated this state of affairs, reinforced it and added new patterns by enrooting it in urban areas. The patron–client networks of the new bureaucracies were not necessarily based on traditional prestige, but on newly created relationships, many of which had their origins in the quest for goods and interests.[12]

Once again, the impact of this situation was profoundly negative from the perspective of constructing citizenship, because instead of recognising and internalising the formal values of the public sphere, individuals came to see it as a screen behind which 'real' processes took place. But matters were more complex than that. Where the opportunity existed (or exists), ethnic networks were generally understood to be secure in the face of the system, precisely because members of different ethnic groups could use group solidarity as a channel of communication and distribution. This development strengthened ethnic identities both because they had goods to deliver and because they offered boundary protection against other competing ethnicities, something that was especially important when the state was seen as having become ethnicised.

The communication aspect of ethnic group solidarity is particularly significant. One of the key functions of ethnicity is to offer not merely a rational-contractual but also an affective environment for communication and action. Members of an ethnic community have different expectations from non-members, believe that they understand each other better, can decode non-verbal communications more efficiently and deal with one another with a higher level of trust. From this perspective, the shortage culture of communism unintentionally reinforced ethnic ties, with self-evident consequences for post-communism.

Verdery offers some instances of how this worked.[13] Thus where an ethnic cleavage already existed, people would tend to allocate

---

[12] János Kornai, *A hiány*, 2nd edn (Budapest: Közgazdasági és Jogi, 1982). 'Limited good' cultures are discussed by Jowitt, *op. cit.*

[13] The relationship between shortage and ethnicity is discussed by Katherine Verdery, 'Ethnic relations, economies of shortage and the transition in Eastern Europe' in C.M. Hann (ed.) *Socialism: Ideals Ideologies and Local Practice* (London: Routledge, 1993), pp. 172-86.

scarce goods to 'special friends' who were more likely to be of the same ethnicity than not; that would tend to reinforce perceptions of clannishness and reinforce boundaries. People sensitive to ethnic boundaries would thus be made more conscious of it by the allusive, ambiguous language of mobilisation in which communications were structured, in which it was assumed that everything had meaning, that every effect had a cause (excluding chance, accident and coincidence), in which national motifs were seen whether they were there or not and in which the nationalist language of discourse was the one that could penetrate the private sphere, whereas the Marxist-Leninist meta-language could not. Hence where the party tacitly or explicitly used nationhood, mobilisation would intensify. At the core of this proposition is that, in essence, because nationhood itself was a cultural good in short supply, people hoarded it whenever and wherever they could.

The core features of communist modernisation have already been alluded to – they constituted a simplified and distorted understanding of nineteenth century industrialisation, but in the process of building this atavistic industrial world the communists also introduced mass literacy, education and the beginnings of a modern infrastructure of communications, including electrification and transport. For the first time in the history of the area, the state had extended its power and its meta-language over virtually the whole of society (some strata, the poorest and weakest, remained below and beyond state power, but this does not affect the thrust of the argument). Furthermore, the communists achieved something that had eluded their predecessors: they solved the problem of rural overpopulation, albeit by brutal shock therapy (a phrase that had not gained currency at the time).

The system was hierarchical and top down, but this was not wholly unacceptable to the newly urbanised peasant masses, for whom the party-state fulfilled the role of their former rural masters. And in as much as the system made provision for their existential needs, it was tolerated and collective consumption was grudgingly accepted. In addition to this, it would be a mistake to see the communist system as having been static. While at the level of theory, the distribution of power remained unchanged, some of its strategic targets were modified with the years.

The redefinition of communism as an ideology no longer committed to pure egalitarianism, the acceptance of stratification (of a 'non-antagonistic' nature) and the turn towards the tacit adoption of consumerist goals of the 1960s constituted a considerable reorientation. These did not, and given the nature of the system, could not add up to shift towards citizenship, but they did provide for greater possibilities for individual autonomy than before and to that extent empowered society. This dispensation, with its particular patterns of one-sided distribution of power, goods, status and language persisted until the collapse of the communist system.

The development that perhaps had the most far-reaching implications for the construction of identities under communism was the failure of integration into a civic identity that would allow individuals to live in harmony with their new new urban environment. Whereas in Western Europe the trauma of modernisation took place against the background of a *longue durée* pattern of urbanisation with established codes of morality and behaviour through which newcomers could make sense of their new and often threatening experiences, Central and Eastern Europe lacked this. Urban development had been sparser and cities had been much less effective in integrating the rural population into urban modes.[14]

The communists set about the building of an urban lifestyle essentially in too short a space of time, without adequate urban resources and with too narrow a scope. The few older cities that existed, like state capitals, were surrounded by semi-urbanised peripheries, not unlike the bidonvilles and favelas of the Third World, while smaller towns were swamped by the rapid building of sprawling, soulless housing estates. This pattern of urban development was not something restricted to the 1950s, but continued up to the very end of communism. The population of Bratislava, for example, more than doubled between 1968 and 1989, leaving behind an urban development disaster that has implications for the social and political identities that currently emerge there.

The pattern of the new identities

The new identities, then, are an uneasy amalgam of elements deriving from the transcendental village community and the romanticised mythic world of communist identity, which was superimposed on the former. The combination is characterised by

[14] John A. Armstrong, *Nations before Nationalism* (Chapel Hill: University of North Carolina Press, 1983).

insecurity, an absence or weakness of the cognitive categories appropriate to the social, political and technological realities with which individuals have to cope and a consequent tendency to decode impressions and interpret meanings by inappropriate criteria. In this ontological void, nationhood came to provide a surrogate, a set of keys to the wider world.

The overall outcome of the imposition of the communist systems on Central and Eastern Europe was, therefore, to create a set of public identities that were marked by major fissures and contradictions. Thus although these societies were pressed into a variant of modernity, they did not have available the choice, the complexity or the change that modernity implies in the West. Society found itself in, as it were, a cheap copy of the real thing. The strategies it developed to deal with this unexpected transformation, as has been argued in this paper, have had an indelible influence on perceptions of the state, of politics and of society's own role and identity in its relationship with both the state and the nation.[15]

When looked at from the perspective of identities under communism, the majority nation had no alternative but to define itself against the party-state. To this end, it constructed boundaries, regarded itself as a separate moral-cultural entity and essentially behaved as if it was a minority, because it was deprived of the power to generate its own strategies and was narrowly confined by what it perceived as an alien body. Thus even though numerically, society constituted the majority, sociologically it was a minority and thus acquired some of the characteristics of minorities.

This history of having been deprived of power has contributed to majority national behaviour under post-communism, in that majorities behave as if they were in mortal danger of extinction, given that they felt that they had been repressed in their quality as nations, that they have survived only by the skin of their teeth and that they must continue in like fashion test the threat should revive. Where a community has lived with the sense of threat, it will go on looking for external dangers, whether they exist or not; indeed, they will create them and sometimes end up the victims of a self-fulfilling prophecy, that the feared threat actually becomes a real one.

---

[15] Heather E. Bellows, 'The Challenge of Informationalization in Post-communist Societies', *Communist and Post-communist Studies*, vol.26, no.2 (June 1993), pp. 144-64.

Where communist party rule began to be diluted, to be 'nostrified' or brought closer to the national aspirations of the community, this attitude was to some extent eased, but only marginally so, because the nation could never be secure in controlling its own destiny as long as the ruler legitimated itself by the non-national ideology of Marxism-Leninism. It was the unacceptability of the combination of nationalism and Marxism that gave rise to the major confusion of national agendas.

The party, never considered the proper agent of nationhood, was neverthless acting in this fashion, which polluted nationhood at the same time as affording the party a limited degree of popularity. No one could be certain as to whether a particular initiative by the party with a national content was authentic or manipulative. The resulting uncertainty generated anxiety about the identity of the nation and content of nationhood. Both of these factors have come to play a major role under post-communism. Ceauşescu's Romania provides a good illustration of these processes. Ceauşescu sought to appropriate Romanian nationalism and use it to legitimate his rule, but the outcome after an initial period of popularity was to make Romanians unsure about what exactly the content of Romanians nationhood was. At the same time, where the nation could define itself against other ethnic groups, it would do so, not least because it was encouraged in this by the party (e.g. Hungarians against Romanians over Hungarian concern over the minority in Transylvania; Romanians against Hungarians over the fear of dismemberment).

For the ethno-national majorities their distorted national identity mediated between them and the state all the same. It created an uneasy relationship, because the gap between the *pays réel* and the *pays légal* was wide and in many respects unbridgeable. People identified with the state, but disliked what it was doing. They expected the state to perform certain tasks like protecting the nation and were irritated when it failed to do so. When party control over the state weakened, as it did at various times under communism, real social aspirations came to the surface. In retrospect, and to an extent this was apparent even at the time, the significance of these periods of weakened party rule – Poland and Hungary in 1956, Czechoslovakia in 1968, Croatia in 1971, Poland again during Solidarity – is that these aspirations were highly homogeneous and highly unrealistic.

Society defined itself as the nation in opposition to the Soviet

Union and its local agents, the party, and conceptualised political action as a confrontational, one-to-one relationship, in which zero-sum games dominated and in which society held the moral high ground. Furthermore, it sought to reinterpret the party's monopoly control of the language of politics into its own more nationally determined mind-set. Thus whenever parties made symbolic concessions to nationhood, these were decoded as gestures likely to lead to the fulfilment of aspirations associated with nationhood, like freedom, which was not, of course, on the agenda. If the party was involved in a dispute with another party which could in any sense be given a national colouring, the opportunity was seldom missed. Thus when in the 1960s, the Hungarian party acted as the willing agent for the Soviet Union in its dispute with Romania, Hungarian opinion tended to see this not as a part of an arcane conflict over Marxism-Leninism, but as a coded reference to the fate of the Hungarian minority in Transylvania.

Furthermore, however much society may have disliked communist rule, its members were inevitably socialised into some of its ways, either positively or negatively. It is a standard proposition that contestants assume one another's features. So it was with the state-society conflict under communism. Communism used the ideology of perfection to legitimate itself and thereby to arrogate total control of power to itself, so society correspondingly defined itself as a single, more or less organic whole superior in its authenticity and morality to the party. One of the most pronounced examples of this was in the Solidarity programme in Poland, which was formulated on the tacit assumption of a very high degree of homogeneity derived from a self- stereotype of a seamless Polish nation to which the party-state was alien.

Society and the state

What society was unable to learn as long as it was locked in this intellectually sterile confrontation was either to deal with the state in a positive way, that is to say not assuming that the state's sole purpose was to exploit society, or to deal with itself in any way other than to assume that any deviation from the norm, any variation in opinion, any diversity was a mortal threat to it, whether intellectually or morally.[16] This, indeed, has been the most baneful

[16] Kazimierz Brandys, *A Warsaw Diary 1978-1981* (New York: Random House,

legacy of the communist experience – the extreme difficulty that post-communist societies have in coming to terms with the diverse interactions that their particular pattern of modernity generates. The communist form of modernity may be a gravely distorted one by Western criteria, but is still a form of modernity in terms of communications, literacy, consumption and aspirations, yet there is great difficulty in dealing with the complexity that this modernity generates. The central problem is that the habits of reductionism, which are informed by nationalist perspectives, have deep roots, with the result that mentalities and the realities of complexity are at odds.

If the foregoing provides something of a picture of the attitudes of national majorities towards the state, the relationship between ethnic minorities and the state is markedly different. While majorities could regard the state as 'their own', even if it did not correspond to how they would like to be, minorities were in a much more sensitive position. They could not identify with the state in the same deep-rooted affective way as majorities, because the state was constituted around the moral and cultural codes of the majority. If the gap between minority aspirations and state provision is too wide, disaffection can result and the chances of stability are thereby reduced. The communist state made matters worse by insisting on its strategy of reductionism and homogenisa-tion, which bore particularly hard on ethnic minorities. From the communist perspective, the minorities question was supposed to have been solved by the 'principled' application of Leninist nationalities' policy, which in practice meant that minorities were to accept formal provision and be content with that. Anything else was interpreted as a challenge to the leading role of the party and subject to political and other repressive sanctions.

What was curious about this communist strategy was that it ended up as supportive of nationalism in a roundabout way. Precise-ly because communism had no intellectually satisfactory answer to the problem of nationhood and nationalism,[17] it was left with verbal solutions which meant little more than defending the *status quo*. The status quo in this context meant that after the end of

---

1983) gives some interesting examples of the informal pressures to conform to a particular view of Polish history exacted by the social milieu.

[17] Szporluk, *op. cit.*

monolithism (1961),[18] existing national majorities would be given something of a framework within which they could find some satisfaction for their aspirations, at least at the symbolic level. But what this communist approach neglected completely was that nationhood, in common with other political categories, was dynamic and subject to change, so that by freezing nationhood in the state in which it found it, it helped to conserve it.[19]

This is not to suggest, as should be clear from the argument marshalled so far, that nationhood did not change at all, but its adaptation was impeded as far as power relationships within national communities were concerned, and it was left with largely the same preconceived heterostereotypes with respect to other ethno-national groups. Indeed, the level and intensity of communication between different ethno-national communities in Central and Eastern Europe were low to minimal. On this basis, it was possible for a tacit alliance between communists and nationalists to come into being after 1968, when the ideological vitality of communism was undermined by the suppression of the Czechoslovak reform programme.

This process was in any case intensified as the communist regimes began to exhaust their enfeebled legitimacy and they turned more and more towards trying to rely on nationalism. This contributed to undermining that legitimacy in the medium term by eroding the communists' credibility, given the inherent incompatibility of the bases of communism and nationhood, but the shift by communist parties did impact on national identities.

It brought nationalism in through the back door like a rather unwelcome relative who cannot be made to leave. The relationship between communism and nationalism, in fact, was based on mutual deception and self-deception. Communists could not use nationalism, as I have been arguing, without undermining their own credibility, so that when they did, they damaged themselves and nationalism by muddying the agendas of both. Yet at the same

[18] See the argument about monolithism in George Schöpflin, *op. cit.*, ch. 5; Jowitt argues that the key turning point was the Twentieth Congress of the CPSU and not the Twenty-Second, but in terms of its effect on Central and Eastern Europe, the second de-Stalinisation proved more far-reaching. See Jowitt, *op. cit.*, p. 251.

[19] Walker Connor, *The National Question in Marxist-Leninist Theory and Strategy* (Princeton University Press, 1984).

time nationalists did themselves little that was good by getting into bed with the communists. Here the mechanism of deception was slightly different. Because the promise of nationalism was vague, because it appealed to the affective dimension of politics, because it controlled a penetrating but unaccountable language game, it tended to imply that more was on offer than was really the case and its propositions could never be tested. It was not falsifiable in the Popperian sense and that was its attraction.

The promise of nationalism was implicit but seductive; being rid of the alien Soviet presence, freedom, prosperity, modernity, being like the West and so on. Yet nationhood in its ethnic dimension plainly could not deliver on any of this, only the complex of interactions mediated through institutions, the functioning of an effective market, political competition, self-limitation, feedback and reciprocity of rights, in a word the bundle of concepts associated with citizenship, could bring this about in the real world (as distinct from the mythic world derived from ethnicity). But as long as the pressure of communism remained in being to impede the emergence of civic ideas, the misty teleology of nationalism was the sole alternative and helped to keep alive an identity which was token of something that was kept suppressed by an intellectually and ethically void communism.

After the collapse

Hence when communism collapsed, these political systems found themselves in a difficult if not indeed impossible situation. Communism was brought down because it had lost its effectiveness and its legitimacy: it was no longer exemplary and binding; the West had taken over that role. It followed automatically that in the moment of the collapse, democracy, the ideology of the victor in the civilisational contest of the Cold War, was the sole alternative. Democracy was received suddenly, without preparation and arrived into a political, economic and cultural arena where the fit between its requirements and what was on offer on the ground was poor. The proposition that democracy would operate smoothly upon introduction was an illusion and it took a while for this illusion to evaporate.

On its disappearance, however, it grew clear that the existential and ontological void could not be filled by citizenship because the institutions needed for citizenship and the political culture necessary to make those institutions function properly were absent.[20] The communists had done their work of destruction well. There was only one force in the field, the one that the communists could neither eliminate nor house-train, namely nationalism. As I have argued, nationalism in post-communist Central and Eastern Europe existed overwhelmingly in its ethnic dimension; the civic dimension was weak to non-existent. The result was that post-communism acquired features and a character of its own, one that can be summed up as 'democratic in form and nationalist in content'.

Indeed, many of the problems besetting Central and Eastern Europe under post-communism can be helfully approached from the perspective of content. What is to be the nature of citizenship, of democracy, of civil society, of rights and duties, of individual and collective provision, together with a host of other questions of a constitutive kind? The difficulty of finding an answer lies in two interfacing fields: the legacy of communism and the nature of ethnic identities.

Over and above the discussion so far, it should be understood that while communism was widely perceived as an alien and failed system, it did neverthless function in real terms. Among its residues is the proposition that people derived at least a part of their identities from communism, whether directly or in opposition to it. Public achievement, for example, career patterns, distinction, intellectual attainment were all in some form or another linked to communist institutions. The relationship between the individual and the state is another area of contradiction. The communist system brought into being a dependence on a state that was not trusted yet desired. The individual looks to the state for provision in both material and symbolic terms and depends on it for status, even while in the absence of a clearly defined public sphere he distrusts it. That state disappeared with the end of communism, and the new legitimating ideology of liberalism, democracy and the market are perceived as profoundly threatening as unknown and unknowable. The disappearance of the structures constructed under communism has left a gap, which many are

[20] George Kolankiewicz 'The Other Europe: Different Roads to Modernity in Eastern and Central Europe' in Soledad García (ed.), *European Identity and the Search for Legitimacy* (London: Pinter, 1993), pp. 106-30.

seeking to bridge by using ethnicity, but ethnicity is inherently incapable of substituting for the state.[21] The result is confusion.

The communist past, as is now evident, cannot be wiped out. The consequences of the distorted modernisation – not least the transformation of the countryside, the introduction of mass literacy and a modern communications system – are irreversible, however uncomfortable this may be for those looking to eradicate the legacy. One way is to turn to the pre-communist past, glorify it and try to promote a view of the nation that is at odds with its own consumption patterns, ways of life and aspirations. The populist calls for a true revolution have their origins here.

The difficulty of the protagonists of ethnicity is that these transformed societies do not have a clear sense of exactly what they want themselves. They do want change, but there is no agreement as to the speed and scope of change. At the same time, much to the chagrin of nationalists, these semi-modernised societies do accept some of the patterns of modernity as imported from the West – in technology, consumption and leisure, for example – and reject attempts to revive an archaic past. The appeal of modernity and existing reality are in conflict with the differentiation demanded by ethnicity. This inner contradiction in the content of nationhood leaves nationalists no alternative but to seek to strengthen the boundaries of ethnic communities rather than infuse them with a new content that would provide a meaning to decode reality. Indeed, the more the patterns of life of different communities come to resemble each other, the more the protagonists of ethnicity have to insist on the differences.

This is the process which informs the frantic insistence on nationhood that has been the single most defining feature of post-communism. In real terms, the material ways of life and aspirations of these different ethnic communities are not particularly different. But the sense that the communities should be different, in order to establish their legitimacy and survival under perceived threats of extinction, accounts for their determination to defend the moral codes that they believe their cultures to represent. The outcome is to have dragged these societies into a cul-de-sac. From this perspective, the bloodshed in former Yugoslavia differs only in

---

21 Jiřina Šiklová, 'Nacionalizmus Közép-és Kelet-Európában', *Valóság* 35:1 (January 1992), pp. 114-16.

degree and not in kind from what is happening elsewhere in Central and Eastern Europe.

The insistence on the defence of the ethnic boundary by using whatever means are on hand does, of course, result in enhancing the general confusion, given that ethnicity cannot provide adequate answers to questions of citizenship and promotes greater instability. There is a serious threat that the state can end up being ethnicised, that ethnic and social minorities are finding themselves marginalised and rejected by the state in which they live and which denies them citizenship rights (e.g. the Russians in Estonia or Latvia) and that in turn reacts back on the majority which sees conspiracies everywhere and creates enemies where there were none before.

Post-communism, therefore, deserves its name. Its character is an uneasy mixture of elements of the past and of the different vision of the future that are on offer. Society is finding it extremely difficult to place these elements in a cognitive framework that would allow it to bring into being the social and political solidarity that could become the foundation for the democracy in the name of which communism was toppled. The pressure from these various different ordering principles is what underlies the problem of building a stable democratic order under post-communism. The emphasis on boundaries and national symbolism generates powerful affective responses, but these are insufficient to provide for the demands for meaning and to answer the challenges that these societies are facing in a period of great turbulence.

The attempts to create political communities relying largely on ethnicity will not produce a Western style democracy, but may well engender types of collectivism that can become the breeding ground for populist-authoritarian system that will take these societies away from the Western model to which they aspire. They will tend to promote thought-worlds that cannot confront the impact of globalisation in communication and consumption. This is liable to result in renewed salience for ethnicity, thereby intensifying the negative spiral in which post-communism finds itself. Thus the likelihood is that instability will persist until these contradictions are overcome.

13

AN ANALYSIS OF POST-COMMUNISM

Anyone looking at post-communism in the states of the Central and Eastern Europe must be struck by the scope of the undertaking. In historical terms, post-communism is one of the most daring enterprises of the twentieth century. The idea of converting a dozen or more countries into democracies in the space of a few years is quite extraordinary from temporal, spatial and cultural perspectives.

The project raises a number of questions, both directly and implicitly, about the nature of politics, the meaning of culture, the relationship between past and present, the intended and unintended consequences of change, the legitimacy of rational construction, the role of elite and societies to mention only a few. The range of responses has been similarly varied. For some, the 'transition to democracy' is a noble cause to be embraced with enthusiasm; for others it is a hostile conspiracy threatening a way of life; alternatively the changes are dislocating and a source of anxiety; for yet others are a form of 'orientalism', an attempt by an exploitative West to foist its ideologies on an alien East.

Further, the fate of post-communism and of the countries that have embarked on the process of transformation raises difficult questions about the nature of democracy and Europe, about how and whether the West can define itself without an alien other that it can regard as external to itself and equally whether Europe or possibly "Europe" is flexible enough to accommodate cultures that are simultaneously alike and unalike. From the perspectives of the Central and East Europeans the undertaking has different parameters and goals. At one and the same time, the Central and East Europeans are looking for security, stability, prosperity, identity, status; everything, indeed, from which they feel history has deprived them, from membership of their elusive Europe or 'Europe', for just as the West creates an image of the East, so the East creates its own images of the West.

The scope of the project is formidable, as far-reaching as the original attempt by the communists to make of these countries societies that would approximate to their Marxist templates. In some ways, it is even greater precisely because there is no single democratic template other than a set of broad principles, diversely interpreted, which will allow the relationship between rulers and ruled to be based on continuing consent. To this extent, every post-communist state is expected to find its own way to an outcome which is only roughly sketched but once reached will, it is hoped, provide for a distribution of power in which fear is dispelled, stability is assured, change is secured, prosperity safeguarded, life-chances more or less equally distributed and freedom for both the community and the individual are in equilibrium. A tall order, then; yet all this is made that much more difficult by the communist experience and the legacy of the pre-communist tradition. There is much to be said for the proposition that if a country wished to move to democracy, it should not start from communism.

Communism can also be analysed in various ways, but few would quarrel with the argument that at its centre was an enormous concentration of power and a homogenisation of society; a conscious cutting of the links between rulers and ruled; an insistence that the state rather than the individual occupied the high moral ground; and the promotion of a pattern of ideological thinking in which surface appearance had to be discarded in favour of more contorted explanations of the world. All these have left their mark. All are in some ways at variance with the assumptions of democracy and are an obstacle to it. Hence the post-communist project has had to begin from a severely disadvantageous starting point and will quite certainly produce a model of democracy different from anything in the West. This is not necessarily undesirable. One of the great strengths of democracy is that so many varied solutions have been tried in answer to the great problematic of taming and civilising power. Each has strengths and weaknesses. The solutions that are currently being worked out in Central and Eastern Europe will one day take their place in this panoply and will be regarded as a legitimate variant of democratic systems.

The base-line, the communist system, however, deserves a closer examination, not least because there is a growing tendency in analyses of post-communism to forget communism. There are many levels of communism, all of which affected these countries in some way or another. It is tempting to go for the easiest – the visible legacies, like the dreadful ring of breeze-block houses that surrounds every major urban settlement – and to concentrate on these. It makes more sense, though, to look at the more abstract levels of communism first in order to try and understand the explanation for the nature of post-communist behaviour and not to derive this explanation from material factors.

Communism, then, can be understood as a failed and distorted experiment in modernisation, but, at a deeper level, it was much more than this. It sought to create a wholly new civilisation and to base this on a fundamentally different way of constructing the world. This is the most persuasive starting point, the moral vision deduced from the original Marxist impulse and the rather different moral order that the communist system of the rule brought into being. It is this level of analysis that provides the necessary insight into the breathtaking daring of the project and the consequent scope of the communist transformation, a scope so vast that it ought place observers of the post-communist transformation under a duty of patience if not humility.

Europe has seen various attempts to construct new moral orders. This is generally a far-reaching enterprise, which involves a radical discarding of history and much or all of the inherited social knowledge that history encodes. It also involves the superimposition of a new moral code on the population and to some extent at least assumes a measure of consent on the part of those affected. Certainly precedent suggests that consent to transformation makes the acceptance of a new moral order far easier, as witness the Protestant Reformation. In the case of communism, however, consent was disregarded from the outset, essentially because the ideology of perfection upon which the new system was built inherently and logically made consent superfluous. Perfection is by definition beyond questioning and automatically presumes consent, hence when this is withheld, those so doing are self-evidently heretics, guilty, offending against a more powerful delimitation of the world. It should be added here that attempts to construct new moral orders have usually taken place when the previous world-views were in a state of decay. What was unusual about the communist experiment was that the system it sought to replace had not decayed, but was in a temporary position of weakness and confusion (the defeat of 1945). Hence the communist project was facing a competitor that would prove to be far more difficult to defeat than its protagonists ever imagined. Not only was the level of consent to communism low, but popular aspirations pointed in an entirely different direction.

There is every reason to suppose that the post-communist states of Central and Eastern Europe have moved on from 'transition' if by transition we mean a fairly rapid progress from communism to democracy. Rather, these political systems have assumed their interim shape and these are unlikely to alter substantially in the forthcoming period. In this sense, post-communism is a real political system, with its own political characteristics, features and dynamic. These features have been conditioned partly by the *longue durée* factors of Central and East European history, by the communist period and, importantly, by the consequences of the decisions taken since the end of communism. At the same time, post-communism must also be seen as a system *sui generis*, not just because no other countries have undergone these particular experiences, but because their political topography cannot easily be located in the field of democracy or authoritarianism; they incorporate elements of both.

They are *sui generis* because of their past, therefore, but equally so because of their projected future. The proposition that democracy can be imported and superimposed on society is attractive to anyone whose temper of mind is sympathetic to democracy, but any analysis of post-communism must reckon with the underlying anxiety that while communism was certainly a non-consensual system, it left a living legacy in terms of culture – habits of mind, expectations, attitudes – that has not decayed quite as fully as was universally assumed in 1989. Furthermore, because sizeable sections of the population were uneasy about the nature of democracy, having had no experience of it, they were potentially or actually open to the temptation of homogenising ideologies and systems built upon them. It is in this sense that, epigrammatically, post-communism is democratic in form and nationalist in content.

Both are important. While there are obviously strong currents of nationalism in the region, the democratic forms that were adopted and to some extent superimposed on these societies, do have some genuine content. The question is the balance between the two. Because this balance varies in time and place, the precise delineation of post-communism is very difficult to make.

Indeed, it has been argued that the post-communist world is characterised by two salient features, both signifying a degree of intermediacy. The first is that with the extinction of Leninism, the post-communist states are in a 'Genesis environment';[1] the second is that they are in a state of liminality.[2] Genesis implies that the nature of the new order is very fluid and all sorts of options are possible. Liminality suggests that elements of the new are mixed with elements of the old; the combination makes the determination of rules extremely difficult.

In essence, the post-communist systems are marked by constant conflict over the most basic criteria of how power is to be legitimated, distributed, applied and generated. One might expect that this conflict would take the form of constitutional crises. In fact, because of the confusion and lack of agreement, the existing rules tend to be weakly regarded and seen as facades for the pursuit of private interests. In effect, there is only a very marginal sense of the public sphere and the public good. They do exist, but they are shot through with distrust, suspicion, disbelief and the conviction that the exercise of power is taking place 'elsewhere', beyond the cognition and control of the individual. In this sense, citizenship is remote from the concept of full political participation as adumbrated by the French Revolution and pursued by Western democracies ever since.

From the foregoing it follows that the political contest is not played out as is usually the case in Western Europe, focusing on the allocation of resources, where the criteria of distribution are largely agreed, meaning that the political battles that are regularly found in the West are fought under rules. Under post-communism, the political contest is about the basic determinants of political organisation, governance and regulation – crucially, involving elements of moral regulation. By way of example, the role of the state in the policing of markets is not settled, so as a result the nature of just profit and unjust profit are likewise not settled. Those active in the economy frequently arrange for their own enforcement of the law and are, therefore, dubbed mafiosi.

Equally the nature and pattern of social aspiration are still under debate. Should people aim to live in an equal society, which for

[1] Ken Jowitt, *New World Disorder: the Leninist Extinction* (Berkeley: University of California Press, 1992).

[2] Zygmunt Bauman, 'After the Patronage State: a Model in Search of Class Interests' in Christopher Bryant and Edmund Mokrzycki (eds), *The New Great Transformation* (Routledge, 1994).

the foreseeable future would mean a relatively modest standard of living or should they accept the growing income differentiation that would enhance capital accumulation? The answer is further muddied because the money accumulated in the post-communist states is usually siphoned off illegally or semi-legally into Western bank accounts, as the local banking system is not trusted.

Theorising the nature of the conflict under post-communism, it can be argued that it is the reproduction of society itself that is at issue. Different social, political and cultural forces, with their own projects and languages of legitimation, are engaged in a contest as to what contours the system should assume, what the inner meaning of democracy is and, vitally, what is to be the role of the nation and of citizenship under the new dispensation. Concomitantly, the language of politics is not agreed upon and, predictably, there are those who may use what is recognised as democratic language in the West but infuse it with a different, say, ethnicised, content. And paralleling these processes, the rituals and liturgies of politics and the saliency or otherwise of myths are similarly a matter for deepest disagreement. In Bulgaria for example: there is still a heated debate as to whether the lion in the coat-of-arms should or should not bear a crown; different meanings are attributed to the crown or its absence.

Another factor in this state of confusion, which exacerbates the situation and makes the regulation of reproduction harder, is the far-reaching inexperience of both politicians and societies. This stems above all from the communist period. Communism had the aim of excluding society from political power, because – so ran the legitimation – the party was already in possession of everything that it needed to govern through its control of history. To this end a far-reaching depoliticisation was imposed, as a result of which neither individuals nor groups acquired any clear idea of political causation, of what could and could not be achieved through political action. This inexperience, once communism had disappeared, made itself manifest in wildly unrealistic expectations and the concomitant apathy when the expectations were not fulfilled (e.g. relatively low turn-outs at elections, the occasional success of populistic promises, cynicism).

A further problem in this connection is the nature of hierarchy and equality. Here communism was wholly contradictory. Formally the communist system was completely committed to equality, but by the 1980s this commitment was overwhelmingly formal and propagandistic. From the 1960s on, various forms of differentiation were accepted and promoted, albeit access to resources tended to be contingent and often enough at variance with the official ideology, not least because access to political power meant prosperity. This gave rise to a form of cognitive dissonance. Formal equality, to which constant reference was made in public pronouncements, was undermined by a rigid hierarchy, which effectively excluded the bulk of the population from access to political participation. It was hard to understand the criteria of social order.

However, this actually signified that egalitarianism was in some respects a desirable aim, so that the reality of differentiation was never internalised as a value, not least because the process by which inequality was structured was opaque. Furthermore, because the value of equality was seemingly guaranteed by the state, after the end of communism the state continued to be seen as the moral centre of equality and equity. Its failure to fulfil this role has reacted back on democratic politics, which is widely seen as having failed society.

The problem does not end there, however. While communism was formally egalitarian and hierarchical in practice, democracy carries an implicit promise of equality (the equality of all before the law, the equality of life chances), even while in reality it is about a very high and intensifying diversity. This development is deeply disturbing for societies which have no experience of coping with diversity, but on the contrary have been habituated to a uniquely high level of stability. The most powerful depiction of this is probably in the concept of the elimination of time in Milan Kundera's *The Unbearable Lightness of Being*.[3]

The shift from a formally egalitarian but really hierarchical society to a nominally equal order is made more problematical, because hierarchy – whatever its drawbacks in terms of limiting choice – does provide the individual with great security and a well-defined position in society. To these may be added a clear and universally understood legitimating ideology to account for success and failure. In this sense, even while the communist system was non-consensual, it was nevertheless real, because individuals derived a part of their social identity from it. Achievements, career

---

[3] Milan Kundera, *The Unbearable Lightness of Being* (London: Faber and Faber, 1984).

patterns, advancement and so on were all measured by the criteria of the communist system.[4]

Another twist to this complex of intertwined norms was that the benefit that society gained from its exclusion was its right not to assume responsibility. Indeed, communism could be defined as a system constructed around the proposition that cause and effect should be obscure and that individuals should have no obligation at all to assume responsibility for what they do. In many ways, this was a very comfortable system and the sudden shift to democracy had laid a considerable burden on people who have had to come to terms with a range of responsibilities and obligations for which they were in no way prepared.

In effect, the communist system was a contradictory norm. It was real for certain purposes, crucially as a negative norm, meaning that real values were derived from it, but it was also rejected. In the context of rejection, answers and meanings were sought elsewhere. In the first place, the societies ruled by the communists sought solace in an increasingly mythicised West; indeed, towards the late 1980s, comparisons with the West were so deeply internalised that this mythicised West was the real yardstick. It was in this sense that the communist system had ceased to be exemplary and binding. But the emphasis here is on the mythicised nature of the West; it was seen as the source of prosperity, plenty, security and so on, but there was no understanding of how these had to be achieved.[5] In this connection, in Central and Eastern Europe an idealised image of the West, sometimes as glimpsed through certain consumer goods or the like, represented the magic by which communism was to be vanquished.

The reception of democracy after 1989, therefore, tended to be collapsed into near impossible expectations of a sudden access to a very high standard of living. When this did not eventuate, on the contrary, apathy and the rejection of diversity ensued.[6] Slowly, very slowly, the myth of the West is being replaced by the reality of the West. This has pluses and minuses. There is a

[4] Jiřina Šiklová, 'Nacionalizmus Közép-és Kelet-Európában', *Valóság*, vol.35, no.1, pp.114-16.

[5] Piotr Sztompka, 'The Intangibles and Imponderables of the Transition to Democracy', *Studies in Comparative Communism*, vol.24, no.3 (September 1991).

[6] *Central and East European Eurobarometer*, no.5 March 1995 (European Commission).

widespread availability of Western goods, together with consumption, technology and leisure patterns (Adidas, Benetton, MacDonalds etc.). Equally, there is now a wider acquaintance with the West than ever before. But the process is simultaneously painful, in that it demands new forms of knowledge, new attitudes, new procedures and so on, few of which are easily acquired. And there is still a certain sense of dependence. In a theoretical way, salvation is expected from the West – currently, through membership of the European Union – and when this is not forthcoming, the response is dismay, disappointment or even a kind of truculence. To this extent, the West is seen as owing the post-communists a duty of care.

A second set of answers to the problem of ontology raised by communism was to look to the past. The mechanisms were similar to the appropriation of the West and its transformation into a mythicised West. Likewise, history was turned into memory, into the remembered and beautified past. The pre-communist systems were seen as rather superior to what they were, their drawbacks were forgotten and, because these systems inevitably placed considerable emphasis on ethnic nationhood, their recall similarly upgraded the role and function of ethnicity. A particularly noteworthy instance of this was the way in which the first Czechoslovak republic, widely seen as a failure in 1948, was upgraded in popular perceptions into a success by 1968.[7] Analogous re-evaluations, sometimes enhanced by the way in which ruling parties sought to appropriate bits of the past for their own legitimation, took place elsewhere. Thus by the 1980s Marshal Pilsudski, the interwar Polish leader, had been informally assumed into the pantheon of Polish political heroes.

Thirdly, post-communist patterns of thought were influenced by religion, not necessarily religion as a body of doctrine and faith, but as a set of values and social norms. Here the prevailing legacy was of Counter-Reformation Catholicism in Central Europe and Orthodoxy in South-Eastern Europe. They both shared certain common ground, notably a stress on hierarchy and obedience, on display and ritual rather than internalisation. In the case of Orthodoxy, this was sometimes extended by a preference for

---

[7] Archie Brown and Gordon Wightman, 'Czechoslovakia: Revival and Retreat' in Archie Brown and Jack Gray (eds), *Political Culture and Political Change in Communist States* (London: Macmillan, 1977), pp. 159-96.

passivity over action; coupled with these was a belief that reality did not lie in appearance (this is the Protestant value system so strongly emphasised by Anglo-Saxon thought) but in what lay beneath the surface.

This had the result that actual social realities could be ignored in favour of a presumed and preferred belief about reality, as for example in the idea that was fairly widespread in the first half of the 1990s that the communist period could simply be ignored and that the fate of these states could be determined by guidelines drawn from the experience of the 1930s. The fact that communism really did effect a thoroughgoing transformation of various social relationships, not least by virtue of the ending of the traditional peasantry, was sidestepped.

Peasant legacy

Lastly, there was the legacy of peasant thought itself. Briefly, the agricultural population in Central and Eastern Europe had no theory of growth, something that was reinforced by Marxism, because traditionally the bulk of the rural population lived at or just above subsistence level and regarded gain and loss as equally balanced. This gave rise to a belief in zero-sum games, that 'my gain is your loss'; the idea that both parties could gain is regarded as, at best, naive. When applied to politics, this system of values makes nonsense of an idea of public good, of public virtues and is very low on the trust that is essential for the smooth functioning of contest and markets.[8]

Overall, these various currents have combined in post-communism to produce a hybrid, which tends to be marked by negative egalitarianism (that all should be brought down to the same level), by a belief that all wealth has been gained illicitly or illegally, by a lack of trust, by impatience and radicalism (the expectation that the state should deliver wealth immediately), by inexperience and ignorance of the nature of politics and political action or organisation and by a propensity to measure politics by moral criteria, that all action is intelligible by the rules of good and evil. The problem with this last proposition is that good and evil are absolute categories

[8] On trust, see Francis Fukuyama, *Trust: The Social Virtues and the Creation Prosperity* (London: Hamish Hamilton, 1995).

and run counter to democratic compromise and the need for tolerance.

These impediments which characterise post-communism are notably difficult for the evolution of civil society, without which – as is widely agreed – it is hard to see a smoothly functioning democracy. The concept of civil society is itself one of some complexity, with a wide variety of definitions. The one to be used here is relatively simple: civil society is to be understood as a process in which the number of political, economic, social etc. actors is increasing and consequently the range of conflicts of interests is spreading. This necessitates the formulation and acceptance of a growing number of criteria for the resolution of these conflicts. At the same time, the role of the state is to supervise civil society in the sense of offering adequate provision for 'hard' legal boundaries, rather than the 'soft' constraints of the communist system in which the exercise of discretionary power prevailed. Only through the consistent application of the rule of law can one conceive of the stability and predictability which are the *sine qua non* of democracy.

The necessary shift from discretion to guaranteed procedures is not at all easy to establish. The habits inherited from the past and crucially the loss of privileges, power and patronage under the new order strongly militate against such a transformation. Once again, the role of the state as the policing agency for the rule of law comes into question, for as already argued, there is little or no trust in the state, its personnel and its criteria. Hence the new modes of conflict regulation are patchily applied and the vital stabilising element of consistency is lost. In the circumstances, post-communist societies can be forgiven their lack of trust. Their inexperience with diversity and with a 'neutral' state makes the task of transformation a daunting one.

Finally in this set of difficulties there is the notion of 'ideological thinking'. This is the phenomenon where the values of society nearly universally expect that every effect has a cause, that there is no chance or accident, for if something has happened, it is because someone has caused it to happen. A moment's thought will show how destructive this pattern of thinking is to democracy. Besides, when everything is caused by someone, the moral imperative is to find the causator and hold him guilty; this intensifies moralisation. In societies where ideological thinking is prevalent, there will be no space for spontaneity and implicit motives will be ignored. Everything will be seen as purposive, all initiatives and developments will be seen as having a single logic and single possible outcome. In effect, post-communism is haunted by massive reductionism and monism.

In thought-worlds where there is no room for happenstance and coincidence, where there is no neutral space, it is extremely difficult to construct compromise, because the automatic assumption of all actors is that others are antagonists and enemies rather than fellow players on the political, economic or social stage. This is the phenomenon that helps to explain the conflict-generating nature of post-communist attitudes. Expectations are geared to hostility rather than compromise and each party will be utterly convinced of the moral superiority of its position. By the same token, the eruption of conflict will then legitimate each party, so that both acquire a de facto interest in the perpetuation of conflict and polarisation. This is observed most vividly in inter-ethnic conflict, where, say, the demonisation of one side by the other is fully reciprocated; the Serb-Croat relationship illustrates this process very well. Tudjman needed Milošević needed Tudjman. As the ex-Yugoslav crisis has begun to wane, so the power of both has begun imperceptibly to decline.

The ultimate difficulty created by ideological thinking is that it makes the very stability and consistency that society is seeking hard to achieve. Societies that construct their cognitions in the ways sketched above find it extremely hazardous to escape from their closed thought-worlds, with the result that regularly the impact of new ideas, new patterns and, importantly, new technologies will be inexplicable. The tendency then is to take refuge in conspiracy theories of the world.

Ironically, what might be said to have begun as a particular way of trying to understand the world, to create cosmos out of chaos,[9] ends up by radically misunderstanding it and thereby generates more confusion in societies that are ill-equipped to cope with the transformation that they are undergoing. Let it be added here that ideological thinking is not something that is easily shed, not something that can be sloughed off by taking thought, as it were. Rather, these patterns of thought have deep roots in the value systems of societies that have been deprived of the

[9] This is the formulation used by Mircea Eliade, *The Myth of the Eternal Return: Cosmos and History* (London: Penguin, 1954)

cognitive instruments for decoding an increasingly complex world. They will remain to bedevil the politics of post-communism for a while yet.

In the political realm the importance of ideological thinking lies in the perpetuation of social credulousness and the vulnerability to simplistic solutions for difficult problems. In particular, it makes societies liable to listen sympathetically to populist discourses and to entrench their political inexperience by impelling them to look for non-institutional solutions. These cannot, of course, actually solve the problems of poor access to power, fear, instability or the like, but they can generate the appearance of a solution; and because populist discourses invariably seek to blame difficulties on internal and external scapegoats, societies are prevented from engaging in the learning process that would eventually allow them to begin to recognise their material interests. Certainly, populist discourses are homogenising and reductionist, so that those who are prey to them cannot begin to embark on the process of understanding the multipolar, diverse, complex reality of the world in which they live.

Then, there is another aspect to the problem of rules. Before a system can function as an overt democracy, the second order rules governing the ebb and flow of power must be set beyond the political contest. It is a basic requirement of consolidation that the rules of the game are unalterable, are accepted by all as not a part of politics; indeed, ideally, they should be taken for granted and treated as 'normal and natural', to be changed only through complex and elaborate procedures. If this does not happen, contestants can and do claim advantage by manipulating the rules to their advantage – electoral regulation, social welfare benefits targeted at particular groups of voters, property share-outs can all be used in this way. The hierarchy of rules is not accepted and rules are not embedded in a widely internalised mode of regulation. On the contrary, they are seen as contingent and there is an expectation that one's opponents will change the rules when their turn comes.[10]

This is very much what is happening under post-communism, although it should be noted that what might be called the outer

[10] Claus Offe, 'Agenda, Agency and Aims of Central East European Transitions' in Stefano Bianchini and George Schöpflin (eds), *Europe and the Balkans: How They View Each Other*, vol.1 (Ravenna: Longo, 1998)

framework of regulation is, broadly speaking, respected. With one or two exceptions (like Belarus), the constitutional order is accepted by all contestants and power is yielded by a party that has lost the elections. But the lack of respect for the rules of the game is serious enough as an obstacle. Crucially, it results in short term thinking, it perpetuates a lack of respect for the rule of law, it engenders cynicism about politics, and it creates a climate in which hidden motives and conspiracies are universally suspected. The outcome is the public sphere functions haltingly and the division between public and private is ignored. The system is rational within its parameters and is self-reproducing. It will be hard to break this cycle.

Before looking at the nature of democratic practice under post-communism in the light of the interlocking set of problems outlined above, it is worth offering a brief model of certain aspects of democracy, for these tend to be taken for granted and to be assimilated to one's own experience of democracy. The proposition on which this analysis is based is that there is no single model of democracy and that the shift towards democratic practice in Central and Eastern Europe has suffered from the tacit collusion between the post-communist supporters of democracy and their Western counterparts, who have, without being necessarily conscious of this, tended to insist that there is only one road to democracy, the one they know.

In reality, there are as many models of democracy as there are democratic countries. They all share commitment to a few basic principles, but the actual implementation of these principles is greatly varied. These principles can be reduced to those of theory and those of practice. The theoretical requirements are, essentially, the overriding need to accept self-limitation, feedback and the proper functioning of self-correcting mechanisms.

Self-limitation

All three are more or less self-explanatory. Self-limitation means not merely the observance of the rule of law, but the recognition and willing acceptance of the unwritten ground-rules of politics. This includes a realisation that the political system exists for the benefit not merely of oneself or one's own interests, but of others, who are fellow citizens and, therefore, entitled to the same rights as oneself. Minorities – social and economic as well as ethnic minorities – should, in consequence, be included in the political decision-making process and, vitally, not suffer consistent closures, whether from the real or the symbolic goods of the state. At the end of the day, self-limitation rests on the understanding that the political system is an enterprise encompassing the interests of all.

Feedback is the principle that governs the relationship between rulers and ruled in a democracy. It implies continuous communication and the readiness on the part of the rulers to govern in accordance with the wishes of population. If these wishes are overridden, the rulers will ultimately suffer. Legitimation is likewise an aspect of feedback, in that it is only through a regular renewal of legitimacy, especially through elections, that rulers can retain their self-legitimation. Without that renewal, their will to rule will erode, as happens in authoritarian systems (communism being the obvious case, but much the same can be discerned from the collapse of the Colonels' dictatorship in Greece in 1974). Feedback, then, implies a readiness to adjust policies in accordance with the will of the people and that, in turn, means that rulers must be ready to explain their strategies to the population.

Self-correcting mechanisms are a significant moment in the functioning of civil society. No state is perfect and the modern state inevitably accumulates power.[11] This is exemplified in the phenomenon of the autonomy of the state over society, when bureaucratic regulation functions in the interests of the bureaucracies rather than for the overt purpose of administration. In these conditions it is important for a society to have the space to adjust its interests, aspirations and imperatives, which may have been distorted by the operation of state power, without excessive state intervention and centralisation.

The institutional arrangements of democracy, on the other hand, are varied. Popular (or parliamentary) sovereignty is presumed in a democracy and this is exercised through representation; separation of powers allows the different parts of the state to operate with a degree of autonomy; the rule of law has already been discussed.

Within this framework, a wide variety of practices can be found. In the first place, there is the Anglo-Saxon model which is formally adversarial though in practice it is increasingly étatist

---

[11] W.H. McNeill, *The Pursuit of Power* (Oxford: Blackwell, 1983).

(e.g. the United Kingdom, Canada). The question then is to determine the effectiveness of popular control over the state. The French model may be described as technocratic, with important popular inputs into the working of the system; the German model emphasises consensus and efficient bureaucracy; the Netherlands and the Scandinavian states are pluralistic and consensual, though there too the state plays a key role in redistribution; the Italian model is still in a state of flux; and Greece is far closer to post-communism than most people would like to admit.

The implication of this argument is that different post-communist states will develop different political institutions and some of these, while democratic, will in reality remain closer to the patterns that have evolved since 1989. In other words, the *sui generis* quality of the Central and East European political systems will not alter significantly. Nevertheless, the democratic achievements of the last few years, as well as the democratic deficit, can be assessed by using the criteria set out above as a check-list.

Thus the fact that up to the end of the century every change of government in the region took place as a result of more or less fair elections can be counted a creditable attainment. There have been no military putsches, no coups d'état, and ruling governments have ceded power when they have lost the elections (Lithuania, Poland, Hungary, Estonia, Bulgaria, Slovakia and in part the Czech Republic illustrate this). Nor has any post-communist state actually abandoned democratic legitimation and tried to employ some form of authoritarian rule, though Belarus is coming very close to this.

The role of constitutional regulation through constitutional courts has come to assume a very high profile role under post-communism and by and large governments respect this. In the West, only the United States and Germany assign their constitutional courts a major role in the political process, but in the post-communist world this is a significant factor. Despite the arguments of some theorists of democracy that constitutional courts, being non-elected, cannot count as democratic institutions, it is fair to suggest that democratic elections are not the only source of legitimation, and the application of rules by the construction of neutral space through consistency and detachment from party politics generates its own legitimation, especially when political systems are still at an early stage of rule-making. The constitutional courts in Hungary, Poland, to some extent Bulgaria and the Czech

Republic have been significant in safeguarding and extending democratic rule-making.

It is a reasonable surmise that throughout most of the post-communist world, and especially in Central Europe (Poland, the Czech Republic, Slovakia, Hungary, Slovenia, the Baltic states), there is a strong commitment on the part of both elites and society to non-violent means of conflict regulation. This is evidently an essential aspect of democracy and without it, a democratic order cannot be visualised. In part, this value can be attributed to memories of the very high levels of coercion under communism, coupled with the rhetoric of force (revolution, class struggle) that communist ideology employed so freely.

At the same time, the tragic events in Yugoslavia served as an awful warning of what could happen if there were a breakdown. The deterrent of this example has certainly been understood in Romania and Bulgaria, where some of the ethnic cleavages could conceivably have resulted in violence, but both ethnic majorities and minorities have held back and applied self-limitation. Even in Slovakia, where the tension between the Slovak majority and the Hungarian minority has been rising, there has been no suggestion of violence or even of civil disobedience (though this latter cannot be excluded).

Where the state of affairs is less positive in terms of democracy is in the civic legitimation of states, as distinct from ethnicisation. Throughout the area there is a propensity to link citizenship with membership of the ethnic nation and to argue that members of ethnic minorities are, in effect, second class citizens. In the case of Latvia and Estonia, a sizeable section of the Russian minority does not have citizenship at all, merely the right of residence. Hence demands for access to political power on the basis of civic entitlement is only fitfully respected and ethnic majorities tend to be suspicious of the loyalty of minorities to the state. This attitude could potentially end up as a self-fulfilling prophecy.

Equally, the commitment on the part of elites to a civic legitimation of the state is contested. By and large, a fault line between left and right can be drawn around this issue (though there are others). On the whole, the right defines itself more strongly by ethnicity than does the left.[12] The legitimation of the state by

12 But confusingly the liberal government elected in Romania in November 1996 was described as 'right-wing', not least by the Western press. Similarly,

ethnicity has certain consequences for ethnic majorities. Above all, an ethnic basis for citizenship tends to obscure the rights of the individual and to enhance those of the collectivity, as embodied in the state, over the individual. Putting the issue somewhat rhetorically, an ethnic nation does not have taxpayers; only citizens pay taxes. In this perspective, the role of reciprocity between rulers and ruled can be marginalised by reference to ethnicity and the customary emphasis on paramount sacrifice and loyalty. Here the post-communist record is patchy. There is widespread ethnicisation, although its extent varies.

Democracy is also legitimated by the international environment. In the 1990s, it is extremely difficult for non-democratic discourses to be heard. It is inconceivable that a politician should stand up and demand that his rule be regarded as legitimate because it is authoritarian; only the language of democracy gains respect and authority. To this extent, the presence and active role of the West helps to sustain democratic legitimation and the various international codes of democratic practice represent a pattern of acceptable behaviour that international organisations are anxious to sustain.

On the other hand, support by the West for democracy has been far less generous than the democrats in the post-communist world had hoped. These elites had thought that the West, Western Europe especially, would move rapidly towards the full integration of the Central and East European states into Western structures. What they have not appreciated is that as a result of the collapse of communism, the West is itself in a crisis of identity and meanings. There is a major and far-reaching contest in Western democracies about the very significance of democracy, about the appropriate distribution of power in a democracy, about the nature and geographical extent of Europe and about transfers of political and economic resources to Central and Eastern Europe. The war in Yugoslavia caught the West unawares and it has come up with inadequate answers.

In conclusion, it is fair to suggest that the post-communist states of Central and Eastern Europe (the situation in the former Soviet Union, other than the Baltic states, is somewhat different) have indeed embarked on a major process of democratic con-

---

Mečiar's government in Slovakia has a strong commitment to ethnic nationhood but is generally known as left-wing.

struction. They have certain achievements to their name, though in this respect the movement towards acceptable democratic norms has been more substantial in Central Europe than in South-Eastern Europe, but none of these states as yet measures up to the criteria that are universal in Western Europe. As against this, given that only ten years have passed since the end of communism, the transformation that has been attained has been considerable.

14

THE RISE OF ANTI-DEMOCRATIC MOVEMENTS

The rise of various authoritarian currents in the post-communist world, especially as exemplified in the electoral success of Vladimir Zhirinovsky in Russia in the autumn of 1993, but also in various other post-communist states (notably nationalisms in Slovakia, Romania, Hungary and Croatia), has come as a distinctly unpleasant surprise for many in the West. Perhaps it should not have done. There were many warning signs and the West itself certainly encouraged anti-democratic forces by its seeming inertia in the face of authoritarian challenges. Still, many people in the West are unable to find an explanation for the apparent paradox that after forty years of communism, sizeable minorities in the post-communist countries – possibly majorities – are opting not for liberal democracy but for another dictatorship.

The explanation for the success of anti-democratic movements in the post-communist world is that communism and its collapse have left a major hiatus in these societies and simplistic answers, such as those given by right-wing and left-wing authoritarianisms, inevitably sound more plausible to sections of these societies than the discourses associated with democracy. The argument to be put forward in this analysis is based on a number of assumptions. In the first place, it will be assumed that the roots of the turn towards authoritarianism are to be sought not in the distant past, i.e. the 'return of history', but in the communist experience and its shortcomings. Second, it will be sought in the post-communist experience and the expectations that the collapse of communism generated. Third, it will start from a set of assumptions about populism, nationhood and nationalism, to the effect that these are authentic political phenomena, not something foisted on an unwitting population. Fourth, it will look at the implications of the transformation, especially at the expectations of revolution and the failure of the end of communism to bring about the expected revolution. Finally, it will also assume that the West could have had a far greater impact on the pattern of post-communist politics than it did and it will offer an argument as to why this did not happen and the consequences of the West's failure for its own political landscape in terms of both the rise of ethno-nationalism and right-wing movements.

The partial modernisation

There is a popular propensity to see the post-communist world as something unchanging, as societies that have been taken out of the deep freeze and that the attitudes and prejudices that were current before the communist takeover have remained miraculously conserved and are now rampant. This ludicrously implies that forty to seventy years of massive upheaval, the extension of the power of the state to encompass the whole of society, far-reaching industrialisation, major demographic change, the introduction of mass education and the impact of the modern mass media have all left these societies unaffected. It does not need much reflection to see how implausible the scenario of suspended animation is in the light of these changes. In reality, the first clue to the patterns of post-communism have to be sought in the particular nature of the modernisation that these countries underwent as a way of understanding the types of societies that have emerged from communism.

In summary form, the central feature of communist moder-nisation was that it was imposed from above and was regarded as alien by the bulk of the population. Although sections of society, notably the beneficiaries of communist modernisation, might have begun by viewing the modernising revolution positively and responded to the promise of a secular utopia with enthusiasm, gradually as the communist system decayed, attitudes changed and, particularly for those who ended up as the losers under communism and its aftermath, modernity itself came to be rejected. In effect, as communism was seen to have failed and to have functioned to suppress rather than enhance aspirations, it discredited its secular objectives. At one and the same time, distorted and narrow perspectives of the West as a viable utopia fuelled this failure.

Given this experience and the concentration of power in the hands of an elite that was increasingly seen as incompetent, significant sections of society felt excluded from the supposed benefits of modernity and were inclined to reject the entire package as alien. This implied that the elites that stood for modernity were themselves low in authority and found it difficult to sustain discourses legitimating democracy once communism had disappeared.

All this was exacerbated by the state of political innocence, not to say infantilisation, in which the communist system kept society. Procedures were opaque, the use of power was arbitrary, routinisation and predictability were at a discount and individuals were not encouraged to assume responsibility for the consequences of their actions. To make matters worse, communism promoted an attitude that to every question there was only one possible answer, all the others were false and, indeed, probably deliberately misleading. This attitude was legitimated by reference to the supposed scientific nature of communism and the crude black-and-white world of a scientific epistemology that claimed to possess all the solutions. The end of communism left these societies with very few guidelines that would serve them in trying to cope with the sudden demands that the introduction of democratic systems signified.

Another illuminating aspect of the communist experience was that it largely failed to create integrated societies, in which the great majority of the population was broadly agreed on a particular set of values, in which there were not deep-seated cleavages and in which horizontal communication between different sections of society, as well as vertical communication between rulers and ruled, functioned reasonably smoothly.

The tripartite division of society proposed by the Hungarian sociologist Gyula Tellér is a useful way of understanding the types of society produced by communism.[1] Tellér suggests that post-communist societies can be divided into liberal, communist and traditional elements. The first two need not detain us for long in this connection, except that their relative strength or weakness is obviously relevant to the size of the traditional segment. Tellér restricts his argument to Hungary, but it is applicable to other post-communist societies too. The liberal segment accepts the values of change, conflict that is mediated by institutions, markets, competition and individual responsibility. The communist segment

[1] Gyula Tellér, 'Döntés elött: politikai vita', *4x4 oldalas: Szabad Demokrata tájékoztató*, no.44 (4 November 1992).

was brought into being by the communist revolution and is necessarily dependent on the state. It prefers collectivist solutions to individualistic ones, but it also accepts that modernity in some form or another is the ultimate and desirable goal.[2]

The traditional segment, on the other hand, rejects modernity and is the strongest political and sociological base for the anti-democratic currents that appear to be gathering in the post-communist world. The characteristics of this segment derive from the shock it experienced through the enforced modernisation of the communist revolution and its resistance to it, coupled with the renewed shock of the collapse of authority with the disappearance of the familiar markers of communism. Its members had failed to internalise the norms of communism but had come to accept the system of symbols, power and hierarchy associated with it, so that the end of communism impacted on them as a major crisis of meanings.

Traditional society can be described as defined by the area's rural past. Traditional peasant and, where appropriate, neo-feudal values survived the communist modernisation, often in the face of the communist attempt at forcible transformation, and continue to motivate sizeable sections of society through cognitive categories that may not necessarily be the most suitable for the actual political conditions. Its ideas are strongly collectivist, negatively egalitarian or hierarchical, anti-intellectual, distrustful of politics — seeing it as an alien and 'unclean' game — and, thanks to its lack of political sophistication, it is vulnerable to manipulation by populist demagogues.

Elements of the past were conserved in the peasant mentality and have mingled with those of the present, retarding it, refracting it and crucially leading to a situation where popular control of power was not the norm, but where a wide variety of illusions were entertained about what could be done *with* power. Where these illusions failed to materialise, explanations and comfort were sought after in compensatory myths. These myths were of a total transformation, and could include aspirations of a very high level of material consumptions, but — being myth-derived — without any

---

[2] I make this argument in somewhat greater detail in my 'Culture and Identity in Post-communist Europe' in Stephen White, Judy Batt and Paul Lewis (eds), *Developments in East European Politics* (London: Macmillan, 1993), pp. 16-34.

sense of the intermediate steps needed to bring them into the real world.[3]

A further irony in all this was that the generally low level of political literacy had the automatic corollary of promoting the role of the state and dependence on it. As these traditional sections of the population found it difficult to come to terms with the complexity of industrial life, they were inevitably forced into a one-way relationship with the incomprehensible state and, willingly or otherwise, they were constrained into an acquiescence in étatism.

Although the emphasis in this section has been on the ex-peasantry, this term is used emblematically and the actual situation varied from country to country. Thus in Poland the peasantry was still very much a reality, largely because of the inability of the communist authorities to complete collectivisation in the 1950s and 1960s. The impact of this still fairly traditional peasantry on Polish political life has been to introduce an element of unpredictability, impatient radicalism and unreliability into an already volatile political scene, as well as to provide a reservoir of support for a conservative Roman Catholicism. In the Czech lands, the absorption of the peasantry into industry took place much earlier, having begun before the First World War, but given the particular nature of Czech industrialisation, a social formation was created that remained isolated from many of the technological and economic processes that might have favoured a more relaxed attitude towards mobility and change. The Czech working class was, therefore, deeply imbued with conservative values of hierarchy and immobility.[4]

In the former East Germany, the transformation was experienced in a more or less colonialist fashion, with West German values and institutions, as well as personnel, being superimposed on East German society. The attitude of the working class was resentful

---

[3] Some of these issues are discussed by Piotr Sztompka, 'The Intangibles and Imponderables of the Transition to Democracy', *Studies in Comparative Communism*, vol.24, no.3 (September 1991), pp.295-312.

[4] Miroslav Petrusek, 'A posztkommunizmus mint szociopolitikai fogalom és probléma' in Václav Belohradsky, Péter Kende and Jacques Rupnik (eds), *Politikai kultúra és állam Magyarországon és Csehszlovákiában* (Turin: Giovanni Agnelli Foundation, 1991), pp.87-105; and Jacques Rupnik, 'The Roots of Czech Stalinism' in Raphael Samuel and Gareth Stedman Jones (eds), *Culture, Ideology and Politics* (London: Routledge, 1982), pp.302-19.

and dissatisfied, with a determination to gain access to the symbols and reality of Western levels of consumption, but hostile to the methods imported from the West. Above all, the cognitive categories of the former East German population made it hard to cope with the new models of expected behaviour and the people tended to retreat into myths, resentment or apathy.

Possibly the most enduring feature salvaged from the rural past has been the deep distrust of the city. Communism imposed a terrible experience on traditional society, which it bore sullenly, unforgivingly and reluctantly, preserving what it could from the past, but changing in unperceived ways as well. This was an altogether different form of urbanisation from that undergone by the West, which was much more organic and effected a fairly successful integration of the countryside by the city. The disappearance of communism thus meant an end to the sense of humiliation and, equally, provided an opportunity for revenge.

The particular irony of this is that whereas in the West, communism was perceived as having created a world of especially soulless industrialisation, remote from the Western experience, for the peasantry that underwent communist modernisation, the distinction between the integrated Western process and the failure of the communist process was non-existent. In this sense, communist modernisation was conflated with Westernisation, coming to be seen as the triumph of the hated and sinful city over the pure and authentic values of the countryside.

The collapse of communism should logically have meant an easy return to those pure values, except of course that the clock could not be put back. Even so, the semi-urbanised masses were ready to give an attentive ear to the ex-peasant intellectuals, who were making false promises of a simpler life. This ex-peasant intellectual stratum deserves special attention. Its members were recruited under communism and enjoyed the rapid upward social mobility that the system provided, but instead of embracing its values unquestioningly, they were repelled by it and had the articulateness to give voice to the lost world, not least because their vision of power was one of a simpler, more straightforward, more transparent set of relationships, where cause and effect were directly related.

The ideology voiced by this intellectual stratum is hostile to modernity, to industry, to the density and complexity symbolised by the city; its most extreme manifestation could be observed in the war of Yugoslav succession. The senseless destruction of Vukovar, Sarajevo or Dubrovnik is best interpreted in this context as the ritual killing of the city. This Serbian example also illustrated something else that was evident to the outside observer: the futility of the war against modernity. But this futility was not at all obvious to the ex-peasantry, who were ready to believe their leaders that a better world was round the corner once the alien, sinful enemies had been extirpated. All this says a great deal about the superficiality of the communist modernisation process, which failed to offer enough of a material, moral or political vision to foster a thoroughgoing integration.

For the post-communist experiment in democracy, the existence of this sizeable, still collectivist-minded and homogenised traditional society does not augur well. Its broad attitudes towards a social and political system orientated towards complexity, change and choice has already been described. Its striking characteristic is its malleability, even manipulability and credulousness, as well as its hostility to opposing points of view. The sections of society that voted for Mečiar's HZDS in Slovakia, the Greater Romania party, the Smallholders in Hungary, the Bulgarian Socialist Party and, of course, the Peasant Parties in Poland can be regarded as having opted in favour of illusory solutions. They are bound to be disappointed with the nostrums purveyed by populist leaders and will continue to be a volatile element in the political spectrum.

The group was further marked by its economic marginality. It had failed to reach the level of existential solidity that had been been achieved by the communist and liberal segments and was conscious that the post-communist transformation was likely to affect its members very negatively. With the severe cutbacks on collective consumption, the group was not only faced with the existential problem of attempting to cope with a diminished standard of living, but even worse, it had to devise new budgeting, earning and similar life-style strategies. In all processes of major change, the sections of society most vulnerable to demagogy are those who have attained a little, but see themselves as losing that little under the new order.

The actual economic transformation was impacting severely on various such groups. The inflation, the shock therapy, the new reordered status differentiation, whereby previously low-status individuals were unexpectedly doing well all combined to accentuate the sense of loss and disenchantment among groups which had in any case very little patience with the kinds of change that were taking place and the objectives of which they were suspicious.

The post-communist experience

The elites that took power from the communists in and after 1989 did so in the name of democracy. The slogan of democracy proved extremely effective in demobilising loyalty to the communist system, largely because it was legitimated by tacit or explicit reference to the success of the West. The interpretation of the West that was current both at the elite and the popular level was, however, flawed. The West was not understood as a complex social, economic, political and cultural entity but as a political and economic success, which had won the Cold War. The externals of high levels of prosperity and sophisticated technology were regarded as the hallmarks of the successful competitor and it is no exaggeration to suggest that for many people 'democracy' was little more than an appendage to the economic triumph. Thus their expectations were that the introduction of 'democracy' would automatically bring with it a Western level of prosperity.

In any case, the new political elites were handicapped by the struggle that they themselves had fought with communism. As in any extended conflict, the contending parties gradually acquire characteristics of the other and the democratic opposition was no exception to this cultural rule. Inevitably, in having to fight a totalising system, the democratic opposition, while placing great emphasis on human rights and democracy, tended to interpret these in a relatively homogenised manner. There were many individual exceptions to this proposition, but overall it is clear, not least from the writings of Václav Havel, György Konrád or Adam Michnik that the counter-elite produced by communism tended to see society and democracy in rather simplistic and idealistic terms.[5]

The new democratising elite was in any case so persuaded of the appropriateness of its democratic beliefs and in its own democratic credentials that it never seriously thought that democracy had antagonists. It proceeded to impose a democratic structure

[5] See Václav Havel, *The Power of the Powerless* (London, 1985) and *Disturbing the Peace*, (London, 1990); Adam Michnik, *Letters from Prison and Other Essays*, (Berkeley: University of California Press, 1985); György Konrád, *Antipolitics* (New York: Harcourt, 1984).

on post-communist countries without any attempt to consult the population. To be fair, there were important external pressures that would have made non-democratic alternatives impossible to legitimate. In the post-1989 euphoria, the West was believed to be deeply committed to the maintenance of democracy throughout Europe and anti-democratic or non-democratic discourses were impossible to articulate at this time. Yet as soon as the impact of democracy began to be felt, it became evident that not all of society was as enthusiastic as had been thought.[6]

The ease with which President Iliescu of Romania was able to manipulate the Jiu valley miners to beat up students demonstrating in Bucharest in June 1990 was an early indication. The poor showing made by Tadeusz Mazowiecki in the Polish presidential elections of November 1990 was another.

The consequence of this was a lack of ability to run a democratic system. It proved difficult to accept that in the real world of power politics, transactions were generally blurred and muddy and that the abstract intellectual and moral criteria that had been so effective in undermining communism – a construct legitimated by intellectual categories and therefore vulnerable to intellectual attack – were counterproductive in a democratic system.

This state of affairs had two outcomes. It resulted in the rapid reemergence of the political sphere as the central area of all activity, coming to resemble the Soviet-type system that had just been defeated. This further meant that the social and economic aspects of the transformation were neglected while the new elites were busily engaging in ever more abstruse ideological and moral battles. Because the new system was legitimated by the language of democracy, society identified "democracy" not as understood in the West, but as the seemingly irrelevant bickering, the empty contests for symbols and moral purity that had no bearing on everyday existence, above all the rapid and continuing economic deterioration. The collapse and disintegration of Solidarity exemplified this process.

The second outcome was that the elite recruited from the democratic opposition was challenged or replaced by an elite that was never seriously thought to exist, namely the nationalist-populist current. Although this was far from clear before 1989, with the

[6] Andrzej Tymowski, 'The Unwanted Social Revolution: Poland in 1989', *East European Politics and Societies*, vol.7, no.2 (spring 1993), pp.169-202.

benefit of hindsight it can be seen that traditional society was paralleled by a traditional elite. This traditional elite, while not untouched by communist modernisation was resentful of it, and emerged on the political scene hostile to both communist and equally to Western modernisation.[7] It may have used the slogan of rejoining Europe but it was dreaming of a Europe that never existed. Certainly, it had no intention of accepting compromise, tolerance or even the complexity that had been brought into being by the lop-sided communist modernisation. It was antagonistic to the proposition that under democracy, transactions were most successfully transmitted through a network of institutions and that the total success demanded by their moral categories was deeply negative in the context of democracy.

What the conflict of these two elites – the democratic and the traditional – brought into being was a kind of political inflation that ran in tandem with the economic inflation. Words lost their meaning, the currency of the political discourse was devalued, the relationship between words and action, between speeches and policies, was obscure and as a result society grew yet more confused and resentful. Democracy was discredited as the new post-communist governments sought to deal with the multiple crises which they faced by the tried and failed method of over-regulation. Both the communist and the pre-communist traditions had been marked by this belief that issuing regulations, directives, instructions and the like was a substitute for action. The post-communist systems drew on these traditions heavily.[8]

In effect, political inflation created a state of affairs where the political sphere made ever increasing demands on the economic and social spheres, offered little or nothing in return and when confronted by its own failures, simply intensified the tempo. The reality was, however, that neither the administrative machinery nor the managerial competence of the elites nor the available technology was capable of coping with the mounting demands of the political sphere in seeking to subordinate all other spheres to itself.

[7] There is an excellent assessment of the Hungarian case in István Márkus, 'Utórendiségünk: gyökerek és gyümölcsök', *Valóság*, vol.34, no.5 (May 1991), pp.1-23.

[8] Attila Ágh, 'A kiábrándulás kora', *Valóság*, vol.36, no.10 (October 1993), pp.62-73.

In the first phase of post-communism, this traditional elite was successful in garnering considerable power, influence and status, though its political incompetence was rapidly exhausting its political capital. The Brazauskas effect – the success of the former communists now relabelled 'socialists' – was one response; the rise of populist nationalism was another.

These two currents were, however, distinct in most other respects. What they shared was that they constituted responses to the chaos created by the interaction of the post-communist elites and the politically inexperienced populations. The success of the ex-communists could be attributed to elements of nostalgia, that at least the communists knew how to run things, to a desire for the order, discipline and administrative competence promised by the ex-communists, and their emphasis on social welfare, which the post-communist elites tended to set to one side in the particular way in which they discussed the market. Crucially, the ex-communists drew on the segment of society that they had brought into being, whereas as the populists looked to traditionalism as their social base. The rise of populism was also closely associated with nationalism and it is to these two phenomena that we turn next.

Nationalism and populism

Some definitions are in order if sense is to be made of populism and nationalism. Populism is extremely elusive, but it is most usefully understood as both a discourse and a set of policies. For the time being, the latter need not concern us in detail, because no avowedly populist government has come to power in the post-communist world, but populist policies involve an element of redistribution by using investment capital for consumption and introducing restrictions on foreign economic involvement. In political terms, populism is anti-individualistic and emphasises movements rather than parties. The discourse and language of populism, however, have definitely made an appearance under post-communism.

For starting purposes, the definition to be followed here is that the heart of populism concerns the use of political power without institutions. It involves a leader or an ideology in which there is a claim for direct access to the individual and an insistence that power, in order to be authentic, should be unstructured. In this context, the role of a charismatic leader can be very significant;

certainly, legal-rational categories are rejected. In general, populist programmes offer their potential supporters more than they can deliver and seek to explain away their own failures, as well as those of the system or situation as a whole by reference to scapegoats, usually scapegoats external to the community (these may be foreigners or an ethno-religious minority).[9]

Anti-intellectualism is evidently an important component of populism. There is a rejection of the complexity of society and socio-political interactions, and this is coupled with what may be a highly forceful rejection of the necessary, complex explanations of what is happening. Under post-communism, the entire matter has been muddied by the behaviour of the post-communist elites as described above. This has created an intellectual and political gap through which populist solutions have come to appear attractive to the social categories vulnerable to this kind of over-simplified world-view.

Conversely this process may well have been strengthened by the sight of intellectuals unable and/or unwilling to abandon the epistemological certainties of the past in favour of a relativised world-view by generating appropriate paradigms for societies equally incapable of making the shift. In this context, intellectuals may also be seeking to preserve the particular status that they have traditionally enjoyed in semi-developed societies, notably the status that derives from the roles as moral legislators.[10]

Further factors in the success of populist mobilisation involve the relationships between the market and the consequent destruction of traditional communities, and between the impact of technological change and alien culture influences. Populist mobilisers can use these factors as a resource and intensify the authentic features of anti-modernism.

Furthermore, there are some unique features of populism under post-communism, deriving from the particular legacies of communism, especially atomisation and normlessness. These unique

[9] This analysis of populism draws on the discussions at the workshop on 'Populism in Politics and the Economy' held at the Central European University, Budapest, 2-3 April 1993 and especially the paper delivered by András Bozóki, 'An Outline of Three Populisms: United States, Argentina, Hungary'.

[10] Zygmunt Bauman, 'Intellectuals in East-Central Europe: Continuity and Change', *Eastern European Politics and Society*, vol.1, no.2 (spring 1987), pp. 162-86.

features can make it easier to initiate populist mobilisation, because the processes of integration into the complexities of modernity were neglected or rejected by communism, leaving societies at the mercy of forces which they cannot readily comprehend. The role of the exaggerated expectations in terms of consumption can also assist populist mobilisation, in that these unattainable aspirations can be manipulated and channelled into backing for populist projects.

Nationalism is often closely associated with populism, indeed in many cases constitutes an integral part of it, but is all the same conceptually distinct. Here, it will be argued that nationhood exists in a civic and an ethnic dimension. When reference is made in common parlance to 'nationalism', the ethnic dimension of nationhood is usually meant. Ethnic nationhood is an authentic experience, in that it has crucial functions in the maintenance of communities, in the definition of identities, in providing expression for the affective dimension of collective life and in the reaffirmation of communities through the symbols, rituals and liturgies of nationhood. This last factor – the acting out of the affective dimension – is also what makes nationhood so powerful and so dangerous a political instrument. Ethnic nationhood is excellent for defining the nature of the bond between different members of a community and equally for marking the boundaries that differentiate them from other communities. But that is where the functions of ethnic nationhood end.

However, while ethnicity is a real experience with genuine and legitimate functions in defining identity and forming community, ethnicity is worse than useless when it comes to matters properly in the civic dimension of nationhood. The civic dimension comprises the rules and regulations that govern the everyday relationship between rulers and ruled and the institutional framework through which these transactions are enacted: matters of representation, taxation, the institutions that mediate between government and society, the codes of conduct that ensure that all are treated as equal before the law.

These matters are quintessentially settled by reference to reason and rational discourse. Ethnicity by contrast appeals directly to the emotions. When questions that belong properly to the civic dimension are transferred illicitly into the realm of ethnicity, the emotionality of ethnicity pushes reason into the background and matters are decided by passion rather than reason. And as cannot be reiterated too often, strong emotions exclude reason.

Under post-communism the civic sphere remains seriously underdeveloped. Even allowing for the devastation caused by communism in this respect, the weakness of the institutional framework and level of trust in legislation and in the administration are low. Unlike ethnicity, the civic dimension of nationhood is not seen as authentic, with the result that citizenship is more a matter of theory, façades and paper provision than legal-rationality. In these circumstances, it is understandable that sizeable sections of the population prefer to pursue their own interests and strategies of power than accept the constraints of legality. The losers in this jungle are easily tempted by politicians who offer them an easy redress.

The combination of these elements – a vulnerable population, the presence of a seductive public discourse that offers quick rewards and the comfort of the pseudo-righteousness of nationalism –is tailor-made to erode democratic stability and, even more seriously, to undermine the self-legitimation of elites that continue to believe in democracy. The policy implications are that the ruling elites not in agreement with populist authoritarianism may well temper their policies in order to avoid isolation, or at any rate they may be inclined to move in that direction for fear of isolation. There are countless examples of this kind of appeasement. The most striking is that of the democratic opposition in Serbia, which has concluded that an anti-Milošević platform would be unviable without a strongly nationalist colouring; this has left Serbian politics in a situation where virtually all political parties use a heavily nationalist rhetoric.

A few words are in order as to the types of authoritarian dictatorship that might potentially be installed. The main characteristic that most of them are likely to share is that of charismatic or pseudo-charismatic leadership. They are not very likely, on the other hand, to attempt establish a totalitarian or totalising ideology with a totalitarian party; the legacy of communism coupled with the hostile international environment would make this difficult. This implies that islands of pluralism could survive behind an authoritarian system using a democratic facade. Their main legitimating discourses would, obviously, be nationalistic and possibly populist. They are only likely to become militarised if the country in question were to be involved in hostilities, as is the case with Serbia and Croatia, both which are running a serious risk of the establishment of military dictatorships.[11]

Revolution and its legacies

The literature on the events of 1989 in Central and Eastern Europe and 1991 in the Soviet Union is still at a loss over how to describe what happened. Various terms like 'revolution', 'transition' or even the anodyne 'upheaval' are used.[12] The Western media have tended to use 'revolution' without much thought as to the deeper content of the word. However, in Central and Eastern Europe revolutions have a much higher prestige than they do in the West. Although there is still a touch of romance attaching to the French Revolution and traditionally the Western left was in thrall to the romance of the Russian Revolution, by and large revolutions are not regarded as desirable ways of effecting political change. For sizeable sections of society in the post-communist world, on the other hand, revolutions are seen as a valid and useful means of bringing about the transformation that normal political channels leave blocked. The weakness of civil society, the corresponding strength of the elites who have traditionally controlled the political sphere, not to mention the use of the legitimating force of revolutions by the communists have created a discourse to which sections of society will listen.

The core of this argument is that the revolution which should have taken place to overthrow communism was aborted by an intra-elite deal, as a result of which society was excluded from power. In this line of argument, democrats and their backers in the West have colluded in a corrupt deal to sidestep the millennial elimination of centuries of injustice and the creation of a new utopia. It is noteworthy that in the initial period after the end of communism, the idea of revolution was largely discredited by its association with 1917 and the communist seizure of power, but as the post-communist elites have failed to satisfy the sections of society looking for a radical improvement in their fortunes, revolutionary solutions have begun to appear more attractive.

---

[11] László Lengyel, 'Útközben: Magyar politika az ezredfordulón', *Politikatudományi Szemle*, (1993), pp.112-34.

[12] The present author's views are set out in *Politics in Eastern Europe 1945-1992*, (Oxford: Blackwell, 1993), pp.253-5.

Here again, it is worth considering the thought-world of traditional society as a way into understanding these ideological constructs. The peasant mind-set was structured by its agricultural activities, its low level of technology, its dependence on the climate and hard manual labour, its economic marginality and consequent limited faith in the future and in the possibility of attainment through its own endeavours. All of this went together with its restricted and largely negative contact with the state and the city, which it viewed as parasitical. Hence change was conceptualised as sudden, massive change, a radical transformation, in which everything that was bad would suddenly be turned into good. The inappropriateness of these cognitive categories as far as the complexity of the modern world is concerned needs no further comment.

Building on this mind-set, which was modified by communism but not reconstructed thoroughly for the reasons discussed in the foregoing, the traditionalist elites have found themselves well placed to articulate a revolutionary ideology to appeal to a minority of society. What is especially noteworthy in this context is that the idea of revolution appeals to currents in the national tradition, the ones that reject compromise as contemptible and emphasise honour and moral purity as the most desirable criteria in politics.

The combination of resentment of the new on grounds of loss of status and economic deprivation with the legitimation derived from revolutions as the ideal method of effecting political change is distinctly uncomfortable and counterproductive from the perspective of democracy. Despite the lessons of history that revolutions generally produce authoritarianism rather than utopia, the tenacity of the revolutionary dream is such that it offers a serious challenge to those committed to gradualism in politics.

The impact of the West

The democrats who took power from the communists had high expectations that their experiment would receive immediate and substantial support from the West. Given their idealism, which had in any case been fuelled by decades of Western statements, they believed firmly that the end of communism would be greeted not merely with verbal backing, but with active measures. Indeed, there was a kind of widespread and somewhat naive faith that these new democracies would be able to "enter Europe" in a very short space of time. "Entering Europe" was equated with membership of the European Community (Union), the arrival of large sums of investment capital and the opening of Western markets to their products, together with political integration and incorporation into the Western security system. It all resembled a vague idea that entering Europe was rather like going into a bar, where the landlord would greet one with open arms and press a drink into one's hand.

Reality was very different and much less favourable. Disregarding the first few months of euphoria, the West's attitude towards the end of communism was hardly that of unalloyed welcome and increasingly more that of sour grapes. The comfortable world of the Cold War, the certainties and verities of the confrontation with communism was over and the West found itself in a major crisis of identity that it still has to resolve. The end of communism may have removed one particular security problem – the danger of thermo-nuclear war with the Soviet Union – but this has been replaced by a host of others with which the West is in no position to cope, whether politically, economically or intellectually.[13]

Not only was the structure of international organisations that existed in the 1990s set up to cope with the problems of the Cold War and ill-suited to deal with post-communism, but Western Europe has found itself in a twofold dilemma. The end of the Cold War has placed the question of the distribution of power and the nature of democratic institutions on the domestic agenda of most if not all these states, the fate of Italy being the most vivid illustration of this proposition, while at the same time the security vacuum in Central and Eastern Europe has posed a question of strategy to which they have no answer precisely because their domestic politics are in a state of turmoil. The economic recession has simply made this situation worse, because investment capital that might have gone to Central and Eastern Europe is not available, even while domestic pressure groups impose restrictions on imports from the post-communist world.

Equally seriously, the West has watched or even turned away from the gathering chaos that appears to be enveloping the post-communist world. At the heart of the problem is the proposition that the territorial dispensation made at the Paris Peace Settlement

---

[13] See *inter alia* several of the essays in Soledad García (ed.), *European Identity and the Search for Legitimacy* (London: Pinter, 1993).

of 1918-20 and largely reaffirmed after 1945 has been brought into question as the post-communist governments and politicians seek to raise political capital by resorting to irredentism. As far as the West is concerned, the post-First World War settlement is sacrosanct and the attempts to alter it are seen with dismay, distaste and contempt. There has been very little effort made, notably in Britain and France, to understand the motives of those seeking change and to formulate policies based on such an understanding.

In reality, by accepting the reunification of Germany, an action that was based solely and exclusively on the national principle, the West tacitly rehabilitated that principle throughout the post-communist world. It was quite pointless for Western spokesmen to say, as they did, that the German case was an exception – a precedent is a precedent. Others are now busy claiming that the precedent applies to them too. German policy predictably stood alone in having a clearer comprehension of what was involved, but after the recognition of Croatia and Slovenia, the other countries of the West have buried their heads in the sand and are refusing to acknowledge the national principle in international politics. A final factor in this mix was that the West seemed to be mesmerised by what was happening in Russia and was ready to subordinate the interests of the Central and Eastern Europeans to its Russian policies, for example by effectively blocking access to Western security arrangements to the Visegrád countries.

The prospects for right-wing authoritarianism, as outlined here, have improved after since the collapse of communism. After the initial, rather naive democratic euphoria, the obstacles to democratic transformation became evident and the attendant social problems came to provide fertile ground for extremist movements of both right and left. For the time being, left-extremist movements remain weak, because of the memory of the communist period, but the revival of the left, with the success of ex-communist parties, came much sooner than most observers would have predicted.

The rise of the right was similarly unforeseen and creates serious dilemmas for democracy, because it raises the prospect of Weimarisation as a possible scenario for some of the post-communist countries. That pattern of development would engender insecurity in Central and Eastern Europe, something that would impact most strongly on Germany, Austria and Italy. The possibility of the Western alliance itself being undermined cannot be excluded as one possible outcome. Another result of the rise of the right in the post-communist world was that it found imitators in the West. The example of small states like Slovenia gaining their independence has evidently been watched with interest in, for example, Catalonia and Scotland, and genocide against the Muslims of Bosnia has been a source of encouragement to racists in the West.

The overall pattern, however, is that the insecurities and instabilities left by the end of communism will persist for many years, that the reintegration of Europe will be a much harder process than was envisaged in 1989-1990, that the domestic travails of the post-communist systems will receive little in the way of support from the West and that appeasement of right-wing authoritarianism will only encourage it to grow by giving it a semblance of acceptability.

15

COMMUNISM AND STATE LEGITIMATION

Four states have disappeared as a result of the collapse of communism and many others have come into being. I want to look at the reason why these states have disappeared, what this says about the nature of state-sustaining ideologies and what the disappearance tells us about the relationship between statehood and nationhood. I will also look at the effectiveness of communism as a state-sustaining ideology.

The four are, obviously, the Soviet Union, Yugoslavia, Czechoslovakia and East Germany. In each case, the survival of the state was linked to communism and the end of communism brought their continued existence into jeopardy. I shall not be looking at the Soviet Union in detail.

Broadly, the construction of political identities can come about in two ways – by ethnicity or by the state. Each gives rise to a different set of loyalties, creates its own panoply of rituals etc. When the two coincide, the mythical nation-state can be said to be in being, but this hardly exists in reality (Iceland may be the sole exception in Europe).

The communist identity

Communism sought to use the precedents of non-communist statehood and nationhood but to establish a different pattern of loyalties between the state and the individual. The template here was the idea of the perfect state that would substitute for the individual in all areas of existence and consciousness, because the individual was imperfect. Only the collectivity embodied in the state could have access to the totality of reason that the Marxist state claimed, creating a total identification with the system and the state. Thus instead of the mythical nation-state, communism would create the ideal 'communism-state', in which *homo communisticus* would be conjoined in a perfect collectivity with all other members of the community. Simultaneously, this process would give rise to a state that would ultimately wither away. The civic and ethnic-bonds of the 'bourgeois' state would thus be replaced by a utopian construct that would function as both.

Is this an effective way of building loyalty? Probably not. The use of the machinery of the state can be very thoroughgoing and leaves a major mark on those affected, but the complete exclusion of society from this process is ultimately counterproductive. However, the impact of communism on society should not be underestimated. It did construct a way of life, a particular pattern of modernity, of expectations and social stratification and, as an amalgam of all these, a kind of identity. This identity was akin to civic identities, in that it lacked a strong underlying affective base, but in as much it was built on a set of shared experiences, involved particular procedures and erected a set of shared goals, it had significant consequences for the way in which people identified themselves and their relationship with power.

At the same time, communism in its attempt to build a noetic state (one constructed on a purely rational basis) deliberately dismissed the element of sacralisation as obscurantist mystification. Can states survive without an element of the sacred?[1] The lesson seems to be that they cannot and that sacralisation, though largely implicit, is derived at least in part from ethnicity and from the civic rituals that the modern state has inherited from its predecessors or has constructed for itself.[2] From this perspective, both the civic contract and ethnicity are, separately and in interaction, more than just a community of shared past and future, they are also the source of a transcendental morality, a mystery that certain processes and events are beyond our comprehension which we accept because we are members of the community.

The collision between the hyperrationality of communism and the aspirations of society were more complex, however, because communism too offered an element of mystery and sanctity, in that although it legitimated itself by reference to reason, indeed as the ultimate repository of reason, it also used implicit reference to myths of social harmony, millennia and other forms of utopian

---

[1] Molnár Tamás, *A hatalom két arca: politikum és szentség* (Budapest: Európa, 1992) [English: Thomas Molnar, *Twin Powers: Politics and the Sacred* (Grand Rapids, MI: Eerdmans, 1988)].

[2] David I. Kertzer, *Ritual, Politics and Power* (New Haven, CT: Yale University Press, 1988).

thinking. The fatal flaw in the communist project from this perspective was that it set up claims that were testable in this world, unlike the claims of religion which are testable only in the next.[3] In this sense, communism undermined its own sacralisation.

Furthermore, the collision between the goals sacralised by communism and those by ethno-nationalism could not be cushioned. These were irreconcilable, the conflict of different moral codes, beliefs, systems of right and wrong, boundaries and so on, which the majority of society would not abandon, even conditionally, so that the communist state was continuously working against the grain of social expectations rather than along them.

Both the implicit and the explicit assumptions of society were at variance with those promoted by the communist state, which meant that it was not behaving in the way that a state should. Indeed, the implicit space of meanings and moral codes for decoding experience was occupied by ideas alien and therefore antagonistic to communism, which, on the other hand, was forever looking to colonise this space itself. This shortcoming was something which the communist sought to remedy by brute force, which thereby in itself undermined the claims of the state to perfect rationality. If the communist state had been perfectly rational, it would not have needed the very high levels of coercion that it did, in fact, employ. Hence this contradiction was a trap, a form of political aporia, from which (by definition) there could be no escape.

In addition, at the practical level, the communists rewrote the political rule book by placing the economy at the centre of political language games. The outcome of this was a certain economy-centredness which displaced the language of politics into limbo, allowed the subterranean language of nationhood to permeate it and thereby created a rigidly separate public sphere (to which society responded with fear and dissimulation), and a private sphere (which was thought to be authentic and meaningful).[4]

Ethnicity and states

In Central and Eastern Europe, the construction of states has

[3] Ernest Gellner, 'Islam and Marxism: Some Comparisons', *International Affairs*, vol.67 no.1 (January 1991), pp.1-6.

[4] Ken Jowitt, *New World Disorder: the Leninist Extinction* (Berkeley: University of California Press, 1992).

invariably been tied to ethnicity, so that for historical reasons the link between ethno-nationalism and statehood has been seen as a causal and necessary condition for the legitimacy and vitality of the state. In each of the three states where this was relevant before the coming of communism, this movement towards matching ethnicity and statehood was in some way diverted, both by the communists and, where appropriate their predecessors, in as much as they sought to generate bonds of loyalty that appeared divorced from ethnicity. In pre-revolutionary Russia this ideology was imperialism; in royal Yugoslavia this was the shared language (Serbo-Croat) and loyalty to the crown; in interwar Czechoslovakia, it was the values of Czech democracy.

With the communist seizure of power, ethno-nationalism was downgraded to a relic of the past possessing no more than cultural significance that would vanish as material conditions were equalised. In Czechoslovakia, this implied notional equality for Czechs and Slovaks. In Yugoslavia, all ethno-national agendas were stringently subordinated to Titoism (self-management, non-alignment, brotherhood and unity, coupled with elite cooperation and repression). In the GDR the superiority of communism to capitalism would give rise to a new communist identity in which the communist element would be stronger than the German (this was later modified). In the Soviet Union, the communist utopia of equality and plenty would compensate non-Russians for the eventual disappearance of their identities and their assimilation into a Soviet cultural universe.

These four states sought to build the bonds of loyalty between the state and the individual in different ways, using a different mix of beliefs, ideologies etc. in an attempt to get away from an implicit ethno-nationalism. In fact, none of them had an alternative, they had to devise strategies to satisfy very particular needs – multi-ethnicity or truncated ethnicity in the GDR. The three states that existed before communism had experimented with other modes of state legitimation, but none had been particularly successful. This may have contributed to a predisposition on the part of elites to try something else.

The coming of communism promised a secular utopia in which there would be equality and plenty, the realisation of the aspirations of the bulk of the peasantry and the working class, which were significant in the Czech lands and East Germany. Sizeable social minorities in the three East European states were prepared to accept this identity, and in each case there was an intellectual stratum ready and able to articulate and define the language in which the new identity was to be structured. However, the communist identity had at all times to compete with the prior ethnic ones and the communist rulers had to devise strategies to house train ethnicity.

To what extent was the Soviet Union a model? It was evidently so, in formal terms, for Yugoslavia which adopted a federal constitution in 1946 and continued with this practice in each subsequent constitution; less so for Czechoslovakia until 1968, which adopted a centralised constitution, leaving only a few residuary functions to Slovakia. East Germany took another route. Initially, it claimed that it was seeking reunification on its terms, then from 1970 or so, it tried to create a separate German identity that in a remote sense resembled the Soviet one, in that it claimed to be different because it was communist and German, indeed the two conjoined into an entirely spurious Germano-communist identity.

Humpty-Dumpty states

All these states underwent sufficiently serious crises to call their existence into question, with sizeable sections of the population looking for alternative state formations. With the Second World War, both Czechoslovakia and Yugoslavia died and had to be reconstituted; Czechoslovakia underwent a major trauma in 1968-9; the GDR was thoroughly restructured after 1953 and in 1961 with the Wall. The Second World War was a major caesura for the Soviet Union, in as much as it was defeated and occupied, with large numbers of its population accepting that defeat with equanimity. The discontinuities are shown in the accompanying table opposite.

Czechoslovakia. The initial flaw in the constitution of the state was built in at the moment of its establishment. The Czechs needed the Slovaks to counterbalance the Germans, but denied the Slovaks the opportunity to establish their own institutions, thereby imposing constraints on their culture and treating it as a *de facto* internal colony. Interwar Czechoslovakia was a Czech state writ large, with all non-Czechs subordinated to a Czech political culture (that this was open, democratic and pluralistic is beside the point).

The ideology of Czechoslovakism had the aim of integrating the Slovaks into a Czech perspective.

	Born				Died
Soviet Union	1917	c. 1941			1991
CSSR	1918	d. 1939	r. 1945	c. 1968	1992
Yugoslavia	1918	d. 1941	r. 1945	c. 1971	1991
GDR	1949	c. 1953, 1961, 1970			1990

Key c.=caesura, r.=restored, d.=died.

Yet in 1938 the state collapsed because the Czechs discovered that they were alone in wanting the state to subsist, and was therefore delegitimated in the eyes of the non-Czechs when the opportunity for this arose.[5] This traumatised the Czechs and after 1945 they looked for a new formula, essentially a Pan-Slav one. The state was linked to the Soviet Union, the Germans were expelled, the Hungarians were suppressed, the Slovaks were subordinated although they were no longer treated as 'Czechoslovaks'. After 1948, the communist legitimation incorporated a Czech one in that there was strong support for communism among the Czech working class and intellectuals.[6] Until 1968-9, Czechoslovakia was a special case, in as much as the communist and ethnic aspirations of the Czech working class and intellectuals largely coincided; the Slovaks were in a different situation, but this did not matter, as they could be overridden. This as one of the explanations for the extraordinary stability of Czechoslovakia during de-Stalinisation.

Slovak agendas, on the other hand, were marginalised. These returned to the political stage in the 1960s, although the Czechs regarded this as a distraction; in a sense they regarded the Slovaks as a distraction throughout the life of the state. Indeed, 1968 can be considered a major caesura for Czechoslovakia, it brought with it a recommunisation, changing the terms of its state legitimation by giving the Slovaks a greatly enhanced role. The enactment of a federal system was the only reform to survive the recom-

[5] This mechanism is dissected at much greater length in my 'Nationalism, Politics and the European Experience', *Survey*, vol.28, no.4 (123), pp.67-86.

[6] Jaques Rupnik, 'The Roots of Czech Stalinism' in Raphael Samuel and Gareth Stedman Jones, *Culture, Ideology and Politics* (London: Routledge, 1982), pp.302-19.

munisation and for many Czechs, the Husak years were seen as 'Slovak in form, Soviet in content'. In other words, there was a current of Czech resentment at the new shape and content of the state.

After the collapse of communism, the new democratic system had to cope with the poisoned chalice of the communist legacy – the very complex federal parliamentary structure that gave a small number of deputies a blocking veto, coupled with a conflict-generating culture that made the system inoperable.[7] In the end, with the 1992 elections, two incompatible versions of the future of Czechoslovakia emerged from the Czech lands and Slovakia, with Klaus and Mečiar receiving an almost identical 30 per cent of the votes. Klaus demanded a firmly federal state in which Czech agendas would dominate; Mečiar wanted much greater real and symbolic recognition for Slovakia within the joint state. Klaus then simply declared that that option was not on offer and for all practical purposes expelled Slovakia. After all, the Slovaks were no longer needed as a counterbalance to the Germans and they were seen by Czech opinion as an economic millstone, a cultural desert and as provincial, tiresome and likely to slow down the Czech Republic's early integration into Europe. The purposiveness of the Czechoslovak state had expired.

Yugoslavia. The state was put together at great speed in 1917-18 without adequate preparation in order to meet the contingent needs of the main actors, the Serbs and the Croats.[8] The Serbs believed that the end of the First World War was a perfect opportunity to expand and to fulfil the ambition for a Greater Serbia, incorporating all the Serbs in a single Serb-run state. The Croats wanted short-term protection from Italy and longer-term security,which

[7] Karen Henderson, *Czechoslovakia: the Failure of Consensus Politics,* Discussion Papers in Politics no.P93/4 (Department of Politics, University of Leicester, August 1993) perceptively points out that while Klaus and Mečiar each received around 30 per cent of the vote in the Czech lands and Slovakia respectively, in global Czechoslovak terms the figures were only $c.23$ and $c.11$ per cent; as she drily notes, this 'does not sound like an electoral mandate to carry out one of the profoundest constitutional changes imaginable'.

[8] Ivo Banac, *The National Question in Yugoslavia: Origins, History, Politics* (Ithaca, NY: Cornell University Press, 1984).

they thought the Yugoslav option would give them. The terms of the relationship were impossibly starry-eyed and marred by misperceptions. In fact, the new state was based on a shared language, shared only in the philological sense, and the Serbian monarchy, with which the Croats found it hard to identify. These divergences led to considerable instability, which was eventually (1929) resolved by the royal putsch, and to a highly centralised state that proved unviable.

In 1941, when Germany attacked, the country fell apart, with only the Serbs ready to defend it. Wartime was a bloodbath which gave the communists the chance of reconstituting the state on the basis of a new formula: the end of inter-ethnic killing; the satisfaction of peasant radicalism; and single-minded resistance and the expulsion of foreign occupation forces.[9] Indeed, there is strength in the argument that in the circumstances only a communist restitution was viable: the previous political order was discredited and the democrats could not agree on a formula; the massive population loss – at least 2.2 million people out of *c*. 18 million – meant that new elites would arise after the war in any case and Tito's wartime programme represented a social revolution that was highly attractive; the communists were the most dynamic element and they were committed to the restoration of the state; and the prestige of the Soviet Russia as the liberator of Eastern Europe and as a Pan-Slav ally was also influential.

Titoism then installed a formalised ethnic equality coupled with strict party control. This was sufficient to see off the threat from the Soviet Union after 1948. A nascent Yugoslav identity did exist, but as the years passed, this identity was irremediably tied to the Titoist order. When that failed, as it did in the 1980s, no democratic alternative was available and the struggle for power among various republican elites tapped into ethnic sentiment as the most viable means of generating support.[10]

The contrast that is sometimes made between Czech and Serbian attitudes is misleading. The Czechs are presented as 'European'

[9] Milovan Djilas, *Wartime* (London: Secker & Warburg, 1977).

[10] Laslo Sekelj, *Yugoslavia: the Process of Disintegration* (Highland Lakes, NJ: Social Science Monographs, 1993); the present author's own somewhat different views are set out in 'The rise and fall of Yugoslavia' in John McGarry and Brendan O'Leary (eds), *The Politics of Ethnic Conflict Regulation* (London: Routledge, 1993), pp.172-203.

and 'civilised', whereas the Serbs are supposedly 'aggressive' and 'barbarian'; even if one accepts these stereotypes, they are symptoms rather than cause. Whereas the Czechs were fully secure in the ethnic foundations of the country once the Germans were expelled, the same could not be said of the Serbs, who tended to see themselves as a beleaguered minority in the Yugoslav context.

The relationship between the Titoist state and the Serbs was structured by the fact that the Serbs were only a plurality in the country, not a majority, and divided between several republics; they had resisted communism in Serbia, but supported it outside Serbia, so that the Prescani were to some extent determining the agendas of the Srbjanci; the state operated deliberately in such a way as to contain Serbian aspirations (campaigns against 'hegemonism' and 'unitarism') in order to allay the fears of the non-Serbs; and eventually there arose a Serbian separatist current, meaning that the Serbian commitment to maintaining Yugoslavia as a single state was no longer unequivocal.

The ideology of Serbian separatism was derived from the proposition that the Serbs had made the greatest contribution and sacrifices to Yugoslavia, that they had suffered as a result of the way in which the communist Yugoslav state functioned, in being denied control over their destiny, that the Serbian nation and its values were being polluted by alien ideas and practices[11] and that communism itself was an anti-Serbian or un-Serbian ideology (for instance, because Tito was a Croat). Hence the Serbs would have to return to their 'true' selves, in the guise of a fairly traditional definition of Serbian ethnicity, based on Orthodoxy, heroism (the determination to pursue a cause of action despite the rest of the world), the glorification of violence, refusal to compromise and so on.

The democratic option existed, but it was weak, because it had to compete with an exceptionally strong ethno-national consciousness that felt itself to have been suppressed.[12] The democratising intellectuals were seen as tainted by the un-Serbian values of Titoism, having come into being as a result of the modernising

11 Milorad Pavić, *The Dictionary of the Khazars* (London: Hamish Hamilton, 1988).

12 This is the 'bent twig' argument, see Isaiah Berlin, 'The Bent Twig: On the Rise of Nationalism' in *The Crooked Timber of Humanity* (London: John Murray, 1990).

policies of the communists, while Milošević came to power with the strategy of salvaging the power of the Serbian *nomenklatura* through the use of nationalism. Also the legacy of republicanisation and the 1974 constitution had created a degree of fragmentation where the focus of the post-Titoist identity was no longer the country as a whole but the republic and that, in turn, raised the question of Greater Serbia and the relationship between the Serbs and non-Serbs.

The German Democratic Republic. There never was any serious alternative to a German identity in East Germany, but the exact nature of that identity posed serious problems for both rulers and ruled. In the first place the SED, the East German party, was in a very different position from its counterparts in, say, Poland or Hungary. It had to compete throughout its existence with another German state, not just the West as a whole, so that it was forced into an unequal contest with a segment of its own ethno-cultural community and to do so from an insecure minority stance. The insecurity was accentuated by two further factors. The SED could never be certain of the loyalty of its own population or of its patron and ultimate source of its identity, the Soviet Union, because for reasons of Realpolitik, the Kremlin could always negotiate the East German state out of existence (as it was apparently ready to do until 1955) or to put pressure on it to pursue policies which the East German leadership regarded as counter to its interests. The presence of nineteen Red Army divisions reinforced this unequal relationship. This acute insecurity, this sense of being triply in the minority, helps to account for the bizarre twists in the East German leadership's strategies of identity creation.

Initially, under Ulbricht, East Germany's position on its Germanness was that it supported reunification on its terms, that when the two German states were reunited, it would be a communist state. This position suffered two major defeats – the uprising of 1953, from which the leadership drew the lesson that society could not be trusted, and eventually it responded with the building of the Berlin Wall in 1961, signifying the hermetic isolation of East German society from West Germany. There was a brief flirtation with Khrushchevism, of looking for a formula that might lead to some relaxation of the severely repressive coercive machinery that the SED relied on, but as soon as the New Economic System began to function, it became evident that greater relaxation would have consequences that the party could not control.[13] With the coming of détente the Kremlin had Ulbricht replaced by Honecker (1970) and obliged East Germany to accept the new policies with gritted teeth.

Honecker had to respond not only to the prodding from Moscow, but also to the West German state's strategy of 'change through rapprochment' *(Wandel durch Annäherung)*.[14] This was profoundly threatening, because East German society was likely to find the West German temptation very seductive. To meet this challenge, Honecker embarked on the creation of an entirely new identity, one that would be differentiated from the West German one by being not *ethnically* German but 'communistically' so. It was an extraordinary gambit. Here were the origins of the surrealistic attempt to construct an East German identity that was separate from West Germany's by reason of being communist, but was supposedly German nevertheless.

This policy involved East Germany in the construction of a separate history with its own panoply of proto-communist heroes, of arguing that the East German nation was German but different because it was communist-German. It was noteworthy that some of the content of this identity contained elements of anti-Polish and even anti-Russian sentiments. The glorification of Prussia and the rehabilitation of Frederick the Great, Scharnhost, Gneisenau and even Bismarck all alluded to an implicit anti-Slavonic sentiment. The proposition that Bismarck was in some way a proto-communist beggars belief.

All the same, this invented identity could never be more than a verbal proposition. It was, for all practical purposes, an attempt to use the functional equivalent of a civic identity, the identity born of the communist state, and to dub it the functional equivalent of an ethnic identity. In real terms, this could be no more than a

13 Ferenc Fehér, 'Kádárism as Applied Khrushchevism' in R.F. Miller and Ferenc Fehér (eds), *Khrushchev and the Communist World* (London: Croom Helm 1984), pp.210-79; David Childs, *The GDR: Moscow's German Ally* (London: George Allen & Unwin, 1983).

14 Timothy Garton Ash, *In Europe's Name: Germany and the Divided Continent* (London: Cape, 1993).

house of cards that had only very limited success in generating genuine attachment and affective bonds. Hence at the moment when communism disintegrated, the East German communist-German identity vanished into thin air. The East German state had no foundations other than communism. The attractions of an all-German ethnicity were vastly more powerful, especially as they were reinforced by the promise of economic prosperity and freedom.

The Soviet Union. In the Soviet Union, the Russians by and large understood the Soviet identity as a Russian one, even if the influential neo-Slavophil current, of which Solzhenitsyn was the best known exponent, denied this. In many ways, the Soviet Union was indeed a Russian state, although one with added elements that had not been a part of the imperial Russian identity of the pre-1917 period. The Soviet Union satisfied Russian ambitions for a world-power status; it insisted that Russian be the universal language of the state, in the armed forces for example, and it was accorded extra-republication privileges as the language of education throughout the Union.[15]

Although after Stalin's death, the superior status of 'Elder Brother' was no longer as explicit as before, Khrushchev's project for the long term merger of all cultures was understood by non-Russians as a form of Russification and probably gave Russians a certain satisfaction, who felt that at the end of the day, the Soviet state was theirs, however much they might have resented some or many of the ways in which it impacted on them. In this sense, communism and the Soviet state did help to sustain a Russian identity and conversely the Russian identity helped to underpin the Soviet Union. For the non-Russians, on the other hand, the Soviet state was alien, its power over them was resented and when the communist ideology that sustained it collapsed, they opted out.

---

[15] Only Russians enjoyed the right to be educated in their mother tongue outside their own republic, the RSFSR, apart from the marginal exception of Armenian-language schools in Georgia. On the general issue of Russian-language education, see Rasma Karklins, *Ethnic Relations in the USSR: the Perspective from Below* (London: Unwin Hyman, 1986).

In all four states, therefore, the existence and identity of the state came to be closely tied to communism and the competition with ethno-nationalism was an ongoing reality. When communism disintegrated, nationalism took over.

Were there alternatives? Possibly, though these were different in each country, invisible because of the ignorance and high expectations of the population and difficult to implement because of the weakness of democratic culture. In the Soviet Union, where the promises of utopia had had the highest prestige, the collapse was correspondingly the greatest. In the GDR, there was a general belief that a democratic and prosperous Germany would result from the merger of both eastern and western German traditions, so that the idea of maintaining an independent but democratic East Germany was a non-starter except for a few intellectual supporters of 'Third Road' projects. In Yugoslavia, the existence of the state was so intimately tied to communism that it could not have survived unless democratic alternatives had been prepared well in advance. In reality, nationalist alternatives were the ones actually prepared. Czechoslovakia had the best chance of surviving as one state and the main reason why it failed was the difference in Czech and Slovak national agendas which then made it impossible for parliamentary and other political institutions work under the new conditions.

The communist experiment in the creation of identities was undermined because it lacked the capacity to construct the affective bonds that sustain states and was too closely tied to performance. As a result, the failure of the communist system in the economy and in technology was far more damaging than in states with a strong echno-national foundation. Communist federations were façades and could not be sufficient to satisfy the demand for autonomy. And the far-reaching difficulty in transforming communist political systems into democratic ones, a process which is likely to take many years, left behind a void that ethno-nationalism, the only surviving competitor on the political stage, could fill.

16

CULLING SACRED COWS? STATE FRONTIERS AND STABILITY

Sacred cows have to be inspected from time to time to see if their sanctity still deserves respect. It may be that the odour of holiness has dissipated or that the beasts have caught foot-and-mouth and that slaughter is the best policy. This loss or decline in the utility of received wisdom can be difficult to see. After all, that is why certain ideas are 'sacred', that they should be beyond question, become a part of what is natural and normal. The argument that follows is that the sanctity of existing state frontiers has attained this status, and that a bit of selective culling might not be entirely out of place.

Lest anyone be very alarmed by having read only the first paragraph of this paper, let them be reassured. I am not about to advocate that all frontiers should now be chopped about, but rather that in certain circumstances this option should not be excluded. Diplomats, employees of foreign service bureaucracies, propagandists from states with something to lose, and other defenders of the status quo should now prepare themselves for the worst.

If we look at what has happened to state frontiers since the Second World War and compare this with earlier eras, it will be evident that they have been frozen. Indeed, they can be said to have ossified. They cannot be changed. They are not negotiable, not a part of the debate. Irredentists and secessionists are on a par with graverobbers and other forms of international low-life. Now this is strange. What is it that has screened frontier change out of our cognitive world? Why have we dropped this potentially useful instrument from our toolbox? If politics is about managing change, promoting stability, and, above all, creating political systems based on consent, then the conversion of frontiers into something static and unthinkable could be interpreted as depriving politics of a procedure that could in certain circumstances enhance domestic and international legitimacy.

The conventional answer concentrates on stability. States, it is said, cannot exist in anything resembling stability if their existing shape and contours can be violated by ill-conditioned malcontents. If nothing else, efficient administration demands at least that. No administration can be sustained if the machinery of state bureaucracy is constantly being changed at the behest of minorities. This might be termed 'the bureaucratic convenience argument'.

Besides, only ethnic groups and ethnically based political movements demand frontier revision, and ethnicity is somehow illegitimate, it lacks the moral virtue of citizenship. Beneath this argument is a tacit and generally covert assumption that in the developed West we have gone beyond ethnicity, and that only primitives, or those who are somehow stuck in a political time-warp, can still resort to anything so hackneyed and degraded.

There is a further hidden argument here, and this has to do with the nature of the modern state. Despite the extensive lauding of civil society, the hard reality of the twentieth century has been the irresistible rise of the state. The Soviet-type system was the apotheosis of this, a system in which the state was the sole repository of rationality and virtue, and where society was by definition retrograde. Western democracies never emulated the Soviet-type system, they would have ceased to be democracies had they done so, but as in all contests, they adopted some of the features of what they opposed. The modern state has incontrovertibly assumed some, I stress only some, of the features of Soviet-type communism, largely in order to construct greater equality through redistribution. Most people would regard this development as positive, but it has had unintended consequences that are now more evident than they were before 1989.

Rise of the modern state

The rise of the modern state has taken several centuries, but with the assumption of various duties previously carried out at the local level, it has expanded its activities in the regulation and supervision of society. This is the core phenomenon of the intrusive modern state. In general, this state is regarded as the norm and those states that are unable to perform this function, for example maintaining adequate control over their territories, are judged weak or suffering from incapacity. Yet this incapacity is, in practice, condoned. Many of the states of the world, notably in West Africa and the Former Soviet Union, are well known to be 'soft': because of 'warlordism' they do not exercise a monopoly of coercion within a given territory and they do not have a monopoly of exacting revenue. No one would dream of denying these geographical entities the right to be called states, with seats at the United Nations and all, even while it is perfectly clear that this statehood, as conventionally defined, is a fable.

In psychological terms this looks like denial. We seem to be decidedly anxious not to confront the real situation and, as cannot be stressed too often, poor analysis produces poor results. Indeed, there may even be a corollary to this proposition: poor sociology produces poor ideology. The suggestion here is that the existence of the state in the particular form that it has acquired in Western Europe and North America is being imposed on the rest of the world for reasons that have more to do with the developed West than anything else. The insistence on the notions of universality of citizenship, on the absolute equality of state provisions, and on the equality of all states once they have been recognized as states by a formal procedure are all pronounced with such fervour that one might be forgiven for thinking that something is being hidden.[1]

The state has been invested with a moral virtue that inheres in it as if by right, as if by its very existence. People widely assume that what the state does is, on the whole, for good. Despite the neo-conservative rhetoric of the 1980s and the legitimating ideology of the United States, the hard reality is that society expects the state to play the role of primary moral, political, economic and cultural agent. In many ways, the democratic state has become the repository of Enlightenment rationality and progress. It is tacitly accepted that the state has access to better information and better decision-making methodology than the individual, so that it is better placed to make strategic decisions. The traditional assumption that society is creative and the state is reactive has been more honored in the breach than in the observance. This state of assumptions, then, gives the state a moral function: in redistribution, say, agencies of state make decisions

---

[1] Mary Douglas, *Risk Acceptability according to the Social Sciences* (London: Routledge, 1985).

not merely to the effect that equality is a positive value, but even more on how that equality is to be achieved, which groups would receive, and which should contribute. This moral role has enormously enhanced the inviolability, crucially the territorial inviolability, of the state. Good government takes place within established borders and any attempt to monkey about with them will automatically mean worse or bad, government, so the argument goes.

The state as repository of moral virtues is, of course, an abstraction. Those who actually control the machinery of the state, the political elites, the members of legislatures, political parties, state bureaucracies not least those who control foreign policy and the armed forces, together with those who take part in the determination of policies are, in reality, the beneficiaries of the high moral status that the state has acquired. Through the procedures of the democratic order and the institutional mechanisms that govern the distribution of power, they make judgments which automatically raise moral issues. This proposition is, however, not acknowledged. On the contrary, considerable effort is expended in not casting the definition of policies in moral terms. The overall outcome of these processes is to give these beneficiaries of moral legislation a clear and generally unchallenged interest in the contours of the existing state.[2]

The broad consequence of the foregoing is that there has arisen a tacit acceptance of territorialism. Territorialism essentially places the territory of the state beyond debate, where it is sanctified and mythicized into something that cannot be questioned because it has a legitimation that places it outside politics. Sometimes, geography becomes destiny: the particular shape that a state has acquired largely through contingent factors of history is presented as so determined by geography. States that correspond to islands are particularly prone to this, as if there is something inherently sinful in dividing an island, e.g. Cyprus. History can also be used in this way. The argument here is that a particular set of frontiers has been inherited from the past and cannot be polluted by being reshaped, regardless of other factors that may obtain. The unsuccessful Hungarian demand for the recognition of the Crownlands of St Stephen was a case in point; the Czechs were more fortunate with the frontiers of Bohemia. An alternative to geography and

[2] Zygmunt Bauman, *Legislators and Interpreters* (Cambridge: Polity, 1987).

history is the demand legitimated by reference to strategy, that a state has to be given a particular province in order for it to have a defensible frontier; the attachment of the South Tyrol to Italy illustrates this.

There is also a rather lower level economic argument. It is widely asserted, with no evidence whatsoever, that a particular territory could not possibly claim independence because it would not be economically viable. This is no more than a fairy story with which to frighten the children. Every territory would be viable economically, but quite a few would be worse off than they are at present. However, when a group has decided that it wants independence, it is quite willing to live with poverty. Lithuania illustrates this proposition with great clarity. Lithuania is indeed a poor country, but that did not deter the Lithuanians from claiming state independence, nor has poverty generated any nostalgia for the Soviet Union. Behind the economic argument, there is another fallacy: that territory represents wealth and power. This was certainly the case in the pre-modern period and even well into the modern era, but nowadays wealth is generated not by land – the flawed belief of aristocrats and peasants – but by information, organisation, and knowledge. In this context, consciousness has yet to catch up with economic reality. Where the two do impinge on one another, as in the debate on the future of the sovereign state in an era of globalisation, every argument is mustered to diminish the impact of a trend that dilutes the effectiveness of the state.

Behind geographic, historical, strategic or economic arguments there lies something deeper, something less directly accessible to the respectability conferred by Enlightenment rationality: the demand for moral worth.[3] Every community expects to be recognised in the world as a bearer of moral values and to be accorded the dignity of an equal member of the community of nations, and nations in the modern world are supposed to be states. It is noteworthy in this connection that American English usage actually conflates the notions of 'nation' and 'state'. This moral worth, however, derives ultimately from the bonds of solidarity and other moral boundaries by which communities regulate their own ex-

---

[3] Donald Horowitz, *Ethnic Groups in Conflict* (Berkeley: University of California Press, 1985).

istence. This brings us much closer to the bone. Communities of 'moral worth' are better known as ethnic groups.

Simply, what existing states are trying to keep veiled is that their own moral worth depends partly or wholly on their ethnic foundations, at some level at any rate, and that if they acknowledge their own deep-level ethnic identity, then it becomes much more difficult to deny the access to political power that flows from ethnicity to other claimants. With this step, we have arrived at the real reason for the petrifaction of frontiers. Virtually every state in the world is made up of more than one ethnic community. The existing world order would be turned upside down if they were all given the right of statehood as currently defined. So rather than redefine statehood, making it more fluid, and diluting state sovereignty, the existing holders of power on the international scene prefer to insist on the inviolability of frontiers instead. This is natural and understandable. They have much to lose.

The consequences of this defense of the *status quo* by the 'haves' is that it makes adjustments that might genuinely promote greater stability through consent much more difficult than they need be. Take the instances shown in former Yugoslavia and the Soviet Union. When the world (i.e. the West) reluctantly accepted that these two states were no longer viable, there was a determined imposition of the preexisting internal administrative borders as the new frontiers. There was neither rhyme nor reason for this, other than the convenience of the West and the determination not to create precedents for other groups claiming independence or territorial autonomy, not least groups of this nature in the West. The outcome is well known: four years of fighting in Yugoslavia and the creation of several states in the former Soviet Union that did not particularly want state independence (in Central Asia, for example) as well as giving hostages to fortune through the inclusion of ethnic groups into another state to which they did not particularly wish to belong (e.g. Russians in the Crimea).

The knock-on effect of this rigidity on the part of the West has been to make inter-ethnic relations more complex than they need be. There are many ethnic groups throughout Europe which would like a degree of autonomy linked to territory but not secession – for example Hungarians in Slovakia and Romania, Turks in Bulgaria, Albanians in Macedonia. However, no majority will even begin to countenance anything remotely linked to territory, for fear that at some future date, the internal boundary could become an external one, that it could lead to disintegration. Slovaks and Romanians are not idiots; they can understand precedents too. The resulting rigidity not only makes it hard for ethnic minorities to gain access to a desirable level of cultural and other autonomy, but actually makes it that much more difficult for the majority to deconcentrate power and construct a democratic distribution of power for ethnic majorities. The very high and counterproductive degree of centralisation on which the above-named states insist is thus to the detriment of the majority. In this way, the agendas of the West, notionally aimed at producing stability, have ended up by diminishing consent and thus creating needless friction.

It will be interesting, and no doubt depressing, to see how the West, the guardian of the international regulation of the birth and death of states, handles new potential cases of demands for independence, like Kosovo and Montenegro. Probably with dismay. There is a deep reluctance even to contemplate the possibility that the historic process of state formation is continuing and that new states might well seek to come into existence. To deny this process frequently leads to friction, in a worst case scenario, to civil war (e.g. Sri Lanka), which paralyses the options of both contestants.[4]

On occasion, ceding a small piece of territory may also bring unexpected benefits. If that piece of land is inhabited overwhelmingly by members of another ethnic group, they should be given the choice of staying or opting out. When a particular city is hopelessly mixed ethnically, then giving it the status of a city-state may be the best solution; there is nothing actually wrong with mini-states, they can work perfectly successfully. In either case, there is much to be gained from diluting the power of the majority which controls the dominant state and giving the minority an option to choose something other than what the majority demands, not the least goodwill and the diminution of friction.

Unchanging frontiers?

Yet the refusal, reluctance, indolence, or complacency of the

---

[4] On Sri Lanka, see two very different approaches: Bruce Kapferer, *Legends of People, Myths of State* (Washington DC: Smithsonian Institute Press, 1987) and David Little, *Sri Lanka: The Invention of Enmity* (Washington, DC: United States Institute of Peace Press, 1994).

West to accept that, as with all else in politics, frontiers too may be subject to change has incontrovertibly resulted in much suffering. In essence, the principle followed by majorities is that if they want security, they must make their ethnic minorities vanish, whether by ethnic cleansing, (e.g. Croatia and its Serbs), or by denial of their existence (Slovakia comes close to this with respect to the Hungarians). The logical conclusion is that instead of adhering obstinately to territorialism and the territorialisation of power, the West as the dominant force in the world should move in the opposite direction; some deterritorialisation of power would seem to be the right answer. How much, in what way this should go, and with what methods would depend on the circumstances. These include referenda, arbitration, leaseback, condominia and symbolic presence, of which a good illustration is that Serbia, though an independent state in the nineteenth century, remained technically under the suzerainty of the Sultan till 1878; to mark this, a single Ottoman flag flew over the Kalemegdan fortress in Belgrade.

A brief sketch of other kinds of instruments to be employed could be useful. First, there is a device which obviously runs counter to the universalism of citizenship, but can in fact resolve much friction without dismantling a state – internal sovereignty. In such cases, a particular territory, yes some territorialisation of power cannot be avoided, has extensive rights of self-government, which include a ban on outsiders settling, and so shift the ethnic balance. The Åland Islands enjoy this status vis-à-vis Finland and the solution has been quite successful. Some South Tyroleans would like this option for themselves, in order to prevent too many Italians from moving into their region. They feel that their ethnic security is best safeguarded by keeping their ethnic majority intact. Until the Italian state accepts that it is simultaneously a state of Italians and Germans there might seem to be some justification for German demands.

Consociationalism or power sharing goes further in the direction of deterritorialisation. The essence of consociationalism is to move away from Anglo-Saxon notions of majority rule and to accept that some power derives explicitly from ethnicity, regardless of the imperatives of universal citizenship rights. This can have positive effects in stabilising multi-ethnic states, though again Anglo-Saxon concepts of adversarialism are replaced by consensus politics. Consociationalism promotes a culture of compromise and accepts the existing territory of the state, but regards power as deriving from all the people as organised by their ethnic identities. On the other hand, consociationalism will only work if there is a fairly high level of trust already in existence. The significance of consociationalism is that it is potentially a model for international integration as pursued by the European Union, in which sovereign states have agreed to pool some of their power in exchange for other advantages.

There are times, though, when consensual approaches will not work, and where the obligations of a single citizenship will be counterproductive because they will be seen by a minority as being structured by the culture of majority. In particular, when polarisation has already begun, where levels of suspicion have begun to rise, the rigid insistence that all the ethnic groups in a territory must live together because the frontiers of the state are sacrosanct creates only instability. In such circumstances, separation of some kind, be it full or partial may be the better answer. Forcing different ethnic communities to live together only generates friction precisely because they have no desire to find compromise or consensus. They are looking to protect the means of cultural reproduction. Bosnia is clearly in this situation and the pretence that it is a single state has little to recommend it. A stricter separation of the two ethno-religious communities in Northern Ireland in order to guarantee the future of both would certainly ease tensions in the province. One of the problems in this connection is cosmetic. The separation of ethnicity from citizenship in terms of power and territory has gained an evil reputation through the abuse of that device by South Africa under apartheid. Apartheid sought to use the veil of 'separate but equal' to promote the interest of whites. This not what is being proposed in my analysis.

There is one instrument in the tool kit that has clearly lost its effectiveness or at any rate is so costly that few states should contemplate. This is irredentism, the acquisition of sizeable new territories. The example of German reunification shows why. Given the integrating and organising capacity of the modern state and the corporate and bureaucratic cultures created thereby, the bringing together of two such entities gives rise to major problems. All states will generate bureaucratic cultures of this kind and few of them are readily compatible. This implies that international integration must be a slow and careful process and that rather than seek to absorb new territories, states should seek to give co-ethnics sympathetic support from outside. This implies that fragmentation, the proliferation of states, is likely to produce greater stability than integration and inversely, that the annexation of territory is likely to create as many problems as it solves.

It looks, therefore, as if the world will have to come to terms with more states rather than fewer, with greater variety and with innovation in problem solving, all of which augur badly for the traditional sovereign state. This is bad news for the protagonists of the predominant Western states, in the United States and in Western Europe. The world has moved on from 1945, and we are now living in an era when the post-1989 realities will have to be made a part of a stable world if that world is, indeed, to be stable.

Part IV. MINORITIES

17

THE PROBLEM OF ETHNIC MINORITIES IN CENTRAL AND EASTERN EUROPE

Ethnic minorities are an all-European issue, though politically the problem is more acute in Central and Eastern Europe. There is a reason for this. The modern democratic nation – the most effective instrument for stabilising ethnic conflict – can be defined as a set of interactive relationships between the state, civil society and ethnicity.[1] Where one or more of these is weak, the other remaining processes will suffer overload, and cannot easily discharge their functions with negative results for democracy.

In brief, the role of the state is to provide stability, predictability and good governance;[2] the role of civil society is to provide articulation for conflicts of interests and the contests for power within society;[3] and the role of ethnicity is to provide for bonds of solidarity, the expression of the deepest levels of identity and cultural reproduction, for the tacit regulation by which a society creates coherence. Hence if ethnicity is expected to be the source of good governance, it will fail the test, because that is not what it is supposed to do. Likewise, civil society cannot be the sole basis for democratic consent, because civil society is the field where public contests for power take place and is structured around

---

[1] This is argued at greater length in Chap.2.

[2] Claus Offe, *Modernity and the State: East, West* (Cambridge: Polity, 1996).

[3] On civil society, see John Hall (ed.), *Civil Society: Theory, History, Comparison* (Cambridge: Polity, 1995) and Ernest Gellner, *Conditions of Liberty: Civil Society and its Rivals* (London: Hamish Hamilton, 1994).

the aggregation of conflict which already presupposes a considerable degree of consent, a shared basis for disagreement.

The problem with respect to ethnic minorities in their relations to ethnic majorities is that while they may accept the state and may take part in civil society, their conception of identity will certainly differ from that of ethnic majorities. This is the source of much friction, which can spill over into conflict and, in extreme cases, into violence (as happened in Yugoslavia). However, given the large number of multi-ethnic states in Europe, what is striking is how little serious ethnic conflict there is. We see the pathologies – Northern Ireland, Basque country, Bosnia – but the fact that most inter-ethnic contact is settled through politics escapes attention. This implies that it is, in fact, possible to find a political solution for such conflicts, provided that the proper mechanisms are established.

The argument advanced here is that ethnic conflict in Central and Eastern Europe is much less pervasive than it appears to be and that the means to regulate it do exist. When this has failed, there is a rational explanation, usually to be found in the concurrent weakness of both the state and civil society. In this context, it is important to understand two key factors. Communism destroyed civil society with an unprecedented thoroughness and the process of rebuilding it, which has been going on since 1989 is slow and painful. What makes the process more difficult than it seems at first sight and explains why parallels with democratisation in South Europe and Latin America are not very enlightening is that the collapse of communism entailed not just the disintegration of an ideology, but the failure of the communist state. Hence the post-communist systems are attempting a historically most audacious experiment: the simultaneous construction of a new state together with a new civil society. Not surprisingly, the role of ethnicity has acquired a saliency in the process that tends to impede the overall project, seeing that ethnicity does have a dimension in the public sphere, but not one that can secure stability, the transparency of power and democracy all on its own.

That said, a number of general political and sociological factors concerning ethnicity and inter-ethnic relations should be explored. First, ethnic minorities in contemporary Europe will not disappear through assimilation. Individuals may assimilate, usually if they migrate, but whole communities will not, because a community that has become aware of itself as a bearer of moral values will not abandon this status. Indeed, the history of twentieth century Europe provides very clear evidence that despite the very high assimilatory capacity of the modern state, ethnic communities have maintained their distinctiveness with great resilience. In a democracy – given the enormous power of the state – ethnic communities need access to political power, to safeguard their cultural reproduction, to gain access to status and value within the state, to secure their "moral worth" as equal bearers of collective moral values.[4]

This signifies that political provision for regulating inter-ethnic relations is an essential aspect of modern democratic politics. Non-democracies do not, of course, need to make such provision, but part of what makes a system democratic is the relationship between ethnicity and state being subject to regulation by democratic mechanisms. This proposition may be unwelcome to proponents of universalism, who see ethnicity as inherently undesirable and would prefer to see it disappear. In reality, the overwhelming evidence of the history of the last 200 years is that ethnicity persists, hence it is preferable to identify its mainsprings in order to prevent it from generating undemocratic outcomes.[5]

In fact, a variety of instruments is available for regulating ethnic relations; some depend on a form of territorial devolution of power (South Tyrol, Åland Islands, Catalonia), while others are based on some kind of power-sharing or consociationalism (Belgium, Switzerland) or combine elements of both. In essence, the purpose of these devices is to give minorities the necessary access to forms of political power to allow them a degree of security with respect to their cultural reproduction and to take their place as equal citizens of the state in which they live.[6]

It is important to recognise that full participation as citizen requires that the members of minority ethnic groups have some access not merely to the institutional level of state power (autonomous organisation, education, culture, recruitment to the

---

[4] Donald Horowitz, *Ethnic Groups in Conflict* (Berkeley: University of California Press, 1985).

[5] Michael Ignatieff, 'Nationalism and Toleration' in Richard Caplan and John Feffer, *Europe's New Nationalism: States and Minorities in Conflict* (New York: Oxford University Press, 1996).

[6] Stéphane Pierré-Caps, *La Multination. L'avenir des minorités en Europe Centrale et Orientale* (Paris: Odile Jacob, 1995).

state bureaucracies and finance), but also to the symbolic aspects of politics (the right to articulate their separateness in the public sphere and have their moral worth recognised). The acceptance of symbolic separateness is much more difficult for majorities to accept, because it appears to threaten their own cultural preeminence. Yet this form of sharing is an inescapable part of democratic self-limitation.

In central and Eastern Europe, there are difficulties with both the institutional and the symbolic level of participation where ethnic minorities are concerned.[7] Ethnic majorities are reluctant to accept that their state, in which they feel they have only recently recovered their sovereignty after Soviet overlordship, is also the state of other ethnic communities, like themselves communities of moral worth.

Segmented states

Particularly acute problems are raised by ethnically segmented states (Macedonia, Serbia, Latvia, Estonia) and states where majority-minority relations carry considerable historical burdens, with each group tending to define itself against the other (Slovakia and the Hungarians, Romania and the Hungarians, Lithuania and the Poles, Bulgaria and the Turks). Less politically acute, but socially tense are relations between ethnic majorities and the Roma, who have embarked on a process of defining their identity politically and culturally in the teeth of majority distaste (Czech Republic, Slovakia, Hungary, Romania).[8]

In general, in these states minority demands are regarded as varying between the dangerous and the impertinent. Thus when representatives of the Hungarian minority in Slovakia presented a list of grievances to the Council of Europe, Slovaks were outraged.[9] When ethnic Albanians in Macedonia sought to establish

---

[7] Urs Altermatt, *Das Fanal von Sarajevo. Ethnonationalismus in Europa* (Zurich: Verlag Neue Zürcher Zeitung, 1997).

[8] On the Roma, see Zoltan Barany, 'Living on the Edge: the East European Roma in Postcommunist Politics and Societies' in Leokadia Drobizheva *et al.* (eds), *Ethnic conflict in the Post-Soviet World* (Armonk, NY: Sharpe, 1996).

[9] On Slovak-Hungarian relations, see Robert Aspeslagh, Hans Renner and Hans van der Meulen (ed.), *Im historischen Würgegriff. Die Beziehungen zwischen Ungarn und der Slowakei in der Vergangenheit, Gegenwart und Zukunft* (Baden-Baden: Nomos Verlag, 1994).

a university of their own, the Macedonian authorities used force to close it down.

This raises an interesting question. Why do ethnic majorities find it so extraordinarily difficult to allow minority language universities? In effect there is only one fully independent minority-language university in Europe, the Swedish-language Åbo Akademi in Finland. On the face of it, the founding and running of a university should be a matter of educational policy, resources and the demand from the minority – something to be settled at the institutional level of politics. A minority of a certain size and an adequate level of literacy should have no problem with providing the intellectual infrastructure for a multi-faculty university, though clearly it will not be able sustain certain rarified areas of research. There are several minorities in Europe which match these criteria, hence the question must arise as to why there are so many more minorities than minority universities.

The function of a university is customarily seen in terms of the quest for the truth, the expansion of knowledge and under-standing and of educating the next generation. In reality, a university is much more than this. Given the enormous emphasis placed on cultural reproduction, on the prestige of high culture and the attainment of moral worth through access to high culture, the university is also a significant locus of symbolic power.

The university symbolises and enables a minority to sustain its cultural reproduction; it gives direct access to symbolic capital for the minority; it provides access to high culture and a collectivity with a recognised high culture cannot be so easily ignored politically by the state; hence the university is a symbolic marker of moral worth both at home and abroad, that makes equal access to power undeniable to the minority. At the institutional level, the graduates of a minority university will demand jobs in the state and other bureaucracies on the same basis as majority community graduates and will want to work largely in their language. The implication of this argument is very far-reaching. It signifies that the minority in question is of equal moral and symbolic status to the majority, hence must have access to the symbolic goods of the state, which means that it has the status of a partner. This adds up to a very significant transformation in the position of the minority and points towards a consociational system, rather than a majority-minority one.

The city plays an oddly contradictory role in inter-ethnic relations. It has both negative and positive facets. It is a negative phenomenon because of the relics of the traditional peasant perspective on the city: that it is an alien, parasitical entity, inauthentic and, crucially, impure. The city as a place of pollution is of vital concern in this context, because this assessment continues to cast a long shadow in the language of ethnic self-definition. The city was traditionally regarded as alien both ethnically and socially – the two were frequently conflated – so that it has the quality of an alien locus with alien practices pursued by alien people – an alienness which need have nothing to do with ethnic differences.

The city is threatening to rural migrants not only because it is generically different – visually, spatially, with respect to vistas and perspectives – but because encounters there are negotiated differently. In small communities, status and authority are by and large ascriptive and derive from the community itself; one knows where to locate 'others', to define who is familiar and who is a stranger. Power is or seems relatively transparent. The terms of conflict and enmity, of friendship and alliance are understood and clear. The rules of engagement are known and not questioned. In the city, this is doubly not so. The rural migrant cannot readily understand the very different rules of city life and finds it all but impossible to accept that these rules are fluid in perpetuity. And when the encounter with the city involves ethnically alien populations for migrants without inter-ethnic skills, the sense of threat and alienation is greatly intensified.

Yet the city also has important positive aspects in this context. If anything is the symbol and reality of modernity it is the city. It is the premier space for collective action and in that sense comes to embody the collectivity itself. There is, equally, a direct relationship between the nation as a political entity and its symbolic expression in the form of a city. The link between citizenship and the city is more than etymological. The city then becomes a part of the symbolic landscape of the nation. In the international context, moral worth is underpinned by the urbanisation that a city generates and the elite capable of taking its place in the world it creates. The city as the locus of specialised knowledge and symbolic capital strengthens this perspective. Without possessing a city it is very hard for an ethnic group to claim full political status, which helps to explain the difficulties experienced by the Roma in seeking to establish themselves.

The particular problems of the relationship between ethnicity and the city in Central and Eastern Europe has several strands. In the first place, the area was characterised by late urbanisation or under-urbanisation. Cities were few and tended to lack the civic autonomies that have evolved in the West. Their relationship to the countryside was much less organic than further west. As a result, they found it harder to play the integrative role, to foster the assimilation of rural migrants into urban and modern ways, that their counterparts in the West have played.

Second, the Central and East European city had a multi-ethnic character until a very recent date. It was only during the communist period that the ethnic homogenisation of the city began to be completed. Homogenisation is significant because it creates an ethnically familiar and uniform space, where inter-ethnic tensions are absent and where, it is believed, the particular qualities of the nation find their route to modernity. Virtually every capital city in the region was multi-ethnic, meaning that the titular ethnic group of a state could never be quite secure in its possession of the symbolic power that they expected to draw from their city. The Baltic capitals are still in this situation. Then, the city merges at one level with the problem of territoriality, in that it is the symbolic projection of territory into modernity, a source of pride and security that the community in question has attained the status of equality with the rest of the world.

Third, the Paris Peace settlement paradoxically ended up by devaluing the city and privileging the rural areas – a strange outcome, because it was expected to assist the region into modernity through the adoption of democratic systems. In reality, the drawing of frontiers in the carving up of the defunct empires heavily favoured the rural populations in determining the ethnic frontiers that were supposed to form the basis of a fair settlement. This left a fair number of cities with an ethnically alien population in a new state, something that left both the majorities and the minorities unhappy. The new majorities proceeded to try to ensure that the cities, now their cities, would acquire an ethnic majority to match the ideal.

The city

Fourth, the city is traditionally seen as the centre of ethnic assimilation by those who control it through their access to real and symbolic power. Assimilation clearly did take place and the city was, indeed, the place where it happened most rapidly. But this was not because the city had a magical assimilatory quality as such, but because those who went there did so to assimilate into urban economic and cultural modes and abandoned their ethnic identities almost as a by-product of migration. In essence, this was the fate of the traditional peasantry which did not possess a politicised consciousness of its ethnicity and was, therefore, ready to give it up in exchange for a higher social status. However, with the disappearance of the traditional peasantry, the process of assimilation is largely finished and can now be seen as historically contingent and not a part of the immanent essence of cities.

All these factors (historical, sociological, cultural, political), even when taken individually, would make it difficult to share a city. Ethnic groups believe that a city is and must be theirs and theirs alone. Members of alien groups entering the city thus find incomprehension and hostility, which is explained by this complex of factors rather than prejudice or, to be more precise, the prejudice has a basis in the rationality of collective existence and cultural reproduction as expressed by the city.

The reality today is that a number of cities in the region are ethnically mixed and that majorities find it extremely difficult to offer accommodation in the symbolic realm to minorities. The establishment of institutions may be tolerated, as long as these are not very visible, but the formal marking out of a city as multi-lingual is universally resisted, for the reasons sketched above. A complete equilibrium in inter-ethnic relations will only come into being, however, when the symbolic dimension of power is respected in the same way as the institutional.

A particularly sensitive problem is posed by the international dimension of the politics of ethnic minorities. Since the end of communism, and plainly spurred on by the catastrophe in Yugoslavia, the West's position on minorities is that these are not exclusively a question for the state itself, but raise general issues of security. This position, which completely reverses the attitudes current before 1989, is unwelcome in Central and Eastern Europe, but is reluctantly accepted – a reluctance that is strengthened by the failure of the West to extend this principle to their own minority problems. One can imagine the howls of outrage if, say, Estonia were to criticise the United Kingdom's policies in Northern Ireland or France's in Corsica. Nevertheless, various mechanisms are in place to ensure that minority issue do not spill over into conflict, notably the High Commission on National Minorities of the OSCE, the Council of Europe and the European Union.

Kin states, ones with fellow ethnics living in another state, are common enough in Europe (e.g. Ireland, Austria with the South Tyrol, Denmark and Germany in Western Europe; Hungary, Poland, Albania, Russia in Central and Eastern Europe). Their attitudes to the home state of their fellow ethnics however, can be bedeviled by the minority question. Here practice varies considerably. Hungary has tended to follow a relatively low-key policy, especially since the election of the Horn government in 1994, while – for instance – the domestic upheaval in Russia has encouraged politicians to see the fate of fellow Russians as an opportunity, thereby creating potential trouble.[10]

Another acute and seldom theorised problem is that of formerly dominant minorities and, correspondingly, formerly dominated majorities. There is a complex of attitudes and experiences that weigh upon majority-minority relations deriving from the sudden, dramatic collapse of a state and the consequent shift in power. Formerly dominant minorities discover that their ethno-cultural identity, which they had unthinkingly assumed would 'naturally' give them access to power, influence, status, social capital and information via their links with the centre, has overnight become a drawback. The Russians in Latvia and Estonia are the most obvious case currently, but the experience of the Hungarians (in Romania, Slovakia, Serbia) after 1918 was similar, as was the case with the Poles in Lithuania after 1945 and this was the fate that the Serbs of Croatia and Bosnia sought to avoid with such fatal consequences in 1991 and after.

Correspondingly, formerly dominated majorities establish their own hierarchies, routines and forms of knowledge. They live with the sense of resentment at having been subjected to colonial rule and look to discharging these resentments on the local representatives of the colonial power, both real and symbolic. Under such circumstances, processes of multi-ethnic accommodation are lengthy, uneasy and, predictably, fraught with misunderstandings.

There has been a great deal of debate on whether or not

---

[10] On various aspects of this problem, see Aleksandar Pavkovit, Halyna Koscharsky and Adam Czernota (ed.), *Nationalism and Post-communism: a Collection of Essays* (Aldershot: Dartmouth, 1995).

ethnic minorities should be given some kind of territorial recognition, by being granted the right to foster their culture in well-defined areas. The objections are the fears – real and perceived – of the majority that such internal boundaries might become the basis of secession. This fear is not groundless, as it was precisely what happened in Yugoslavia, Czechoslovakia and the Soviet Union. But the question is deeper and more complex. Territory is more than just a piece of real estate, it is also deeply symbolic of the political power of an ethnic group, a universal acceptance of its moral worth and a guarantee of its cultural reproduction. It is noteworthy here that diasporas are weak at least in part because they lack the powerful symbolism of their own territory, like the Roma.

In conclusion, it is worth underlining three things: first, ethnicity and the politics of inter-ethnic relations have returned to the European agenda for the foreseeable future. They will not disappear, so it is vital that political solutions be found to manage the problem. Second, these solutions exist, have been tried and tested and, with modifications, can be introduced in Central and Eastern Europe. But, third, the pivotal problem of politics in the region is not so much ethnicity as such but the weakness of the state and of civil society which would constrain ethnicity to operate within democratic channels. Here the picture may be gloomy, but it is far from catastrophic.

18

MINORITIES UNDER COMMUNISM

It can be taken for granted that minorities did not prosper under communism. The communist system was dedicated to the homogenisation of society and anything that deviated from the officially determined norm was regarded as a threat. This proposition applied not just to ethnic minorities, of course, but to social minorities as well, but the focus in this analysis will be on the problem of how communist systems dealt with minority ethnicity.

Thus the central assumption for this essay is that communism disliked diversity and did little or nothing to construct mechanisms that would allow societies to come to terms with the changes that the communist inspired transformation actually brought about. Ultimately, communism offered a few rather ineffective methods for resolving the problems of diversity: suppression through coercion or threat of coercion, discretionary concessions that could in theory be withdrawn at any time and some formal provision for minority life. This did mean that communist systems offered recognition for ethnic minorities, something that was not the case with social minorities, but essentially that was as far as communism was prepared to go.

This position derived logically from the underlying assumptions of the communist ideology and system. Class was the dominant form of social consciousness and ethnic identities were an expression of false consciousness that would eventually disappear. In reality, of course, these ethnic identities proved singularly resilient and the ruling communist parties had no answer to their survival.[1]

In formal terms, communist minority policies were based on the compromise that Lenin had made with the multinational state that he had inherited from the Tsars. Lenin's attitude was that national identities would eventually disappear and, in fact, they

---

[1] On ethnicity and its political functions, see Walker Connor, *Ethnonationalism: the Quest for Understanding* (Princeton University Press, 1994).

would go more quickly if ethnic groups could be shown that the Soviet state had more to offer than ethnicity could. To this end, he allowed, even encouraged, the construction of ethnic communities, giving them languages and other forms of cultural infrastructure that they lacked before. However, all this generosity had a proviso: the content of these minority cultures had to be determined by the ruling communist party. This was the meaning of the formula 'national in form, socialist in content'.[2]

Lenin's policies were taken over by the newly established communist systems in Central and Eastern Europe, although they were modified in practice. The crucial modification was the one taken tacitly from Stalin's reformulation of the ruling ideology, that the Soviet Union might be committed to the creation of a secular utopia, nevertheless that utopia was to be strongly Russian in expression. In essence, this meant that the dominant ethnic group in the state could project its own ethnic agendas through the new system – even if it was strongly permeated by the language of communism – and insist that minorities adhere to the ethnicised local version of the system.

However, as far as the minorities were concerned, the communist seizure of power was something of a caesura for in the years immediately preceding the consolidation of power by the communists, the wartime and post-war governments were pursuing strongly nationalist policies and this left its mark on minority thinking.[3] In the first place, the Holocaust and the post-war expulsions of Germans and others on the basis of collective guilt created a sense of insecurity in the minorities that were left behind. As far as they were concerned, a precedent had been set. The coming of the communists then changed the equation. Overt discrimination on the basis of collective guilt was ended, but communist oppression then followed. As against this, expulsions clearly affected the majority as well, in that having participated – directly or indirectly – in an act of ethnic cleansing, the majority was to some extent caught up in an attempt to justify its actions.[4]

[2] For details see Paul Goble, 'Three Faces of Nationalism in the Former Soviet Union' in Charles A. Kupchan (ed.), *Nationalism and Nationalities in the New Europe* (Ithaca, NY: Cornell University Press, 1995), pp.122-35.

[3] On the historical background, see Raymond Pearson, *National Minorities in Eastern Europe 1948-1945* (London: Macmillan, 1983).

[4] Bradley F. Abrams, 'Morality, Wisdom and Revision: the Czech Opposition

A sense of mutual insecurity, fear and suspicion of 'the other' was in place.

The striking aspect of the relationship between the communist state and ethnic minorities was its unevenness in terms of power. All the high cards appeared to be in the hands of the party-state, from absolute control of the instruments of coercion, such as money and employment to the tacit support of the ethnic majority. In these seemingly hopeless circumstances in the face of the might of the state, minorities ought to have thrown in the towel and accepted assimilation. Individuals certainly did. But ethnic collectivities as a whole did not. Indeed they survived the communist experience of distorted modernisation, though with many deep-seated fears as to the nature of the political system and of politics as such. On the whole, minorities under communism saw themselves as suffering under a double disadvantage – they were oppressed by communism and equally they were oppressed as members of a minority. Needless to say, this argument did not find favour with members of ethnic majorities. Overall, therefore, minority insecurity over survival and as a moral community was exacerbated by the communist order. At the same time, the experience of the communist period points towards another conclusion. Once mobilised into a consciousness of their ethnic identity, ethnic groups are quite extraordinarily difficult to eliminate. If even the machinery of the totalising communist state proved incapable of achieving this, less harsh systems would find it yet more difficult to do so.

Hence the communists, relying on the Leninist principle, assumed that ethnic identities were a relic of the bourgeoisie and class inequality, so that the egalitarian policies of communism would result in their rapid disappearance. In the meantime provision would exist for the formal – rather than substantive – articulation of ethnicity, but this would be restricted to a few areas, mostly of culture, like language use, education and the coopting of a few ethnic minority leaders into formal institutional structures. Otherwise, ethnic minorities were expected to conform to the dictates of the party and to its leading role. What minority institutions were brought into being or allowed to survive were to operate as transmission belts, to propagate party ideology and policy.

Given the very high levels of repression in the early years of communism, ethnic minorities had very little alternative but to accept what they were given. In any event, the formal provision was not entirely unsatisfactory for some members of minorities in that it was an improvement, or appeared to be, on the pre-communist ethnicised state strategies, which regarded ethnic minorities as a threat to the integrity of their state and their identity. In the interwar period, communist parties had attracted considerable minority support by championing minority rights (this was seen by communists as a tactical device to weaken these states, but the minorities did not understand it in this way) and some memories of this persisted.[5] In this sense, minorities had some hopes that the communists really would end national op-pression, as they promised and that under communism they would be able to assume their rightful place in the system; this was clearly the case with the Hungarians of Romania after 1945, but it informed attitudes in Yugoslavia and Slovakia as well.

Stalinism

Stalinism disabused them of this belief. For the communist leader-ships, all identities which they did not control were a potential or actual threat to the principle of coercive unanimity which they regarded as the essence of equality. On this basis, anything that did not conform to a narrowly defined criterion of equality – male manual workers using relatively simple technologies[6] – as to be eliminated as a hostile conspiracy. This enforced homogenisa-tion of society, The Terror, did succeed in freezing social and ethnic identities for the time being, but could not extirpate them entirely. Social stratification, including the restratification generated by communism itself, became visible with the end of monolithism in 1961,[7] but this left ethnic differentiation in an awkward position in terms of both theory and practice. While social interests could

---

[5] R.V. Burks, *The Dynamics of Communism in Eastern Europe* (Princeton University Press, 1961) gives details.

[6] I deal with this point in *Politics in Eastern Europe, 1945-1992* (Oxford: Blackwell, 1993), chap. 4.

[7] See my argument in *ibid.,* chap. 5.

just about be accommodated under the Khrushchevian dispensation, ethnicity could not be, seeing that it was anomalous in terms of the long term aims of the system. It was seen as a direct challenge to the tenets of Marxism–Leninism, given that Marxism had always preordained them to disappearance.[8] Hence, communist authorities vacillated between formal provision and repression of minority aspirations and, in effect, ended up close to the standpoint of the majority nation, that minorities represented a threat to communist and nationalist power; in the case of Ceauşescu's Romania, this was explicit; elsewhere it was implicit but clearly understood.

The interaction between communist parties and the national (or nationalist) elites was, in fact, more complex than appeared at the time or later. In a very real sense it can be argued that the nationalists were in a tacit alliance with the party, because they understood that whatever else the party might be doing, it was controlling the state and was thus the agent of protection for the majority ethnic community. This was only marginally important during the Stalinist period, but once Khrushchev had begun to encourage the ruling parties to find some kind of an accommodation with the populations over which they ruled, the Central and Eastern European political scene changed. The parties now had some leeway in arranging their relationship with the ethnic identities of the state. This was the context in which the tacit alliance came to be born.[9]

In these circumstances, formal minority representation – through cultural organs, minority language publication and minority representatives in parliaments, Central Committees or rarely, politbureaus – proved to be ineffective. The full weight of the communist state, once aimed at a minority, was hard to offset; in consequence, minority representation (Csemadok for the Hungarians of Slovakia or the Councils for the Hungarian or German nationalities in Romania, for example) withered on the vine and were increasingly emptied of content. In so far as they had any function, it was largely symbolic – a demonstration by the communist state that it recognised the existence of minorities but was not ready to do anything substantive about them.

---

[8] Roman Szporluk, *Communism and Nationalism: Karl Marx versus Friedrich List* (New York: Oxford University Press, 1988).

[9] For greater detail see *ibid*.

The alliance had various implications. It provided the ruling party with a measure of support and, by making low-key allusions to national and nationalist referents, it could mobilise a degree of popular backing. Romania under Ceauşescu was the clearest example.[10] If nothing else, the party could count on an element of consent which had previously been absent. From the minority point of view, on the other hand, this gradual, implicit but very real shift away from the a-national or anti-national stance of the party was rather bad news. Inevitably, minorities came to be seen as a negative factor in the state and came under pressure to assimilate or abandon their ethnic distinctiveness. The consequence of this shift for ethnic minorities was to force these groups in on themselves, to lead them to fight a rearguard action for what they saw as survival and to intensify their distrust of the state, which they saw as increasingly ethnicised.

Furthermore, the overall antagonism to diversity had another unintended outcome. It blocked the potential for the evolution of cross-cutting, multilayered identities. Individuals saw themselves very largely as members of an ethnic groups and not much else. The multifaceted character of modern societies, something that was enhanced by the massive economic and social transformation engendered by communism, was not and could not be accompanied by an equivalent redefinition of identities. As the officially sponsored class identities were emptied of anything other than formal quality, ethnicity became the dominant mode of social self-perception.

In terms of identity formation, the experiment in the construction of a communist society can be regarded as a historic alternative to the civic identities that dominate Western democratic systems.[11] The communist experiment may have failed, but its legacy lives on and the way in which it impacted on ethnic minorities demands investigation. Essentially, as has been suggested, communism was a highly reductionist and homogenising system; the identities that evolved in response to it tended to be similarly simplified. However, given that large parts of the population came into deep-level contact with the state and had their life chances

[10] On Romania see Robert R. King, *Minorities under Communism* (Cambridge, MA: Harvard University Press, 1973)

[11] See pp. 128–44.

and life strategies shaped by the communist system, inevitably, these newly forged identities were marked by communism.

As far as ethnic minorities were concerned, the communist period saw their integration into the ambit of the state and that state was, of course, a national state, so that the supposedly communist modes were largely permeated by the ethno-national traditions of the state in which they lived. The communist *Gleichschaltung* was certainly far-reaching, but it never succeeded in eliminating the national quality of these systems. In this sense, the communist modernisation had a major and probably in-eradicable impact on minorities – they had been socialised, moder-nised and politicised (or depoliticised) by the state in which they lived and consciously or not, they adopted its modes and mores, its administrative habits and political vocabulary. In this respect, the communist surrogate for civic identities proved effective in bringing a degree of integration into being and binding some – though not all – of the loyalties of the minorities to it.

Where minority life was less than satisfactory however, was in its range of possible choices. Here the double jeopardy was very clear, notwithstanding differences deriving from the size and set-tlement pattern of a minority. A group of several hundred thousand could generate a critical mass of activity and thus extend the range of choice, whereas a group of under a hundred thousand would find that its existence as a minority would be diluted by the impact of the majority.

Thus, by way of example, the Hungarian Szeklers of Transyl-vania – around 700,000 strong and living in a compact area of settlement – could continue to lead an overwhelmingly Hungarian life, while the Germans of the same region, around 400,000 after the end of the Second World War but scattered throughout southern Transylvania, found the twofold pressure too much and gradually they abandoned their struggle to maintain a German life. The presence of West Germany which was prepared to offer them an alternative home was also significant in this context; Hungary was not prepared to accept very large numbers of its co-ethnics. After the collapse of communism, the number of Germans continued to dwindle and by the mid-1990s, it was probably below 80,000 and falling.[12]

[12] Figures from Michael Shafir, *Romania: Politics, Economics and Society* (London: Pinter, 1985). In the summer of 1994 I visited Prajmar, near Brasov, where I

In practice, though, minority provision was very restricted and formalised. The communist state offered minorities some schooling in their mother tongue, usually up to secondary level, though the number who progressed from primary to secondary level tended to diminish. Here a difficult problem has to be assessed. The state generally claimed that the reason why provision never matched the statistical number of the minority was that minority parents preferred to send their children to majority language schools, as a means of improving their career prospects. In other words, they were choosing natural assimilation. Minority intellectuals, on the other hand, would argue[13] that if the state were more open-minded about its language provision in general, then members of the minority could expect equivalent career prospects even in their own language. This dilemma has not disappeared with the end of communism.

The core of the argument points towards another problem – what is to be the social composition of the minority. Centrally, cultural reproduction is greatly enhanced if the minority has the capacity and the political space to construct a reasonably wide range of social roles, and be able sustain intellectual, commercial, bureaucratic, religious, political and other activities, i.e. those available to the majority, which is in any case one of the models for minority self-perceptions and aspirations. Hence minorities will look to find ways of expanding their range in this sense.

Indeed, as communist states grew to rely more on ethnicisation as a source of power, seeing that the communist ideology, welfarism, and other modes of legitimation were exhausted,[14] the existing instruments of minority cultural reproduction tended to be downgraded. Minority language schools were merged with majority language schools or closed altogether, often on the basis of some educational reform that may or may not have been spurious. Minority publications were obliged to abandon any role of fostering minority culture and to be nothing more than the transmitters of whatever the communist majority wanted propagated at the

---

was told that whereas the German population of the village had once been over 3,000, it was now around 80.

[13] In private conversation with the author.

[14] See my *Politics in Eastern Europe, 1945-1992* (Oxford: Blackwell, 1993), especially chapters 7 and 8.

time. Self-analysis by the minority, attempts to place the economic, social or cultural development of the minority into any kind of scientific context, were frowned on or blocked entirely. Essentially, communist policy adopted a position that either explicitly or implicitly denied that any minority problem existed at all and, therefore, any attempt to raise one by members of the minority could be said to constitute nationalist propaganda.

Poland and Hungary, both close to being mono-ethnic, offered an interesting contrast in this connection. In Poland, the party-state adopted a stance that was close to asserting that there were no ethnic minorities of any kind in the country at all, implying that the few non-Poles – perhaps 1 million in all in a population if 38 million by the 1980s – were due to disappear.[15] Consequently, the emergence of a German minority in the 1970s in the sense of a rising number of persons who claimed the right to emigrate to West Germany on the grounds of the German ethnicity, was a serious shock to Polish opinion. Similarly, the tentative expressions of minority existence during the Solidarity period were not well received. Hungary, by contrast, never denied the presence of small numbers of non-Hungarians, and claimed to offer more than adequate cultural provision for them. In reality, schooling in the minority languages never went beyond a few hours a week and other cultural activities were formalised and restricted.

Furthermore, as the communist system settled down to a post-Stalinist, more routinised existence, it shifted away from the dogmatic use of power towards a more nuanced, more fluid order. In this context, the rise of the discretionary use of power became central. Although in theory everything was formally decided according to the rules of the party and the official ideology, in reality – with variations from country to country – a certain amount of negotiation was possible. This affected minorities, though given their generally weak position in the hierarchy of power, they benefited from such discretion rather less than the majorities.

However, it was occasionally possible to publish a book or an article in a minority language (thereby contributing to minority culture), sometimes it was possible to do a deal with officialdom

[15] Chris Hann, 'Intellectuals, Ethnic Groups and Nations: Two Late-Twentieth-Century Cases' in Sukumar Periwal (ed.), *Notions of Nationalism* (Budapest: Central European University Press, 1995), pp.106-28, deals with the case of the Lemko.

to keep a minority language school from being closed or merged and so on. The problem with this system lay precisely in its discretionary nature. Nothing could be institutionalised, there could be no guarantees that the future was in any way safeguarded. The result was that concessions could do little or nothing to satisfy minorities as to their deeper existential fears; and these fears are still in place in the context of post-communism.

Whenever groups or individuals are largely excluded from power, they seek to remedy this by whatever means are to hand. Under communism, one of the most significant such instruments was symbolic politics.[16] This had two purposes. One was to try and gain some concession from the system and the other was an assertion of one's own continuing existence, a demonstration that the minority still lived and thus had the right to be recognised as a community with its own values. The problem with symbolic politics is that it is not all that effective. It may satisfy (briefly) the affective dimension in those participating in such action, but it has precious little effect on those holding power. What it does, though, is to polarise relations between the minority and majority. When the minority uses its symbols – flags, celebrations of its past, festivals etc. – the majority sees these forms of assertion as a direct attack on its own integrity and values. The result can be very negative because it can result in polarisation. Thus the Serbs of Kosovo regarded the right of the Kosovo Albanians to fly the Albanian flag (though varied by having to bear a red star) – which they enjoyed by the late 1980s – as a major affront, in as much as it was read as a symbolic denial of the Serbian quality of Kosovo. In this sense, though the Albanians might have derived some psychological satisfaction from flying their flag, it did not improve their access to power or material resources, even while it infuriated the local minority (which was at the same time a part of the national majority).

Urbanisation

There is another aspect of the relationship between communism and ethnic minorities that demands scrutiny. The modernising revolution instituted by communism saw urbanisation as the

[16] David I. Kertzer, *Ritual, Politics and Power* (New Haven, CT: Yale University Press, 1988).

primary instrument for the social transformation that was the over-arching aim. The city, the socialist city, was to be the crucible of the new socialist man (and woman too, but communism never paid its dues to gender differences). In the first place, the communist vision involved a homogenisation in social terms, yet the rapid – even overrapid – urbanisation of the communist period had im-portant consequences for ethnicity as well.[17]

Even before the coming of communism, the city had been used as a means of assimilation. Peasants of various ethnicities would make the journey to the city and, in exchange for the higher status of urban existence and some guarantee of material benefits, would abandon their original ethnicity and assume the ethnic codes of the majority population. Vienna, Budapest, Prague, Lwow and other major urban centres all had this role. Under communism, this process was accelerated, but the results were not quite as clear cut as they had been before 1939. The problem was twofold. Most of the peasantry streaming into the cities in the 1950s had already acquired some kind of an ethnic consciousness and was loath to give it up. Second, the communist provision for formal ethnic identity impeded assimilation, in that it offered migrants the opportunity to retain their ethnic allegiance, or at any rate some of it.

Besides, as has been noted, communist urbanisation was rapid and thus less effective, in that large numbers of rural migrants coming to the city were better placed to constitute the critical mass that would enable them to hold on to some of their original ethnic identity. While in largely mono-ethnic states this was not a problem, in multi-ethnic ones it could be. Not least it meant that the communist authorities had to swamp the city to ensure that the majority ethnic group could overwhelm minorities. Ex-amples of this can be cited from Romania, Yugoslavia, from the Soviet Union and Slovakia. Thus Bratislava was traditionally a tri-ethnic city (Slovak, German and Hungarian), but in the 1970s and 1980s, its population doubled and the incomers were almost exclusively Slovak; the Germans had been expelled after 1945 and the Hungarians disappeared from sight. The non-Slovak minority was simply condemned to invisibility and, indeed, the new migrants were highly intolerant of non-Slovaks, seeing them

---

[17] György Enyedi, 'The transition of post-socialist cities', *European Review,* vol.3, no.2 (1994), pp.171-82.

as a threatening manifestation of the alienness of the city. Similar patterns could be found in Cluj, Košice and various Soviet cities. The pattern in Croatia was also interesting, in that sizeable numbers of Serbs moved to the major cities – Zagreb, Rijeka, Zadar – and integrated into urban ways, which to some extent meant adapting to Croatian ways. Over time, they tended to define themselves as 'Yugoslav' rather than as Serbian and it was only with the crisis of 1991 that they found themselves forced to redefine themselves as Serbian.

Overall, the experience of minorities under communism paralleled other patterns that the communist system created. Society had been marginalised, indeed treated as a minority, and once the system had disappeared, it responded with a sense of uncertainty and insecurity about social roles and responsibilities. Because ethnic identities are based on the deepest levels of belonging, all ethnic communities have generally conserved their ethnicities and have resisted attempts to break these down. Correspondingly, in the aftermath of communism, they have reacted positively to those who have sought to offer guarantees on the basis of ethnicity, regardless of the polarisation that would follow. The outcome has been a rise in ethnic identification and the shift towards the use of the codes of ethnicity in situations where these had little to offer, such as the distribution of power and the resolution of conflict. The ethnicisation of the state, a phenomenon increasingly to be seen in states like Romania, Slovakia or Latvia, means that only members of the ethnic majority have any chance of access to power, that political power is monopolised by the ethnic majority for its own purposes, that the symbolic and liturgical aspects of the state are appropriated by the majority and that the cultural reproduction of the majority becomes the overriding concern of the state, now permeated by majority interests, while ethnic minorities are marginalised by all the means available to the state apparatus, legal, administrative, political, economic and so on. In the long term, ethnicity is not sufficient on its own for the creation of stable democratic responses, only civic loyalty and equality before the law can achieve that, but the nature of the communist experience, and the particular patterns of majority-minority relations that it gave rise to go some way towards explaining the reasons for the upsurge of ethnic nationalism under post-communism.

19

ETHNIC MINORITIES IN
SOUTH-EASTERN EUROPE

Ethnic minorities: the nature of the problem

Ethnicity has always been a fact of political life in the world, particularly in South-Eastern Europe, but only since the collapse of communism has it returned to the West's political agenda. Hence the relationship between different ethnic groups living in the same territory will remain on both the regional and the local political agendas for many years to come.

Various approaches have been taken to the problems of multi-ethnicity, many of them incompatible with even the semblance of democracy. The tension generated by inter-ethnic relations can be utterly destabilising and, furthermore, even when an acceptable settlement has been reached it does not necessarily last. Unless all the parties involved in a multi-ethnic relationship are aware of these dangers and are prepared to work towards a solution on an ongoing basis, friction will persist and can spill over into greater or lesser crisis.

Inter-ethnic crises almost always have an international dimension, given that most ethnic groups have 'kin' in another state. Besides, in the 1990s the international community has come to recognise that observance of democracy and human rights constitutes the best guarantee of stabilising ethnic relations and that has given rise to pressures on domestic political behaviour that were not present before the collapse of communism.

There are particular problems in inter-ethnic relations in South-Eastern Europe and these will be looked at in detail in this analysis; they give ethnic identities in the Balkans certain highly individual features.

Religion – which is singularly intractable to bargaining and negotiation – plays an unusually salient role in the self-definition of ethnic groups for historical reasons; this was always an area of major religious cleavage lines and the Ottoman Empire used religion as its primary mode of organisataion. The intractability of religion lies in its claim to an exclusive revelation, which profoundly influences the way in which people regard others outside their group, even when the dogma has been lost and all that remains is identity and the boundary between insiders and outsiders.

In reality, religion does more than this. It leaves a residue that continues to influence styles, forms of expression, perceptions of the acceptability or otherwise of conflict and, correspondingly, of harmony. Patterns of social and political thought, the categories in which a community defines itself and its understanding of the good life are similarly affected by the mediated legacy of religion. Crucially, the memory – often implicit rather than explicit – of apostasy or conversion shapes a community's sense of security about itself and its existence. Where there is a well established history of regular conversions, and in the Balkans this was not unusual, the problem of loyalty and betrayal come to play a key role in the self-image of a community.

Identification with territory, which can sometimes have a positive function in easing tensions if a clearly demarcated area is accepted as properly associated with more than one group, by and large does not have this role in the Balkans, where on the contrary territory is seen as the exclusive possession of one group only. Competing claims exacerbate this.

Language, regarded as such a self-evident marker, is not so definitive. As between the South Slav languages, the transition from one to another is straightforward, so that language on its own is not enough of a marker. While the language boundary is clear as between unrelated languages (Greek, Albanian, Romanian, Hungarian) and the Slavonic languages, bilingualism makes identity shifting possible and is, indeed, practised. Low level bilingualism where only low cultures with small vocabularies and social know-ledge are concerned assists this process.

Furthermore, the culture of violence and the forcible suppression of differences have a long tradition in the region, one that is far from dead. All this implies that identities are readily changed, they are not innate and fixed for all time as nationalists would have one believe, with the result that it is easy to harbour fears about the survival of the ethnic group as an entity, to suspect others of making inroads into one's own ethnic 'substance' and, generally, of acting as a threat.

Majority-minority relations are reciprocal and interactive. There is little point in trying to understand what is happening only by looking at the minority, for this effectively decontextualises the essence of inter-ethnic politics. The political, cultural and social context of the minority is the majority and to some extent vice versa. Each side tends to define itself by an image, usually negative, of the other.

Overall, the need for workable solutions to the politics of inter-ethnicity is acute, so that it is particularly vital that the dynamics and characteristics of ethnicity and the political interplays related to it are fully understood in a meaningful sense.

Throughout Europe and obviously in the Balkans, ethnic majority-minority tensions have been a fact of life and in the eyes of many Western observers, undesirable. It should be stressed at the outset that Western analyses have been hampered by an interlocking set of misperceptions about ethnicity, so that even if the data concerning a particular area of the Balkans are well-known, without a deeper insight into the nature and functioning of ethnicity, the facts on their own are not necessarily revealing.

The central proposition concerns the persistence of ethnicity. In the modern period, since South-Eastern Europe came to the consciousness of the West in the second half of the nineteenth century, there has been awareness of inter-ethnic tension, though it was seldom interpreted that way. Rather it tended to be seen as religious intolerance or sometimes as imperial oppression or as social conflict or flawed language policies; anything, indeed, but ethnicity. In this context, analysis is badly served by both liberal and Marxism assumptions concerning the nature of human motivation.

Marxism explicitly, and liberalism implicitly place their central emphasis on material interest and both accept a certain universalism which is uneasy with the particularism of ethnicity. They tend to dismiss ethnic allegiance and political action based on ethnicity as 'ephemeral', as a 'protest' and cannot see that in many circumstances, ethnicity is central to human attitudes and to the political action that ensues.

This proposition demands investigation. Why does ethnicity persist, what is it its role? The core of the answer lies in the nature of group solidarity. Broadly, there are ad hoc groups held together by a shared interest – economic, material, financial – and, at the same time, there are groups based on the ties that go beyond easy negotiation, that are built around the unwritten, unconscious, unarticulated but real needs of belonging. Once it is accepted that individuals have a basic need to belong to communities in conditions where they do not have to negotiate and renegotiate their everyday activities, but can take the rules governing interaction for granted, the inner springs of ethnicity become clearer.

Collectivities evolve over time and regulate their affairs; that regulation then acquires both a normative and a definitive quality. People accept the rule, determine what is right and what is wrong by the rules so absorbed and then define who they are by their observance of those rules. They will assume that this process is 'natural', that this is a universal norm. This means that contact with other groups which determine their 'naturalness' differently, will generate perplexity, possibly antagonism. Crucial in this process is that it is imperceptible, that the regulation of the community is not conscious. Indeed, attempts to make it so will frequently be resisted as threatening group solidarity.

Markers of identity

Further, the group will sustain its existence by a series of rituals and by establishing various markers that differentiate it from other groups. Every community has rituals, every community determines its existence by reference to symbols which are effectively a way of celebrating the continuity of the group, marking it, reasserting it for the members of the group. By the same token, generally somewhat more consciously, groups will define themselves by a variety of markers; language, religion, history are only the most obvious of these. In essence anything can be a marker, from dietary laws and dress codes to cosmologies. It is important to note here that attachment to rituals and symbols persist even when the original faith that gave rise to them has faded. Essentially, rituals are a way of maintaining solidarity without establishing consensus, a way for members of a group to work together even when they are in disagreement.

Groups maintain themselves, furthermore, because group existence generates a body of knowledge that is transmitted over time, so that individuals do not, as it were, have to reinvent the wheel, but grow up equipped with a range of ideas through which they can make sense of the world. Ethnicity is a form of social capital.

Once argued in this way, the resilience of group identities and the determination of groups to maintain themselves in being becomes intelligible, group identity is rational in its own terms. The linkage between group identity and the problem of ethnicity is not wholly clear, however, until the element of politics is introduced. Groups have existed since time immemorial and maintained themselves in a variety of ways. With the rise of the modern state, however, group identities were projected outwards, the number of those involved in the group grew and, at the same time, the state (the ruler) expanded its range of tasks.

Crucially, as the state expanded it looked for a higher level of loyalty as well as a higher level of taxation and conversely society expected a greater say over how it was ruled. This transformed the relationship between rulers and ruled and the latter increasingly defined itself around its experience of political power. The relationship between the state and society was, therefore, argued in terms of the group and of the proposition that individuals who shared the group loyalty, who belonged to the same culture, should share the same political authority. Culture and politics should be the same.

Thus whether the state preceded modern ethnic consciousness and generated a political consciousness (as in Western Europe) or whether political consciousness was mobilised normatively in terms of ethnicity on the basis that all members of a particular ethnicity should have their own state (the Central and Eastern European model), ethnicity gained a saliency in politics that it had not had before. Indeed, there much to be said for the proposition that nationhood defined in these terms constituted the first mass political identity.

The vital conclusion to be drawn from the foregoing is that ethnicity will persist into the foreseeable future. It will not disappear under the impact of greater prosperity. Indeed, while in some circumstances, wealth can indeed blunt the edge of inter-ethnic tension, in others it can generate it (e.g. Slovenia, Lombardy, Catalonia). Again, it should be stressed that ethnicity precedes economic well-being rather than deriving from it.

What follows from this is that any attempt to resolve majority-minority relations with the tacit or explicit expectation that over time these will so far diminish in friction as to go away is an error. Even in the ideal case of Switzerland, inter-ethnic tension exists, although there are countless excellent methods for diluting such tensions.

Nor is there much mileage to be had from the comments that are frequently heard, to the effect that contain communities have lived together peacefully for centuries and would do so again if left alone and not stirred up. This analysis is vapid to the point of inanity. For pre-modern communities, ethnicity was not as central as it has become today because political power was not structured around it. The coming of modernity (especially communications) has transformed the picture in terms of the self-consciousness of communities and this will not diminish. Modernity essentially affects all the ethnic communities of South-Eastern Europe and, to make matters more complex, was largely brought about by the communist transformation. People can only be 'stirred up' if they feel that there is something to which they might respond, like fears as to the future of the community; mobilisation must have reasonance if it is to work.

The nature of the modern state has to be understood at this point in order to make sense of what follows. The pre-modern state sat comparatively lightly on society. It lacked the capacity to penetrate it, to organise it, to extract resources, to militarise it and to regulate it; it tended to use pre-modern means, like brute force for extraction, and rituals and liturgies to maintain cohesion. The modern state, on the other hand, has very far-reaching capacity to rationalise both the individual and the group. Crucially for this analysis it structures identities around a particular set of policies, procedures, bureaucratic forms and modes of governance. These invariably leave an impact on those affected and over time, mere bureaucratic arrangements acquire a timeless "natural" quality, which those affected make their own, integrate into their body of social knowledge and come to regard as central to their way of life.

This proposition, it should be stressed, impacts on populations regardless of ethnicity. Ethnically diverse groups can thus acquire a shared political identity whether they recognise this or not. In this way, given time, the state can shape identities and can even attract the loyalty of various ethnic groups, as long as their ethnicity is given some space, some means of articulation. In effect, the modern state has been a signal success in the field of integration. Communism, with its highly invasive, hyper-etatist concept of the role of the state was correspondingly more effective than the more liberal democratic state.

A brief analysis of the impact of communism in this context is valuable here. Communism did bring about the transformation of a number of key factors – the end of the peasant problem, modern industrial working methods and urbanisation, modern communications, a centralisation of power and status and a rather simplistic attitude towards diversity and change. In essence, communism implanted a belief – or strengthened it – that questions could be answered in a black-and-white fashion, that there was invariably a single right answer to every question and opponents were enemies. At the same time, it also brought with it a certain pattern of ideological thinking: that every effect has to have a cause, that there are no accidents, no coincidence, chance or happenstance; conspiracy theories of the world are a very short step from this. Equally, disagreement quickly escalates and turns into conflict.

All this makes the culture of compromise extremely difficult to establish and, equally, implies that a Western style modernity with all its variety, uncertainty and ambiguity is highly difficult to absorb. At the end of the day, one is left with the inescapable conclusion that communism left these societies unequipped or ill-equipped to face the problem of diversity. And without a readiness to accept diversity, it is hard to predict much success for democracy.

It is common ground that while short-term solutions in ethnic issues may be found in non-democratic political systems, these are seldom likely to last. Methods like oppression or hegemonic control may create stability for a while, but will not solve the problem. Indeed, when applied to inter-ethnic relations, tension will merely be swept under the carpet to revive with much greater force at a later date (the suppression of the Croatian 'mass movement' in 1972 is a good example). The implication of this is that lasting solutions to inter-ethnic problems have to be consensual. These are quite clearly best achieved through democracy.

A great deal is currently argued about 'transition', the nature of democracy under post-communism, whether there is a democratic deficit or not. Rather than rehearse these arguments, the assumption in this analysis is that by and large democratic forms have, indeed, been adopted but their democratic content is frequently still weak. Crucially, three necessary conditions for democracy – self-limitation, feedback and self-correcting mechanisms – are only barely met, particularly in the context of inter-ethnic relations. They are not wholly absent, but weakly observed. The implication of this proposition is that with the strengthening of a democratic culture, something that necessarily requires time, relations between ethnic groups should improve. Indeed, it is hard to see how it could be otherwise. Before an ethnic minority can validate its existence, status and aspirations in the eyes of the majority, the majority must have acquired the self-confidence and self-awareness to recognise that the minority is an inescapable and not automatically damaging aspect of its own identity. That, in turn, means that there has to be a civil society.

Civil society is, once again, a much debated expression. It is used here in the sense, implied above, that there exists a politically significant core in all ethnic groups which is ready to accept a growing number of political (cultural, economic, social, religious etc.) actors, other ethnic groups included, that the contest for resources and status will be continuous and that new ways of resolving those contests will have to be established. In this sense, civil society is as much a process as a state of being.

Finally, some mention has to be here of history or, to be precise, of memory. Memory is a part of the shared body of social knowledge which a community will not surrender readily. It is a part of its identity. Hence no amount of argument that the perceived history of a particular group is 'false' or 'spurious' or 'imagined' is likely to convince that group. If anything, it will see these arguments as an attack on itself and reinforce its boundaries. However, time can soften memory and certain events can be forgotten, even if they are there in the storehouse ready to be revived; this will happen, though, only if the group feels itself under threat. An example of softening: during the nineteenth century, relations between Hungarians and Croats were fairly dire (Jelačić, inter-ethnic massacres, oppression by Budapest etc.), but these memories have almost entirely disappeared and play no role in respective inter-ethnic attitudes.

The important matter in the context of memory is if one group feels that it has been historically humiliated by another, if it has the sense that it is diminished in terms of its 'moral worth' by reason of the existence or actions of another. In such situations, the sense of injury is generally so strong that it is very hard to remedy except by extraordinary means, almost invariably symbolic

and ritualised. The mutual perceptions of Hungarians and Romanians approximate to this state of affairs; President Iliescu's call
for a historic reconciliation will need a great deal of work by
both parties if it is to have any serious effect. The Albanian
presence in Kosovo along with the sacred sites of the Serbian
national identity is similar; Albanians may find it very difficult to
empathise with Serbian feelings on this issue. Other people's sacred
ground seldom resonates.

In inter-ethnic disputes of this kind – and they are legion in
South-Eastern Europe – both parties will seek to legitimate their
positions by reference to the same past but to a radically different
memory. There is, in effect, only one way out of such deadlock:
to deny either party the resource of memory, to stop them from
using the past if they want to achieve anything in inter-ethnic
relations. This goal is very hard to attain, given that the past is
a key constituent element of identity and identity is not open to
bargaining. So a will on both sides to begin movement in the
direction of an agreement is essential.

Understanding the intricacies

It is worth noting that too much of the Western discussion of
inter-ethnic relations concentrates on the pathologies. There are
successful cases too, but these seldom receive the attention they
deserve, presumably because they are less newsworthy. There are
two broad points to be made here: the post-communist systems
are very young, and are severely handicapped in respect of constructing democracies because of the communist legacy; and
secondly even mature democracies have found it a severe challenge
to cope with inter-ethnic relations; indeed, one has actually come
close to breaking up on this issue (Canada). In this context, any
and all solutions compatible with democratic practice should be
considered in the context of South-Eastern Europe, albeit with
the full awareness that ideas plucked from one political culture
may be as pie in the sky in another.

There is a general tendency on the part of those caught up
in an inter-ethnic dispute to argue that the characteristics of their
particular case are unique, that no outsider could possibly understand
them because they are felt so deeply and that parallels from elsewhere
are completely irrelevant. This kind of claim to exceptionalism
should be firmly resisted. The slavish application of the experience

of one situation to another is futile, but there are general principles and theoretical insights in the field of ethnicity that are widely applicable and the lessons of one case can be helpful in illuminating another if this is done judiciously.

So, there are some general methodological considerations and these deserve attention. The first of these is that prevention is better than cure. If an ethnic group begins to assert itself, to raise its consciousness, it is certainly preferable for the ethnic majority to recognise this and make the cultural concessions that will preempt political mobilisation, by, say, making fairly generous educational provision and offer a few symbolic gestures, like bilingual place-names and street signs. This may not work for ever, but it could prevent considerable trouble later by creating a cooperative climate. This state of affairs probably applies to the Greeks of Albania, the smaller ethnic groups of Macedonia and Romania and possibly even the Hungarians of Vojvodina. Roma communities throughout the region would currently be satisfied with provision along these lines.

If this opportunity is missed, and political mobilisation along ethnic lines has begun, then the majority will find the best solution in making some political concessions. Here the right combination of material and symbolic measures is usually the most effective. Special financial grants to minority life, the promotion of some well known minority activists to positions of importance and visibility in the state, using the minority language in certain functional areas of the administration and, maybe, allowing the minority to display its own flags, coats-of-arms and other symbols can go a long way towards securing the loyalty of most members of an ethnic minority. It is very important in this connection that members of the ethnic minority should be treated in such a way as to be able to avoid a charge of collaboration. The majority has a role to play in this. Probably the Turks and Pomaks of Bulgaria would accept this level of solution, also the Muslims of Greece, as well as the Muslims of the Sanjak.

If, however, these opportunities for settling matters easily have been missed, and the two sides are deeply entrenched in opposition, then the political lines have to be so clearly drawn that territory comes into the equation. This is much more painful for the majority. The role of territory in ethno-national consciousness deserves careful scrutiny. Whereas before the coming of modern ethnic nationalism, states swapped territory freely, this is no longer the case, because territory is not just a piece of real estate, but a part of 'the sacred homeland', usually wreathed in mystical allure. Note that Western states are not exempt from this sacralisation of territory (Shakespeare's 'this precious stone set in the silver sea' still resonates). The net result is that the very idea of ceding territory, even when in ethnic terms it might make a great deal of sense, is absolutely unthinkable.

Here is an illustration from outside the South-Eastern European area. From this perspective, it would make much sense for Estonia to cede Narva to Russia; its population is overwhelmingly Russian (*c.*95 per cent), Narva is directly on the border, and besides it is an economic disaster area. A notional cession might well generate Russian goodwill and reduce the size of the Russian minority in Estonia by around a half of the total. But these considerations are anathema, as they run counter to the territorial integralism of the Estonian identity.

All ethno-political identities share this territorial integralism. So anything that smacks even remotely of a territorial arrangement is rejected with a near-hysterical vehemence throughout the post-communist world. This includes local territorial autonomy and does so for a good reason, for which the West is responsible. The collapse of both Yugoslavia and the Soviet Union was determined along pre-existing territorial divisions and the lines drawn by the communist authorities were taken as sacrosanct by the West, even when the outcome was an ethnic, geographical and maybe even a historical absurdity (e.g. the Crimea). Essentially the errors of the 1918 Paris Peace Settlement were reimposed on Central and South-Eastern Europe in 1991.

These two factors combined (sacralisation and the fear that an internal administrative boundary could become an international frontier), it is suggested, underlie more than anything else the utter refusal of any post-communist state to countenance territorial autonomy. The autonomy of the Gagauz area in Moldova was, presumably, feasible only because there was no possible kin-state to which the Gagauz could attach themselves.

Yet once the polarisation has begun, the minority will look for guarantees of its security and survival in terms which will certainly include some territorial arrangement, whatever it may be called. By and large, territorial autonomy is not only a no-go area for negotiations, but is seen as a provocation by the majority. In theory, if both sides were willing to drop the symbolic aspect of territoriality and concentrate on practicalities, a local government reform which was reasonably fair-minded towards the minority – unlike the Slovak administrative reform with respect to the Hungarian minority – could work. Low-level local government boundaries should be drawn in such a way as to ensure that a minority that lives in such an area is not reduced to a small and inconsequential fragment after the redrawing, in consequence of which it can be denied any administrative language rights, but it is vital that local government districts are regarded as such and are not given any symbolic territorial aspect.

But the symbolic and psychological aspect of territoriality is not the only argument against it. Modern states are dynamic and this dynamism involves geographical mobility. In other words, members of an ethnic group will frequently find that they will have to look for work, opportunities, careers and status outside their own denominated areas. If a territorial arrangement is in force, they will find it very difficult to demand educational and cultural provisions outside their own area, implying that the cultural reproduction of the entire group would be affected, given that it is usually the most energetic who move. This means that a preferable solution for minorities is that cultural, educational and administrative provision should be made for them throughout the territory of the state as long as they reach a certain minimum percentage in that area, say 8 per cent (the Finnish solution). In this sense, the territorially delimited solutions adopted in Wales, in the South Tyrol and the extraordinarily broad-minded educational regime in the Prekmurje in Slovenia (where both Hungarians and Slovenes learn both languages) may turn out to be traps rather than the generous arrangements that they are customarily seen to be.

Finally on this issue, there is a broad sociological point to be made about land and power. Traditionally, both the aristocracy and the peasantry regarded land as the best security and source of power. In the modern period, this is evidently a fallacy. Information, symbolic capital and the ability to shape ideas are far more significant in the generation of power. Nationalists, however, are caught in the grip of the past, only partly because of their relative closeness to their peasant antecedents in South-Eastern Europe, and continue to insist that land is power. Not surprisingly, they find alternative sources of power profoundly threatening, because these alternatives are entirely outside the range of what is understood to be proper.

The key assumption in all these suggested arrangements is that existing frontiers are inviolable. There is, as half suggested above, a tacit Western belief that this is the least troublesome way forward. This proposition should, however, be explored with greater rigour. The Western stance is derived very largely from the deep con-servatism of the international order, which is severely hostile to new states coming into being in any way other than decolonisation. Possibly fortunately, no one succeeded in reconceptualising the end of communism as a form of decolonisation; the implications would have been very far-reaching. Hence the rather more tradi-tional approach to secession came into play. There were one or two cases of this after the Second World War (Bangladesh, Sin-gapore), but they were rarities. This explains the shock and fear of the West at the rise of possible new states. The three Baltic states could just about be swallowed, though that took place with much reluctance, but the collapse of Yugoslavia and the Soviet Union was another matter.

In any event, conservatism persisted and various instruments in the international tool kit were forgotten, notably plebiscites, boundary commissions and arbitration. Internal frontiers would become international frontiers and that was that; so where the definition of new frontiers could not be avoided, the nearest administrative demarcation to hand was chosen, regardless of sui-tability and long term stability. To be fair, some of the internal boundaries in former Yugoslavia did have long term historical sanction, but that does not mean they were ideal in the 1990s.

This has left a legacy where a sizeable number of people have become citizens of states that they might not have wished to become, had they been given the choice. This state of affairs has brought about the present situation, in which different ethnic groups are obliged to live together, whatever the circumstances. This has had a very significant and little understood outcome. It has upgraded the role of citizenship and, less self-evidently, has imposed on South-Eastern Europe of a universalising Western value citizenship over ethnicity, again regardless of suitability.

This is the somewhat unpromising raw material from which the states of South-Eastern Europe are obliged to invent themselves very rapidly as modern democratic states, without the period of apprenticeship that the West underwent. The implications of the task that these states faced were enormous: they had to construct new ways of life, new political cultures, new legal, political, economic and other codes acceptable to all the inhabitants of state territory in a very short period of time and beyond that, to do so against the crippling legacy of communism.

In reality, the states of South-Eastern Europe had their own, rather different traditions of citizenship, one that was much more ethnicised than in the West and any modification to this was accepted only at Western insistence, usually more on paper than in reality. In essence, states defined their citizens according to ethnicity, which in the Balkans was usually non-territorial and with religion and language as the salient criteria. Communism changed the concept of citizenship, in that it gave the population certain relatively low-level social-welfare provisions, but not entitlement or empowerment vis-à-vis the state and certainly no sense of obligations towards the state or any sense that all the inhabitants of a particularly territory shared identically in obligations, loyalty and rights. A sense of shared community with non-members of the ethnic community was equally absent.

Ethnic outsiders were regarded as a threat, as alien, as potential or actual subversives whose professions of loyalty to the state were distrusted and disdained. The rules of democracy as understood and practised in the West, implying that all the inhabitants of a given territory were equal in the eyes of the state, were and are seen as naive. Ethnic outsiders are either a potential threat or an actual one. From this perspective, ethnic minority rights are not just meaningless but profoundly destabilising. This has unwelcome implications. Because the destructive quality of inter-ethnic relations is a reality and because such destabilisation impacts on Europe as a whole, the entire South-Eastern European area has to be monitored to ensure that the ethnic issue does not erupt into overt crisis. The construction of citizenship can, therefore, be expected to be a long haul.

Having said this, it is essential to add that Western support for inter-ethnic détente can be helpful, that over time it can lead to a stand-off between majority and minority and that stand-off can itself acquire the quality of a status quo. In this connection, it is also important to recognise that neither majorities nor minorities are homogeneous, that only in cases of extreme polarisation will there not be a spectrum of opinion in each group, which implies that there are currents of opinion ready to try and find a solution.

The trick is to give these currents the political authority and power to take decisions and make them stick.

Ethnic parties

A brief discussion of ethnic political parties is relevant here. There is a line of argument which holds that such parties are incompatible with democracy, that in a democracy all citizens have the same relationship to the political system regardless of ethnicity. This is nonsense. It is a self-serving argument used by majorities to attack ethnic minority parties. Besides, not only do several Western states accept ethnic minority parties (the United Kingdom, Spain, Italy for example), but such parties can be helpful in giving ethnic minorities a sense of security, a representation of their interests that might otherwise be denied them and a symbolic presence while constraining the majority to confront the multi-ethnic nature of the state. There is no automatic guarantee of success. Not least, ethnic minority parties are very difficult to integrate into the political process, they are easily depicted as extremist and it is difficult for them to launch political initiatives, as these can be readily isolated by a hostile majority. Nor is it easy for them to find political allies, because sympathetic liberal parties of the majority are usually very sensitive to charges of selling out on the national issue. Furthermore, ethnic minority parties inevitably homogenise the ethnic minority in terms of its interests, choices and aspirations, making internal debates within the minority harder. Equally, the existence of such parties can legitimate the operation of much harsher nationalist parties on the part of the majority, which argue that their stance is made necessary by the presence of the minority party. This phenomenon is, of course, an outcome of ethnicisation, but the ethnic party may well be held responsible for it. Still on balance, despite all these disadvantages, it is preferable to allow ethnic minority parties than to ban them; a ban would drive the minority into subterranean ways of articulating their interests.

From the perspective of the ethnic minority, all majority parties, regardless of their ideology and programme, are to some extent ethnic majority parties; ethnic minority interests are not and cannot be of primary concern to them, their values and ethos are permeated by and constructed around ethnic majority modes, with which minorities are at best uneasy. This is frequently reflected in the names they choose, like the 'Liberal Party of Ruritania' or 'Ruritanian Social Democracy'. However civic these political parties may seem to be, at a deep level they incorporate the assumptions of the ethnic majority.

The sociology of minorities is important enough to consider separately. There is a vague, untested assumption that all minorities are much the same, that they are made identical by being in a minority. Certainly, there are shared features like having to define one's identity on a daily basis in opposition to the majority (this in reality is Renan's *'plebiscite de tous les jours'*) and, therefore, their priorities will be much more singlemindedly focused on cultural reproduction than the majority's. But very often minorities differ markedly from one another in their social composition, their history, their attitudes, their successes and failures and their view of the majority.

Majorities find it especially difficult to accept competition in terms of 'moral worth', of cultural status, of international recognition, of being taken seriously by the West. There is an implicit majority view that a minority should remain a minority in all respects and should, above all, accept its understanding of the outside world through the perspectives of the majority. The idea that a minority can communicate politically and culturally with the West, for example, has frequently aroused great indignation and suspicion. Thus the Albanians of Kosovo came to be regarded by the Serbs as a threat in part because they established links with the outside world. Equally it was a considerable shock to the Serbs to discover that the Muslims of Bosnia were able to field a sophisticated team of politicians, speaking fluent English and dealing with their Western counterparts on equal terms.

The issue of moral worth also affects other areas. From the perspective of educational policy, there is no reason why an ethnic minority should not be able to run its own university. But attempts to found one (by the Albanians in Macedonia, the Hungarians in Romania) run up against a variety of obstacles which cannot be explained in terms either of higher education policy or technical legislative reasons. The deeper reality is that ethnic majorities assume that in one country there can only be one high cultural language and cultural life has to be conducted in that language. Attempts by the minority to gain equality on this terrain are deeply threatening, because they seem to place the minority on the same moral and cultural footing as the majority, and that is unacceptable because of everything else that might follow by implication, like complete access to power and status and the actual sharing of the state with the minority. The minority sees these endeavours as completely legitimate, as an exercise in proper cultural reproduction and interprets the manoeuvres of the majority as manipulative.

A survey of viable and non-viable methods

A useful taxonomy of ethnic conflict management is the one developed by two Western political scientists, John McGarry and Brendan O'Leary.[1] They put forward eight ways in which ethnic conflict can be approached. The present analysis elaborates on their eight-fold division.

The first two categories are *genocide* and forced or voluntary *mass population transfer*. Clearly, these are incompatible with democracy, but they are used in South-Eastern Europe and, indeed, there is a long tradition behind them. The idea underlying this 'solution' is that an ethnically cleansed state is likely to be more stable, better integrated, less troubled by the continuous problems of multi-ethnicity and so on. There are no moral qualms about killing or expelling large numbers of ethnically alien people precisely because they are ethnically alien. Hence, this method is the ultimate rationality of ethnicism, harsh but guaranteed to produce results.

This last proposition is a misconception. While at first sight ethnic cleansing may, indeed, produce the desired result, in reality it does not generate security. The problem is memory. Mass expulsion or transfer relocates large numbers of people who are welded together by their experience of an inexplicable collective trauma, who now define their identity by having been expelled and who will regard those who expelled them as in some ways their demonised other, their evil *alter ego*. Nor do expelled groups fade away. The general international experience is that after the initial period of shock, the expelled group recovers – indeed, recovers demographically – and regroups.

The expelling community, for its part, can never quite come to accept that its action was not as successful as it thought. Not only because some members of the expelling group are likely to have second thoughts about the brutalisation involved, but even

---

[1] See their *The Politics of Ethnic Conflict Regulation* (London, 1993).

more because the survival of the expelled group in a reconstituted form is like the return of a ghost, a perpetual reminder of something that collectivities would prefer to forget, an act of mass cruelty. No community likes to think of itself as barbaric and the resurgence of an expelled group is a reminder precisely of this. Furthermore, expulsion sets a precedent of which the expeller is only too aware. What could be done to one group could be done to it too. This then creates a set of mutual fears and hatred, a sense of threat and failure that neither group can do much to allay other than through a major act of symbolic reconciliation and remorse.

There are many examples from the history of the twentieth century to back up these propositions, the most obvious being the Holocaust. Others which can be cited include the expulsion of the Sudeten Germans, of whom there are at least as many today as were expelled (and killed) after 1945 and who have gained recognition as a 'people' (*Volksstamm*) in Germany, thus confounding those who thought that they would simply assimilate. Czech-German relations remain troubled to this day. The Palestinians are outside my geographical remit here. In South-Eastern Europe, the Greek-Turkish population exchange may have been voluntary, but it was experienced as forced by those involved; it would be hard to assert that it has solved the problem of relations between the two states and two ethnicities. The emptying of the Krajina does not mean that the problem of the Serbs of Croatia has disappeared, whatever Croatian nationalists may dream to the contrary. And, of course, in Bosnia the legacy of the killings and ethnic cleansing will haunt the area for decades, making political solutions very hard to envisage.

There are two interconnected sub-sets of this category. One is where the demographic reproduction rates of the two communities are so disparate that one group concludes that the massive growth in the size of the other means that it has lost the ethnic game, that its ability to ensure its cultural reproduction has been undermined. It will then probably either emigrate (the Serbs of Kosovo before 1991) or will go into internal emigration (the Germans of Prague before 1938). The other is where a group does have a kin state to which to migrate and decides that the country where it lives currently makes it cultural reproduction impossible (Germans and Jews of Romania after around 1959). Once the process has begun, it tends to accelerate very rapidly.

Partition and secession. Although in certain circumstances, especially where a territory controlled by one ethnic group has a solid majority of another ethnic group, partition might be a useful way of dealing with the problem, the internatioal order is deeply antagonistic to it. Secession and integration with another state, furthermore, creates problems of integration for the newly enlarged state. The state-generated identity discussed above does not disappear overnight, indeed it persists for generations to make the rationalisation of the new state that much more difficult. Awareness of this may to some extent inhibit secession. The reunification of the two German states is the clearest illustration of this proposition; an East German identity will last for many years and that fact will continue to affect German politics in ways not expected by West Germans. This factor is evidently relevant to the Albanians of Kosovo and Macedonia. Their political identities and experiences have been conditioned by Yugoslavia and by Serbia and Macedonia respectively; unification with Albania itself would pose as many questions as it would solve. Much the same applies to the Hungarians of Serbia and Romania. In all probability, attempts to integrate the Republika Srpska into rump-Yugoslavia would run into analogous difficulties. These already exist with respect to Montenegro. The only case for frontier changes is frontier rectification, where a small area is transferred to another state, but the symbolic cost of even this would be so high that it is unthinkable; besides, it would not solve anything major.

The other objections to secession have already been mentioned in the above, with one exception. It is impossible to draw genuinely clear ethnic dividing lines. There will always be minorities left on either side of a new boundary. Even in the Croatian-Hungarian case noted above, there are small minorities from both groups on the 'wrong' side of the frontier. This raises the issue of the minority within the minority. Communities of this kind tend to be highly conscious of their marginal status and to be particularly acutely aware of their endangered status, so often they will resist change with especial ferocity. The Serbs of Kosovo are a good illustration. Overall, secession and partition do not appear to be very successful means of solving ethnic minority tensions, unless inter-ethnic relations are so acutely tense that it becomes last resort.

Assimilation and integration. The distinction is that integration means two groups living side by side, each retaining its ethnic identity but sharing a set of political foci and state-generated symbols, whereas assimilation implies that one group abandons its ethnicity entirely and accepts the identity of the other. Occasionally assimilation involved both groups abandoning some of their ethnicity and merging them in a higher identity, like 'Soviet' or 'Yugoslav' but these do not appear to be on the table in South-Eastern Europe today.

Classical assimilation which flourished at a particular moment of history is now very largely a matter of the past. Essentially those who assimilated did so under two distinct conditions: they had to undertake a journey, usually migrating from the country to the city, but sometimes overseas; and they abandoned peasant status in exchange for that of urban worker, implying a better, more secure standard of living. During the course of these two concurrent processes, many individuals were ready to give up their ethnic identities, which they saw as a part of their peasant status, for a new ethnicity, which they associated with getting on in the world. The key here was the trade off. Assimilation signified a major social, cultural and moral transformation. Furthermore, the assimilating group had to make the terms of assimilation reasonably open. It helped if there was no serious religious boundary between the two groups (Protestant Slovaks could become Protestant Hungarians, but it was much more problematical for Orthodox Romanians to become Catholic Hungarians). The same applies with even greater force to a perceived racial distinction, as in the case of the Roma. But this assimilation process is exhausted because the traditional peasantry is no more; there is virtually no one left to be assimilated. Individuals, not least the children of ethnically mixed marriages, might assimilate, but collectivities as a whole will not.

The policy implication of the end of assimilation is that assimilatory policies are futile and counterproductive. They will irritate the minority without having much effect. Nor will they attain their other, covert aim, that of blocking the emergence of an ethnic minority intellectual stratum and thereby impede the group's cultural reproduction. It may make it harder, but the group will still continue to exist. The decapitation of the Hungarian minority in Slovakia after 1945, mostly through a partial population expulsion and exchange, illustrates this argument. The Hungarians evolved a new intellectual stratum, one as determined as ever to maintain its Hungarianness.

In South-Eastern Europe, given religion as the threshold, assimilation was always a difficult matter. It is very hard to see how a nominally Muslim Albanian could ever become a Serb or a Macedonian and actually be accepted as such. Much the same applies to Hungarians in Romania. The Muslims of Bosnia, many of whom did accept either a Serbian or Croation identity have found that their identity of origin was never fully forgotten; the fate of the urbanised Serbs of Croatia was analogous. On the other hand, the so-called 'Slavophone Hellenes', the ethnic Macedonians of northern Greece can and do assimilate, because they share religion, and there is only a linguistic threshold to cross. But despite enormous pressure on them by the Greek state to declare themselves Greek and to stop speaking their language (the existence of which is denied), it persists. In effect, linguistic and other forms of assimilation no longer take place and states would save themselves a good deal of trouble if they could bring themselves to recognise this.

Hegemonic control. This is, for all practical purposes, the standard model. One ethnic group, as a rule the largest, gains control of the state and uses the machinery of the modern state to dominate all other ethnic communities. This is so common that it hardly needs further analysis. Its essence is to make a challenge to the power of the ethnic majority unthinkable; exclusive control of the coercive apparatus, the symbols of status, power and rewards, some cooperation of minority elites and the construction of a mind-set in which domination is accepted as the norm are needed to sustain a regime of this kind. It is not quite incompatible with democracy (e.g. France under the Third Republic). It just depends on the level of coercion employed. What needs to be said here, however, is that patterns of domination vary, that some ethnic majorities will allow more space than others and that these can go through change in time as well. In these conditions, minority strategies will also vary, but in almost all cases they will be aimed at persistence, survival and endurance.

Further, the success of hegemonic control will also depend on the level of consciousness, sophistication, literacy, social knowledge, aspiration and political skill of the minority. Where the majority is successful in keeping these in check, its ability to exercise control will be that much higher (the relationship between the Bulgarian majority and the Turkish minority exemplifies this situation). But in all probability this is likely to be a declining asset. As social capital expands, it becomes ever harder to deny it to a minority without denying it to the majority as well. An example is Information Technology: it is possible, say, to keep access to the Internet out of the hands of the minority but that will almost certainly mean that the majority will be prevented from enjoying it too.

In *arbitration*, a neutral third party is accepted as an intermediary by both ethnic groups. McGarry and O'Leary use this category more restrictively than seems useful; in this analysis, it will be employed to cover a range of neutral, third party interventions, both domestic and international. The essence of arbitration is that both sides to a dispute conclude that they should find a way out and that they are prepared to subordinate their power, authority and aspiration to an outsider. This demands a fairly high degree of trust and willingness to avoid degeneration into conflict. Arbitration can be exercised by mediators on an *ad hoc* basis (Holbrooke's shuttle diplomacy) or on a more permanent basis, like the work of the High Commission on National Minorities (as in Macedonia). An alternative arrangement arises when ethnic groups accept that a constitutional court has sufficient independence from the ethicised political machinery of the state to enable a minority to live with its decisions.

This definition more or less clarifies the advantages and disadvantages of arbitration. Both sides have to have some degree of commitment to preventing the conflict from becoming worse. In South-Eastern Europe, arbitration can be helpful as one particular instrument of conflict management, but it has to be deployed with others if it is to be effective.

Territorial arrangements. Federal and cantonal. Some of the drawbacks of territorial arrangements have already been sketched, but it is worth stressing again here that in the present climate of mistrust in South-Eastern Europe, any attempt to institute a solution along these lines would encounter only rejection and would exacerbate rather than improve the situation. As a matter of fact, ethnic federations tend not too work too well, because they generate aspiratons for autonomy that cannot be fulfilled, together with distrust based on fear of secession. In practice, federal solutions work well for mono-ethnic states with regional differences, like Germany and Australia.

The final category is *power-sharing* or consociationalism. When territorial arrangements are impossible, either because relations are too polarised or because the ethnic groups in question are too large, then a non-territorial bi- or multinational solution is the only option on the assumption that the state intends to resolve its problems in the framework of democratic stability. This, in essence, is consociationalism or power-sharing, a system in which all the ethnic groups have certain entrenched powers and practices (elite accommodation, proportionality, minority veto, access to state power in both real and symbolic terms).

Power-sharing is an extremely difficult trick to pull off. It can be done though, but it demands positive antecedents and a good deal of political skill, not least the ability of all politicians to convince their electorates that power-sharing is the least bad option, that separation would be worse (e.g. lead to civil war). The central feature of power-sharing is that each and every group must be able to practice self-limitation and see beyond its own aspirations to those of the others. Possibly, it helps if the power-sharing habits are established before the full coming of modernity – certainly the successful Western cases all share this feature (Switzerland, the Netherlands, Belgium, Finland, Austria).

In the post-communist world the dice appear to be loaded against consociationalism. The legacy of the communist and pre-communist past, weakness of identification with the state or even more vitally, suspicion on the part of the strongest group that other groups are not committed to the state, plus the ideological mind-set and the propensity to see conflict rather than compromise as the norm all militate against power-sharing. Having said this, it is hard to see any other solution working in the long term, given that all the ethnic groups are determined to have their share of power as the guarantee of cultural survival and reproduction. Macedonia, Romania, Serbia (with respect to Kosovo) and, of course, Bosnia (if it survives) are obvious candidates with poor prospects.

Broadly, there are no easy answers to the problem of inter-ethnic relations in South-Eastern Europe. The difficulty of the answers lies not only in their complexity and variety, but also in certain

Western attitudes which are impatient of the time needed and crucially of the alienness of South-Eastern Europe. There is an underlying, tacit assumption that the post-communist world can be assimilated to Western norms in a very short space of time. After all, the protagonists of the approach would have us believe, these states have adopted Western-style political systems and held elections, so why on earth are they not Western, like normal people? They are not because they are not.

Over time they can come to resemble Western political systems – after all, this has happened with other former non-democratic states – but they must be given the support, not just material support (the easy solution) but political, intellectual and cultural support (more difficult). In this connection, the short-termism of the West is a serious obstacle. It takes a major crisis for the West to wake up to the need for action and early action would have prevented degeneration into crisis (Bosnia is a classic example).

On the other hand, Western pressure on the states of South-Eastern Europe is essential to prevent ethnic tension from boiling over. These states are indeed open to Western influence, and identity politics, for all that it is driven by emotions and other imperatives not open to bargaining and compromise, is seldom absolutely intractable. Few states will risk total isolation. The fate of Serbia in this connection is an awful warning.

At the end of the day, just as majority-minority relations should be seen holistically, as part of a single set of processes (despite the temptation to treat them in isolation from one another), so the relationship between the West and South-Eastern Europe is a reciprocal one, even when states appear to be utterly recalcitrant. Transformation into Western-style, especially Anglo-Saxon democracy is probably not feasible, but better treatment for minorities, meaning improved stability, is, though it will take time. Solutions do exist and they can be introduced into the political tool-kit of the region. They will not work automatically, but will require regular maintenance. The question is, to continue this metaphor, whether or not the West is willing to offer the necessary after-sales service. If not, breakdowns and worse are to be expected. And then the West will again have to provide a repair service.

20

MINORITIES AND POST-COMMUNISM
A POLITICAL AND SOCIOLOGICAL ANALYSIS

The problem of nationhood, nationalism and ethnic minorities in the post-communist world has emerged with an unexpected and unpredicted virulence. Western policy, while not wholly paralysed, is permeated by a sense of helplessness about the seemingly infinite complexity and violence engendered by these issues which as far as the West is concerned, had been regarded as long dead and buried. In a very real sense, the era that was thought to have closed with the Paris Peace Settlement of 1918-20 has resurfaced and the solutions devised then have come under renewed scrutiny.

Furthermore, the entire communist experience has marked Central and Eastern Europe in a very different way from the experience of Western Europe. In the West, the ethnic question returned to the political agenda in the 1960s in a relatively muffled form, having at various times beforehand been successfully or unsuccessfully repressed or coopted by processes of nation-state building. In the post-1945 order, Western democracies were able to absorb these old-new pressures into the democratic process, albeit with some manifest failures like Northern Ireland. This was not replicated and, indeed, could not be in Central and Eastern Europe. The heart of the difference between the two halves of Europe is the contrasting approaches to citizenship. Whereas in the West citizenship has been defined in such a way as to allow ethnic pressures some play within the political system and offer them a degree of representation in the system, the newly emerging democratic systems in Central and Eastern Europe have yet to construct a sufficiently sound institutional basis to make a parallel definition of citizenship feasible.

Because of the far-reaching destruction of social and institutional frameworks under communism, public identities are frequently defined by ethno-national criteria regardless of whether this is appropriate to the situation or not. Thus, by way of example, economic issues should be resolved by applying the criteria relevant to economics; there is a definite propensity under post-communism, however, to define all questions by ethnic criteria. Time and again, ethno-nationalists are able to use economic issues like poverty or backwardness as a way of mobilising support by using discourses like "we are poor because aliens or foreigners have conspired against us", rather than giving economic problems explanations rooted in economics. The consequence is a confusion of agendas, one with very dangerous results, because the true function of ethnicity – one of its functions at any rate – is to make provision for the collective acting out of the affective elements that exist within every society.

The proposition being offered in this analysis, therefore, is that while ethnicity is an authentic experience with genuine and legitimate functions in defining identity and expressing the underlying moral codes that have a strong constitutive role in the make-up of every community, ethnicity is worse than useless when it comes to matters properly in the civic dimension of nationhood. The civic dimension comprises the rules and regulations that govern the everyday relationship between rulers and ruled and the institutional framework through which these transactions are enacted – matters of representation, taxation, the institutions that mediate between government and society, the codes of conduct that ensure that all are treated as equal before the law.

These matters are properly settled by reference to reason and rational discourse. Ethnicity by contrast appeals directly to the emotions. When questions that belong to the civic dimension are transferred illicitly into the realm of ethnicity, the emotionality of ethnicity pushes reason into the background and matters are decided by passion rather than reason. And, as cannot be reiterated too often, strong emotions exclude reason.

These propositions have acquired a special urgency in the case of the post-communist countries of Central and Eastern Europe because, as already suggested, communism destroyed the nascent civil societies that were coming into being before and after the Second World War. The attempts to construct alternatives to communist party rule and the develop social autonomies, like Solidarity in Poland, were structured by the conflict with the totalising ideology and power of the communist system and, as happens so frequently, ended up by adopting some of features of the communist system, above all in the emphasis on homogeneity and moralising.

The political functions of nationhood and nationalist ideologies in the region are in any case different from those in the West. While in the West, as a broad pattern of development, citizenship evolved in the eighteenth century before modern nationalism or grew in tandem with it and, equally, the gap between the cultural and political units was not excessively wide, east of the Elbe, however, political power and culture were severely divided.

During the nineteenth century, various sub-elites battled with ruling empires to construct their own states in the name of nations that had yet to be mobilised, so that these sub-elites were forced to rely on the one political resource that they had at their disposal – ethnicity. This historical background helps to explain the strongly ethnic character of nationhood and of state legitimation in the region. The subordination of Central and Eastern Europe to communism exacerbated the situation, because the nations of the area by and large came to perceive communism as a new alien overlordship and opposition to communist rule was increasingly vested in nationhood. In the circumstances, it was very difficult for any civic dimension of nationhood to emerge. Consequently, these states have emerged into post-communism singularly unprepared for democracy.

Indeed, it could be said that the correspondence between communism and the needs of democracy could scarcely be less appropriate. Communism eliminated all possible civic institutions and codes of conduct, it turned these societies into civic deserts where the micro-level patterns of behaviour were governed by mistrust and characterised by atomisation. It was hardly unexpected, therefore, that ethno-nationalism should have acquired the saliency that it did; there was no other identity in the public sphere that could have played this role. Some communist regimes themselves contributed to this development by their use of nationalism (Ceauşescu in Romania).

Democratic forms, nationalist content

As a result, the democratic discourse and institutions adopted by these post-communist states to some extent remained empty forms or were filled by other, non-democratic content. A crucial aspect of this was the problem of representation. An ideal democratic government acts as the legatee of all its citizens and seeks to act in such a way as to meet the aspirations of the majority. The post-communist governments, on the other hand, have a different approach to the question of representation. Either explicitly or implicitly, they tend to regard representation as something based on ethnicity and therefore to deny it wholly or in part to non-members of the ethnic majority. Broadly speaking, post-communist governments take the view that they do not represent citizens, but the nation. Various consequences flow from this, mostly to do with the downgrading of the civic dimension of nationhood and the intensification of ethnicity, including in areas where ethnicity serves only to import a strong emotional element into public discourse and policy formation. Several of the post-communist constitutions (Slovak, for example) are quite explicit in linking ethnicity and citizenship, to the advantage of the majority, thereby putting a question-mark over the benefits of citizenship and the chances of identification as far as the minority is concerned.

The Slovak case study

The Slovak experience in fact illustrates a number of these processes very clearly. Despite Slovak and Czech being mutually comprehensible and a historical tradition of borrowing from Czech culture, the Slovaks preferred to define their modern, nineteenth-century identity as something different from that of the Czechs. The experience of the interwar period, when they were defined as 'Czechoslovaks', members of the same nation as the Czechs though speaking their own language, tended to reinforce this sense of being dominated by their politically more powerful and culturally stronger neighbour. Indeed, there is a sense in which Slovaks tended to define that experience as akin to colonial domination. The Czechs might retort that without their incorporation in Czechoslovakia, the Slovaks would very probably have been assimilated by the Hungarians – the Slovak-inhabited areas had been a part of Hungary until 1918 and very substantial numbers of Slovaks had become ethnically Magyar – but this did not impede a generation of Slovak intellectuals from claiming that their status in the first republic had been subordinated to Czech agendas. Under communism, there was strong opposition to 'Prague centralism' and the post-1968 dispensation gave the Slovaks a separate status and access to development funds which resulted in the rapid industrialisation of Slovakia.

After the 'velvet revolution', both Czechs and Slovaks were committed to looking for a solution to the problems that had beset the relationship, but a workable compromise eluded both parties. The Slovaks sought a far-reaching autonomy, including a recognition of their 'sovereignty' and repeatedly used their blocking veto in the Czechoslovak federal assembly to achieve this. The 1992 elections were largely fought on the issue of the future of the relationship between the two nations. Unexpectedly, the new Czech leadership decided that it would no longer accept the anomalies of the *status quo* and offered the Slovak a restricted choice – either federation, with Slovak institutions subordinated to Prague, or independence. As a result, the Slovaks found themselves with an independence that they did not particularly desire and for which they were woefully unprepared.

The new Slovak state found itself faced with a series of dilemmas. It was economically weak, it was politically inexperienced, it was short of competent administrators and it was led by Vladimir Mečiar, a prototypical ethnic entrepreneur, who was prepared to use every ethnic trick to maintain himself in power. The particular ethnic agendas of the Slovaks, the lines along which ethnic mobilisation could readily take place, were self-definition against the Czechs as oppressors, and against the Hungarians who were seen as having humiliated the Slovaks historically and, to make matters worse, a minority of whom continued to inhabit the southern strip of the country, in the areas bordering Hungary.

Indeed the dream of an ethnically pure Slovakia remained just that because around a fifth of the population of the new state was made of non-Slovaks: Hungarians, Roma, Ruthenes. Slovak nationalists resolutely set their face against this fact and sought to promote the ideal of an ethnically pure Slovakia. It was this dynamic that underlay the constant friction with the Hungarian minority, over bilingual road signs, for example, which the Slovaks, using the administrative machinery of state sought to block at every turn and which brought Slovakia into conflict with the Council of Europe, a body taking an increasingly active role in the protection of ethnic minority standards. Slovak self-definitions were complicated by a realisation that Slovak culture was a late-comer in Central Europe, that it was relatively anaemic by comparison with either Czech or Hungarian. A large part of the

Slovak population was first generation off the land and politically and culturally very inexperienced and thus prey to every demagogic device, so that concepts of ethnic tolerance and compromise were difficult to sell to a sociologically insecure population that looked for instant solutions. Friction with non-Slovaks was inevitable, as the newly promoted Slovak intelligentsia looked towards homogenising solutions. Mečiar and his party, the HZDS, as well as the Slovak National Party, were in the forefront of depicting the Hungarians as a threat to the integrity of Slovak territory and using allusive language to imply that Slovakia's economic, political, and social problems were somehow to be attributed to the minority. This line of rhetoric appealed especially to those sections of the Slovak majority which were materially threatened by the transformation, namely the new urban strata in recently industrialised centres like Martín, Žilina or Banská Bystrica.

Minority strategies

Taking the Slovak case as a paradigmatic illustration, this means that ethnic minorities in similar situations tend to be either entirely or largely excluded from the symbolic and affective constitutions of the state and to live in the state concerned in a situation of grudging toleration, in many respects as second class citizens, even though all the civic duties (taxation, military service etc.) that are exacted from other citizens fall on them equally. In these circumstances, it can easily be imagined that over time ethnic minorities grow disenchanted with the state of which they are citizens, but of which they do not feel that they can be citizens in the same way as members of the majority can. The Russian minority in Latvia, for example, is classic case of this kind, where even access to citizenship has been very difficult.

The self-definition of majorities and minorities and the identities derived from these experiences will differ in a variety of ways and the stability of a political community will depend on the extent to which the gap between the two can be bridged. In broad terms, national majorities will tend to regard their state as exclusively theirs especially in the symbolic-affective areas. They will accept that non-members of their ethnic community may live on state territory, but even when practice is very tolerant, they will be inclined to patronise the minority, regard their demands as in a way a deviation from the norm and insist that the majority's way of doing things is 'natural'. Multiculturalism is not a proposition that most members of an ethnic majority will accept automatically and even where the majority has come to terms with the presence of a minority and sees itself as ready to share in some aspects of minority culture, there will be little attempt to understand the minority culture and minority concerns in their entirety.

The problem of autonomy

The question of autonomy has repeatedly surfaced and resurfaced in this connection. It has to be said that its impact has been overwhelmingly negative on majority-minority relations. Autonomy can be defined as operating at three levels, personal, cultural and territorial. All three have political, cultural, legal, administrative and other related implications. Personal autonomuy suggests that the individual should be free to define his or her own ethnic identity and that the state should recognise this and use the machinery of the state in such a way as to avoid discrimination on ethnic grounds. This is broadly the state of affairs in several West European countries. There are no particular privileges or special provisions that flow from personal autonomy, but where a flourishing private sector operates, it allows individuals to run their affairs and use their money to organise schools, churches, clubs, newspapers, political parties and the like for the maintenance and defence of ethnic activities. Personal autonomy does not imply that the ethnic group as whole is recognised as having a collective identity with repercussions for the political system as a whole.

Cultural autonomy is more complex. It does involve a structured relationship between the majority and the minority and the explicit recognition by the majority that the ethnic minority has a separate legal and political persona. The precise ordering of this can vary considerably, but some kind of a recognised collective identity for the minority is a *sine qua non* of cultural autonomy. One of its central implications is that members of the minority, by virtue of that membership, can share in the tax benefits of the state, that their citizenship is understood as defined by loyalty to the state and to the ethnic community and that there is no contradiction between the two. In cases of this kind, the state will make provision for schooling in the minority language, it will allow bilingual administration where this is appropriate and it will take care to ensure that members of the minority suffer no discrimination by virtue of their ethnicity. Cultural autonomy can be interpreted to mean that members of the minority will benefit from these provisions throughout the territory of the state, so that wherever members of the minority live, they will be entitled to education in their language if they so choose. In practice, of course, this is in an ideal-typical situation and, quite apart from the expense, is often unrealistic. Furthermore, in a variety of situations, cultural autonomy will come to overlap with territorial autonomy.

Territorial autonomy takes the argument a stage further. It designates particular areas where an ethnic minority is concentrated and declares that in these districts, the minority has the right to pursue its strategies as it chooses. This state of affairs can involve the creation of a local assembly, possibly even a presumption of minority monolingualism, all of which will be supported out of state funds on exactly the same terms as provision for the majority. The Statute of Autonomy enjoyed by Catalonia comes close to this, as does the minority provision for Swedes in the very special case of the Åland Islands, where members of the ethnic majority (Finns) are forbidden to settle. The Swiss system of three-tiered government – the commune, the canton and the federation – solves the problem in another way. Almost all Swiss communes are monolingual, as are most cantons, but the state as a whole recognises three official languages (German, French and Italian) and special provision is made for Romansch.

In the post-communist world, on the other hand, autonomy is universally interpreted by majorities as a covert demand for secession. The proposition that a particular area should enjoy special status is anathema to members of ethnic majorities, who reject minority claims as an attack on the integrity of the state. In part, this is attributable to political inexperience and in part to the crudity of post-communist political thinking, the legacy of atomisation and the propensity to see all political contests in zero-sum terms. In essence, the word autonomy is automatically understood as a claim to territory and the distinctions made above are dismissed as sophistry. This is explicable in the context of post-communism with its excessive but inevitable overemphasis on ethnicity as the sole road to political, social, and cultural salvation, the confusion of ethnic and civic agendas, the propensity to understand the world as a series of conspiracies and the deep distrust of diversity.

Diversity and weakness of cognitive instruments to deal with it may be regarded as the core of the explanation for the difficulties caused by ethnicity in the post-communist world. Communism was a singularly poor apprenticeship for democratic compromise and tolerance, because it emphasised homogeneity, black-and-white thinking and the kind of epistemological certainty that insisted that in each moment of choice there could be only one answer. The relativisation of values, the reflexivity of modern life (the process whereby group identity is continuously restructured by the information that a community receives about itself), the continuous construction and reconstruction of identities that are an established feature of Western life remain very alien to the post-communist mind-set.

Territorial and migrant minorities

A distinction should be made here between long-settled minority communities with a well established area of habitation, especially those that have lived in a particular area since before the coming of modern nationalist mobilisation, and minorities arising from relatively recent migration. The latter will generally encounter a variety of obstacles to integration, but it will not be regarded by the majority as a threat to the integrity of the state. Long-settled minorities associated with a particular territory, on the other hand, will generally be the object of some suspicion in the eyes of the majority, for fear that the link between the minority and the territory will result in the dismemberment of the state.

This is evidently a key feature of majority attitudes in the broad area of nationhood. Closely linked to this is the reluctance to perceive minority demands as justifiable. In well established democracies, these demands may be granted, but the majority will tend to see such concessions as derogations from a self-affirming norm. Where the majority–minority relationship is less effectively regulated by citizenship, there will be a strong tendency towards the ethnicisation of the state. The state will be run overwhelmingly in the name of and for the benefit of the majority, citizenship and ethnicity will be conflated and the minority will be excluded from the rights, though not the duties, of the former.

Minority attitudes start from the basic proposition that a minority is in a position of weakness in the face of the majority which is seen as controlling the state. Consequently, the energies of the minority will be aimed at redressing this perceived imbalance. Given that the ground rules are essentially in the hands of the majority, minority politics will tend to consist of continuous adjustment to majority initiatives unless the *modus vivendi* between the two parties allows the minority a good deal of autonomy.

Where the constitution of the state and its politics is reasonably open-minded, transactions between the two can take place in the civic dimension, thereby reducing the role of ethnicity in the relationship. In such cases, minority self-definitions can be partially depoliticised and the relationship between the two sides become moderately relaxed. Both parties, however, must understand the written and unwritten ground rules of such an arrangement. There will be invisible boundaries that neither side should cross and both will have to exercise considerable self-limitation. In the process, the minority will have to abandon certain aspirations, like full self-government and statehood, in the name of compromise and stability. The majority, for its part, will have to recognise that by incorporating the minority, it must deny itself the complete fulfilment of its particular aspirations concerning the particular territory it controls. The alternative is the ethnicisation of the state, which has far-reaching negative effects on both, notably mutual fear and suspicion and the threat of constant friction. Minorities in ethnicised states will, in general, lose out on both the swings and the roundabouts.

Members of such minorities will be denied access to the highest positions in politics, the armed forces, diplomacy, administration and so on, and they will probably not receive their due of the symbolic and material goods of the state. They might well conclude that the state has been ethnicised by the majority and that as a result they are permanently excluded from the benefits of citizenship. This was quite evidently what happened between the Albanians of Kosovo and the Serbian majority after Milošević's rise to power. The Albanians concluded that the Serbian state excluded them from both the symbolic and the material benefits of statehood and they began to devise alternative strategies.

The exacerbation of conflict

Under post-communism, there are a number of exacerbating factors operating. One of these it what might termed the 'conflictogenic' or conflict-generating nature of post-communist politics. Given the legacy of communism and the absence of trust, individuals will start out from a position that others, whether in the political realm or not, are potential antagonists and that only a frontal assault on their opponents can safeguard whatever interests are at issue. If both parties to a contest start from this base line, then the underlying set of shared assumptions that make compromise possible will be absent and conflict will inevitably be the outcome.

Such conflict will then in turn legitimate each of the antagonists, who in a polarised situation will find that their antagonist is essential to give them the status and power that they seek. The difficulty with a state of affairs of this kind is that it promotes zero-sum games, black-and-white value systems, in which minorities are almost bound to be the losers because, by virtue of being in minority, they will lack the power to validate their interests.

Once the disenchantment on the part of a minority has begun, however, the majority will see this as confirmation of their suspicions, namely that the loyalty of the minorities was always suspect, that their commitment to the state was conditional and that, in reality, the minority constituted a fifth column, a danger to the integrity of the state, because their true loyalties were elsewhere. This attitude is reinforced when co-nationals of the minority live in close proximity, like across the border. This, of course, is a classic example of a self-fulfilling prophecy. The majority treats the minority as a danger to the state and, by reason of their being so treated, the minority gradually turns into that danger through processes of polarisation and exclusion.

At the centre of the majority's fears is loss of territory. The modern European state is uniquely unable to come to terms with the idea that it might lose territory, although in pre-modern times this was a widespread experience. Loss of territory was not a welcome experience, but it had not acquired the near-catastrophic quality that it has today. The change is centrally to do with the rise of the modern nation-state which has sacralised territory into 'national territory', something that cannot be lost under any circumstances.

The Hungarians of Slovakia

The issue of territory is complicated by ethnicity, but it is not a purely ethnic issue. An ethnic majority which for some reason has come to rule over territory inhabited by members of another ethnic group will automatically include that territory into their concept of the national territory and ignore, if not indeed resent the presence of an ethnically alien minority there. Southern Slovakia illustrates this perfectly. The frontier between Slovakia and Hungary was drawn in 1920 along the Danube by strategic criteria, not ethnic ones. The ethnic frontier ran well to the north of the state frontier, leaving a sizeable number of Hungarians in Slovakia. Nevertheless, for Slovaks, the Danube frontier was rapidly sacralised into 'national territory' and the presence of the Hungarians there was regarded as a source of both symbolic and power-political risk.

Some added data should be noted here. In 1918, the then Slovak leadership offered Budapest a Slovak-Hungarian frontier that followed more or less closely the ethnic frontier, but this was discarded in favour of a strategic frontier with access to the Danube, incorporation of east-west railway lines and annexation of a series of towns with a Hungarian majority on economic gounds. In consequence large numbers of Hungarians found themselves on the wrong side of the state frontier. After the Munich agreement in 1938, under the First Vienna Arbitration, the ethnically Hungarian areas were reincorporated into the Hungarian state, but these were returned to Czechoslovakia at the end the Second World War. Today, this strip of southern Slovakia has a slight Slovak majority, roughly in the proportion of 8:7 making its reincorporation into Hungary an impossibility, quite apart from the political, economic and cultural burden that such a reincorporation would pose. This implies that hotheads apart, there is no serious interest in Hungary in changing the frontier between the two states, but it is very difficult to convince Slovak nationalists of this, given their assumptions about the nature of states and nations.

What is especially ironical about this difficult and aggressive relationship between majority and minority is that the suspicions of the majority are almost invariably unfounded. A key distinction in this context is that between integration and assimilation. Integration refers to the acceptance of the dominant political codes and procedures of a state; assimilation is the internalisation of all cultural norms and the acceptance of assimilands by the assimilating majority as fully equal in all respects.

Majorities underestimate the integrative capacity of the modern state and, because they define their own identity so strongly if not indeed completely by ethnic criteria, they cannot and will not understand that a minority that has lived in a particular state for a period of time will acquire some of the civic and, for that matter, political habits of that state. One of the most striking aspects of the experience of the twentieth century and the modern state is that even where members of an ethnic group are subjected to serious discrimination, they will only turn against that state in quite exceptional circumstances.

Here again the experience of the Hungarians of Slovakia is instructive. Almost all of the ethnic Hungarian-inhabited territory attached to Czechoslovakia in 1920 was returned to Hungary by the First Vienna Arbitration of 1938. These ethnic Hungarians were less than overjoyed by their reintegration into the Hungarian state and would have preferred some aspects of the Czechoslovak system to be retained. The Czechoslovak identity of these Hungarians was, of course, strengthened by their reattachment to Czechoslovakia after 1945 and, despite very severe discrimination between 1945 and 1948, at no time did they consider reintegration into Hungary a desirable option; they wished to remain in Czechoslovakia. The consequences of the end of the Czechoslovak state may, however, modify this, overwhelmingly because the new Slovak state has given the ethnic Hungarians little incentive to identify with Slovakia.

This implies, logically, that when a state has suddenly disappeared, the civic identities that it has inspired and generated will likewise vanish. This process results in a gap, a quest for identification with the new state to which they are now attached and a new set of civic meanings. Unless the state in question recognises this gap and offers the ethnic group in question a measure of affective identification, the minority will look to fill the gap by ethnicity. It will look to the moral and cultural values of the ethnic community to provide meanings in a moment of crisis and disorientation. Processes of this kind could be seen in Yugoslavia, Czechoslovakia and the Soviet Union.

For the most part, minorities prefer that the political formulae – the constructive characteristics of the state – are interpreted in a broad rather than a narrow fashion, so that they can be included in it. Their loyalty to the state in question is generally so high that it will outweigh ethnic considerations, unless they are directly excluded and/or possibly subjected to genocide. They have learned a particular way of dealing with the state authorities, in handling matters of administration and all the myriad issues that arise in a modern state.

This is very different from the relationship between the subjects of pre-modern state, whose contacts with the state were few and generally negative. As far as the pre-modern peasantry of Central and Eastern Europe was concerned, these contacts were essentially restricted to paying taxes, being conscripted into the armed forces and being treated badly by the gendarmerie. In a modern state, the contacts between the individual and the state are multiplied a thousandfold. For what it was worth, contact between the individual and the communist state were particularly intense, simply because of its totalising nature the communist state sought to impinge on every aspect of life. Not surprisingly, the relationship between the two grew in density, so members of the same ethnic group living in different states have fewer points of contact than they generally realise. By way of example, Hungarians from Rumania are foreigners in Hungary and citizens of the Hungarian state are increasingly regarding them as such.

The failure of assimilation

But if the modern state has scored a singular success in the area of integration, it has done badly in the area of assimilation. Indeed, as a general rule, it can be proposed that once an ethnic group has acquired a certain cultural consciousness of itself as a separate group, it will be all but impossible for the state (controlled by the majority) to eliminate that cultural consciousness and to transform their ethnicity.

The assimilation of individuals is certainly feasible, but entire communities have proved extraordinarily resilient in the face of assimilatory attempts by modern states and even where cultural reproduction is made all but impossible – by obstacles placed in the way of a minority to develop its own intellectual stratum for instance – assimilation does not follow. And where individuals assimilate, the possibility that their descendants may dissimilate cannot be excluded. Linguistic assimilation is generally regarded by nationalists in Central and Eastern Europe as the most effective way of ensuring that a minority should disappear. It should be noted, however, that this is not an automatic guarantee of success. The language may then be restricted to household use or even die out over time, but consciousness of a previous ethnicity will seldom disappear completely.

The failure of assimilation is, as a rule, badly taken by majority nationalists, who then may attempt to quicken the pace by further repression, indeed by the elimination of all minority institutions, notably those related to education and culture. It is noteworthy that even under the full repressive apparatus of the totalising communist state, as in Romania vis-à-vis the Hungarian minority, which succeeded in ensuring that a sizeable section of the intellectual stratum of the minority emigrated in the 1980s, the reproduction of the minority has persisted.

There have been cases, however, where minorities – having lost the demographic game to a majority – do appear to have given up and to have accepted that there was no future for them. The Germans of Romania and the Serbs of Kosovo fall into this category, even if the Serbian state has tried very hard to prevent this. In both these cases, however, the key factor seems to have been the existence of a potential country to which migration was possible (Germany and Serbia respectively) and, it seems to be the case that once a minority concludes that it cannot sustain itself demographically in the face of the majority, it will abandon what is, after all, invariably a struggle and leaves.

Much of the above analysis would point to the desirability of majorities treating their minorities as citizens rather than as subjects belonging to another ethnic group and thus to be regarded as inferior. But there is a further cluster of factors indicating the advisability of such a policy. These are concerned with domestic and international stability. It is self-evident that a contented minority, one that feels that it has a stake in the state in which it lives, will be far less likely to pursue policies or survival strategies at variance with the interests of the majority. Indeed, stability based on ethnic compromise will undoubtedly strengthen a state rather than weaken it. This is a proposition that most nationalists, who approach the problem from the perspective of identity and the passions associated with identity, are likely to reject, even if the evidence points entirely in the opposite direction. Switzerland is the clearest success story in this context, but others can also be mentioned, notably Finland and the ethno-religious Protestant minority in the Irish republic. In all these cases, the majority made significant concessions and defined citizenship by non-ethnic criteria, to the benefit of all concerned.

The international aspects of the problem parallel this state of affairs. Where an ethnic minority lives across the frontier from a state made up of its co-nations it will be far less likely to be attracted by irredentist policies if it is made to feel that the state in which it lives as a minority gives it equal access to both the material and the symbolic goods of the state. The majority state may keep a watching brief over the fate of its co-nationals, but it will seldom interfere in such circumstances. The Germans of the South Tyrol and Austria or the Swedes of Finland and Sweden illustrate the proposition. Repressive ethnic majorities, on the other hand, have to live in an atmosphere of suspicion that their neighbour is constantly looking for opportunities to weaken it and to use the minority as a Trojan horse. That in turn sets up a vicious circle of repression and suspicion which is very difficult to break. Slovakia and Hungary have been in danger of entering this process, as well as Poland and Lithuania.

Ethnically mixed areas pose particular problems which are at least sub-acute, but can easily become acute, especially if the area is the scene of relatively recent immigration or has been the scene of some other major socio-economic transformation. The super-imposition of an authoritarian system intended to create the semblance of outward order will come to be regarded as counterproductive at the moment of relaxation. In mixed areas, it is important that the cultural boundaries between the two (or more) groups be perceived as clear and secure, so that each ethnic group has a sense of when it is crossing that boundary. Thus the more markers available, the easier boundary maintenance is.

While the socio-economic change is taking place, members of ethnic groups (ethno-national, ethno-religious) evidently need the sense of security associated with group membership, because so many of the codes of morality and behaviour will be under threat from the transformation. Hence a strong sense of some identity will acquire particular significance under conditions of transformation. Members of a group have to know who they are while the adjustment is taking place. This matters less when such a transformation affects pre-modern peasantry rather than semi-modern or fully modern groups, that is those who have already made the symbolic journey from the countryside to the city, who already have a clear consciousness of who they are. As far as the latter are concerned, this consciousness may well be called into question by their arrival in a multi-ethnic context which is at one and the same time different from their previous place of habitation and equally their previous socio-economic status.

The persistence of boundary markers

When, however, two groups each with a separate consciousness but possessing few markers find themselves in proximity and are undergoing socio-economic transformation, there is bound to be trouble. Precisely because the groups are close (e.g. not separated by language) and the assimilation of one group by the other is feasible, they will resent the appearance of advantages enjoyed by the other – for this is a matter of perception – and will look to make up the advantage when the opportunity presents itself. At the same time, the leaders of each group (political, intellectual) will do everything in their power to safeguard the group's identity and to persuade the group that 'the other' is a source of threat – in a word, it will be demonised.

As long as the superimposed order holds, this will not matter, but under the veil of tranquillity, group identities will clash and resentments will accumulate, and even when the resentment is properly directed at the modernising processes of uprooting, disruption and the consequent disorientation of values, it will be ethnicised. Both Northern Ireland and Bosnia-Hercegovina illustrate these processes.

The bloodbath in Bosnia-Hercegovina illustrates perfectly the analysis offered in the foregoing. The boundaries between Serbs, Croats and Muslims are weak and permeable, but are perceived as real. There is no language barrier; there exists a high rate of inter-marriage; there is an urban elite that accepts integration and thereby seems to have betrayed the group by disregarding the boundaries and thereby has deprived the groups of their leaders and allowed the leadership to fall into the hands of marginal men, extremists and ethnic entrepreneurs. The result is that those members of the group, the socio-economically weak or less privileged, for whom boundary maintenance is important, will create their own new and sanguinary ways of achieving this.

However, there are, other, less extreme examples than the tragedy of Bosnia-Hercegovina. Northern Ireland, while extremely unpleasant, does not begin to compare in death and destruction. On the other hand, the relationship between Jews and non-Jews in Hungary offers another illustration of the processes involved.

Culturally there is nothing to differentiate the two groups, yet each group is conscious of its own identity and of the different identity of the other. The characteristics attributed by members of one group to the other are not automatically negative, but they do serve to maintain boundaries in a situation which is politically tranquil.

The Slovaks in the Czech Republic

Another interesting case which might at first sight fall into this category is that of the Slovaks of Czech Republic. In reality, it is marked by other characteristics, as we shall see, and this state of affairs is unlikely to change in the future. Until the separation of the Czech and Slovak Republics, the Slovaks living in the former had no distinctive status – they were simply migrants, often living in the Czech lands for shorter or longer periods, but with their home base in Slovakia. With independence all this changed and the Slovaks of the Czech Republic found themselves in the position of a minority. The evidence to date, however, does not in any way suggest that this has given rise to any serious political difficulties. On the contrary, these Slovaks appear to have opted voluntarily for remaining in the Czech Republic and thereby gradually to abandon their Slovak identity. Certainly, there was little to indicate that they would demand minority rights or establish ethnic parties.

The explanation for this quiescence, for this seeming readiness to abandon their Slovak identity must be sought in historical, cultural-linguistic and material factors. Czech-Slovak coexistence and, indeed, cultural assimilation have a long history, predating the foundation of the Czechoslovak state in 1918. Over the last century many Slovaks have accepted a Czech national identity; T.G. Masaryk was partly Slovak by descent. The proximity of the two languages undoubtedly helped in this process. A Slovak does not have to cross a serious linguistic threshold to become Czech, although the Slovak language has traditionally enjoyed a rather low status in the eyes of Czech speakers. Nor is there a religious boundary to be crossed. Like the Czechs, the Slovaks are mostly Roman Catholic with a minority being Protestant.

The shared civic identities, the habits acquired by having lived in the same state since 1918 are an added factor in this respect. But probably the single most significant explanation for the low level of Slovak self-articulation was that they opted to remain in the Czech Republic voluntarily. There was no territorial issue involved, they understood what they were doing at the time when they took their decision, they knew that they would stand to benefit from that decision by choosing to live in a state with a higher standard of living and with a better chance of early integration into Europe, that they would retain whatever status and achievement they had acquired in career terms and that generally as a life strategy, integration with probable assimilation in a couple of generations into a Czech identity would serve them better than returning to Slovakia.

Viewed through his perspective, the Slovaks of the Czech Republic are a migrant minority and a not a territorial one. This raises one further point of speculation. Are the Slovaks of the Czech Republic likely to follow the dynamic of North American migrants, that after some generations they will seek to rediscover their Slovak roots and attempt to construct a Slovak culture as a subset of Czech culture? This possibility exists, but is likely to happen only if the Czech majority continues to insist on maintaining a distinction against the Slovaks and blocks assimilation, something for which there are no precedents: by and large, once linguistic assimilation was complete, Slovaks were fully accepted by Czechs.

Otherwise, the statistics are against the maintenance of a separate Slovak identity – there are approximately 350,000 Slovaks in a population of 10 million Czechs and many of them are in mixed marriages, implying that their offspring will be Czech. Czech identity is both strongly ethnic and civic, again implying that the fate of the Slovaks in the Czech Republic is likely to be assimilation. It is noteworthy in this connection that for the first time in their history the Czechs are living in an ethnically homogeneous state and the evidence to date, still fragmentary at the time of writing, suggests that the Czechs majority finds it a very agreeable state of affairs now that it has to make no effort to deal with diversity. Hence rather than the North American model, one should probably look at the fate of the descendants of the Polish migrants to France as the likeliest scenario for the Slovaks; they are completely integrated into a French cultural identity and Polishness for them is only a sentimental memory.

Policy issues

Since the collapse of communism the West has put together a series of statements and documents that can be presented as something approximating to a 'European standard' in the treatment of minorities. The Copenhagen Declaration of June 1991 is the most significant of these formulations. A number of issues are noteworthy here. After the First World War, the West initially opted for a complex minority regime, which was supposed to be supervised by the League of Nations. This was widely seen as having failed. After 1945, minority questions simply disappeared from the broad political agenda and European integration through the Common Market mechanism was expected to resolve the ethnic issue. This did not happen, as we have seen, and the consequence has been to force the West to return to a reconsideration of ethnicity and minorities as important policy problems. However, unlike the period of 1918-39 the problem currently tends to be viewed through the perspective of international security rather than collective rights. In particular, there is a more or less explicit proposition that ethnic minority questions cannot be seen as a purely domestic political issue and that where inter-state relations are affected, the international community as a whole has an interest in seeing that they are resolved peacefully.

In policy terms, the question arises whether the West can do very much and if so, what. In this connection, it is important to recognise that the lesson of the Yugoslav crisis is that the West will only intervene militarily over questions of ethnicity and conflicts deriving from disputes over the treatment of minorities in quite exceptional cases. However, in situations before polarisation has begun, Western pressure can be effective and useful. The West can monitor the treatment of minorities by majorities and use political influence to ensure that discrimination is curtailed. The activities of the Council of Europe and the High Commissioner on Minorities of the OSCE are particularly good examples of this. Individual Western governments can likewise offer their services as honest broker when a dispute threatens to get out of hand. It is especially important to understand that preemption is better than cure, that early intervention is likely to be far more effective than a search for *ex post facto* remedies. This implies that the West should maintain a watching brief over potential and actual minority questions and that it should use private and public pressure to this end. Underlying all this is the factor that until the civic dimension in the post-communist world is stronger and deeper, ethnicity will continue to play a far more significant and therefore dangerous role than is the case in the West and that the West has a clear interest in preventing these from coming to a head.

PART V. THE ETHNIC FACTOR RECONSIDERED

21

ENGLISHNESS: CITIZENSHIP, ETHNICITY AND CLASS

Civic nationhood

The distinction between the civic and ethnic dimensions of nationhood is an extremely valuable one. *Inter alia*, it allows one to theorise the variable responses that groups make to different political and cultural experiences; it provides insights into a wide range of closures; it extends the range of analysis into sub-state nationalism and the nature of the difference between the assimilation and integration of ethnic minorities; it illuminates some of the interaction between civil society and ethnicity; and crucially it throws into relief the way in which identities are constructed by the activity of the state and the patterns of shared response to that state by those who live under its rule. Although civic identity is customarily identified with democratic states, in reality all states, regardless of the political ideology and political system, have an analogous impact on their subjects. Indeed, it can be argued that even communism functioned as a pseudo-civic identity, in that it sought to impose a particular, ideologically driven identity on the populations ruled by communists, that of Soviet man.[1] This brought into being a variety of similar responses which are largely, though not precisely, shared by the post-communist states.

Effectively, the concept of civic identity has its pedigree in the theoretical work that argues that the impact of the state on

[1] See pp.176-86.

identity formation was central in the rise of nationhood,[2] an approach that has been criticised as ignoring or underestimating the role, impact and function of ethnicity.[3] In this perspective, it can be viewed as a classic legacy of the Enlightenment and anti-Enlightenment debate. It ties in, further, with the debate on Western and Eastern nationalism. In the work of some scholars, nationhood and nationalism in the West are characterised as civic and democratic, while in the East (wherever that may be – in the non-West), nationalism is nasty and authoritarian.[4] The *locus classicus* of civic nationhood is the French Revolution, which was committed to the liberty, fraternity and equality of all its citizens. The implication of the foregoing is that as well as analysing civic identity in its relationship to democracy with its overtones of civil society, one should also think in terms of a state-driven or 'étatic' identity, which is marked by a variety of characteristics and, crucially in this context, interacts with some of the ethnic imperatives and conserves them to give rise to a somewhat ethnicised citizenship.

In the contemporary world, however, there is a certain subsurface moralising about ethnicity in the West. By and large there is a tacit, sometimes explicit, assumption that democratic states are free of the 'taint' of ethnicity and that the democratic nation treats all its citizens equally, regardless of ethnicity, religion, creed, race, etc. One of the arguments to follow is that things are not quite as true as they might seem at first sight and that civic identities can, indeed, hide quite significant non-civic agendas and identities. Englishness is one of these.

So the civic model *tout court* was always somewhat deficient. It underestimated the impact of the state, particularly of the interventionist modern state, upon the emergence of shared patterns

---

[2] Charles Tilly (ed.), *The Formation of the National State in Western Europe* (Princeton University Press, 1975); Michael Mann, *The Sources of Power: The Rise of Class and Nation-States, 1760-1914* (Cambridge University Press, 1993).

[3] Anthony Smith, *The Ethnic Origins of Nations* (Oxford: Blackwell, 1986).

[4] Hans Kohn, *Nationalism: its meaning and history* (Princeton, NJ: Van Nostrand, 1955) and John Plamentaz, 'Two Types of Nationalism' in Eugene Kamenka (ed.), *Nationalism: the Nature and Evolution of an Idea* (Canberra: Australian National Press, 1973) are prime examples. Leah Greenfield, *Nationalism: Five Roads to Modernity* (Cambridge, MA: Harvard University Press, 1992) is not too far from this position.

of identity. Likewise, it undervalued the role of the dominant ethnic group and hence of ethnicity in states supposedly legitimated by a civic ideology. And by associating it with democracy, indeed coming very close to making it a necessary condition for democracy, those taking this position for all practical purposes made democracy the preserve of a few West European polities, plus the immigrant states of North America and the Southern hemisphere. All this might be thought just a little Anglo-Saxon in its unstated assumptions.

Not only is it Anglo-Saxon, it is also inaccurate in that it mistakes surface appearance for underlying mechanisms. There is, of course, a strong civic identity in the Anglo-Saxon world, but this civic identity is insufficient on its own to explain the nature and workings of political and cultural interactions in these polities. Much the same principle applies to France, although there the relationship between civic and non-civic elements is somewhat differently arranged.[5] Indeed, if one looks carefully at every European democracy, including those universally acknowledged to be 'stable' and 'mature' democracies, an ethnicisation will unquestionably exist, at however deep a level, to provide the cohesiveness that a purely civic identity does not appear able to do. Lest anyone jump to the conclusion from the foregoing that this analysis is about to slide into a paean of praise for ethnicity, let me offer the reassurance that this is not its thrust. Rather, I shall seek to establish the complex and frequently unacknowledged interdependence between the civic and ethnic dimensions and thereby hope to make clearer some of the processes in the exercise of power.

Even when a civic identity presents itself as civic and denies its ethnic content, this is no more than a self-legitimating discourse, probably a reference to a foundation myth, like the French Revolution or the constitution. In reality, whatever the original impulse, these polities have found that a degree of ethnicisation of the civic identity is essential to provide the cohesiveness without which the modern state finds it very hard to survive. The very intrusiveness of the modern state and the demands that it places on its citizens implies that a notional civic contract lacks the capacity to take the strain that this growth of state interventionism brings with it. Then, while ethnicity is undoubtedly vague with respect to

[5] Rogers Brubaker, *Citizenship in Nationhood in France and Germany* (Cambridge, MA: Harvard University Press, 1992); David Miller, *On Nationality* (Oxford University Press, 1995)

any programme that may be derived from it, it does imply that all members of the ethnic community share in it equally. In that sense, a somewhat inchoate theory of equality can be derived from ethnicity, certainly one that reinforces that much more explicit equality in citizenship.

Hence the real political community that constitutes the state inevitably has ethnic as well as civic quality. Crucially, a polity that is founded exclusively on a civic contract cannot avoid the dilemma of consent, of what would happen when some of the citizens withdrew their consent from the state. Some cement stronger than civic loyalty, therefore becomes necessary. The insurance policy is usually, though not invariably, provided by ethnicity.

Despite the claims to universalism derived from Enlightenment rationality, some sense of a shared culture – the bases of ethnicity – were present in the origins of nationalism even in the most civic of polities in Europe (France, England, The Netherlands), so that the civic-ethnic dichotomy is evidently better seen as a spectrum, as a matter of emphasis. If this is accepted, then it follows that civic systems are open ethnicisation, as has in fact happened, as in France.[6]

The key problematic is that citizenship, as defined at the turn of the eighteenth century, required the ending of access to political power by right of birth and opened it to all citizens, to all members of the polity. The undertaking was awesome, because it demanded trust on the part of the rulers that the newly enfranchised citizens would not use their newly acquired power to destroy the representatives of the old regime and that a culturally divergent group would not use its power to flout the rules of citizenship and demand a special, politically privileged status for itself. To that extent, it was crucial that in these civic polities there should already exist a reasonable degree of cultural homogeneity. In France, this was achieved by the revocation of the Edict of Nantes and the extension of the culture of the Ile de France to the remainder of the realm; in England, as I shall argue, a different approach was adopted, which accepted some deviation from the English norm (like a separate legal system for Scotland), but secured the necessary cohesiveness by other means.

[6] Eugen Weber, *Peasants into Frenchmen: the Modernization of Rural France, 1870-1914* (London: Chatto and Windus, 1977)

It should also be noted that the late eighteenth or early nineteenth century state did not need the degree of cultural homogeneity that it required later. The proposition in this context is that as the demands of the state on the citizens intensified, so did the degree of uniformity it imposed. True, the state created some of the uniformity itself, but it had long been recognised that the higher the level of shared culture, the easier governance would be.[7] Those who share a set of cultural values and recognise one another as fellow members of the same solidarities would obviously accept higher duties to each other than with respect to non-member, thereby making it easier to legitimate the exercise of power. This rule obtained then and obtains still.

But none of the foregoing deals overtly with the relationship between the civic and ethnic dimensions of nationhood. The first difficulty was how a culture was to be understood; the second was whether and how this understanding was to change; and the third was to what extent the relationship between the civic and ethnic elements was to be made explicit.

Cultures are to be understood as systems of moral regulation that are sustained over time by a variety of means, not least the sharing of myths and symbols that create solidarity but do not impose a consensus.[8] Cultures can thus exist in both time and space without any particular need for political involvement; many continue to do so. What changed in the eighteenth century, however, was the rise of the interventionist modern state that places a far greater set of burdens, expectations and obligations on the individual and the collectivity than its agro–literate predecessor.[9] The problem of consent to be ruled, and therefore regulated, taxed and recruited (or conscripted), thus became correspondingly more urgent.

In essence, the device of expanding the political community and calling it the 'nation' solved some of the problem but not all of it. The increasing demands by the state on the ruled, the growth of state power and the will to use it, together with the transformation of territory as a source of raw materials (as well

---

[7] Niccolo Machiavelli, *The Prince* (London: Penguin, 1961).

[8] David I. Kertzer, *Ritual, Politics and Power* (New Haven, CT: Yale University Press, 1988).

[9] Tilly, *op.cit.*

as the traditional arguments of prestige and manpower) created a new web of interrelationships, linking rulers and ruled with territory. Each of these categories carried some baggage from the past. The baggage of the state was that it had exercised power with only a minimum of consent and this state of affairs had to be modified. Society had a set of beliefs as to what it regarded as 'normal' and 'natural' and insisted that the political order conform to these imperatives. And territory, previously seen as a resource, generating power and prestige, that rulers could freely exchange through dynastic alliances and peace treaties, now became the location for interactions between rulers and ruled and was metamorphosed into 'homeland'.

The explanation for this change is partly functional. As the pre-modern agro-literate state was gradually turned into the intrusive modern state, it assumed wider and deeper powers and the organisation and operation of this power was invariably understood as territorial. In the context, compactness and contiguity of territory became significant, given the existing levels of communication. Indeed, it is hard to see how it could have been anything else, given the West European state's feudal antecedents. Feudalism is understood here as the organisation of power around a hierarchical system of territorial units in a region where land was scarce and, therefore, had to be closely regulated.[10] Then, there was a clear link between land as a physical asset, its agricultural output and wealth. To this can be added the prestige to be derived from the possession of territory and territorial titles as a central cultural imperative; indeed, there is an argument to be made that because of the historically very early efficient regulation of land, the association between the exercise of power and delimited territory gave territorialism in Europe an unusually precise, delineated quality that land does not necessarily have in other parts of the world. However, the symbolic possession of the land does not automatically go with the ability to organise the territory concerned with maximum efficiency (by the criteria of the time). The improvements in organisation and communication, not least through the printing revolution, made this feasible.[11]

---

[10] John Armstrong, *Nations before Nationalism* (Chapel Hill: University of North Carolina Press, 1982).

[11] One does not have to accept the whole of Benedict Anderson's arguments to see the significance of this emphasis on print capitalism, see his *Imagined*

This changing interrelationship between land and power was crucial in the eighteenth century as the modern state began to expand and extend its extractive and rationalising capacity. This capacity may have declined a little in the late twentieth century with the rise of globalisation and the overloading of state capacity, but the decline is only partial and in any case the symbolic legacy has yet to ebb. In essence, then, the eighteenth century saw the confluence of a series of processes that linked culture to territory to power to organisation to communication, so that cultural power was firmly territorialised and territory was equally firmly understood as the *sine qua non* of power. The outcome of this state of affairs was that culture as moral regulation became inextricably intertwined with the exercise of power, each shaping the other, something that had not been the case previously, seeing that it had been the rise of the modern state that had altered the equation and created a nexus between the two.

None of this might have mattered so much had this transformation not been attended by another related political change; the rise of the modern state created the need for a new form of legitimation and this was organised around the idea (sometimes ideal) of the nation. In sum, the nation symbolised political participation, the extension of access to political power for all because the nation – the mediaeval *natio* – has always constituted the body politic, the *corpus politicum*, which enjoyed monopoly rights over power. But for the newly redefined nation to move towards the ideal of political power for all, something else had to happen. There had to be a new order which guaranteed a much higher level of trust between rulers and ruled. After all, no ruler is going to share power if he thinks that those who are to be newly assumed into power will use it to string him up from the nearest lamp-post. The creation of trust only became necessary with the new consensuality; pre-modern systems needed much less mutual trust and could be run in a for more coercive fashion. If legitimation was the will of God, then so was coercion.

What is of signal importance in this connection is that the rules of social solidarity, the basis on which obligations are founded, encode the rules for reciprocal relationships in what circumstances A owes an obligation to B, especially in the context of a tacit

Communities, 2nd edn, (London: Verso, 1991).

societal obligation, is regulated by the implicit ground rules that every collectivity generates. The civic dimension of nationhood, and thus the mutual obligations of citizenship that link individuals to one another and to the state, are conditioned by the rules of reciprocity inherited from ethnicity. These can change over time, but the change is usually slow; where it is rapid, there will be gaps and dysfunctions. The impersonal norms of the Anglo-Saxon public sphere have their origins in the pre-modern patterns of England. They can be grafted on to other societies, but that does not mean that the graft will take. In sum, if the original ethnic codes of reciprocity and trust are weak, if trust is not given easily to strangers, then the civic dimension of nationhood will likewise be weak. This does not mean, however, that polities without an impersonal public sphere will fail; rather, reciprocal obligations will be constructed in other ways, even while the appearance of an impersonal public sphere will be sustained for formal consumption. Thus patron–client systems will function in analogous ways, as will those of the *nomenklatura* or family loyalty. The outcome will not be an Anglo-Saxon type of civic obligation where everybody pays their taxes and accepts a high level of bureaucratic regulation without demur, but such different systems will have their own imperatives that are equally appropriate in ensuring cultural reproduction.

Nevertheless, it is not suggested here that citizenship as such as unimportant. It did provide a route towards a greater sense of participation in politics, which then made government easier – consensual government is easier than non-consensual[12] – and simultaneously created a basis for yet greater cohesiveness. Potentially, the new system could become inherently self-sustaining, as has largely been the case.

The problem, therefore, was the establishment and maintenance of this trust. Trust is a fragile commodity, it could easily be lost or gained and, crucially, if it is based solely and exclusively on negotiated consent, it becomes subject to the withdrawal of that consent. This is the notional essence of the civic contract, that hypothetically all the contracting parties could at some point withdraw their consent, especially if they are supposedly sovereign. Withdrawing from a contract, on grounds of non-performance,

[12] John Hall, *Coercion and Consent* (Cambridge: Polity, 1994).

say, may be acceptable in the commercial world (though it hardly adds up to good practice), but it is absolutely intolerable for a political community which has to have a sense of stability that the rules will not be rewritten without a very good reason indeed.

This proposition applies not merely to the fate and neck of the ruler but equally to the fate of the territory in which a particular political community – now a territorialised community, as we have seen – lives. Notionally, in a purely contractual system, if a region decides that it wants to secede, there is nothing in logic to prevent this (in some circumstances, secession may even be desirable); however, from the perspective of territorialisation, of stability, cultural reproduction and the entire process of ensuring the material and non-material aspects of a community, the proposition is utterly unacceptable. Securing the stability of territory, therefore, becomes a priority of the very highest order.

How better to attain this than to make it unthinkable by virtue of making it inconceivable, by making territory an integral part of what is 'normal and natural' ? What the transformation sketched above achieved was to make the existing territory inhabited by a political community part of the unquestioned and unquestionable tacit assumptions by which every community lives and by which it defines itself. But to get there from here, as it were, required various methods for making territory-as-real-estate into territory-as-norm.

Crucially to ensure trust, the rulers had to root the same definition, perception and assumption of trust in the entire population. This could be reached by a variety of instruments – assimilation and integration, ethnic cleansing or redrawing the frontier. In much of the existing literature, there is an implicit assumption that 'nationbuilding' – the process referred to in the previous sentence – was (and is) a civic affair.[13] In reality, this is not so. The attainment of trust demands something more enduring than a civic identity which can be called into question on the basis of non-consent. It must be accompanied by the unstated but powerful affective bonds that underlie citizenship.[14] Above all, trust requires

---

[13] Walker Connor, 'Nation-Building or Nation-Destroying' in *Ethnonationalism: the Quest for Understanding* (Princeton University Press, 1994) discusses the relevant literature.

[14] Maurice Keens-Soper, 'The Liberal State and Nationalism in Post-War Europe', *History of European Ideas,* vol 10, no.6, pp.689-703.

ethnicity or a functional equivalent – the shared memories, codes of communication, moral regulation that ethnicity (or its equivalent) represents. The outcome of this endeavour has been contradictory. There is indeed something that can be called a civic identity. People can and do identify with states through their institutions and state norms, but this is seldom sufficient.

States that fail to go beyond this civic identification generally find themselves in trouble. At the same time, because democracy demands limits on ethnic articulation – excessive inputs from the affective dimension distort the procedures of democracy – ethnicity is downplayed and unacknowledged. In the real world, the supposedly civic quality of democratic state institutions is heavily permeated by the codes of ethnicity.

Take France which prides itself on being a strongly if not solely civic polity, that anyone who is a citizen of France and has acquired the political knowledge that goes with citizenship is thus French. This is self-serving nonsense. Frenchness is marked by a thoroughgoing ethnicism, the institutions of the French state are constructed around a French identity, though legitimated by reference to a myth of universal rationality, which effectively excludes non-French modes. The legacy of the past – of – say, the values of Descartes, Pascal, Voltaire, the Jacobins, Napoleon and so on – make France quintessentially French. All who want to be French must accept these values in the name of citizenship.[15] It is not a bad deal, incidentally. Assimilation, to call the process by its true name, does confer all the rights and duties of French citizenship on all who assume it, as well as a stable, secure identity, and the majority generally respects this. There are derogations from the norm only with communities which are manifestly not willing to become quite as French as the majority would like or are so perceived (Muslims). The terms of assimilation are, of course, determined by the majority.[16]

A counter-example is Canada. For a variety of reasons Canada would not or could not develop its own ethnic identity – indeed, it made a virtue out of necessity and argued that its purely civic identity was the essence of Canadianness – with the consequences

---

[15] Allen Bloom, *The Closing of the American Mind* (New York: Simon and Schuster, 1987).

[16] Rogers Brubaker, op.*cit.*

that there was nothing that could transcend the affective bonds of Anglophone and Francophone identities (the allophones adjusted as and where they had to). This Canadian civic identity is proving itself insufficiently resilient to take the strain of Francophone aspirations for secure cultural reproduction in overwhelmingly Anglophone North America. With the benefit of hindsight, it is probable that because no serious attempt was made to construct a Canadian identity that would integrate both language communities – admittedly, not an easy undertaking at the best of times – the community more fearful for its future would look for the most effective means of securing its reproduction and in the current circumstances this could still mean independence for Quebec. Under the conditions of a civic contract, the withdrawal of Francophone consent to remaining in Canada is fully within the logic of the civic identity.

The counter-factual argument here is that a much stronger, affective Canadian bond would have solved the problem that has bedevilled a modernising Quebec, that of ensuring an alternative, 'Canadian' model of modernity, rather than the American one that the Anglophones accept. From the Francophone perspective, this is a serious danger, because there is too little to separate a modern (and thus thoroughly North American) Francophonia in Canada from an Anglophone modernity, with the perceived threat that Quebec's French culture would eventually disappear. The core of the danger is that language is the only boundary marker as the two cultures are being largely homogenised. Under these conditions, a civic Canada cannot provide the necessary guarantees that the Francophones feel they need; indeed the threat of a single Anglophone culture is, in their eyes, being promoted by Anglophone Canada. In effect, Canada is the problem, not the solution; had there been a Canadian ethnic identity, the situation could have been very different.

What these examples show is that without a shared ethnic culture – or ethnicised culture – that is accepted as dominant by most or all of the citizens of a particular polity, the integrity of the state will be in jeopardy. Hence it follows that the civic identities that mature democracies proclaim to be civic are determined by the ethnicity that is necessary for the political cohesiveness demanded by trust. It should be added at this point that while the teleology of ethnicity is misty, as a principle ethnicity insists that all members of the ethnic group share equally in its ideals, values and instruments of cultural reproduction. This equality is then a vital aspect of democracy, especially with respect to democracy in the modern state, which is intrusive and exigent, and creates entitlement on the basis of what looks like citizenship, but is in reality an ethnicised citizenship. Without this notional equality, democracy is hard to organise, though as we shall see, it is not impossible if the necessary cohesiveness of society is attained by some other means.

Cultural reproduction

Much has already been argued in this analysis using the idea of cultural reproduction, so that this particular concept demands further elucidation at this point.[17] In essence, the starting position for making sense of this concept is the proposition that cultures exist as systems of moral regulation which bind individuals together. From these systems cultures draw the nature of the bonds of solidarity and loyalty, the dividing line between good and evil, the continuous construction and reconstruction of coherence and the means by which the community defines its meanings. It follows, therefore, that communities will defend their system of moral regulation, which they understand as forms of social capital, of communication and of the determination of identity. This explains the persistence of ethnicity and civic nationhood.

Then, it is through belonging to a community that individuals as members of a collectivity are able to make selections and choices, to identify criteria, to be empowered to take certain processes for granted, meaning that they do not have to define and redefine what they are doing and why. The complex of myths, rituals and symbols is a primary instrument of community maintenance. By participation in the mythic world and rituals of the community, whether consciously or not, the members of the community ensure that it persists in time; they are thus engaged in cultural reproduction. This process cannot be avoided. No one has total rationality, so that selection is essential and the criteria of selection are socially determined. Hence the mechanism should be seen as self-sustaining. And it sets limits to self-awareness.

Furthermore, the selection applies not only to the criteria of action and values, but also to establishing the boundaries of the

---

[17] Pierre Bourdieu, *The Field of Cultural Production* (Cambridge: Polity 1993).

community, to deciding who is a member and who is not, what the bonds of obligation are to non-members (if any) and crucially what the community allows to be made visible or keep hidden at any one time. If there is some particular idea of proposition or process that would endanger cultural reproduction, the community will collectively and through ways that are not made conscious to its members simply dismiss them, they will not be 'readable'.[18] Hence outsiders to a community will regularly be able to see patterns and realities that members cannot and which the latter will actively dismiss as non-existent.

Applying the idea of cultural reproduction to nationhood, therefore, is a fruitful way of seeing how and why nations survive and, indeed, seem to flourish, despite the repeated attempts to write them off by the legatees of the Enlightenment, the liberals and the Marxists, both of whom seek to marginalise nationhood and national identities as 'irrational'. Political action and mobilisation along national cleavages are similarly downgraded as temporary or as protest movements that will die away,[19] because their aims are in conflict with the goals of Enlightenment rationality.

Equally, examining the mechanisms of cultural reproduction will also show that processes hidden from the community will persist and that even when certain features of a community are identified, the identification is itself a way of ensuring that it persists, because the identification and any critique are directed at the wrong target. By way of example: in every attitude survey Hungarians emerge as by far the most pessimistic society in Europe. They are occasionally upbraided for this by more gung-ho outsiders. Hungarians themselves will discuss their pessimism with a mixture of pride and despair, but there is no serious attempt to theorise it. It may well be that expecting the worst has a stabilising function. During the communist period, responsibility was divorced from cause and effect and was imposed politically. Presumably, pessimism evolved as a defence mechanism, though it must have drawn on earlier traditions. Currently, it is firmly anchored as an internalised

[18] This process is analogous to the ideas elaborated by Thomas Kuhn, *The Structure of Scientific Revolutions* (University of Chicago Press, 1962), about the shifting nature of paradigms. See also Mary Douglas, *Risk Acceptability According to the Social Sciences* (London: Routledge, 1985).

[19] Joseph Rothschild, *Ethnopolitics: a Conceptual Framework* (New York: Columbia University Press, 1981).

norm. Its functions are partly apotropaic, partly a way of coping with the very rapid changes of post-communism, partly a declaration that individuals cannot and will not assume responsibility because too much is outside their control and partly a device for coping with the opaque and unpredictable world in which Hungarians live. In that sense pessimism is a part of cultural reproduction.[20]

Englishness

This sketching of some of the theoretical issues should help to provide an analytical introduction to the problem of Englishness. The data from which one can put together a set of seemingly unrelated symptoms for a diagnosis are these: for two generations and more, English political debate has concentrated on the issue of class, especially in the demand for the creation of a classless society. Every political party has adopted the classless society as its slogan yet regardless of what governments and elites seem to do, class remains as the central constitutive factor of English society. Why? Then, the mid-1990s saw the beginnings of a debate on Englishness.[21] Again, why? Paralleling this latter debate was the growing street level articulation of an English, as distinct from a more or less time-honoured British, identity. This too required an explanation. Last, there is the question of Europe; why has the opposition to Europe been quite so emotional, quite so bitterly unreasoning? And what, if any, are the links between these symptoms? What do they portend?

The question of class is, indeed central. The set of questions posed above cannot be answered directly, head-on as it were, but has to be tackled laterally. What is class in contemporary England and what is its function, why has it seemingly resisted all attempts at a modernisation? The answer has to lie in an unexpected area. Class in England has survived because regardless of what people say, it has a role and function in cultural reproduction that is hidden from view by the power relations encoded in it. Despite appearances to the contrary, class allows people a very

---

[20] See also the argument on fatalism in Michael Thompson, Richard Ellis and Aaron Wildavsky, *Cultural Theory* (Boulder, CO: Westview, 1990).

[21] A good deal of this was found in *Prospect*, a newly launched journal almost tailor-made for the purpose.

high degree of security regarding their identity. One can derive a very firm sense of who one is, who one's fellows are, what are the reciprocal obligations owed to others and so on from class. [22] Furthermore, class status provides a ready-made and universally acceptable explanation for failure, something which is extremely important in all social systems. In effect, class provides ways of orientation in society.

If this somewhat unexpected proposition is accepted, then things become much clearer. Class survives because the great majority of the population likes it that way. People are comfortable with their class status, however much they may complain about it, because it constitutes a form of social capital and a body of cultural knowledge. These are not abandoned lightly. Consequently whatever people may say about class in public, at a less than conscious level they are engaged in reproducing it. The essence of the argument in this context is that all societies engage in forms of tacit cultural reproduction, through the myriad forms of social interaction that they consider 'normal' and 'natural'. [23]

Take speech and accent, for instance. This area is notorious for its pitfalls. Yet too few people are ready to accept that by being able to identify the class position of another speaker of English-English, one is immediately able to bring into operation the exact social code which reinforces both speakers' class identities and thereby contribute to the maintenance of the process. The term 'English-English' is rather clumsy, but it is used explicitly to exclude all the other varieties of English, like Scots, American or Australian; the term 'E-English' will be used from here on. In E-English, people will hardly ever mix RP 'received pronunciation' and basilect (less prestigious varieties of speech) and when they do, the listener will be perturbed, as if someone were upsetting the natural order of things, which incidentally they are. [24]

But the process goes well beyond accent, despite the fact that it is accent that receives so much of the attention.

Speakers of E-English engage in a highly complex definition

---

[22] On some of the problems of solidarity and reciprocal obligation, see Michael Ignatieff, *The Needs of Strangers* (London: Chatto and Windus, 1984).

[23] Michael Billig, *Banal Nationalism* (London: Sage, 1995); Mary Douglas, *Implicit Meanings* (London: Routledge, 1975).

[24] John Honey, *Does Accent Matter? The Pygmalion Factor* (London: Faber and Faber, 1989).

and redefinition of the context in which they communicate in order to avoid transgressing class boundaries. As a result, communication is shot through with ambiguity and understatement, E-English regards it as a virtue not to say what one means, but to convey that meaning in a roundabout way, so that neither party to the communication will be put in an awkward position with respect to the other. The central and highly revealing social taboo is causing embarrassment and being embarrassed; communication has evolved to avoid such situations. Thus it has become impossible to say 'no' in E-English. There is a panoply of acceptable periphrases, like 'I'm terribly sorry' through 'I'll have to come back to you on this' to 'You don't want to know that'. The turn of phrase is elaborate and roundabout and much of the meaning is conveyed by tone, facial expression and body language.

There is every sign that this process of elaboration is dynamic and that it is far from over. Certainly, communication has grown much more complex over the last three or four decades, precisely the period when the traditional class-structure did not break down exactly but regrouped and adapted. The class hierarchy that emerged from the Second World War was already fraying at the edges and under attack from the post-war Labour reforms, but it held its own, for example with slogans like 'It's back to normal' aimed at getting women out of the labour force and back into the home. Almost certainly because the process was continuously controlled by the existing elites who intuitively or consciously saw that a retreat was preferable to a defeat, the class closures were subtly redrawn. The surge of anger that came through the 'Kitchen Sink' school of literature (most notably the plays of John Osborne) basically proclaimed the disappointment of those who had been through a successful upward mobility[25] and then discovered that power and status still eluded them, because in the interim the goalposts had been moved.

That has essentially been the story ever since the 1950s. However strong the push for social mobility may be, those who benefit only *seem* to benefit. Access to status and the influence that goes with status, which is incomparably more important than money in the process of setting agenda and thus exercising power, never really slipped from the hands of establishment. Even when the

[25] Bryan Appleyard, in *The Pleasures of Peace: Art and Imagination in Postwar Britain* (London: Faber and Faber, 1989), takes up some of these themes.

establishment widened recruitment, those now assumed into it were socialised into its supple and resilient ethos which had one overriding aim, its own unquestioned and unquestionable survival as the dominant value system.

Nothing shows the resilience of this ethos and those who are its bearers more vividly than the fate of the two great assaults – perhaps this should read 'apparent assaults' because they both contributed to the strengthening of the system – in the 1960s and in the 1980s. The 1960s attack came from the left and attempted to use education as its instrument. This had a good deal going for it. Education has been one of the primary means of enhancing upward social mobility throughout Europe ever since the Enlightenment and before and, besides, it appeared to have produced good results immediately after 1945, though these were flawed by leaving a sizeable residue of the working class behind without any opportunity for social mobility.

Hence the educational reformers of the 1960s found a simple solution – too simple, some might say – extend educational opportunities to all and create a truly comprehensive system. This endeavour, however, ran into a number of obstacles which were sufficient to derail the reform. First, the reform had two separate objectives: the democratisation of recruitment and the democratisation of the content of education, which tended to mean a shift away from the traditional understanding of standards. Then, the middle classes, who might well have accepted the former, baulked at the latter because they saw their own cultural reproduction threatened, and in consequence either opted out or did what they could to delegitimate the reform.

The entire project failed because it misunderstood the nature of the problem which was not education as such but class. The fact of class was, of course,. recognised, but in the context of the time, class was interpreted in a largely Marxist or *Marxisant* way, overwhelmingly in material terms. The proposition that class had ramifications into status, values and, crucially, identity was either not considered at all or was dismissed as obscurantist mystification. The after-effect of the attempt to break down class through education, however, has cast a long shadow. Education continues to be seen as a potential instrument for achieving social change and the process sketched in the foregoing is rejected. Because those formulating policies for change operate inside the mind-set of Englishness with all its baggage of cultural reproduction, it is extremely difficult for all concerned to see class for what it is, as a source of identity. The outcome is a reinforcing of class boundaries. Class status is evidently not merely a function of interest, but also of a complex set of interrelated identities, which depend on one another for their reproduction. No direct assault will change this state of affairs.

The other great attempt to transform the nature of class hierarchies came in the 1980s with Thatcherism. In its simplest form, this proposed to make status, above all class status, open to acquisition through wealth; or to be slightly more precise, to speed up the process whereby class status can be bought. Traditionally, new money takes about a generation before it is fully assumed into the class hierarchy and even then certain closures operate against it. The Thatcherite project proposed to eliminate the time element and to give the newly wealthy instant access to status. It encouraged money-making as away of opening up the economy to new energies. Not surprisingly, the existing beneficiaries of the hierarchy were alarmed and mounted a very successful vanguard action to delegitimate the new aspirants. The aspirants were roundly denounced for 'greed', a term that was brilliantly effective because it subsumed condemnation of vulgarity (a traditionally right-wing closure) and of individualism (which satisfied the left). In any case, money-making proved vulnerable to an economic downturn and the challenge was effectively seen off by the end of the 1980s.

The pretext for the Thatcherite centralisation of the state might have been efficiency and accountability, but it also ensured that the paternalistic state, constructed around English ethnic codes, would not be challenged.[26] The quite extraordinary concentration of power in the machinery of the state can also be interpreted as a device to protect Englishness. If the localities were to acquire power, this could be used to challenge the existing modes of cultural articulation, as they could constitute alternative forms of social and cultural capital. By vesting moral regulation in the state, tacitly insisting that the state is the ultimate repository of rationality, a paternalistic ethos is sustained, one that is derived from implicit models of Englishness and which does not even acknowledge its own name. This English étatism cannot be located in the left-right

---

[26] On centralisation, see Simon Jenkins, *Accountable to None* (London: Penguin, 1996).

spectrum, but is automatically accepted by all political parties and public opinion. The rhetoric of the right can be firmly disregarded here.

Yet at the same time, the state has operated in a sufficiently supple way to contain Scottish and Welsh aspirations, even if this was increasingly being questioned in the 1990s. In effect, a complex double bluff has been played out. Whereas traditionally in common parlance the state was referred to as England, by the 1990s it was widely called Britain, but the content was the same. There was a universal assumption that what went on in England was the British norm; the expression 'British law' for example is meaningless, given the separate legal system in Scotland, but it is widely used.

This nominal projection of English norms onto the rest of Britain has been very significant in allowing the maintenance of a system that has enough leeway in it to satisfy Scottish and Welsh cultural reproduction. If England had been ethnicised, it is hard to imagine that the transformation of Wales into an officially bilingual region could have been countenanced; it took place very largely without a serious debate in London at all. Similarly, the separate legal and educational system in Scotland, together with a range of Scottish institutions that function quite differently form England could be accepted because English ethnic norms did not arise and the class hierarchy was not affected. Scots are very largely outside the English class system and the Welsh are partially so. Hence the Scots and the Welsh have been able to sustain an ethnic identity within a nominally British but in reality English state because Englishness was not primarily ethnic.

The key issue with respect to Englishness and class, therefore, is that every attempt to make serious inroads into the class hierarchy hits the obstacle of the class hierarchy and the class hierarchy invariably proves strong enough to win. *Prima facie* this is puzzling and cannot be understood in terms of class only. One has to look at the entire context in which these contests have taking place and this is where one has to abandon classical pragmatic English analysis and ask deeper, more probing questions about the precise nature of the relationship between Englishness and class.

English identity, then, is intimately bound up with class. At every turn, the English are engaged in a complex ritual around class status and the more they do this, the more they ensure that class is what determines their identity. Whether the activity in question is supportive of class or rejects it, what is happening turns on the issue of class and ensures that it is understood in that way. It is in this sense that Englishness is deeply bound up with class. As already noted, this is not class in the Marxist sense, far from it. The class nature of Englishness is about status, identity, culture and security, for that is the true, underlying explanation for why class has resisted all attempts to change it: class status gives the great majority of the members of English society a very clear and very secure identity. The system offers very high levels of cultural cohesion and creates a sense of coherence and order at a time of far-reaching change. The last thing that any member of this integrated system wants is to change it. Of course, this has a negative side. It blocks equal access to power.

Various things flow from this identity, not least one's position in society, one's status, patterns of communication (it is far easier to communicate with fellow members than with non-members) and the expectations of social achievement. Crucially, class status provides the individual with a ready-made explanation for low achievement, as well as success. It is a not only a highly tenacious and fully functioning system, but it is so deeply internalised, so thoroughly a part of one's everyday existence, that it can be justifiably regarded as the functional equivalent of ethnicity. George Mikes, the archetypal insider-outsider, famously observed that while Continentals had a sex life, the English preferred a hot water bottle;[27] this could be adapted along the lines of, while the Continentals have ethnicity, the English have class.

It is this near-protean adaptability of the class system that safeguards its status as the English equivalent of ethnicity. The social, political, economic and moral dilemmas and perspectives that are structured by ethnicity elsewhere are all but automatically, 'normally' and 'naturally' defined in terms of class in England. This explains the persistence of class through all the upheavals of the twentieth century. It operates subtly, its beneficiaries generally act without any conscious intention of imposing class closures and restating or redefining cleavages; they do not have to, they are functioning inside a self-reproducing system. This allows it a remarkable regenerative capacity.

---

[27] George Mikes, *How to be an Alien* (London: André Deutsch, 1958).

Class as defined here can give way on a whole variety of detail as long as it can retain the essence of what it stands for and what it offers in a mediated, more or less covert form. When the pressure to extend recruitment becomes irresistible, those newly recruited discover that true status and the power that goes with it have shifted to somewhere shadowy and unassailable. No one will argue in favour of class privilege explicitly, of course, but there has been a consistent underestimation of its tenacity, not least because its reality, foundations, significance and strength are misidentified. In effect, class has disguised itself and made itself less visible. There is no ostentatious class display or privilege, but covert markers of accent (only the first level trip-wire), vocabulary, dress codes, life styles are used barely consciously to the same end and result. Class status is marked out, even though people are aware of this only when something jars.

The central proposition about the English class system is that it fulfils a crucial need for far too many people for them to be ready to dismantle it. Social institutions which are authentic in the sense that they fulfil a need have an autonomous ability to survive and to adopt new forms which gain acceptance without any overt discussion of what has happened.

Despite its negative image by the criteria of equal access to power that democracy presupposes, the class system does have at least one highly positive consequence for the domestic stability of England. Virtually every other modern state is defined – often explicitly, sometimes not – in ethnic terms. England is rare, subordinating ethnicity to class, and this has helped to make the country relatively open to migrants, exiles and other foreigners. They do not fit into the class system, at any rate not immediately, and they do not threaten it either. While there is low level differentiation by skin colour and quite extensive verbal abuse of blacks, the race problem is nothing like as serious as it is in the United States or even France or Germany, where the integration of immigrants poses far-reaching questions about the nature of the ethnic self-definition of the majority. The fact that blacks perceive the class system as racist is irrelevant in this context.

There is, however, a new and far more dangerous threat to Englishness; this is the threat of Europe. The nature of this threat is, as might have been expected in the light of the analysis in this paper, persistently misunderstood. Those hostile to European integration oppose it in terms of defending sovereignty, or to be more precise 'sovereignty'. But this is a complete decoy. There is no such thing as sovereignty and even states which pretend that there is find that the price they pay in terms of isolation is impossibly high. The moment a state signs any international convention, even the Universal Postal Union, it has given away a part of its sovereignty, which means that the entire concept is negotiable. So the issue is not 'sovereignty' but something else.

Here is the real difficulty. As long as Europe was nothing more than a trading competitor, Englishness could coexist with it, it did not pose a challenge in terms of a new hierarchy of status and access to power. But a Europe of a European Union most certainly does. It implies that the time-honoured way of Englishness, with its tacit emphasis on class hierarchy, is potentially subject to erosion. New forms of knowledge, new concentrations of social capital, new definitions of status can all be derived from EU membership. This is what the Eurosceptics have instinctively understood and that is why their attack on 'Europe' is so determined. They may not construct their arguments along the lines made here, but they are quite correct in their intuitions that further integration into Europe will mean the end of Englishness as it has existed for the last two centuries or more.

The anti-European slant of Englishness is nothing new. The deeply-held belief in English pragmatism ('we are English because we do not have theory') and the corresponding rejection of theory as alien and Continental are, in reality, a counter-ideology of their own and have a long history.[28] Common sense may be presented as non-ideological; in reality it is an ideology that says that by concentrating on what is immediately in front of us, we can agree, but we ignore whatever may disturb this process. It can be summed up as 'if it works it's good' or less kindly as 'a pragmatist is someone who doesn't know why he's doing what he's doing' (or she for that matter). Pragmatism stresses agreement to disagree and the acceptance of ambiguity. These mechanisms

---

[28] David Simpson, *Romanticism, Nationalism and the Revolt against Theory* (Chicago University Press, 1993). For Linda Colley, *Britons: Forging the Nation, 1707-1837* (London: Pimilico, 1992) the emphasis is on the Protestant religion, on loyalty to the crown, a sense of territory and the shared experience of war and the proposition that these were powerful enough to transcend separate English, Scottish and Welsh identities. My own feeling is that Britishness overlay these but, as history has shown, never eliminated them. The reasons are argued out here.

are very helpful in sustaining class hierarchy, because the exclude potential challenges by, in effect, declaring them to be outside class and thus beyond the purview of Englishness, i.e. un-English. It is striking how ineffective 'common sense' is outside English culture. A good illustration is Northern Ireland, where repeated attempts to find agreement by fudging issues have produced disastrous outcomes. Fudging issues is excellent where the contestants are English; it will simply not work in a place like Ulster where clarity and literalness are the highest value.

This 'I am a plain man' attitude is a very strong value in Englishness. Evidence can be found in the rejection of anything theoretical as 'waffle', as 'vague', as 'empty and meaningless'.[29] By the criteria of Englishness, this is true. But whether theory really is as empty of meaning as these rejections would insist is another matter. What does matter is that by virtue of being English, theory is and must be rejected. The result is well-known but is not understood and, actually, cannot be by English cognitions, because to do so would provide the means for decoding the English class system and that could be unbelievably threatening for all concerned.

The penultimate link in this chain is the nature of popular perceptions and self-definitions. Here we find something of a paradox. Whereas for the higher levels of the class hierarchy, Englishness is about the sentimentalised symbols of identity – the proverbial warm beer and cricket on a summer afternoon – or about a moralising and moralised programme like Orwell's decency and tolerance,[30] at the lower levels of the status order there is a much harsher, clearer and obviously ethnicised self-definition. This is the constituency to which the unmistakably nationalist tabloid headlines appeal. The ones trotted out during the Euro

[29] There is a splendid example of this kind of rejection by Peter Jones in his attack on academic jargon, *Times*, 25 May 1996. What is very striking in this polemic is how unself-aware the author is, how deeply committed he is to a literalist view of the world and how strongly he rejects abstraction because abstraction demands a more complex vocabulary that he is willing to countenance. He would, of course, reject any suggestion that the use of language can encode patterns of power and authority.

[30] Roy Porter, (ed.) and his contributors explore some of these themes in *Myths of the English* (Cambridge: Polity, 1992).

96 football competition illustrate this ethnicisation vividly, particularly through the creation and recreation of anti-German ethos.

For the middle classes, unwelcome though these manifestations of a rather nasty kind of Englishness may have been, they were made to disappear – cognitively blanked out – by being waved away as a kind of slightly regrettable *joie de vivre* indulged in by the lower orders.[31] The dismissal was certainly too easy. The fact, for fact it was, that large numbers of people responded to the headlines and decked themselves out with the flag of St George, the red cross against a white background, the ancient but then largely forgotten flag of England, indicated a strong resonance. The flag was something new. Previous expressions of Englishness, like the Last Right of the Proms, used the Union flag which does not have explicitly English connotations. It cannot be excluded, incidentally, that the use of the St George's flag could have been copied from Scottish football fans, who have been draping themselves in the lion rampant and the flag of St Andrew for years.

These outcroppings of visible Englishness, however, were preceded in time by the slow maturing of a much more serious popular sentiment that was given no outlet, no articulation except on rare occasions. Reverence for royalty was one aspect of this, but the genuine wave of support for the Falklands war was something else again and, indeed, it was exceedingly unwelcome for the higher strata who intuitively understood that ethnicity, with its fairly clear egalitarian agenda and hostility to status by birth, threatened their status on the class ladder. And, probably, that was one reason why the middle strata, led by the intelligentsia,[32] were so utterly unrelenting in their attacks on the one politician

---

[31] The ability of collectivities to screen out unwelcome phenomena – unwelcome because they threaten one's received self-image – should never be underestimated. It is revealing that the highly influential book edited by Eric Hobsbawm and Terence Ranger, *The Invention of Tradition* (Cambridge University Press, 1983), which had the ostensible purpose of unmasking 'ancient traditions' as modern frauds, avoids any dissection of the English. The implication is that the English do not have the unfortunate diseases which beset Scots, Welsh, Continentals *et al.* (as it were).

[32] That is, the chattering classes. I know that one never, but never refers to those with specialised knowledge as 'intelligentsia' in the British context, because this would imply that knowledge carries a position in the class hierarchy, and under the rules of Englishness this is not the case.

who recognised the mobilisatory strength of English nationalism, Mrs Thatcher.

So, summarising the evidence of the foregoing, there exists an explicit English ethnic sentiment, but it is confined to the lower strata and did not traditionally find the kind of higher level articulation that is standard elsewhere in Europe. Intellectuals had been bought off with a social status that was high enough to keep them quiet but not so high as to let them set much of the moral agenda. The agendas of Englishness continued to be determined by those at the top of the class hierarchy. In consequence, the existence of a kind of low status ethnic Englishness was not a real threat as it stood.

The change in the decade of the Thatcher government and thereafter is that slowly, not inevitably or irrevocably, a middle-class Englishness is beginning to find its voice and the process will sooner or later encounter the low-status Englishness sketched above. This high-status Englishness is being actively mobilised by the Eurosceptics, who are therefore deeply engaged in the construction of an ethnic Englishness against Europe. There is a certain irony in the argument that Englishness in the broad European sense is coming into being by reason of anti-Europeanism, but this will hardly be without precedent. What is strikingly more intriguing is that the campaign is implicit and obviously unaware of the unintended consequences of what is being done.

Yet by articulating and mobilising Englishness in order to defeat 'Europe', the Eurosceptics are not only finding a measure of resonance, but are equally setting in train processes that could certainly transform the bedrock of Englishness as presently structured by class for ever. Ethnicity, as argued, accepts a degree of class hierarchy, but places the emphasis on the notional equality of all members of the ethnic group. This creates a cohesive loyalty and solidarity, which allows for the devolution of power, even while equality remains notional, given the affective bonds involved. The class structure of Englishness, while excellent in providing stability and clarity of identity, is weaker with respect to trust and has thus necessitated a significantly less generous devolution of power.

Crucially, the English elites cling determinedly to the now antediluvian concept of parliamentary sovereignty and will have no truck with popular sovereignty, virtually a *sine qua non* for a modern democracy. The implication is that Englishness as currently structured has adapted very badly to the needs of modernity – the impersonal norms, the interchangeability of persons – because its codes continue to be governed by class, which presupposes certain qualities that are inherent in birth. The proposition that the entire community could be trusted with equal access to power is, therefore, intuitively recognised as dangerous to the existing dispensation. The difficulty is that the deference that went with class, the acceptance of class as 'normal' and 'natural', has eroded somewhat at the lower levels of the status hierarchy, but no alternative mode of Englishness has yet emerged. The outcome is confusion and that coarsening of social interactions on which so many have remarked.[33]

Thus the state of play (a very English metaphor) in the late 1990s is complex, contradictory and stands at a crossroads. If the Eurosceptics are successful in mobilising an anti-European English ethnicity, and come to weaken the roots of class by offering a seemingly viable alternative, there will be a period of turmoil during which class will be replaced by new hierarchies, new forms of social capital and new cultural codes. There will also have to be changes in the existing structures and institutions of politics. Scotland may well decide not to participate in a United Kingdom that is governed by a new-minted English ethnic nationalism, placing the question of consent high on the agenda. An England outside the European Union will be very unattractive for some, who will look for an alternative. Citizenship will self-evidently be transformed both as to form and content. Black minorities and other immigrants, protected hitherto from excessively harsh closures by their exclusion from the class hierarchy, will discover what English racism is really like. And, the ultimate irony, the existing beneficiaries of the class hierarchy, those at or towards the top of the tree of status and influence, will discover that the Eurosceptics' attempt to save England from the depredations of Europe might actually end up by making England more European than it has ever been.

---

[33] For instance, Richard Hoggart, *The Way We Live Now* (London: Chatto and Windus, 1995).

22

YUGOSLAVIA: STATE CONSTRUCTION AND STATE FAILURE

The particular dilemma and tragedy of Yugoslavia might be described with only a little cynicism as the product of a major historical error. In a very real sense, the state was founded on a weak basis because of a set of serious misunderstandings, some of them deeply structural, others contingent and derived from a cognitive screening out of long term factors by short term ones. Indeed, there is a case to be made for the proposition that the concentration on short term problems can produce really major headaches in the long term.

The above argument needs to be grounded in both the interpretation of the nature of state foundation and the actual historical data. How states come into being or how they fail tends to be an under-investigated area, yet the success or otherwise of the modern state does to a very considerable extent depend on the actual contingent circumstances of its birth. There is an argument to be made that such contingent factors continue to influence its operations, not least through its foundation myth which generally encodes something of the purposiveness of the state in question. When the purposiveness of a state remains caught in the contingent factors of its birth and if it cannot readily transcend these, the chances of its success are diminished.

All this raises a further question or set of questions to do with what states are actually for and whether the purpose of states has changed over time. Here the key moment is the rise of the modern state. Whereas the pre-modern state was static and could operate with a fairly high degree of coercion, the modern state, because it is dynamic, presupposes a much higher level of consent. After all, the modern state has quite extraordinary expectations of its subjects: that they entrust it with a high level of power to organise, to regulate, to rationalise, to tax and to coerce and that generally they trust those who exercise power over them. This is extraordinary because it assumes that rulers and ruled concur in the broad aims of power, that the ruled believe that power will not be exercised to their detriment but to their advantage. Democracy is the most developed form of this dispensation, but other modes of establishing consent are also possible, though as economic and technological change advances, the intensity of two-way exchanges must increase too and democracy is the most effective way of achieving this.

Hence the function of states in the modern world is to act as a framework for the exercise of power in a fast changing world, to provide stability and make provision for change. They way in which a state establishes its rules, both implicit and explicit, will shape the patterns of power and simultaneously the aims which the exercise of power is intended to serve. What is critical in this context, however, is that the state cannot shape the aspirations of society *in toto*. Society has its own agendas, its own expectations and moral imperatives; states must heed these or else come up against the problem of consent and the withdrawal of consent. State failure can be seen as the loss of consent to be ruled by that particular state.

So how, then, is consent to be attained and maintained? The classical answer is that consent between rulers and ruled is achieved through the civic contract which is encoded in the doctrine of state sovereignty. The population of a particular state is said to have consented to that state, the rulers of which regard themselves as ruling only by virtue of that contract and thus consensually. A moment's thought will show that this does not deal very effectively with the problem of dissent. While dissent from policy issues can be readily integrated into the concept of the civic contract, the withdrawal of consent to the state as such cannot. Indeed, and this is the particularly significant lesson of Yugoslavia, although states in Europe look well established, immanent and unquestionable, their existence in their present form is under challenge in several places and should not be taken for granted.

Those in power have a vested interest in preempting the very question of the existence of the state and seek to do so by making the existing dispensation unquestionable, by making the status quo 'normal and natural' and thus cognitively beyond challenge. But that is not the same as an explicit, overt civic contract. That is an altogether different process, one used widely in the world, that of making certain questions unaskable by sacralising them.

Sacralisation can take various forms. It can be attained by creating and maintaining a state over a very long period of time, so that its origins are vague and the population accepts it as the only possible form of living. France falls into this category.

However, there is generally more to sacralisation than a straightforward cognitive closure. The really effective way of constructing consent is to base it on culture. And it is at this moment that this analysis arrives at its most controversial point, the linking of consent to ethnicity. In essence, the core of the argument here is that one of the features of a shared culture is that it encodes the bonds of solidarity that tell the members of a collectivity what their tacit obligations are to one another, what they share and what they do not. Crucially, solidarity does not presuppose consensus.[1] Indeed, solidarity makes a range of disagreement possible by establishing the outer boundaries of disagreement. But when it comes to the establishment and maintenance of states, the function of solidarity is to exclude the questioning sketched above. The name given to this cultural solidarity is ethnicity.

Ethnicity has its own purposiveness. Once in being, an ethnic community will do virtually everything it can to ensure that it survives and it employs a very wide range of instruments to ensure its cultural reproduction.[2] The ultimate aim is to gain universal recognition for itself as a community of moral worth, as a bearer of collective values on the same terms as all others.[3] At the end of the day, moral worth is about imposing a pattern on the world that gives meaning to the myriad conflicting impressions and experiences that individuals encounter in their lives. Ethnicity is a central means of creating coherence and order in what would otherwise be chaos.[4] Through this coherence, individuals recognise mutual bonds and obligations. They acquire moral worth in their own eyes by being members of a community of shared solidarity.

Thus the solidarity that underlies ethnicity is the central element in ensuring that consent to the state remains in being. People

[1] David I. Kertzer, *Ritual Politics and Power* (New Haven, CT: Yale University Press, 1988).

[2] Pierre Bourdieu, *The Field of Cultural Production* (Cambridge: Polity, 1993).

[3] Donald Horowitz, *Ethnic Groups in Conflict* (Berkeley: University of California Press, 1985).

[4] Mircea Eliade, *The Myth of the Eternal Return: Cosmos and History* (London: Penguin, 1954).

who share an ethnicity also share an understanding of what their community is and what the metaphorical and physical boundaries of that state are or should be. By and large, members of the same ethnic group do not seek secession, indeed they will not have the group consciousness which could give rise to the questioning that might produce secession.

So what, then, are the bases of ethnicity? There is a range of answers to this question, and again the answers given today are more complex and more sophisticated than they were a century ago. One can debate the nature of ethnogenesis, but as far as Europe is concerned, an ethnic group has to have an awareness of itself as a collectivity, a sense of its own past and future and a set of markers by which it differentiates itself from other groups. All other factors are contingent. Some ethnic collectivities will make use of various materials, like say language and religion, while for others these are less important. What is significant is the actual quantity of usable materials. Where these are plentiful, especially where the shared past is dense and complex, the identity fashioned out of it will reflect this.

The palette of choice is significant too. The greater the range of raw materials, the more easily a community will be able to adapt to different challenges. It is important to recognise in this context that self-definitions are not fixed, but will shift according to circumstances, that these identities are fluid and seemingly opportunistic. This is one of the aspects of collective identities that underlies the charge of their having been invented and of their being intellectually impoverished.[5] In fact, invention will only operate where there is resonance; the past that is used must be recognisable by the collectivity in question as theirs. As long as a particular strand in the self-definition remains capable of energising the population, as long as it prompts a moment of self-recognition, it will be effective.

A further problem, of particular significance with respect to Yugoslavia, is that of overlaps. It can happen that more than one group will lay claim to a particular piece of history or language or religion as a badge of identity. In such situations, there will certainly be a contest and maybe conflict. Given that any conflict

---

[5] Eric Hobsbawm and Terence Ranger (eds), *The Invention of Tradition* (Cambridge University Press, 1983).

of this kind will be about the deepest levels of identity, it will inevitably be bitter and seen as highly threatening by those involved.

It would, however, be misleading to regard ethnicity as the sole determinant and creator of group political identities. Much of the debate about nations and nationalism omits a key aspect of the nature of nationhood: the state and civil society are also vital in the construction of identity, indeed, given the nature of the modern state, it is very hard to see how the activity of the state could fail to transform identities in various ways. The modern state has an enormous capacity to reshape the way in which a society regards itself, through legislation and through moral suasion, not least through its control of the educational system.[6] It is, in fact, at this point that the coincidence of interest of the state and ethnic group is clearest. The ethnic group has an overriding concern in its own survival, in its cultural reproduction. The state has an equivalent concern in ensuring the reproduction of consent. The two meet through the medium of education, where much of this reproduction takes place.

The outcome of this state of affairs is that individuals of different ethnicities can acquire the same state (étatic) identities. They have been socialised into dealing with the state in a particular way even when their consent to the state may not be wholehearted. Their expectations of how a state functions, what it can and cannot do have been shaped by that state experience. This adds up to an identity which can divide groups of the same ethnicity and, can create differences that will persist over very long periods of time. An example is Romania, where political patterns, notably voting behaviour, in Transylvania (a part of Hungary until 1918) are markedly different from those in the Regat.

What emerges from a study of states, their success and failure, is that success requires that they have a legitimating ideology that is capable of mobilising and remobilising consent, in other words that the population feel that the state continues to articulate their deepest aspirations. The coincidence between the legitimating ideology and the aspirations does not have to be perfect, but the gap cannot be too great, otherwise the existence of the state is endangered.

By and large, state failure is not much studied. Yet any closer

---

[6] Ernest Gellner, *Nations and Nationalism* (Oxford: Blackwell, 1983).

look at the history of Europe in the twentieth century will show that it is more widespread than it appears. If the criteria of state failure are taken to be complete disappearance, the loss or acquisition of territory (gaining territory is a problem because it creates major tasks of integration and transformation of state purposiveness), foreign conquest or loss of empire, then Switzerland is the only state in Europe to have not undergone this trauma. The implication is that states are far more fluid than they seem, that changes are a part of the political repertoire, but because state failure really is traumatic, everything is done to screen out this reality.

This proposition also says something about how the European political tradition deals with the problem of non-consent. Although coercion is not unknown (e.g. the Spanish Civil War was fought at least in part about the relationship between Castile and the Basque country and Catalonia), the general European approach is reluctantly to accede to secession and new state formation. The period between 1945 and 1991 (the end of the Soviet Union) was unusual in that this fluidity was temporarily frozen because of the Cold War; that era is definitively over and Yugoslavia is one of the casualties.

The third element of the modern nation is the civic dimension, the nature of civil society, citizenship and the complex web of interactions between different groups and between individuals, groups and the state. Society acts on the state and vice versa; conflicts of interest are settled by the criteria that a particular community has evolved. These conflicts are settled much more easily when all the members of the community in question share a set of cultural norms, i.e. they share the same ethnicity. Because ethnicity encodes some of the deepest moral assumptions and aims of a collectivity, there is a general tendency for intra-collective communication to be more effective than communication with non-members. This does not mean that such communication is impossible, just that it is more complex and more likely to result in misunderstanding.

What is significant about the impact of civil society on nation-hood is that where society is well-established and self-confident, it finds it easier to take its own existence and identity for granted and does not have to concern itself with its own survival and self-reproduction. This makes it much easier for a nation with a strong civil society to live with the codes of other ethnic groups. Correspondingly, where civil society is weak, that self-confidence will be weaker too and the nation in question will be much more inclined to see issues in ethnic terms.

When the lessons of these theoretical consideration are applied to Yugoslavia, the flaws in that state – flaws that were built into the state from the outset – become clearer. This argument is not aimed at suggesting that the experiment in setting up a South Slav state was doomed from the outset; rather, that its founders seriously underestimated the extreme difficulty in running a multi-ethnic state in the modern world. Again, it is not argued here that this was outcome of malign intentions. The flaw derived from a misunderstanding of the nature of nationhood, crucially because of the reductionist definition that was employed.

The argument in favour of the South Slav state was that all the South Slavs share an ethnicity and, therefore, they should all be in the same state. The word 'ethnicity' was not, of course, used at the time. The term then current was 'race', a word without the extraordinarily negative connections that it bears today. But the content of 'race' was only partly biological. Its essence was language. The universal assumption in the analysis of nation-hood was that people speaking the same language were members of the same nation and should in consequence be living in the same state, hence the South Slavs (generously including the Slovenes and Macedonians in the same language group) were all members of one nation.[7]

This initial assumption was the single most important flaw in the creation of Yugoslavia because it ignored all other factors in the make-up of nationhood. Serbs and Croats spoke the same language, hence they were all member of the same nation and should, therefore, be living in the same state. As a syllogism this may work, but as sociology it was poor stuff. And, as cannot be emphasised too often, any ideology based on inadequate sociology will be faced with the choice of either abandoning its project or constructing the conditions that would then justify the ideology. In the South Slav context, this meant homogenising the various different ethnicities until they really were one.

To be fair, this was not quite so outrageous at the time as it appears today. Such projects of social engineering were common enough in the nineteenth century, as dominant ethnic groups

---

[7] Ivo Banac, *The National Question in Yugoslavia* (Ithaca, NY: Cornell University Press, 1984).

sought to assimilate weaker ones through their control of the state and the educational system. France is the classic example, but neighbouring Hungary had made a similar attempt; the Hungarian failure should have served as a warning to the South Slavs, but it was ignored, largely because they were misled by the question of language.

Exclusive emphasis on language meant that other key elements of identity were ignored and, when they interfered with the project, were suppressed. Of vital significance in this connection was that the Croats – the most important dissonant actor – really did have very different experiences from the Serbs and that their identity, the way in which they defined themselves as a community of moral worth, could not be reconciled with the vision of Yugoslavia held by the Serbs. The outcome was stress and friction. Despite the shared language – to which I shall return – there were many other markers and aspirations that separated the two communities.

In the first place, while the Croats did indeed launch the entire concept of Illyrianism, the basis of the South Slav idea, Illyrianism was not the only Croatian project. The nineteenth century saw the formulation of Croatian Rights as an alternative vision of the Croatian project, in which Croats were clearly and unmistakably different from the Serbs,[8] but the contingent circumstances of 1918 made this position inaudible.

Second, the Croatian identity was heavily marked by the experience with Budapest. While the Croatian perspective on Hungary tends to be negative, the reality is that the bulk of the Croatian elite acquired its view of politics in the struggle with Hungary and, to some extent, with Vienna. A Croatian elite with certain political skills, especially those of bargaining and legalism, had come into being and it had constructed an identity in which the nature of political communication was to that extent predetermined. There was an expectation that bargaining would produce results, even if those results were not necessarily what

---

[8] Djurdja Knezevic, 'The Enemy Side of National Ideologies: Croatia at the end of the 19th century and in the first half of the 20th century' in Laszlo Kontler (ed.), *Pride and Prejudice: National Stereotypes in 19th and 20th Century Europe East and West* (Budapest: Central Europe University Press, 1995), pp.105-18.

the Croats had set out to achieve. The Croatian étatic identity already existed.

Third, the Croats had a longer term historical and literary tradition of their own, one marked by contact with Venice, Vienna and the German-speaking world. A Croatian way of creating coherence was already in being. This too marked them out as different from the Serbs.

Finally, and rather importantly, there was religion. The difference was not merely the obvious one, that of differences between Eastern and Western Christian dogma. Rather, religion gives rise to a mediated identity derived from religion and religious styles. The ways of making the world are heavily influenced by the dominant religious identity of the community in question. In essence, as a result of the Counter-Reformation in the seventeenth century, much of Central Europe was re-Catholicised on a Protestant basis, that is to say that Catholic and Protestant values were in conflict. The Catholicism that resulted gave saliency to certain features of style and content. These included an emphasis on hierarchy and obedience, on display, on form over content, complexity over simplicity, the attempt to include all phenomena even if they are left unexplained and to gloss over inconsistencies. Counter-Reformation Roman Catholicism accepted the 'complexity of opposites', the *complexio oppositorum*, in which doctrinal opposites are brought into a kind of order so that unity may be enhanced.

The Serbian experience was wholly different. The Serbian experience had been one of resistance by force and the successful establishment of the Serbian state in the face of Ottoman hostility. The state experience and étatic identity of the Serbs was one of rather low levels of integration, given the limited of capacity of the Serbian state (poor-quality bureaucracy, high levels of illiteracy, corruption, tendency to ignore regulations, personalisation of politics). At the same time, the Serbian project was regarded as unfulfilled, in as much as sizeable numbers of undisputed Serbs continued to live under Austria-Hungary (Croatia, Vojvodina, Bosnia).

For the Serbian elite, this was a classic irredenta that had to be brought into the Serbian state by the equally classic methods of expansion through force and conquest. This last factor was highly significant in 1918, because the contingent events conspired to create precisely this symbolic experience. Threatened by Italian expansion, a section of The Croatian elite called on the Serbian government to send their armed forces into Croatia and Slovenia. What was experienced as liberation by the Croats was integrated into Serbian experience as yet another military expansion.

The question of language still misleads some observers. Their position is a simplistic philological one and does not differ from the nineteenth century position. According to the argument, people who speak the same language as defined philologically all belong to the same nation. The problem is that language as a cultural, let alone political phenomenon is quite different from philology. Although many people dismiss the role of politics in the definition of language, it is real enough.

After all, philologically the language of the United States and the United Kingdom is the same, the difference between them has arisen through politics and geography, but it is more than real enough. The same is true for France and Wallonia, where there is not even a sea boundary to separate one from the other. The cultural aspects of language show that over time, the different experiences of two communities speaking the same language philologically differentiates their language as well, as words begin to acquire different meanings, carry different emotional charges and evoke different responses. From this perspective, Serbian and Croatian were culturally different languages and culture, as argued in the foregoing, has a central role in the definition of nationhood through ethnicity. This set of differences between the two dominant ethnicities that made up Yugoslavia constituted the first and greatest flaw in the new state.

Then, the next integrating factor in the new state was to be the monarchy. This proposition again shows that it came from a different era, but monarchy was widely believed to have stabilising qualities that republics lacked. Possibly the sacralised quality of kingship lay behind this, the belief that despite the secularisation undergone by Europe since the Enlightenment, some kind of divine sacrament endowed monarchs with a higher political sense than mere presidents could command.

Whatever the truth or otherwise of this argument, the difficulty in the case of the South Slav kingdom was that Serbs and Croats had different expectations of kingship in the light of their pre-1918 experience. For the Serbs the monarch was theirs; for Croats he was emphatically not theirs, given that he had resided in Vienna and Budapest. Furthermore, when they approached the king, they expected him to be relatively detached with respect to the Croats and not to adopt a strongly centralising position which ignored their wishes. Not surprisingly, the monarchy rapidly lost whatever legitimacy it may have had in the eyes of the Croats.

To these deep-structural flaws can be added the contingent errors of perception and practice made by both Croatian and Serbian actors. Many of them certainly were errors and not antagonistic machinations, but such was the mutual sensitivity that there was no space for error and each move was interpreted in the harshest light. To take one example, the Croatian elite concluded that the Constituent Assembly of 1921 was so determinedly anti-Croat that there was no point attending. This was fairly clearly not the case.

Serbian attitudes were still comparatively fluid and there was still room for argument. In the absence of the Croats, however, the Vidovdan constitution really was highly centralising and did ignore Croatian susceptibilities. This was a self-fulfilling prophecy that came true. But, having said that, the decision to promulgate it on St Vitus Day, 28 June, a day heavily redolent of Serbian modes and perceptions (Battle of Kosovo Polje in 1389, anniversary of the assassination of Franz Ferdinand in 1914), was tactless, to say the least. It confirmed Croats in their belief that they had been right to stay away and legitimated their fears.

The remainder of interwar history simply moved along these predetermined lines of polarisation. Each step taken by one side or the other confirmed the actors in their conviction of the malign, intransigent, hostile nature of the other. Compromise was impossible with such people. The only answer, they believed, was force and yet more force. In effect, it was not until a significant part of the Serbian elite came to recognise that centralisation would not work, that the Croats would not be homogenised into Serbian modes, that some kind of compromise could be sought. But the 1939 *sporazum* (the compromise between Serbian and Croatian elites) was too late, Croatian attitudes had hardened and there was virtually no support left for Yugoslavia.

The events of the war are vital in understanding several processes. Central to these is state failure and refoundation, but to these should be added the scars of the war itself,[9] a conflict that became

---

[9] Milovan Djilas, *Wartime* (New York: Harcourt, Brace, 1977).

an inter-ethnic massacre that, in the immediate aftermath of the war, to some extent delegitimated violence as an acceptable instrument of politics and to create an atmosphere in which inter-ethnic cooperation was no longer anathema. The destruction of the old elites contributed to this change. In reality, the events of the war should be seen as a deep gulf between old and new, which made possible various options previously unthinkable. The communists both seized the opportunity offered by this gulf and contributed to the new options.

When they talked of a new order, they meant it. The new order would give rise to a new state radically different from the old, in which the ills of the old order would be swiftly remedied. The communists also enjoyed the immense advantage of having been untainted by the state failure and of their association with what appeared at the time to be the most successful and most dynamic ideology of the new world. This strength was also their greatest weakness. Any ideology and movement attempting to build a new world faces a key problem which it generally ignores – the past.

Because the revolutionaries are themselves suffused by their belief in the order that they are bringing into being, they assume that they are untainted by the old and that everyone else will readily accept the new world that they are creating. This establishes a Manichean mindset, in which the legacy of history – the real, living, authentic past – is dismissed as hostile conspiracy, because of the vain attempt to eliminate history itself. In reality, bits of the past will always live on and successful political projects are those that manage to graft the new onto the old without serious discontinuities. The Yugoslav communists were not interested in these subtleties, they already had the answer in the refounding of the state, with its completely different purposiveness and foundation myth. In this endeavour, they overlooked, as they were bound to, one fatal flaw. By tying the existence of the Yugoslav state to communism, they predicated that existence on the perpetual success of communism. In 1945 it was clearly impossible to envisage a time when communism would be so eroded that its weakness would threaten the future of the state; but by the mid-1980s, this was not quite such an extraordinary proposition.

To these structural weaknesses in the communist project, there should be added two others. In the first place, communism was a direct descendant of Enlightenment rationalism and communists believed that rational construction was not only viable, but expressly desirable. Implicit processes were denied or written off as legacies of the past. Obstacles that existed in the form of values and attitudes different from theirs were dismissed as irrational or alien or hostile. Second, the entire Marxist project had a very particular and peculiar relationship with ethnicity. At the level of theory, the two are incompatible, in as much as Marxism insists that the individual's primary and original identity, aspirations and world-view are derived from the material base. Ethnicity derives it from culture. Hence the persistence of ethnicity faced Marxism with two insurmountable problems: how to account for the survival of ethnic identities and what to do with them.

The solution was to define them as relics of the past and to give them formal existence as something that would wither away. This intellectual trap left Yugoslavia's communist rulers incapable of dealing with the resurgence of ethnic identity politics except by suppression, which then revived the responses of the interwar period. The consequence was that they were incapable of building a system that would give genuine expression to the ethnic reality of Yugoslavia and of allowing these realities some space within communist hegemony. Of course, that would have meant a formal dilution of the community ideology, hence of their legitimacy to rule, so it was not a step that could be taken until the very end.

The alternatives were unfortunate. Ethnic identities were initially suppressed and a Yugoslav identity was superimposed over them. But as the effectiveness of communism as a system waned, an off-stage ethnicity became more and more an accepted point of reference. The official language of politics was marked by an ever growing gap between the condemnations of ethnic nationalism and its reality. That gap too helped to undermine the legitimacy of the system and the state.

The central difficulty was that for Yugoslavia to be able to survive as a state, the communists would have had to collude in their own political demise and act as midwives to a democratic order; and they would have had to do it before the erosion was too far advanced, in other words before they saw any reason for it. This was evidently too much to expect.

To the foregoing, there are a number of contingent factors to be added as instrumental in the collapse of the state. The first of these was the role of Tito himself.[10] Tito was pivotal in the refoundation of the state and central to the maintenance of its cohesion. At the same time, unfortunately, he proved too limited in his vision to recognise that the Yugoslav order that he created would, after all, have to come to terms with ethnic identities and to allow them some room in politics. The various ethnic communities of Yugoslavia had not been superseded by the communist Yugoslav identity – an étatic, pseudo-civic identity – because it could not substitute for the real and symbolic bonds of solidarity that ethnicity provided. Tito was too inflexible, too much a captive of his authoritarianism, too caught up by his own towering authority to be able to recognise the true sociological processes that his own very real successes had launched.

Then, Tito's enormous prestige, authority and power brought with it the major disadvantage that it was all but impossible for a reasonably open-minded and sophisticated successor generation to take its place. Tito, like the jealous despot that he was, saw to it that it was third and fourth grade politicians who succeeded him. The post-1971 purges saw the best successor generation taken off the political scene to be replaced by party hacks. This proved to be a tragedy, because the system that Tito constructed could only be made to function by him or someone like him. After his death in 1980, the system drifted, the centre failed to hold and the power of the republics waxed. Increasingly, the reality of power was out of alignment with the purposiveness of the state.

Further, neither Tito nor Kardelj, chief ideological tailor to the system, had a true understanding of conflict and of the ways of resolving it.[11] Crucially, because they both understood ethnicity as a malign relic of the past, they were incapable of seeing the need for building instruments of ethnic conflict management. Tito had two ways of dealing with ethnic conflict – suppression and personal intervention. Neither would he do anything to establish routinised procedures accepted by all in the field of inter-ethnicity. The outcome was that the ethnic distribution of offices, resources

---

[10] Stevan Pavlowitch, *The Improbable Survivor: Yugoslavia and its Problems, 1918-1988* (London: Hurst, 1988); Milovan Djilas, *Tito: the Story from Inside* (New York: Harcourt, Brace, 1980).

[11] Paul Shoup, *Communism in the Yugoslav National Question* (New York: Columbia University Press, 1968).

and prestige was random, unpredictable and became a source of conflict and unregulated contest rather than one of reassurance. The experience of other multi-ethnic systems is unequivocal on the need to routinise an ethnic key. Titoism refused to do so, because it believed that ethnic identity was inherently negative.

The outcome of this was that elites, for whom an ethnic identity, along with a Yugoslav identity, was authentic tended to give saliency to the former. This process was much enhanced by the grave weakening of the federal centre after the 1960s. Once the power of the secret police was broken with the fall of Alexander Ranković and attacks on 'unitarism', the code-word for Serbian power, gained ground, the republics emerged as serious centres of power. The 1974 constitution secured this new arrangement by accepting the republican veto.[12] Consequently, it was perfectly rational for elites to adopt a republican identity and these were to some extent inherently ethnic (other than Bosnia-Hercegovina).

As these elites increasingly identified with republican power, they adopted its symbolic and real characteristics. It was at this point that the absence of a legitimate expression of ethnic identities in the public sphere turned into a real threat. These identities were authentic, they informed politics, but they had always to be disguised by another language, by another political vocabulary. The only way out would have been to recognise these identities as real, to provide the mechanisms for reconciling them and gradually to transform the system from a pseudo-consociational one to a real consociationalism. But that came up against the rock of the communist ideology, the one upon which the state itself was to be shipwrecked.

The only counterweight to these republican elites was the federal bureaucracy and the armed forces. Neither could be the core of an all Yugoslav identity because they drew their legitimacy from the ruling ideology and once that was gone, their position was fragile. The spectacle of JNA, the Yugoslav armed forces, looking for a political home in the summer of 1991, after Croatia and Slovenia had opted for independence, illustrated this process vividly and with a tragic outcome. The seceding republics had no further use for the JNA, which they saw as inherently pro-Serbian, and which saw them as destructive of Yugoslavia. The

[12] Leonard J. Cohen, *Broken Bonds: Yugoslavia's Disintegration and Balkan Politics in Transition,* 2nd edn (Boulder, CO: Westview, 1995).

gap in perceptions was evident – for the Croats and the Slovenes, 'Yugoslavia' had become symbolic of Serbian power, while for the JNA, the Yugoslav state was an essential entity to make its existence valid and legitimate.

The nature of non-elite ethnicity was just as relevant. In the immediate aftermath of the war, it is reasonably clear that war-weariness and disgust at the inter-ethnic killing had led many people to concluded that their ethnic identities were less significant as a source of meaning than had been the case before the war. Until the 1960s these ethnic identities coexisted with a Yugoslav identity, even when people continued to identify themselves with their ethnic affiliation. The question then arises as to why this Yugoslav identity declined. Even at its peak, it was never able to attract even 10 per cent of the population (those who returned their identity as 'Yugoslav, nationally undetermined' in the censuses).

The explanation has to be sought in a number of factors. First, there was the process of republicanisation already mentioned. Just as republics attracted elites, so they attracted non-elites too.[13] This did not mean, at that stage, that the ethnic identity excluded the Yugoslav one, but the former gradually gained in its power to resonate. Some of this had to do with the failures of the system, both the failure to construct meaningful inter-ethnic mechanisms and in the general sense, that as ethnicity was slightly illicit, its place in the official Yugoslav order was never clear, it could pose as a superior alternative without having to put its cards on the table. Ethnic identities could promise much as the 'normal and natural' order without being called on to deliver.

Then, ethnic identities prospered through the failure of the Yugoslav one. Yugoslavism as a doctrine was too closely bound up with communism and, given the propensity of communists to centralise power, it was associated with Serbian power. This made it hard for non-Serbs to see a genuinely all Yugoslav identity as attractive to them. The Yugoslav identity was an étatic identity that, by definition, had limited democratic content. As long as the Yugoslav state was non-democratic, the identity that it propagated was similarly non-democratic.

---

[13] Laslo Sekelj, *Yugoslavia: the Process of Disintegration* (New York: Columbia University Press, 1993).

This applied even to the much vaunted slogan of '*bratsvo i jedinstvo*' (brotherhood and unity) the supposed cornerstone of 'nationalities policy'. The slogan was always imposed and not assumed voluntarily. There was always an element of threat and coercion behind it: 'if you are not nice to your fellow Yugoslavs, we have ways of making you nice'. Indeed, the first direct intervention by the JNA into Yugoslav politics was over the Croatian crisis of 1971. This element of coercion effectively removed any incentive for people to learn inter-ethnic accommodation from below. Traditional, pre-communist modes of such accommodation coexisted, sometimes uneasily, with brotherhood and unity, but neither was adequate and neither had full legitimacy.

To these factors there should be added the sociology of Yugoslav urbanisation. As everywhere else in the communist world, industrialisation was rapid and undertaken without much thought for its consequences.[14] Urban ghettos were built and rural migrants were decanted into them, with all the attendant ills that are so familiar from every other part of the world. Crucially, no attempt was made to construct an urban identity that would respond to needs of these migrants, how they were to conduct themselves as urban workers and citizens, other than a vague proletarian identity (this was less clear-cut than in the Soviet world).

The outcome was the ruralisation of the city. Rural modes, rural thought-worlds, rural values and attitudes persisted. Central in this connection was the persistence of ethnic allegiance as the key source of meanings. Contact with members of other ethnicities reinforced it rather than diluted it. It was only in cities where there already existed a tradition of inter-ethnic accommodation from before the communist period that ethnic relations could be regulated.[15] Time helped to some extent. Where members of two communities had lived in the same tower block for a couple of decades, this might make matters easier, but even then, when the decisive test came after 1991, it turned out that suspicion and hostility prevailed over tolerance.

Once again, the absence of a clear-cut Yugoslav identity that was relevant to inter-ethnic relations and was felt to be authentic

---

[14] Andrei Simic, *The Peasant Urbanites: a Study of Rural-Urban Mobility in Serbia* (New York: Seminar Press, 1973).

[15] Dževad Karahasan, *Il centro del mondo. Sarajevo, esilio di una città*: (Milan: Il Saggiatore, 1995).

proved to be a far-reaching flaw in the system. It meant that once the system came to be tested, there was only a minority prepared to stand up for it. The majority was either actively hostile or passive or open to mobilisation along ethnic lines and at that moment, all the myths of the ethnic order could be brought into play; these proved to be stronger, as they generally are, than the actual ground level experience of accommodation. Yugoslav counter-myths were too feeble to have much effect.[16]

Finally a word about the international context of Yugoslavia. International support for states helps them to remain in being and to overcome the threat of state failure. States help one another almost instinctively, presumably on the tacit assumption that the failure of one state is a reflection on them all. Yugoslavia was undoubtedly the beneficiary of this approach. In the interwar period the Yugoslav state came to be seen as a stabilising factor in the Balkans, as the instrument for keeping the lid on otherwise troublesome and quarrelsome ethnic groups[17] and it reassumed this role after 1948 as the non-Soviet communist state that kept the Soviet Union out of the Adriatic.

Even when the doctrine of human rights began to make headway in Europe, Yugoslavia's poorish record was simply overlooked on strategic grounds. The kind of criticism that was levelled at other communist states, like Czechoslovakia, was regarded as 'undesirable', not least because the Yugoslav authorities were successful in presenting their dissidents as ethnic troublemakers (e.g. those imprisoned in the post-1972 purge in Croatia and their counterparts in the other republics). The same went for Yugoslavia's tilt towards the Soviet Union, as in 1967 when it granted Warsaw Pact aircraft overflying rights to supply Egypt in the Six Day War; the West simply ignored this. The Yugoslav leadership, for its part, used its adherence to the doctrine of non-alignment to generate prestige and support in the Third World.

From the international perspective, therefore, Yugoslavia's problems began when its roles as intermediary and as buffer state between the West and the Soviet Union began to lose their value in the mid-1980s. The attempt to construct a European identity and legitimation for Yugoslavia – the intermediary role was too

---

[16] See pp. 67-82.

[17] Rebecca West, *Black Lamb and Grey Falcon* (London: Macmillan, 1942).

great to sustain by that stage – could not gain much support because of the legacy of the past and the country's adherence to a communist legitimation. Nevertheless, when the cracks in the edifice of the state grew visible the West ignored these and continued to back a state that was enjoying less and less domestic support.

It is open to question whether earlier Western attention to Yugoslavia in 1989-90 might have preempted the polarisation that led to the collapse. The level of intervention needed would have been very far-reaching and the will to intervene in this fashion was not there. Besides, by 1990 the West was suffering from bureaucratic overload as communism was collapsing generally and the question of German unification arrived on the agenda.

Furthermore, there was a real Western fear that allowing Yugoslavia to break up would serve as a precedent for the disintegration of the Soviet Union. There is a lesson to be drawn from all this. International pressure is seldom sufficient to maintain a state if it lacks domestic legitimacy and if the consent to sustain is absent. This lesson, it would appear, has still to be absorbed by the West. The attempts to enforce the Dayton Agreement and keep Bosnia in being are strangely reminiscent of the way in which Western attitudes are marked by a belief that whenever possible states must be sustained, whether their domestic bases justify this or not.

23

POWER, ETHNICITY AND COMMUNISM IN YUGOSLAVIA

The rise and fall of Yugoslavia between 1918 and 1991 clearly illustrates the proposition that states require a cohesive set of ideas and identities acceptable to the bulk of the population by which to legitimate themselves. In most cases in Europe, states are based on a single dominant ethnic groups which frames the underlying set of ideas that provide the purposiveness that institutions need for their survival. Yugoslavia is significant because no one single ethnic group was in a position to act as the basis for the state and as a result, two alternative concepts were attempted. They both failed.

The first of the two, inter-war Yugoslavia, rested on the two not wholly mutually supportive pillars of language and monarchy. They both had antecedents in the nineteenth century with significant consequences for the twentieth. The central concept of statehood that emerged in Central and Eastern Europe after the reception of nationalism in the first half of the nineteenth century was the equation of language, nation and state. Although this proposition was frequently stated as an incontrovertible fact by nationalists, in reality it was a programme. Indeed, all three elements were programmatic and ignored other aspects of the existing cultural and political order, something which could be said of many programmes.

Taking the question of language first, it was by no means self-evident in the region that language meant in all respects the same thing as intended by the protagonists of linguistic nationalism in the West. The difficulty in Central and Eastern Europe was that with the exception of Polish, none of the languages of the area enjoyed an unbroken history as a medium of high cultural and political communication. While many of them had had some kind of a mediaeval or early modern existence as the language of a court or literature, this had generally fallen into desuetude and they existed only as series of peasant dialects.

343

Consequently the construction of a language as a cultural medium required an act of will. This was undertaken by the intellectuals who were just then entering the political scene and thereby secured themselves a solid status and base for power. In this respect, the definition of these old-new languages – Czech, Hungarian and in the South Slav lands, Serbian, Croatian and Slovene – was an act of rational construction, with opportunity for claims to power being smuggled in with hidden agendas. Nationalists might claim that all they were doing was reviving long-suppressed languages and thereby providing opportunities for the spirit of the people to find expression, much as Herder had proclaimed, but the way in which a language was defined unquestionably had implications for the size and population of the nation and state that these nationalists were seeking to call into existence.

In the South Slav lands this problem was acutely complex because in strictly philological terms, using the spoken language on the ground as the benchmarks, the entire Slavonic speaking Balkans constituted a single language area. Slavonic dialects shaded off into one another and by linguistic criteria no fundamental distinction could be made between the dialects that eventually became Slovene, Serbian, Croatian, Macedonian and Bulgarian. When the nineteenth century intellectuals began their endeavours, therefore, their decisions were to have far-reaching results both culturally and politically. With Slovene and Bulgaria, these issues were resolved by the activists of these proto-nations opting for variants that were recognisably different from their neighbours. Macedonian is a separate issue that only emerged as a key factor after the Second World War. The problem of the Serbian and Croatian languages, on the other hand, bedevilled relations between these ethnic groups virtually from the outset. The essence of the relationship was that in the nineteenth century a group of Croatian intellectuals decided to opt for the particular dialect of Croatian (Stokavski) that was closest to Serbian in the conscious belief that in consequence, the groups would come to constitute a single nation and thereby eventually find statehood together.

The Illyrian idea

This became known as the Illyrian idea, which attracted considerable support from among the Croats, who found the thought of Serbian backing against Vienna and Budapest rather congenial.

A minority of Croats, however, rejected this and argued that the Croatian nation was separate and different from the Serbs. This division of opinion was never fully settled, but during and immediately after the First World War, the great majority of the Croatian elite opted for Illyrianism and Yugoslavia, although it should be noted that Stjepan Radić, the future leader of the Peasant Party, rejected it from the outset. The Croats had constructed an identity that overemphasised language and understated the significance of history and religion (Roman Catholicism).

The Serbs likewise came to accept the Yugoslav idea, but did so with a different history and with different agendas. This requires further refinement. Under Ottoman rule, the Serbian patriarchate at Peć became the only Serbian institution and the identification between the Serbs and Orthodoxy grew very strong during the centuries. As far as language was concerned the Serbs all effectively spoke the same Stokavian dialect, but politically could be divided into two broad groups, the Serbs of Serbia proper and the Serbs of Austria-Hungary.

The former lived in the Kingdom of Serbia, which had successfully carved out its independence from the ailing Ottoman Empire in the nineteenth century and added new territories, inhabited mostly by Eastern Orthodox Slavophones, who were easily integrated into the Serbian national ideal. The Serbs outside Serbia, the *precani*, in the Vojvodina, Bosnia and Croatia, shared the language and religion of the Serbs, but their politics was determined by different considerations: relations with Vienna, with Budapest and, where appropriate, with the Croats.

They identified themselves as Serbs by language, religion and history; the role of the memory of the glorious defeat at Kosovo, which marked the end of the mediaeval Serbian state and the conservation of this memory through the great cycle of oral ballads can hardly be overstated in this context. What the Serbs were reluctant to accept, however, was that other South Slavs, speaking the same language as themselves, could have a substantially different culture. There was a clear tendency on their part to see the Croats as Catholicised Serbs, who would return to Serbdom once the error of their ways was demonstrated to them. Alternatively, they expressed reservations about Illyrianism, which they regarded as an attempt by the Croats to denationalise the Serbs.

The strongest current among the Serbs, as represented by the great cultural innovator, Vuk Stefanović Karadžić, was that all speakers of the Stokavian dialect were Serbs. In this way, there arose two diametrically opposed conceptions of the South Slav nation: the Croats' Illyrianism, which sought to include all the South Slavs while recognising some of the differences among them, and the Serbian one, which was purely linguistic and ignored cultural, religious and historical factors. By the mid-nineteenth century, the Serbian state was influenced in the direction of expanding its power over all speakers of Stokavian, whom it regarded as Serbs. This unification of the Serbs would take place under the Serbian monarchy, as the only possible counterweight to Austria.

The role of the Serbs of Croatia

The Serbs of Croatia were both subjects and objects of these processes. They looked back on a tradition of separateness defined by the Military Frontier, which was directly under the jurisdiction of Vienna, and which gave them an identity of their own. They were uneasy about the rise of Croatian nationalism and tended to look simultaneously towards Serbia, Vienna and Budapest, especially in the last years of the nineteenth century, when the Hungarian government relied on them heavily as a political base.

In the early years of this century, at a time of growing tension within the monarchy, the project of Croatian and Serbian cooperation against Budapest was born. Eventually this was to culminate in the wartime Corfu Declaration, the basis of a South Slav state agreed among the leaders of the three main protagonists, the Croats, the Serbs of Croatia and the Serbian leadership.

The new state came into being on 1 December 1918 and was based, as sketched above, on the principles of one language giving rise to one nation, and the Serbian monarchy which was now elevated to an all-South Slav kingdom. Indeed, the state was initially called the Kingdom of Serbs, the Croats and Slovenes. It was inevitably based on serious mutual misperceptions on the part of both Serbs and Croats.

Both language and monarchy fell into this category of misunderstanding, but this was exacerbated by differences of style and aspirations derived from different historical experiences. The Serbs insisted on establishing Yugoslavia as a unitary state and were impatient with any suggestions of federalism. They were able to write this into the Vidovdan Constitution not least because

Radić insisted on boycotting the constitutive assembly. Vidovdan – St Vitus Day, 28 June – was the day on which the Battle of Kosovo was fought; its significance as a symbol of national affirmation for the Serbs was enormous, but its adoption as a Yugoslav symbol was an ominous indication of how the Serbian elite viewed the new state. This emphasis on a unitary state was hardly surprising. Unitarism had been the key Serbian experience. By the same token, the Croats' political experience had been precisely the opposite: continuous argument with Vienna and Budapest from a recognised position of a separate political existence.

On the language issue, the new ruling elite was dominated by Serbs and Yugoslav-inclined Croats (as well as Slovenes, of course) and it was decided early on that these two ethnic groups were in fact one nation and that they spoke one language, Serbo-Croat. The 1921 census did not ask questions about national allegiance and returned Serbo-Croat speakers as a single majority.

The monarchy was, as agreed, the Serbian monarchy writ large, but with very little evidence that the king, Alexander, had any understanding of the need to appear in a different light to his Croat subjects. He shared the view of the Serbian elite that Croats were essentially the same as Serbs and where they behaved in an unexpected, non-Serbian fashion, this was occasioned by ill-will or other deviancy or political disloyalty. This attitude was underpinned by the historical baggage which the Serbs brought with them: the idea that the new state must be strong, unitary, centered on Belgrade and run by Serbs. There was no suggestion of proportionality or any redefinition of the state ideology in a way that would satisfy the Croats. In fact, pro-Yugoslav Croats accepted this with few reservations, not least because parts of Croatia, notably the littoral, were under threat from Italy and the Serbian connection provided a vital defence.

Croatian political culture

Not that the Croats were without baggage of their own. Crucial in this respect was their experience in their struggle against Vienna and Budapest, which had been legalistic and argumentative. The Croatian discourse was couched in terms of petitions, pleas, counter-pleas and the like, which left the Serbian elite, to whom this was alien, perplexed and impatient. Any detached examination of the relationship between the Prime Minister Nikola Pašić and the leader of the largest Croatian party, the Peasant Party, Stjepan Radić would leave the impression of a *dialogue des sourds*. It was as if the two leaders were discussing entirely different matters; the political process was not helped by Pašić's lack of imagination and Radić's mercurial, unpredictable behaviour.

The Serbs felt that the Croats could never be satisfied with what was on offer, while the Croats felt cheated that Yugoslavia did not mean the hoped for liberation through statehood, but a new semi-colonial dependency, made all the worse by the fact that the Serbs operated by a very different set of ground rules from the one that they had learned in Budapest. Nor were matters helped by the monarch, who intervened indirectly in politics whenever he thought that royal or Serbian interest were affected. Finally, the Serbs of Croatia were initially euphoric, but gradually concluded that the new dispensation did not bring them as much as they had hoped. Matters were resolved in a highly negative way with the murder or Radić in 1928 actually on the floor of the Yugoslav parliament (he died two months later – he was shot by a deputy who insisted that he could no longer tolerate the way in which Radić insulted the honour of the Serbian nation). The Croats took drastic revenge. In 1934 two Croatian gunmen murdered Alexander in Marseilles, where he had just arrived on an official visit, and the French foreign minister who was a accompanying him for good measure too. Before this, using Radić's murder as the pretext, Alexander had suspended parliament and instituted a royal dictatorship, from which the Croats felt themselves excluded. The agreement of 1939, known as the *Sporazum*, came too late to reconcile the two parties and when Germany invaded Yugoslavia in 1941, responses from Serbs and Croats were very different. The former resisted, the latter used the opportunity to establish a state of their own. The event clearly demonstrated that the Yugoslav state lacked the support of the Croats, essentially because neither linguistic nor monarchical legitimation gave them enough of an interest to attract their backing, but on the contrary, spurred their opposition.

Partisans and the war

The collapse of Yugoslavia was followed by four years of war. The war years were extraordinarily and predictably cruel in which the pent-up frustrations and passions of the inter-war years, the sense of humiliation felt by the Croats and the sense of betrayal felt by the Serbs were released. Three main currents emerged. The new rulers of the Croatian state (known by its initials, NDH– *Nezavisla Državna Hrvatske* or Independent State of Croatia) embarked on a policy of constructing an ethnically pure Croatia by genocide and many thousands of Serbs were massacred. The Serbs in Serbia rallied behind the monarchy, as represented by the Četniks, while those in Croatia joined the communist-led Partisans. As the war unfolded, the Partisans offered the clearest and most attractive programme. In essence, they were successful in creating a threefold legitimating myth: that they were the only truly committed force dedicated to fighting the foreign occupation forces; that they were the true representatives of inter-ethnic peace and reconciliation; and that they would most effectively achieve the aspirations of the radical peasant masses, which had been largely excluded from the politics of the interwar period. Neither the Croatian nationalists nor the Četniks were able to match this dynamism and persuasiveness and the Partisans emerged from the Second World War as double victors. They expelled all the foreign occupation forces and they defeated their enemies in a civil war. In 1945, they were definitely the masters.

The post-war order was consciously built on the proposition that the pre-war system had failed, that a revolution had taken place and that the new communist ideology was the wave of the future. The self-confidence and energy of the new rulers were unquestionably bolstered by their unshakeable belief in communist ideology and practice: that class was invariably more significant than nation and, say, a Serbian worker could by definition not have different interest from a Croatian worker. Where a nationally differentiated interest was perceived, this false consciousness could be corrected by agitation and propaganda, by resocialising the population and by ridding society of its reactionary elements. Nationhood, in this belief system, was a bourgeois device aimed at dividing the proletariat and at preventing it from recognising its true interest of proletarian internationalism.

The other elements in the mix included the enormous prestige of the communist leader, Josip Broz Tito, who was of mixed Croatian-Slovenian descent but always regard himself as a Yugoslav. To the Tito factor should be added the prestige derived from victory in the twofold war and the associated prestige of the Soviet Union among a population who had been sympathetic to

Pan-Slavism and tended to regard the Soviet Union as the revitalised Slav power. Among the Orthodox, this was enhanced by the traditional role that Russia had played as the protector of Orthodox Christians in the Balkans. The practical arrangements made by the communists – they established a nominally federal system that remained under the very tight control of the communist party – derived from these factors. The underlying idea was that communist ideology would serve as the unifying formula to hold the different nations together and that Leninist organisation would provide the cement. Consequently the reduction of ethnicity to its cultural aspects was intended to be a first step in the direction of a political order in which ethnicity would eventually disappear.

In 1948 the new Yugoslavia faced its first major test. Stalin launched a political assault on the Yugoslav communists, whom he regarded as far too independent, and expected that they would crumple. They did not do so; on the contrary they were able to mobilise support from virtually all elements in the country, very largely on the tacit argument that Yugoslavs had not fought for their independence in order to see themselves subordinated to the Soviet Union. This was effective, but it undermined internationalism, especially as it involved communist Yugoslavia in a conflict with the fountainhead of internationalism, the Soviet Union. This conflict represented the first shift in Yugoslavia's ideology in the direction of relying on a form of nationalism, the ideology of the state as a state worth keeping in being for itself, in preference to having it merged in some kind of a proletarian super-state.

Emerging successfully from the confrontation, Tito and his lieutenants realised that they would need to transform their own legitimating ideology and, as much by good luck as by conscious planning, they hit upon the idea of a communism not dependent on the Soviet Union, something that was an epoch-making innovation at the time. It boosted their legitimacy, especially when it was buttressed by self-management at home and non-alignment abroad. Both these ideas were used as differentiating factors intended to enhance a Yugoslav identity. As long as tight political control by the party – renamed the League of Yugoslav Communists in 1952 as a (merely) symbolic move away from Leninist democratic centralism – was in place, ethno-national identities could not find any space for political expression. Indeed, in the immediate aftermath of the wartime killings, the strict policy of the party in clamping down very hard on anything that might remotely threaten its monopoly attracted a certain amount of approbation when it affected nationhood. The proposition that Serbian, Croatian, Slovenian and other identities should fade away, except perhaps as cultural relics, received a measure of popular approval.

One move by the party, however, was to have far-reaching and ultimately fatal results, a classic illustration of the law of unintended consequences. This was the creation of a federal system. Initially, these newly established republics were no more than façades. Real power lay with Tito, his close associates and the party. Gradually the republics acquired identities of their own and came to see themselves as real loci of power. In the early years it did not matter. There were no significant differences between, say, Slovenes and Serbs and anything that arose could be settled by Tito. But by the 1960s, this arrangement would no long operate quite as smoothly as it had before. The origins of the 1960s crisis was a seizing up of both the political and the economic machinery.

In a sense, the communist rulers of Yugoslavia were the victims of their own success. They had stabilised the country, created a system which had more than a degree of legitimacy, as well as international recognition, and they were well on the way to in-dustrialising parts of Yugoslavia, in particular the northern republics of Croatia and Slovenia. A threshold had been reached in politics, economics and in society which would require a redistribution of power; how much, in what way and by what criteria then became a matter for debate. This debate was to give rise to the first really serious internal crisis of the post-war era, the Croatian crisis of 1971.

The reforms of the 1960s

The crisis of the 1960s, which was to culminate in the events of 1971, was extraordinarily complex and involved arguments over democratisation, Marxism, socialism, nationhood, efficiency and marketisation. Its centre was the question of what kind of a state Yugoslavia was to be. No attempt will be made to disentangle any of this complexity here, nor any assessment of the crisis, only an examination of the way in which it impacted on the role of ethnicity and of the policies brought to bear on it. The key starting point is worth restating. All the participants, despite the subsequent rhetoric, started out from the assumption that Yugoslavia would remain in being as a state and that it would continue to be ruled by a self-managing Marxist ideology. The difficulty was that both these notions could be open to a variety of interpretations.

By the early 1960s, the Croatian communist leadership, supported by the Slovenes, but also by the liberal Serbian intellectuals, had begun to challenge the centralising, hard-hat Partisan generation, that took a view of change as being something threatening and could always block proposals for reform by reference to the communism that it controlled. Indeed, a wide variety of interests could be hidden behind the façade of communism and by reference to the Partisan struggle. It should be understood here that the Partisans could hardly be accused of possessing a very high level of political sophistication. They had come from the villages to sweep away the old, corrupt, exploitative order, found a seemingly perfect recipe in communism, a tailor-made leader in Tito and carried with them all the baggage of the simple messianistic world of the epic struggle against the enemy. They were quite unsuited to ruling an increasingly complex society but were not about to yield power to those who were. Hence if the party condemned some manifestation of discontent as 'nationalistic', they simply accepted it and used the tough methods that they always had to eliminate it.

The preeminence of this elite was strengthened by another factor that was almost unique to Yugoslavia in the communist world. Not only was the *ancien régime* discredited, but its representatives had very largely disappeared. They had died during the war or had gone into emigration, with the result that the new elite had a fairly free hand in determining the patterns and codes of elite behaviour, which they took overwhelmingly from their radical peasant beliefs and from communism. Neither predisposed them to patience, subtlety and compromise. Yet while this elite firmly believed that it was creating a new, anti-national communist identity, in reality matters were more complex. Whatever people's ostensible motives might have been, those affected by communist policies did not automatically abandon their ethnic identities and a Serbian official would continue to be perceived as a Serb, however much he might protest that he was acting out of communist conviction. This phenomenon was particularly acute in Croatia, where a clear ethnic pattern was established under the communist veil. The Serbs who joined the Partisans to escape the Ustaša massacres automatically emerged as the winners in the post-war order and were highly influential in the Croatian party and the instruments of coercion. For them, these institutions were seen as a guarantee that the Serbs of Croatia would never again be menaced by fascist genocide, as well as of the success of communism through which ethnic discrimination ended. It should be noted that not all the Serbs of Croatia were communist, but the leadership was very strongly so, and was able to impose its will on the rest of the community.

Thereby they simply ignored the unarticulated Croatian response, which was an expression of an experience of frustration and humiliation, and resentment that Croats could not even be trusted to build communism on their own, but had to do it under Serbian tutelage. The fact that majority of communists in Croatia were Croats did not disturb this picture. Nor was the Croatian view of the world helped by the widely propagated thesis about the 'Ustaša nature' of the Croatian nation. For all practical purposes, any expression of Croatian identity could be branded and delegitimated in this way, regardless of the content and regardless too of other interests that might be served by such condemnation.

While in Croatia, the Serbian minority's economic interests had merged with the structures of communist party power, in Yugoslavia at large, two significant coalitions of interest had come into being by the 1960s, both of which had an ethnic, as well as a non-ethnic, base. At this time the economy was beginning to slow down as extensive resources were exhausted, the political factories – enterprises subsidised for political purposes, mainly in the underdeveloped southern republics – were proving unecono-mic and the shift of excess rural population to town was producing unemployment or underemployment. It was clear that this system could not be sustained for long without dire consequences and in 1965, the reformers succeeded in pushing through a major economic reform; they were opposed by the conservatives, who recognised that their economic resources and sources of power and patronage would be threatened if the reform was successful.

Reform, conservatism and ethnicity

What was striking here was the line-up. The reformers were mostly concentrated in Croatia and Slovenia, though they also had some strength in Serbia, whereas the conservatives were in the other, less developed republics. Hence the republican structures, which Tito and Kardelj, the Yugoslav party's long-serving ideologist, had intended to be nothing more than administrative agencies, were increasingly acquiring real political content and given that the republics did have an ultimate ethnic base, the arrival of the ethnic issue on the agenda could not be long delayed. When it occurred, it showed that attempts to eviscerate the ethnic elements of nationhood and to overlay them with an all-embracing Yugoslav identity had failed.

Yugoslavism deserves a short discussion in this context. It was launched by Kardelj, who acted as a kind of ideological tailor for the Yugoslav party throughout his long career – if the party needed a new ideology, he would run it up; if it wanted it shortened or a hem taken in or a turn-up removed, he would invariably oblige. In the 1950s, the need was for a justification of federal domination and Yugoslavism met the bill. It had several aspects – history, language, class, in all of which a single Yugoslav variant was distilled and then declared to have been the authentic version and imposed in the population. Despite about fifteen years of socialisation, this endeavour failed, partly because of its inherent implausibility, partly because of the memories it raised of the inter-war period and partly also because of the crass way in which it was enforced. The proof of the pudding became evident precisely at the moment when the covert ethnicity of the 1950s emerged into the daylight in the later 1960s.

The reformers discovered that despite having the best of the intellectual argument, plus the windfall advantage of the own-goal scored by the conservatives when Alexander Ranković, the federal minister of interior, was found to have bugged Tito's residence and was sacked, thereby removing many constraints on the political sphere, the conservative forces could not be so easily overcome. Their ethnic and political base was in the southern republics, fearful of the winds of market competition; in the armed forces (JNA) fearful of republican power; in the veterans' organisations, fearful of losing their privileges; and in the instruments of coercion, fearful of coming under direct political control. The result was stalemate, neither side was strong enough to defeat the other. In 1969 the Croatian leadership sought to break the log-jam by using popular support, which automatically meant reference to ethnic aspirations. They moved in the first instance against their local conservatives (the Žanko affair), many of whom were ethnic

Serbs; the affair was automatically interpreted by the local Serbs an initiative directed against them. This was true, but again it was partly ethnic and partly to do with power derived from the communist victory. The difficulty was that the dispute could only be argued out in the discourse of Titoism, which of course had no room for ethnicity.

What transformed the reformist–conservative conflict in the 1960s was that for the time being Tito was neutral. This neutrality removed a vital curb on the Croatian leadership, which by 1970 was openly encouraging the population in its attempt to garner power. Croatian opinion, long suppressed and grappling with the burden of humiliation, both symbolic and real, immediately began to push for a restoration of its national world, especially in the symbolic realm, much to the alarm of the Serbian minority. This development could then be used by the conservatives to delegitimate the Croatian strategy in communist terms. In effect, there was a conflict of codes, with the ethno-national discourse perpetually denied legitimacy by those who controlled power and thus the language of public discourse in Yugoslavia. In a sense this was understandable. The moment that a communist ruler permits the use of nationalist language, his own credibility as a communist will be undermined, given the theoretical incompatibility between nationalism (basing its ultimate rationale on culture) and communism (on class).

The Croatian nationalists who challenged the party leadership did so on a variety of grounds. What threatened to be the most disruptive or was perceived in this way was the question of language. As suggested above, philologically there is nothing to differentiate Serbian from Croatian, and this was given a programmatic quality by the Novi Sad agreement of 1954, signed by Serbian and Croatian intellectuals at the height of the campaign in support of Yugoslavism. This proposed that there was one Serbo-Croat language which existed in two variants, each of full validity. But when the Croatian intellectuals began to inspect the dictionary of the language published in Belgrade, they discovered that words in the Croatian variant were frequently described as 'dialect', so much so that some of them denounced the agreement and began work on the development of a fully-fledged Croatian literary language. An orthographical dictionary of Croatian was subsequently suppressed as a source of conflict between Serbs and Croats. The attempt to differentiate Croatian identity linguistically was a clear indication that self-definition by language retained its force as an expression of identity in Central and Eastern Europe, however artificial such initiatives might initially be. In the case of Croatian, the newly revived medium took root.

As the Croatian strategy unfolded, however, the Zagreb party leadership discovered an unpleasant reality deriving precisely from this point. On the one hand, they were put on the defensive *vis-à-vis* the conservatives, given that it was difficult for them to ward off charges of nationalism in a system that regarded – and had to regard – nationalism as a most serious deviation. Then, on the other hand, they found that however far they might go in placing themselves at the head of a national-patriotic movement, they could never be fully accepted as the authentic agents of nationhood, but were perceived as fellow travellers, so to speak. They were always vulnerable to being outbid by those who were genuinely nationalist and this was exactly what happened. Nationalists, unlike the Zagreb leadership, were not concerned with heeding the limits and contortions required of those who sought to enfold their national appeal in pseudo-Marxist language; they could appeal directly to national aspirations. This process immediately brought the key issue of communism to the agenda in the form of a threat to the party's monopoly of power, a challenge to the leading role of the party. It was this development that finally convinced Tito to throw his weight behind the conservatives and purge the Croatian leadership at the end of 1971, threatening them with military intervention. Tito then went on to eliminate 'the rotten liberals' from other republican leaderships in an attempt to return to authentic Marxism. This heralded a renewed Marxist attempt to control the ethno-national issue.

Republicanisation and the 1974 constitution

So far this chapter has concentrated on the Serbian-Croatian conflict as the core of the national questions in Yugoslavia, but it is appropriate at this point to expand the perspective and to look at the issues raised in the context of other national groups as well, because they tended to gain increasing saliency in the 1970s, particularly as a result of the 1974 constitution (another of Kardelj's excursions into the intellectual rag-trade). The new experiment sought to reestablish the central party as the dominant actor in politics, but it recognised that genuine forces were released in the 1960s which would require some satisfying. These forces would as far as possible be restricted to the republican level and even within the republics, self-management would be upgraded through greater power being given the communes (*opština*) and the enterprises, in the hope that they would emerge as the true foci of power, loyalty and identity, thereby transcending ethnicity. The external limits of the system would be safeguarded by the armed forces, now formally declared the guardians of *bratstvo i jedinstvo* (brotherhood and unity), the code words for the integrity of the state against nationalist challenges. This political order was fleshed out by a revitalisation of the secret police, the reintroduction of political criteria in employment through having to meet nebulous criteria of 'moral-political fitness' for various appointments, the re-ideologisation of education, and symbolic campaigns to reenact unity, for example in the numberless films churned out in the 1970s to celebrate the Partisan victory and thereby to reinforce the message of unity in arms under communist and thus anti-nationalist leadership. Trials of those accused of nationalism were particularly tough in Croatia, with long prison terms of four years or more being the norm. This was the time when Franjo Tudjman served his first prison sentence; he served a second one in 1982-1984.

The crucial unintended consequence of the 1974 constitution was republicanisation, a process whereby the republics increasingly became the true centres of power at the expense of the centre, something they were able to do through the introduction of the republican veto in federal affairs. By the 1980s Yugoslavia consisted of eight separate sub-polities (the six republics and the two provinces). The republican parties never lost control of their own *nomenklaturas*, but they were able to deflect some of the initiatives of the centre and increasingly they had to legitimate themselves through a mixture of self-managing ideology and the republican interest. This latter was a curious hybrid of regionalism and ethnicity, inevitably so given the original ethno-cultural content with which the republics had been endowed, so that ethnicity, which has seemingly been buried by the 1971 intervention, returned by the back-door.

The republican constellation was not what it had been though. The great innovation of Titoism had been the creation of new nations as a means of resolving ethnic competition; promoting the inhabitants of particular areas into nationhood removed the

object of such contests from the political scene. By the 1970s
the nations had begun to assume a reality and acquire authentic
support from those affected.

Matters did not change immediately after Tito's death in 1980s.
For a while the post-Tito leadership attempted to rule as if Tito
were still alive. Various symbolic reenactments of his personal
authority were tried and criticism of the late president was prohi-
bited. Decisions were made collectively and consensually in that
republicanisation meant the republican veto. But it was evident
that this system could not work without Tito's authority, as the
republican interests were growing without there being any effective
countervailing force. It was now difficult to avoid the conclusion
that the institutional arrangement left behind by Tito was deficient
not only in that it required a semi-monarchical figure like himself
to make it work, but also that the absence of either an effective
all-Yugoslav identity and an all-Yugoslav interest made the problem
of constructing a new political formula insurmountable. The process
of decay was accelerated by a number of contingent factors.
Yugoslavia's economic situation deteriorated steady, as it had exhausted its extensive resources and the system proved weak in
generating new ones; foreign loans kept the economy ticking
over, but only at the cost of mounting indebtedness. Then, the
party's legitimating myths were beginning to wear out. Whereas
in the 1960s, the Titoist package of self-management and foreign
policy success through non-alignment attracted a measure of support, this was less and less the case by the 1980s. It was much
the same with the myth of the Partisan struggle; to a generation
born after 1945, what happened during the war had little relevance.
And the key proposition, that the communists were the most
effective in resolving the national question, was similarly under
threat from republicanisation.

Still, some of the successes of the Titoist solution continued
to hold. Macedonia was one instance. Before the war, Slavophones
of the Vardar valley were described as Southern Serbs and the
area was run as a *de facto* colony by the Belgrade authorities. In
the terms of the language they spoke, these Slavophones could
opt to become either Serbs or Bulgarians or Macedonians and,
being Orthodox Christians, religion was not an impediment.
During the war Macedonia was annexed by Bulgaria, and the
Partisans – in order to mobilise support – promised the Macedonians that they would receive recognition as an independent

nation in its own right. This move gave the Macedonians a vested interest in both Yugoslavia and in the communist variant of Yugoslavia that Tito established. Hence communism operated hand-in-glove with nationalism in Macedonia. Communist support for the declaration of autocephaly by the Macedonian Othodox bishops (autocephaly has universally been seen as a mark of independent nationhood in the Orthodox world) was a good case in point. Macedonian intellectuals busied themselves with creating a new language different from both Serbian and Bulgarian and constructing a history and literature, again with considerable success. So much so that towards the end of communism, Macedonia was a stable factor in the Yugoslav equation, because its overriding interest was in using the Yugoslav state framework as a protection against Bulgaria, which did not even recognise its autonomous existence.

The evolution of a Muslim nationhood was a parallel and in some ways even paradoxical device used by the communists. Muslims of Serbo-Croat mother tongue (speaking the Stokavian dialect) and living in Bosnia-Hercegovina, had a weak national consciousness before the war and they tended to graviate towards whoever was in power (before 1918, they were one of the bastions of loyalty towards Vienna). In the early years of Titoism, the communists did not really know what to do with the Muslims; in the 1953 census, the only category they could use was 'Yugoslav', but by the 1960s the category 'Muslim' was introduced, and as a result many of those who had previously defined themselves as Serbs now declared themselves Muslim; some remained Croat. The net result was that in the 1961 census, they were returned as the largest ethnic group in the republic for the first time, at the expenses of the Serbs, who took this shift rather badly.

On the other hand, the establishment of the Muslim national category did achieve a long term aim. It resolved the national allegiance of this group by giving it a separate identity and thereby ended the competition between Serbs and Croats, both of whom had entertained hopes that the Muslims would join them. During the wartime Croatian state, which included Bosnia, they were defined as 'Croats of the Islamic faith'. Both Serbs and Croats entertained the belief that at the end of day, the Muslims would opt to join them. Had one of them been successful, it could have claimed the whole of Bosnia-Hercegovina on ethnic grounds at the expense of the other rival. This scenario was now bankrupt.

Yet at the same time the notion of creating a nation on the

basis of religious adherence, especially when it was promoted by communists, was astonishingly contradictory. It cut across the formal consistency of Titoism and weakened the legitimating power of its ideology, while it simultaneously moved ethnic criteria to the foreground of the public stage. This contradictory posture applied to Macedonian nationalism as well. There must have been at least some people in Serbia, Slovenia or Croatia who would have asked themselves why it was permissible for Muslims and Macedonians to promote their ethno-national identities, but it was a major political deviation when they did so.

Something similar applied to Kosovo, though with important variations. By the 1980s, the Albanians in the province had come close to achieving parity with the other nations of the country. This political shift authomatically raised major and intractable issues, notably it questioned the tacit South Slav nature of the state. The word 'Yugoslavia' means 'land of the South Slavs' and although under Titoism a Slav identity was never an overt symbol in the legitimation of the state, it undoubtedly existed at the affective level. Besides, Albanian assertiveness provoked serious questions about the very deep-seated emotional significance of the province in the Serbian view of the world, as the cradle of Serbian civilisation. Matters were exacerbated by the near-colonial regime run by Ranković and the secret police in Kosovo between 1944 and 1966, which created far-reaching resentment among the Albanians. The disproportionately high Albanian birthrate, the highest in Europe in the 1970s and 1980s, pushed the Kosovo Serbs into a demographic minority, to the extent that many of them to concluded that they had no future in the province and emigrated. Finally, the reforms of the post-1966 period, like the establishment of an Albanian-language university in Pristina, permitted the Albanian intellectuals to begin mobilisation and to organise the population into a Yugoslav-Albanian national consciousness. In reality, there could be no long term place for such an identity in a Titoist or a Slavonic order.

The Serbian response

The processes described in the foregoing had a major unintended consequence – the rise of a Serbian separatism. The Serbs had seen themselves as the strongest pro-Yugoslav element in the country, but by the 1970s a group of Serbian intellectuals were beginning to question the value of this status. They argued that the Serbs had always made the greatest sacrifices for Yugoslavia, but had gained little from it; that as a nation they had sustained defeat after defeat (in Croatia, in Bosnia-Hercegovina and in Kosovo); and, perhaps, that they might now reappaise their support for Yugoslavia, certainly as constituted at the time. This line of thinking was associated with the writer Dobrica Ćosić and it found expression in the Memorandum of the Serbian Academy of Sciences in 1985, which subsequently came to be perceived as having prepared the ground for Milošević's strategy in the 1980s. Serbian separatism was relatively uninfluential until Milošević took power in an internal party coup in 1986. Until then, it had to compete with the remnants of Titoism, which enjoyed support in the federal administration (obviously, this justified its continued power), armed forces (likewise) and also with a relatively well established liberal reformist current, which despited the defeats of 1972 (the purge of Nikezić) still claimed the loyalty of a significant section of Serbian intellectuals.

The year 1987 can be taken as one of the hinges of post-war Yugoslavia. It marked the moment when the republicanisation process of 1974 culminated in an unbridgeable split on the future of the civic aspects of Yugoslav politics (as distinct from the ethnic ones) and implied that it would be increasingly difficult to maintain the state as a single polity. As already argued, republicanisation was initially kept in check by the federal party, the armed forces and to some extent the federal government; until Tito's death in 1980, his towering personality was more than enough to resolve conflicts, mainly by simple intervention. What he said went. Unfortunately no one could succeed him, despite somewhat pallid attempts by the federal defence minister, Nikola Ljubičić and the secretary of the party, Stane Dolanc, to don Tito's mantle.

In reality, there was a stand-off between the centre and the republics. The former could no longer exercise superior power over the latter, once again, with the consequences, as sketched, of the republican leaderships increasingly referring to their tacit ethnic base as a source of power. Nevertheless until 1987 the system was still broadly similar throughout the country, in as much as republican parties (leagues of Communists) exercised a leading role and eliminated challenges to their monopoly. The results were at times highly contradictory. Central legislation was frequently ignored by the republics, even when they had actually agreed to it (e.g. the stabilisation plan of 1983) and as the 1980s wore one, there were growing divergences in how the different republican parties interpreted their leading role: some were neo-Stalinist (Bosnia-Hercegovina), others were very relaxed (Slovenia). It was clear even at the time that this state of affairs was so unstable as to be untenable. In fact, it was the Slovene party which broke ranks and gradually permitted a shift towards one-party pluralism.

Slovenia moves towards democracy

Although the Slovene changes were argued in non-ethnic terms, it was understood in Ljubljana that Slovenia was in a position to determine its own fate and that this would be done regardless of the interests and opinions of other Yugoslavs. I received this message very clearly during a visit to Ljubljana in 1986. It was not clear whether those involved fully recognised that a move in this direction would mean accepting an ethno-national foundation for the new Slovenian order. One-party pluralism, as it turned out, was only an instrument of transition towards pluralism proper and, in a short period of time, the Slovenes were pressing for a far-reaching autonomy with an increasingly explicit ethnic message. A part of this message, however, was non-ethnic and implied that Slovenia was committed to establishing a democratic order. They felt that this could not be done within a Yugoslav framework.

This proposition was never spelled out, but it was unmistakable from the way in which the Slovenes approached the problem, in that they rapidly gave up any idea of transforming the rest of Yugoslavia, which would probably have been beyond their abilities in any case. Hence the Slovenes' democratisation project carried within it the hidden message that as far as Ljubljana was concerned, the communist legitimation of Yugoslavia was finished and at that point the sole alternative was national independence, coupled with statehood. The Slovenes did not, of course, shift in this direction overnight, but their attempts to maintain a single Yugoslav state declined in enthusiasm as each of their initiatives met with a rebuff from Belgrade, both on nationalistic and on neo-Titoist grounds. The confederation plan of October 1990 was the last gasp of Yugoslavism.

From the Serbian vantage point, the situation appeared to be quite different. Just as in Slovenia, the Titoist system was widely perceived to be, if not exactly bankrupt, certainly eroded in its capacity to command loyalty and support, but the mechanisms of erosion were different. The catalyst was Kosovo, where demonstrations by the Albanians in 1981 were followed by a rising emigration of local Serbs. This emigration produced a deep shock in Serbia, something that was enhanced by the result of the 1981 census, which returned an Albanian population in Kosovo of around 90 per cent.

The reaction was on outraged Serbian opinion, which could not bring itself to accept that ethnically they had lost the game and that the most sacred of Serbian lands was now in no way culturally Serbian. The visceral, racist anti-Albanian response of the Serbs – strengthened as it was by the religious cleavage, the Kosovo Albanians being largely Muslim – not only had its historical roots, with Muslim Albanians substituting for Muslim Turks in this mythologically suffused mind-set, but it was spread by the Serbian media, which used the Kosovo issue to claim autonomy from political control.

The simultaneous challenge of a sense of national injury and the threat to communist power was exacerbated by the growing economic crisis, to which the Serbian leadership had no answer. It rejected proposals for moves towards democratisation, like the redistribution of power and the introduction of market conditions, as this would have undermined its power and privileges, as well as resulting in the probable collapse of many enterprises. In the event, Milošević captured the leadership of the Serbian party and rapidly moved to consolidate his position by repeated reference to Serbian nationalism and the grievances of the Serbian nation. His liberal opponents were vanquished and the Titoists saw their opportunity to salvage their power by joining him. A new neo-Titoist-cum-Serbian nationalist political formula was well on the way to being born.

Milošević had Yugoslavia-wide ambitions. He rejected the demo-cratising programme of the Slovenes and insisted that only through a recentralisation could the economic crisis be resolved. None of the other republics was prepared to accede to this, especially as they increasingly understood it to be a revived Greater Serbian programme, albeit it was argued in terms of both Titoism and pan-Serbianism. Fears of the latter were enhanced by the way in which Milošević dealt with Kosovo and Vojvodina, both technically provinces within Serbia but *de facto* enjoying the powers of a republic. In 1988-89, Milošević put an end to this status. His supporters chased away the Vojvodina leadership – a coalition of hardliners and neo-Titoists who were united in seeking to maintain an authoritarian regime in Novi Sad – in the 'yoghurt revolution', so-called because the Vojvodina apparatchiks fled when they were pelted with yoghurt cartons by an angry crowd. Montenegro was an analagous case; it was a full republic, not a province of Serbia and its inhabitants have always considered themselves Serbs, though a minority of Montenegrins have sought to develop a separate Montenegrin consciousness. The ousting of the leadership began at more or less the same time and Kosovo followed soon after, both processes being completed by the spring of 1989. Thus Milošević effectively controlled the whole of Serbia and Montenegro as well, which put him in a strong position to dominate both federal state and party organisations.

Milošević and the other republics

This assault on Tito's legacy appalled the other republics, but they ultimately found themselves powerless to stop it. Milošević successfully exploited the ambiguity of the situation, in which he could use party and state structures to promote Serbian nationalism. There was no answer to this, because the legitimating force of Titoism was largely exhausted and the only alternative was nationhood and democracy, the Slovenian road, but communist leaders lacked the ability and the plausibility to adopt this model. For all practical purposes, by 1989-90, the future of Yugoslavia as a single state had a major question mark over it. If Yugoslavia could not be held together as a communist state, was there an alternative? It was evident that Milošević's Greater Serbian variant was unacceptable to the rest of the country and that the communists from the other republican leaderships would have to be replaced before an answer was available.

This answer was given in 1990. In essence, in parallel to and to an extent influenced by the collapse of communism elsewhere in Central and Eastern Europe, the Yugoslav communists were eliminated from power in republic after republic as free elections were held. Democracy represented the death-knell for Yugoslavia because it implied consensus and there appeared to be no way to bring the Serbs to accept a compromise. Elections were held in Slovenia and Croatia in the spring of 1990, in Bosnia-Hercegovina and Macedonia in the autumn; in all cases the communists lost and ceded power to various nationalists, who proclaimed themselves democrats as well. In Serbia, Milošević was well entrenched and was able to control the electoral process in December 1990.

It should be noted that in both Croatia and Serbia the electoral system influenced the ethnic composition of the new legislatures. The voting was a first past the post, two ballot system; this allowed large parties to maximise their votes and produced the result that in Croatia Tudjman's Croatian Democratic Alliance (HDZ) won 205 out of 356 seats (57 per cent) with only 41 per cent of the popular vote. Nor did it help matters that Serbian minority divided its vote between the reform communists and the overtly Serbian parties. In the Serbian elections, after two rounds Milošević's reform communists ended up with only 48 per cent of the vote, but this brought them 194 out of 250 seats (77.6 per cent); the voting was marred by various irregularities and a boycott by the Albanians, which obviously boosted Milošević's total.

The previously mentioned confederal plan was put forward jointly by the Slovenian and Croatian leaderships in October 1990. It constituted the only attempt to transform the country on the basis of democracy. The plan proposed that the six republics become independent states in alliance, with some common institutions and all decisions to be taken unanimously. It was not taken very seriously by Milošević and, conceivably, the authors of the plan knew this too, so that it was put forward more as an alibi than anything else. From that time on, the disintegration of Yugoslavia was no longer a question of if but of when.

In looking back on the process, it is striking that the key role in pushing for greater devolution leading to disintegration was played not by the Croats but the Slovenes. Throughout 1988-9, there was a shrill dispute between Belgrade and Ljubljana, which confirmed the Slovenes in their belief that there was little to be gained from persevering with Yugoslavia. They concluded that the Serbs in general and Milošević in particular were incapable of compromise and step by step the conviction grew that they would be better off outside the Yugoslav framework. There was, indeed, a certain correlation between the growth of democracy and the turning away from Yugoslavia, above all because both the old and new leaderships found it more congenial to rule by consent, enjoying a popularity denied to communities and this experience ineluctably pushed them to rely on their ethno-national base. As Slovenian nationhood was thrust further into the centre of the political stage, the Slovenes too found it more difficult to compromise or at least found fewer reasons why they should look for some kind of an agreement involving give and take. True, at no point was Milošević ready to give; this made matters much easier for the Slovenes. Ironically, by contributing to raising the temperature, the Slovenes ended by making matters much worse for the Croats. Slovenia could always be detached from Yugoslavia with comparative ease, as it enjoyed a relative prosperity and good connections with the West, not to mention the fact that there was no minorities question to complicate relations, but for Croatia, as argued already, the Yugoslav connection was far more intricate.

Croatia and the armed forces

Two other factors require discussion – the fate of Croatia and the role of the last Titoist institution, the armed forces. During the period when the polemics and tension between Serbs and Slovenes were mounting, Croatia remained quiet, indeed it was almost a bastion of Yugoslavist loyalty. It took till the end of 1989 for the Croatian party to concluded that free elections, on a multi-party basis, could not be put off any longer. There were several reasons for this caution. It was far harder for the Croats to envisage full independence than for the Slovenes, given that there were Croatian minorities in Bosnia-Hercegovina and the Vojvodina; the Croatian leadership was full of trepidation at any move liable to lead towards democracy, because it understood that this would revive the issue of nationhood, something which had caused the crisis of 1971; and the Croatian communist leadership must have realised that in the event of any real move towards independence, the whole question of the Serbs of Croatia would leap back to the agenda with a vengeance.

This difficulty did not trouble their successors, who in the first flush of victory in April-May 1990 behaved with complete tact-lessness and incompetence towards the local Serbs. Indeed, they adopted policies virtually calculated to mobilise Serbian opinion against Zagreb. They quickly adopted the symbols of the wartime independent state, on the proposition that these had always been the Croatian symbols, and ignored the Serbs' susceptibilities. More seriously perhaps when they began to purge the *nomenklatura*, the Serbs went first and, in some cases, Croatian members of the *nomenklatura* remained. In general, they did very little to reassure the local Serbs that Croatia would be a democratic state in which there would be enough space for Serbs to live as they wanted, with their own ethno-national agendas and symbols, like the Cyrillic alphabet.

Possibly the greatest error of all was that Tudjman made no attempt worthy of the name to build up a moderate Serbian leadership in Croatia, with which he could do a deal. On the contrary, it was as if he was doing everything to polarise the situation. When the Serbs presented their demands, these were dismissed and they were told that only cultural rights were on offer, there could be no question of any territorial autonomy. And to rub it in Croatian policemen were sent to the heavily Serbian inhabited areas like the Krajina. In a very short period of time, moderate Serbs were marginalised and the hardliners from the rural areas seized the leadership. They were much less sophisticated and were not inclined to listen to arguments about compromise. Indeed, in their world view, their worst fears were confirmed: for them it was a return to 1941 and soon the air was full of cries of 'the struggle against the fascist Croats'.

From this state of affairs it was a very short step to the *ad hoc* alliance with the armed forces, which turned out to be the fuse that eventually set off the fighting in the summer of 1991. The armed forces for their part viewed the disintegration of the country with dismay. They saw clearly that without a Yugoslavia, they would have no role and their power and privileges would be transformed into an insubstantial pageant. From an early date in 1990, the armed forces intervened in Croatia ostensibly and to some extent genuinely to protect the Serbian minority. It was a good case of political actor looking for a role and finding it regardless of the consequences.

The attitude of the JNA was a mixture of military professionalism, Titoism and, given that around two-thirds of the officers' crops was made up of Serbs and Montenegrins, with many of the Serbs from the minorities outside Serbia, pro-Serbian sympathies. The armed forces, therefore, took the Slovenian and Croatian declarations of independence in June 1991 as acts of treason and decided to put an end to it by direct intervention. In other words, they insisted that the protection of *bratstvo i jedinstvo*, with which Tito had charged them so long before, was still their valid role, utterly regardless of the very different circumstances in the early 1990s.

This explains the initial intervention in Slovenia, which turned out very badly through military incompetence, and the subsequent intervention in Croatia, which seemed to have a much more definite purpose. In reality there were at least three such objectives: the restoration of Yugoslavia in the Titoist mould; the protection of the Serbian minority; and support for Milošević's strategy of creating a Greater Serbia out of the Serbian-inhabited areas of Croatia, Bosnia-Hercegovina, plus Montenegro, Vojvodina and Kosovo. The armed forces vacillated around these three, something which helped to explain the hesitation and inconsistency with which it pursued the war. Without a clear political direction – and there was no government behind the armed forces to provide this – and without a political purposiveness of its own, the JNA's involvement seemed senseless. It was almost as if it fought simply to demonstrate its own existence. *Bellum gero ergo sum.*

Milošević too found himself in the position of having to run ever faster in order to remain in the same place. His particular genius in 1987 and after was to offer promise after promise of 'salvation' to Serbian opinion, which he never had to keep, but to achieve this, he had to keep raising the stakes. It began with Kosovo, continued with Montenegro and Vojvodina, and then oscillated between a Serbian dominated Yugoslavia and Greater Serbia. To achieve his aims, he was perfectly prepared to use the JNA in Croatia, while fully understanding that their interests were only temporarily coincidental. The motives of the armed forces were vague and uncertain; Milošević was protecting his own power and power base. His legitimating ideology could not be anything other than a Serbian one and beyond a certain point, Serbian opinion would not support his project of the Greater Serbian Yugoslavia, hence his shifting between the two.

In the final analysis, the chances of converting Titoist Yugoslavia into a democratic Yugoslavia were never very good. The failure of the two previous attempts to hold the country together – linguistic-monarchical and communist – meant that the conditions imposed by the various actors would be severe, almost certainly too severe. The necessary agreement on the benefits of keeping a Yugoslav state in being was absent, and communism collapsed too suddenly, at different rates of speed in the different republics, for the various republican elites to find common ground.

Then again, the democratic traditions in the different republics varied widely, with the Western aspirations of the Slovenes being in stark contrast to the volatility and political inexperience of the Serbs. The chance factor was also relevant – neither Milošević nor Tudjman was fitted for the role of holding a complex state together at a time when it was riven by the deepest tensions and contradictions; Milan Kučan, the communist-turned-democratic president of Slovenia, was. And the one institution with a genuinely all-Yugoslav purposiveness, the JNA, had no interest in democracy. Keeping Yugoslavia together was always going to be a very difficult operation; a democratic Yugoslavia would always have been nearly impossible. And the nearly impossible was not on offer when it was needed.

24

HUNGARY AS KIN-STATE

Anyone looking at the broad canvas of post-communist international affairs must be struck by the comparative calm in Hungary and the turmoil of post-Yugoslavia. There is, of course, regular speculation about the Hungarian minorities living in Serbia, Slovakia and Rumania and the relationship between these groups of ethnic Hungarians and Budapest as a source of instability. All the same, while there has certainly been friction between Hungary and its neighbour, the overall situation has remained relatively calm and Hungary's behaviour towards its co-ethnics has been in complete contrast to that of Serbia. These two patterns illustrate the potential range of responses currently open to kin-states in the post-communist world.

To some extent, the relative calm in Hungary is a direct consequence of the upheavals in former Yugoslavia. Hungary and its neighbours seem ready to go some distance to avoid bloodshed and to try and find a political solution to what will always be a complex relationship, despite repeated outbursts of nationalist polemics and rhetoric.

Kin-states, that is states with sizeable numbers of co-ethnics just across its border, living as citizens of another state, are to be found in many parts of the world, not just post-communist Europe. Such states will always be sensitised to the problems and aspirations of these co-ethnics. And the state in which they live, the home-state, will likewise be concerned about the loyalties of these ethnic minorities. The Hungarian case has the unusual feature of being very longstanding, so that Hungarian attitudes can be studied over time.

The basic data are these. After the collapse of Austria-Hungary in 1918, the old kingdom of Hungary lost large chunks of its territory to the successor states, Czechoslovakia, Romania and Yugoslavia (as well as smaller areas to Austria and even two tiny pocket-handkerchiefs of land to Poland). Much of the territory lost by Hungary was inhabited by non-Hungarians, but what most Hungarians found it hard to take was that around 3 million ethnic Hungarians found themselves living in the successor states, often in the immediate vicinity of the Hungarian state.

This loss of empire led Hungary to side with the Axis powers during the Second World War. It regained sizeable parts of the lost areas between 1938 and 1941, only to lose them once more in the post-1945 territorial dispensation. Under communism, the ethnic Hungarians became a taboo subject and over time, Hungarian society grew used to having lost the territories, though it retained an active interest in the fate of their co-ethnics. There are about 0.6 million ethnic Hungarians living in Slovakia; somewhere between 1.7-2.0 million in Romania (the figures are contested); and *c.*0.35 million in Serbia. There are smaller and politically less important minorities in Ukraine, Slovenia, Croatia and Austria.

With the collapse of communism, the new government that took power in 1990 under the prime ministership of József Antall pursued a policy that was virtually the polar opposite of that of the communists. The Antall government put the fate of the ethnic Hungarians first among its foreign policy aims, much to the alarm of the home-states. Both these processes were summed up when Antall declared himself the prime minister ('in spirit') of 15 million Hungarians, which includes those living beyond the frontiers of the Hungarian state, and by the universally negative response to this from Bratislava, Bucharest and Belgrade.[1] Certainly, Antall's formula seemed to imply something like a dual loyalty for the ethnic Hungarians, both to the state of which they were citizens and to the Hungarian state.

Antall's policy declaration was no doubt intended to send a message to the Hungarian minorities that the Hungarian state would no longer neglect them in the way that the communists had. Yet as well as doing this, Antall's message that he was the 'prime minister' of all Hungarians was also subject to interpretation by the home-states and they understood his words very differently.

---

[1] In fact, there are not 15 million Hungarians. The population of Hungary is 10.4 million, but well over 500,000 of these are not ethnic Magyars, but Roma (Gypsies), Germans, South Slavs, Slovaks and Romanians. Even if one includes Hungarians in the diaspora, in North America and Western Europe, it is difficult to arrive at a figure of 15 million. This statistic should therefore be understood as a national myth.

Not least, it was a political and legal absurdity for Antall to have claimed that he was the prime minister of Hungarians who were not citizens of the Hungarian state and who did not vote for him (or against him). A more experienced politician might have thought more carefully about the wording of his message.

Yet despite its inexperience, the Antall government did have one major ethnic success story to its name, the treaty with Ukraine. In exchange for the absolute inviolability of the Hungarian-Ukrainian frontier, peaceful means included, the Ukrainian government has guaranteed extensive rights to the *c.* 160,000 ethnic Hungarians who live in Transcarpathia. This treaty could undoubtedly have a model function.

In fact, despite repeated polemics between Hungary and its neighbours, the relationship between Budapest and the other three capitals never deteriorated to a crisis. Friction there has been aplenty, but all sides seemed ready to recognise that there was more to lose than to gain by letting matters escalate.

The ethnic Hungarian minorities themselves are one further political actor to be assessed in this complex game. It would be wholly misleading to assume that their interests are identifiable with those of the Hungarian state, far from it. Indeed, one can almost go so far as to suggest that there is more than a degree of tension between Hungary and the Hungarians of Romania, who have a strong and clear-cut identity of their own. It is fair to say that all the minorities have sought to use Budapest for their own purposes, which did not automatically coincide with those of the Hungarian state.

Public opinion in Hungary itself responded to this four-year process in a somewhat contradictory fashion. Although initially there was a good deal of sympathy for Hungary's co-ethnics, gradually, as the Antall government emphasised the fate of the minorities as a central objective in its foreign policy strategy, Hungarian opinion began to tire of this rhetoric. Antall's party, the Hungarian Democratic Forum (MDF), became Péter Boross's party after Antall's death (1993). In the 1994 elections the MDF's vote dropped to 9.6 per cent from 42 per cent in 1990. One of the reasons for such severe punishment was that Hungarian society had had enough of a government that seemed more concerned with non-citizens of Hungary than with its own voters. This gave the new Hungarian Socialist Party-Alliance of Free Democrats (SZDSZ) coalition, under the prime ministership of Gyula Horn which took power after the 1994 elections, a strong base from which to launch to more conciliatory foreign policy. Horn explicitly declared that he was the prime minister of 10.4 million Hungarians.

The Hungarian connection is a complex one and there are various answers as to why, despite the occasional alarms, it has not led to a full-scale crisis. Some of the answers are structural; the very complexity of the Hungarian connection makes all the participants move with caution, seeing that outcomes are very uncertain. The complex web of political relationships operates on at least three levels. There is the relationship between Hungary and each ethnic minority; that between Hungary and the government of the state of which the minorities are citizens; and there are the attitudes of the minorities themselves to the Hungarian state. Each of these basic relationships is further complicated by political and power relationships internal to the various actors. Thus the relationship between the Hungarian government and Hungarian opinion, between the Hungarian minorities and the government of the state in which they live and within the Slovak, Romanian and Serbian majorities all help to make these interconnections highly complex and sensitive.

Furthermore, the presence of the West, to which both Hungary and the home-states look as a source of both political and economic support, acts as another inhibitor. Integration in the West is conditional on the reduction of tension and various Western organisations, not least the High Commission on National Minorities of the OSCE and the Council of Europe, have played an active role in minimising it.

At the same time, it should be noted that most if not all of the political actors in the Danube region have only limited experience of the politics of compromise and it has taken them time to acquire the necessary experience. The communist system, with its emphasis on clear-cut, black-and-white attitudes, was hardly the best school for the new breed of post-communist politicians who have had a completely different set of tasks to tackle. Post-communist politicians have had to learn on the job and there is little doubt that they have made many mistakes.

Not least, their task has been made more difficult by the way in which a minority of politicians have listened to the siren call of extreme nationalist sentiment as the easy way of mobilising political support. In every post-communist state there is a well-defined constituency of members of the ethnic majority who will listen to nationalist demagogues: as a rule, those who have the most to lose by the transformation from a communist to a democratic-market system. István Csurka in Hungary, Ghreoghe Funar in Romania, Vladimir Mečiar in Slovakia and, of course, Slobodan Milošević, have all played the nationalist card from time to time. What is especially noteworthy in this connection is that in Hungary, Csurka failed completely at the polls, whereas his opposite numbers have propered to a greater or lesser extent.

There are several lessons to be drawn from the Hungarian case-study: in the first place, while it is extremely painful for all the members of an ethnic group to be divided among two or more states, it is possible for all concerned to come to terms with this and to move away, however slowly, from the traditional imperative of the nationalists to unite all members of a nation to a single state. The Hungarians since 1918 admittedly have had to accept that membership of the cultural community (the ethnic group) does not have to mean automatic membership of the political community (the state), but it is a lesson that other divided nations might care to note. This does imply, though, that time is a key factor in this context.

The role of elites is another relevant factor here. There have been two major transformations of the ruling elite in Hungary (in 1944-48 and 1989). Different elites have rejected or espoused the policies of their predecessors, resulting in changes in public opinion formation in Hungary and thus in the nature of popular pressures on the Hungarian government. As the experience of the Antall government shows, there are limits as to how far a government can go against the grain of public opinion.

Budapest has been gradually learning that it can achieve more for its co-ethnics by patient negotiation than by megaphone diplomacy. It is clear enough that this is ultimately easier for Hungary, an ethnically near-homogeneous state, than for the successor states, given that the latter have the far more difficult task of constructing a multi-ethnic system that will satisfy both majority and minority. Running a multi-ethnic state will work only if the emphasis is on citizenship as the primary constituent factor determining the relationship between rulers and ruled. If ethnicity is given this role, the minority will inevitably see itself as disadvantaged, because by definition it cannot share in the political goods of the state in the same way as the ethnic majority. The role of the kin-state is limited in this area. There is a very little that Hungary can do to promote the emergence of a civil society in other states. At best it can do its utmost to avoid giving a pretext to extremists for mobilising along ethnic lines and thus impede the strengthening of citizenship. Perhaps this should be seen as a facet of democratic self-limitation.

The way in which a kin-state treats its own minorities can also be a relevant factor affecting the kin-state/home-state dynamic, particularly where – as in the Hungarian case – roles are reversed and the kin-state becomes a home-state for minorities from its neighbours (Slovaks, Romanians, South Slavs, Germans; the Roma are not important in this context). Here, Hungary has sought to establish a relatively liberal minorities régime, partly as an aspect of democratisation, but partly also to serve as a moral justification for its stance towards the Hungarians in the kin-sates.

A particularly sensitive area of kin-state–minority relations turns on how the kin-state government deals with a political organisations of the kin-minority. This concerns issues like subsidies to political parties, to minority publications, to the enhancing or downgrading of the status of minority politicians and to the way in which kin-minority affairs are treated in the kin-state electronic media (under government control) and print media (largely free of government control). This can be especially significant during elections in the home-sate, when support from the kin-state can actively influence electoral outcomes in another state. And the exposure given to ethnic minority leaders in Hungary can have and has had an impact on the inter-state relationship between Hungary and its neighbours.

In this connection, the fragmentation of Hungarian foreign policy during the Antall period was not helpful. In many respects, Hungary had four separate foreign policy making bodies, the Foreign Ministry, the Ministry of Defence, the Prime Minister's office and the Office for Hungarians Abroad. Not all of this was negative. Relations between the Hungarian and Romanian defence ministries have been close and much better than in other areas. But overall, the fact that Hungary did not operate a coherent foreign policy was unhelpful to Hungary's image in the West, *vis-à-vis* its neighbours and probably did not help the minorities either. The broader implication of this point is that it is essential for kin-states to speak with one voice, which implies that different governmental agencies should accept that there be a hierarchy in the determination of foreign policy priorities.

Furthermore, the process of fragmentation is not all one-way. The ethnic minorities can and do use the Hungarian state for their own purpose. This is a complex relationship with political, economic, cultural and psychological dimensions. To take the last first, regardless of the political colouring of the Hungarian government and the mood of current opinion in Hungary, there will always be a sense of residual unease about the ethnic Hungarians. How this expresses itself will vary, but it will definitely involve a measure of guilt that Hungary is not doing enough for the ethnic Hungarians. For the ethnic Hungarians themselves this presents an opportunity to play on this guilt and to use it for their own purposes. There are, of course, limits to this game, but it is real all the same. Politically, the relationship is involved, in that it affects different political groupings in the successor state (as in Slovakia) or within the ethnic Hungarian organisation (as in Romania and Serbia). These different political groups will appeal to their counterparts in Hungary for moral and practical support. A good example of this was the way in which the electronic media in Hungary reflected the election campaign in Slovakia in 1992 or 1994. The various competing political groups within the Hungarian minority naturally sought to use the Hungarian media to their advantage. It is ultimately impossible for Hungary to be neutral – indeed the very existence of the Hungarian state is perceived as an irritant by its neighbours – but whether Hungarian television exercised sufficient discretion, sensitivity and impartiality is still an open debate.

There is always a danger here that a political party in Hungary which enters this game of using the minorities for its own purposes will tend to overemphasize its minority policy, to the detriment of other policies. Clearly, this was the trap into which the MDF was led. The alternative is to underestimate the significance of the minority issue and to ignore it; the SZDSZ's position was not too far from this. Gaps of this nature allowed the different ethnic Hungarian groups to appeal to the diversity of the Hungarian political scene and generate other political benefits. Cultural funding is evidently among the most important. It would be helpful, though very difficult to achieve, if all the Hungarian groups concerned – in Hungary and in the successor states – were to recognize the complex nature of the processes and to move with care and sensitivity in this area.

Economic factors have undoubtedly played a role in these processes as well. First, attitudes in Hungary towards the minority Hungarians were clearly influence by the presence of Hungarians from Romania on the labour market in Hungary. The fact that minority Hungarians were prepared to work for lower wages was strongly resented. Second, rather more indirectly, Hungarian opinion may also have been informed by the difficulties that Germany has had in integrating East Germany. If the largest, wealthiest and most powerful state in Europe should find the absorption of territory so painful, then – the argument goes – what chance would Hungary have if any of the minority-inhabited areas were to be reattached to Hungary? In this context, despite the pain of the loss of empire imposed on Hungary in 1918-20, the fact that it brought an ethnically homogeneous Hungarian state into being could be seen as a blessing in disguise.

The Hungarian case sheds light on the principles by which the kin-state determines it policies. Here the Budapest government has several factors to balance. It must satisfy Hungarian public opinion; it must pay heed to the cultural needs of the ethnic Hungarians; it must do this with sufficient sensitivity to avoid raising the hackless of the ethnic majority and the governments of its neighbouring states; and whatever it does, Hungary must also be aware of the demands of international and regional stability, something which the West is monitoring with greater awareness of the dangers of destabilisation through ethnic conflict than was the case before the disintegration of Yugoslavia. In this sense, Hungary has a fourfold responsibility. The Antall government discharged this responsibility with only partial success. It will be interesting to see how the Horn government fares in this area.

25

HUNGARY AND ITS NEIGHBOURS

Preliminaries

The problem of the tripartite relationship involving Hungary, its neighbours and the ethnic Hungarian minorities, although largely neglected in Western writing during the Soviet period, is clearly the second most sensitive security issue in Central and Eastern Europe after the war of Yugoslav succession; through this war, Hungary might indeed have become involved in a wider conflict. Ethno-national disputes, and these are already entangled with other issues which are not strictly anything to do with ethnicity (e.g. the Gabčikovo-Nagymaros Barrage – GNP), could readily engulf all aspects of inter and intra-state relations.

The role of the West in this respect is clearly a highly influential one, both as mediator and as a source of moral-political support for democratic forces that look for solutions through negotiation rather than through zero-sum games and violence.

History

By the Treaty of Trianon, Hungary lost about two-thirds of its territory to its successors.[1] This constituted a twofold loss. Territory,

---

[1] At the time, in 1920, these were Austria, Czechoslovakia, Romania and the later Yugoslavia (Kingdom of Serbs, Croats and Slovenes until 1929). A tiny strip of land was also ceded to Poland. Between 1938 and 1945, Hungary regained territories as a result of which most ethnic Hungarians were reincorporated in the Hungarian state, together with some non-Hungarians, but with Hungary emerging from the Second World War as 'Hitler's last satellite', none of these gains could be kept. The Trianon frontiers were left undisturbed except for the so-called Bratislava bridgehead, three villages on the southern bank of the Danube which had to be ceded by Hungary to Czechoslovakia in 1947. With the division of Czechoslovakia in 1993, Hungary's neighbours were Austria, Slovakia, Ukraine, Romania, Serbia, Croatia and Slovenia. Ethnic Hungarians lived in all these states, but these communities were insignificant in Austria, Croatia and Slovenia. There was no particular problem with the *c.* 200,000

meaning prestige, status and power had to be ceded, but so also did large numbers of ethnic Hungarians, in severe violation of the Wilsonian principle of national self-determination. In Hungary, Trianon is still regarded as a major catastrophe for which France is held responsible as the patron of the Little Entente and as the dominant element in the occupation of 1919. Many Hungarians are reluctant to accept that peacemaking in 1919-20 was a crude process, legitimated in some respects by the principle of national self-determination, but based also on *Realpolitik* and pragmatism. Even less do they understand that the proclamation of the Hungarian Soviet Republic in 1919 lost Hungary whatever residual sympathy it might have enjoyed among the Entente powers.

The shadow of Trianon as the 'unjust peace' continues to darken Hungarian politics to this day. However, this is not intended in any way to suggest that Hungarian attitudes have remained unchanged since 1918. Between the wars, integral revisionism ('return everything') dominated Hungarian thinking, but with the disappearance of the *ancien régime* that had ruled Hungary since time immemorial as one of the consequences of the Second World War, a metamorphosis began. The strategy of their *ancien régime* had manifestly failed. The essence of this strategy was to look for alliances with any state prepared to support Hungary's claim for territorial revision (initially Italy, then Germany). However, this strategy never made the distinction between all the territories lost by Hungary (the Crownlands of St Stephen) and the territories inhabited by ethnic Hungarians; in 1945 it was evident that integral revisionism was bankrupt and Hungary could begin to come to terms with the loss of empire.

Various new currents surfaced, three of which were noteworthy: Danubian cooperation, ethnic minority defence and communism. Although the last of these emerged the winner, the first two left traces on Hungarian thinking that have not disappeared entirely. None of the successor states pursued policies that were particularly sympathetic to the ethnic Hungarians, but communism froze the status quo and thereafter the question of the *c*.3.5 million ethnic Hungarians played only an occasional role in domestic and international politics. Leninist nationalities policies did little to solve the problem of majority-minority relations, except at the level of rhetoric.

---

strong Hungarian community in Ukraine.

In Hungary itself, the question largely disappeared from the overt political agenda and the Kádár régime insisted with particular emphasis that this should remain so as far as public consumption was concerned. The most that the communist government was prepared to do was to keep a watching brief on the minorities. Only gradually did policies change. In the 1960s, Kádár's idea was that the problem of the minorities could be subsumed in a Danubian cooperation project, but this died away for lack of support. In the 1970s the Hungarians tried a bilateral approach, signing agreements with the successor states that minorities – all minorities, including those living in Hungary – would constitute bridges between Hungary and its neighbours. This strategy was moderately successful with Yugoslavia, less so with Czechoslovakia, but led nowhere with Romania. By the 1980s, there was growing readiness on the part of the Hungarian government to try to internationalise the problem, by raising it in various forums, like the ECSC, but this had very limited support. Overall, the collapse of communism left public opinion unprepared for the question of how Hungarians in Hungary should approach the problems, difficulties and demands of the minorities in the successor states.

From the perspective of the successor states, the question looked very different. As far as Yugoslavia was concerned, the Hungarian minority was never much more than an irritant, partly because Yugoslav politics were dominated by the Serb-Croat question and partly because the Hungarian state was least interested in this minority. Nevertheless, when the opportunity arose in 1941, Hungary joined Germany in the dismemberment of Yugoslavia and reannexed the Bačka, as well as two small pockets of land from Croatia and Slovenia.

Immediately after 1945, the communists instituted a brief policy of revenge (massacres, imprisonments) and the settlement of Serbs and Montenegrins in the main Hungarian-inhabited area, the Vojvodina. The minority was thereafter largely ignored. It was noticed only when some single issue surfaced, but this was rare. The key aspect of the minority was that it was sociologically weak, being made up largely of peasants and lacking an intellectual stratum ready to articulate ethnic demands and threaten Serbian hegemony until the 1970s, by which time the Vojvodina was ruled by a rather hard-line régime dominated by the former Partisan settlers. The toppling of this régime by Milošević in 1988 was experienced by the Hungarians as a liberation and restrictions on their activities were imposed only gradually.

In Czechoslovakia, once again, the problem of the Hungarian minority was a peripheral one, both between the wars and after 1945. During the first republic, the central concern of the Czechs was twofold: to establish a democratic state and to make this a state permeated by Czech ideals. This made it necessary to find a solution to the German problem that would enable the Czechs to dominate the state without the appearance of doing so. This was function of 'Czechoslovakism', the proposition that Czechs and Slovaks constituted a single 'Czechoslovak' nation, which had a numerical preponderance in the new state. The Hungarian question was an appendage to this state of affairs. From the Czech perspective, the existence of the minority and the revisionist policies of Hungary formed a useful pretext for denying the Slovaks the federation that they had been promised, because a federal system would have been a security risk. The device also to some extent encouraged Slovaks to regard the Hungarians as a serious rival, antagonist and enemy, as a result of which the Slovak national ideology became markedly anti-Hungarian. The construction of the post-1918 Slovak identity and self-image used anti-Hungarian elements as a 'safe' component. Thus the period of forced assimilation (1867-1918) was projected backwards historically and it was argued that the Hungarian state had always sought to assimilate the Slovaks and that Slovakia had suffered under the Hungarian yoke for a thousand years. The oppression of the Slovaks by the Hungarian aristocracy was reinterpreted as an ethno-national relationship rather than a class one, in which ethnic self-identification was marginal, seeing that Hungarian peasants were just as oppressed as Slovak ones. The reannexation of the ethnically Hungarian southern Slovakia by Hungary after Munich, as a result of the First Vienna Arbitration in 1938, merely confirmed these perceptions of the Hungarians as the greatest enemies of the Slovaks.

After 1945 the situation changed radically in consequence of the adoption of a 'Slavonic' ideology by the reconstituted state. On this basis, the Germans were expelled and the Hungarians were subjected to severe repression (denial of citizenship, confiscations, some explusions, forced labour in the Czech lands, no ethnic institutions of any kind). The years 1945-8 completely traumatised the Hungarians of Slovakia, as might have been expected, but ultimately the repression did nothing to solve the sense of Slovak selfhood and its sense of inferiority and weakness vis-à-vis both Prague and Budapest. In summary, the newly rising Slovak élite could never forgive the Hungarians, whether as members of the minority or of the Hungarian state, for having come so close to assimilating them. This was the core of the Slovak trauma and it became an organic feature of the Slovak national self-image and identity, one that was transmitted during the communist period and played a key role in underpinning Slovak fears after 1989.

The communist *coup d'état* of 1948 put a gradual end to the repression, but there was never any question of the Hungarians being given fully equal rights to Czechs and Slovaks (in so far as the word 'rights' could in any way be appropriate to a communist system). Czechoslovakism was abandoned, the Slovaks were recognised symbolically as a fully equal constitutive nation in the state, but were denied the power that the Slovaks felt that they should have by a communist centralisation that was interpreted as a Czech centralisation. In this context, the Hungarians once again had the politically useful function of being a target of Slovak resentments.

In 1968 the Hungarians minority sought, but was not granted, equal treatment; after the suppression of the Prague Spring, Slovakia was granted a good deal of autonomy under the new federal arrangement after 1969. The Slovaks used this space to strengthen their own national identity, which they tended to interpret in material terms. This was the time when the population of Bratislava grew enormously, from around 200,000 to somewhere under half a million; the rapid pace of expansion shows in the disastrous socialist dormitory suburbs that now surround the city and are held up as a negative example of urban planning. The growth of Bratislava had a symbolic function. Slovakia was now a serious political actor and, therefore, it had to have a serious capital. Much the same went for the heavy industrial base that was built in northern Slovakia; it was an exercise in quantitative expansion with symbolic overtones.

As far as the minority was concerned, the more or less autonomous Slovak leadership tried to weaken the cultural institutions of the Hungarians, by seeking to close down schools, for example. This was not wholly successful, but the constant assimilatory pressure was not without consequences. The expulsions of 1945-8 had principally affected the educated elites; subsequent Slovak pressure went some way towards blocking the reemergence of an ethnic Hungarian elite and the sociological profile of the minority showed that peasants and workers predominated to a much greater extent than among the Slovaks.

The situation was different again in Romania, where the proportion of Hungarians was smaller than in Slovakia, but where their absolute number (contested, but certainly around 2 million by the 1970s) made the problem a qualitatively different one. There were other factors, too, that differentiated the situation in Romania from the other successor states and, to an extent, made the Hungarian problem a central one for the Romanian state. Before 1914 Romania had been an ethnically almost pure country and the state was constituted on this basis. Citizenship depended on Romanian ethnicity and, for example, Jews were automatically denied citizenship since they could never become Orthodox Christians.

The emergence of Greater Romania in 1918, therefore, was simultaneously a triumph and a trauma for the Romanians. On the one hand, they had finally achieved the great objective of Romanian foreign policy and national pride, the reunification of the three Romanian lands of Wallachia, Moldavia and Transylvania, and were successful in incorporating all possible ethnic Romanians into the new state by expanding into Bessarabia and southern Bukovina.

One the other hand, for the first time Romanians were obliged to share their state with sizeable numbers of non-Romanians, of whom the Hungarians were the most numerous, but there were many others, notably Germans and various Slavonic minorities. For many Romanians, the proposition that individuals who were not ethnic Romanians and Orthodox Christians could be fully fledged members of the state and entitled to all the rights of citizenship was alien and repugnant. Two groups were regarded with special disfavour, Jews and Hungarians. We can leave the question of Romanian-Jewish relations to one side here, but the relationship with the Hungarians was historically difficult and convoluted. The two states had been neighbours for many centuries, both had suffered at the hands of the Ottomans, but the Hungarians had clearly emerged better prepared for the onset of modernity in the nineteenth century than the Romanians. Throughout much of their modern history, Romanians had perforce been obliged to regard Hungary as their window on the West; the first book printed in Romanian was published in Budapest, for example.

At the same time, most Regateans – Romanians from the Danubian provinces – had come to regard Hungarian rule over Transylvania as cruel, oppressive and unjust, so that its incorporation in 1918 was celebrated as a measure of great historical justice and compensation for the humiliation of defeat and occupation by the Central Powers during the First World War. The invasion of Hungary in 1919 as a part of the anti-communist intervention campaign by the Romanian army and the occupation of Budapest for several months was felt to be just revenge, but left deep resentments in its wake among the Hungarians.

At the affective level – the level where collective emotional responses resonate – the symbolic power of Transylvania in the Romanian mind-set cannot, therefore, be overestimated. The Romanian-Hungarian relationship was further complicated, however, by the fact that Transylavania was seen by both ethnic groups as a symbol of their existence as a community. The Romanians argued that the presence of ethnic Romanians in Transylvania after the withdrawal of Roman legions had been the key factor that ensured their survival as an independent ethnic and cultural community. The Hungarians claimed with equal fervour that the semi-autonomous Transylvanian state of the seventeenth century, which signed the Peace of Westphalia of 1648 as an independent entity, represented the continuity of Hungarian statehood during the period of Ottoman occupation. From this perspective, the union of Transylvania with Hungary in 1848 was the logical outcome of many centuries of development.

This confusion of issues of identity and emotions made it virtually impossible to disentangle issues of legal rights, property, land reform, language usage, education and so on from state sovereignty and territorial revisionism. Indeed, the relatively centralised system set up in Romania after 1918 might formally have been justified in terms of territorial security, though in reality it was as much about extending Regatean norms to Transylvania, including to Transylvanian Romanians, as anything else.

However, while Belgrade and Prague had only relatively weak minorities to deal with, the Hungarians of Transylvania were a different matter. Not only had they been the rulers of the province for centuries, and thus possessed the self-confidence of traditional legitimation, but in addition the community had markedly higher educational, cultural and economic standards than the Romanians. For the average Romanian from the Regat, a journey to Tran-

sylvania was (and to an extent still is) a cultural shock, because
it looks and feels different; also an alien language is widely spoken
there. It was a far more complex matter to subordinate this community to the norms of the Romanian state than the integration
of the untutored peasants of the Vojvodina was for the Serbs.

Against this background, the return of two-fifths of Transylvania
by the Second Vienna Arbitration of 1940 was completely traumatising for Romanian opinion, and, for what it is worth, the
new frontier was far less satisfactory from the ethnic standpoint
than the one between Hungary and the Slovak state drawn in
the First Vienna Arbitration of 1938. The recovery of northern
Transylvania became a major war-aim for Romania and it influenced the Romanian elite in their acceptance of communism,
in effect because the deal offered them by the Kremlin in 1945
was either a reintegrated but communist Romania or a semi-
democratic Romania without northern Transylvania. The Romanians opted for the former.

The coming of communism was more complex than this, however, and the role that the Hungarian minority played in that
process influenced their treatment for the whole of the communist
period. In 1945-6, the leadership of the Hungarian minority came
to the conclusion that Marxism was the most effective guarantor
of their future as an ethnic community and threw their weight
behind the communist takeover. It is generally agreed that the
success of the communists depended on Hungarian support; non-
communist Romanians have never forgotten this.

On the other hand, Hungarian calculations went awry and the
communist Romanian state was not prepared to provide the space
in which a strong, self-confident minority could sustain its institutions and generate its own political norms and power. The
aim of the Romanian party-state was to whittle away the power
amassed by the Hungarians and they were successful in this by
the 1970s.

Ceauşescu's severely repressive policies had an impact on the
entire population of the country, but the Hungarians felt that
they were at a twofold disadvantage, in that they were repressed
in their ethnicity, as well as their civic identity. The late Ceauşescu
regime (1971-89) increasingly used the Hungarians as a propagandistic target and sought to bolster its own fading strength by
relying on anti-Hungarian nationalism. The systematisation project
of 1987-9, which sought to reduce the number of villages in

Romania by half, was widely viewed by Hungarians as a measure directed against them, although it impacted as harshly on ethnic Romanians as well. The legacy of the Ceausescu years, which created a deeply negative stereotype of Hungarians among Romanians, became a central part of the adjustment process in the politics of post-communist Romania.

After communism: the Hungarian perspective

The Hungarian government when newly elected in 1990 was completely inexperienced and made a fair number of errors in handling the problem of the minorities in the successor states. It started from the assumption that the communists had shamefully neglected the national question and that Hungarian opinion was determined that historic wounds should be healed. In this context, the task of the new nationally minded government was to act as protector of the Hungarian nation, regardless of where its members lived, both morally and politically. As a matter of fact, neither assumption was correct. The communist government had, in fact, taken an interest in the fate of the ethnic Hungarians, though it acted in a very low key fashion, and, second, Hungarian public opinion was not primarily concerned with righting the wrongs of Trianon. That was first and foremost an intellectual issue.

An early statement by the new prime minister, József Antall, that he was the prime minister 'in spirit' of 15 million Hungarians was guaranteed to inflame suspicions that Hungary had political designs on its neighbours, that at the very least the Hungarian state would play an active role vis-à-vis the minorities and would thereby interfere in the internal affairs of the successor states.[2] Another early statement that Hungary's defence policy would be that of all-round defence likewise did little to reassure them, despite repeated reassurances that Hungary would never seek to change frontiers by force.

The difficulty with Hungary's policies was that sometimes the government and, to an even greater extent its nationalist supporters, failed to make a clear distinction between ethnicity and territory, thereby regularly creating the impression that it did, indeed, have an interest in the redrawing of the frontier. In an already heightened

---

[2] Antall's statement was made on 13 August 1990, reported by MTI of that date.

atmosphere of suspicion, where nationalism was used equally actively as a political resource in the successor states, the occasional statements that Hungary had no desire to change frontiers tended to be dismissed as disingenuous or as propaganda aimed at the West. Extreme nationalist publications like *Szentkorona* and *Hunnia* were constantly making such inflammatory calls, though they were marginal to the mainstream of Hungarian politics.[3] In effect, internal Hungarian debates were seized upon the successor states as evidence of hostile Hungarian intentions.

A word on the make-up of the ruling coalition is appropriate at this point. One can largely disregard as marginal the minor partners of the Hungarian Democratic Forum (MDF), the Smallholders and the Christian Democrats. However, the MDF itself was a coalition, something that was far from usual under post-communist conditions. Its main elements were the national liberals, the Christian Democrats and the radical-nationalist populists. Antall himself belonged to the Christian Democrat tendency and had established a complete preeminence over the party. The national liberals were, on the other hand, rather weak and weakened further by the rising tide of impatience that propelled the populists into the foreground.

Their leader was the writer and demagogue, István Csurka, whose ability to touch on sensitive nerves had gained him a considerable following, one that he was able to mobilise to take to the streets. Csurka's ideology was a vague but thoroughgoing radicalism. He believed that Hungary had been 'robbed' of its revolution thanks to the peaceful transfer of power in 1989-90 and called for a complete redistribution of power. At the same time, he made emotional appeals in the name of the Hungarian nation and the national spirit and called for national unity as a way of overcoming the existing difficulties experienced by the country. His attitude to the question of the Hungarian minorities was more oblique than anything. He was not an explicit revisionist, demanding frontier changes, but in the atmosphere of suspicion, allusions and hints that he dropped could be understood as tantamount to that. One example of this was the interview that

---

[3] Indeed, the editor of *Szentkorona,* László Romhányi, was sentenced on charges of incitement for his anti-Semitic and anti-Romanian articles, Hungarian Radio, 8 February 1993, BBC *Summary of World Broadcasts,* EE/1610 B/5 (11 February 1993).

Csurka was reported as having given to the Zagreb paper *Globus* (26 February 1993), in which – according to the report – he said, 'I do not say that we do not have territorial claims and these are legitimate, *vis-à-vis* Baranja and Vojvodina', although he then added that because of Hungary's economic and military weakness it was unable to realise these claims.[4]

Furthermore, by raising the temperature on the minorities question, Csurka was looking to effect radical changes in Hungary itself, a clear instance of using the minorities problem with another aim in mind, something that spokesmen for the minorities themselves complained of repeatedly. On the other hand, within the MDF Csurka's position was not as strong as it had been assumed. At the MDF Congress in January 1993, Csurka's support was shown to be limited and Antall was successful in repulsing the offensive that Csurka had launched the previous summer.[5]

It should also be understood that Csurka may have had popular support on domestic social issues, but it was minimal on the question of the minorities. Indeed, there was more than a measure of fear and resentment of those members of the minorities who had resettled in Hungary and were regarded as parasites taking jobs from Hungarians. In terms of popular backing, a fairly widely offered guesstimates suggested that Csurka's support did not exceed 2-5 per cent of the vote and not all of these supporters could actually be mobilised to cast their votes.

By 1993, however, the debate in Hungary on the Hungarians of the successor states had changed its quality.[6] The initial basis of official Hungarian concern, democracy and human rights, was no longer felt to be adequate by nationalists in Budapest, who

---

[4] As reported by Hungarian Radio, 26 February 1993, BBC *Summary of World Broadcasts* EE/1627 B/1 (3 March 1993).

[5] Edith Oltay, 'Hungarian Democratic Forum opts for Centrist Policy', *RFE/RL Research Report*, vol.2, no.9 (26 February 1993).

[6] A good illustration of this was the softening of the attitude of the Defence Minister, Lajos Für. In February 1992 he declared that the Hungarian government and parliament should do everything in their power using legal and diplomatic means to guarantee the survival of the minorities (MTI, 20 February 1992). A year later, he was giving repeated reassurances to Hungary's neighbours that the Hungarian state had no hostile intentions towards any of them and that the role of the country's armed forces was solely to protect the territorial integrity of the state. Hungarian Radio, 16 February 1993, BBC *Summary of World Broadcasts*, EE/1617 B/10 (19 February 1993).

argued that the position of minorities was bad and deteriorating. Consequently, there was an undercurrent of opinion that preferred a much more active policy, possibly even going as far as advocating territorial revision, albeit through peaceful means. It should be stressed that this was not official policy, but there were no forthright official denials and Hungarian policy tended to be ambiguous. Towards the end of 1992, there were repeated rumours that among other policy options, the government was considering extending the rights of citizenship and voting to all ethnic Hungarians, regardless of where they lived. In a statement in Munich, Géza Entz, head of the Office for Hungarians Abroad, was reported as having said this and adding that he expected that the necessary framework would be in place by the 1994 Hungarian elections.[7] Any such moves would set off stentorian alarm bells in all the successor states.

There was another aspect of this problem that the nationalists in the successor states preferred to ignore. The spectrum of debate in Hungary was wide, positions differed and these differences were freely articulated in the press. However, nationalists outside Hungary ignored the fact that opinions expressed in a debate should be understood in that context and tended to attribute a homogeneity to Hungarian opinion that was certainly misleading and distorted. Thus when official spokesmen said, as they regularly did, that Hungary had no territorial demands on any of its neighbours – the foreign minister, Géza Jeszenszky did this, for example, with respect to Romania in an interview with *Romania Libera* (22 February 1993) – this would be discounted as disingenuous and deceptive tactics by the Hungarians. In many respects, the counter arguments of the Hungarians deserved attention, that the atmosphere was so strained that regardless of what they said, there would always be somebody in the successor states ready to find some devious conspiracy in their public utterances.

It should also be understood that in many respects one of the countries that would suffer directly from any territorial changes would be Hungary itself. While out-and-out nationalists might dream of returning to the pre-Trianon frontiers or at least to the Second World War frontiers, analysis not based solely on ethnicity would show that Hungary would experience extreme difficulties

[7] Hungarian Radio, 24 December 1992, BBC *Summary of World Broadcasts*, EE/1573 A2/1 (29 December 1992).

in reintegrating any territories putatively ceded by any of the successor states. A worst-case scenario for Hungary would be if, hypothetically, Romania were to agree to return Transylvania. The problems of economic, political and social integration would be insurmountable and if this hypothetically enlarged Hungary wished to keep its democratic institutions, it would have to become a joint Hungarian and Romanian state, something that few people relished. Indeed, it has been suggested by Budapest wits that if Hungary's neighbours wanted to ruin Hungary for good, they should simply return all the Hungarian-inhabited areas to Budapest's jurisdiction. The result would be a disaster and many people in Hungary understood this explicitly or implicitly.

A further aspect of Hungary's policies was the way that the small minorities in the country were dealt with. Under the communists, there was some element of using the minorities as a kind of alibi, of claiming that they were very well treated in order to show up the successor states. It was hard for the post-communist state to avoid a similar approach, but the formulation of a new draft law on the minorities, which was agreed in March 1993, was in part genuinely based on the principles of human and collective rights.[8]

It took some time for the Hungarian government to formulate a defence doctrine and a defence policy based on it. This was put before parliament in March 1993 and firmly stated that the Hungarian republic had no predetermined enemies and that it looked to pan-European and regional cooperation as the most favoured framework within which problems could be solved. This would include the sensitive issues of ethnic minorities as well, which 'cannot be regarded as falling with the exclusive sphere of internal politics of the state involved' and should therefore 'be resolved through active international cooperation'.[9] Furthermore,

---

[8] The draft was agreed by all the parliamentary parties and sent to the organisations of the minorities. It proposed self-government for all the minorities, to be funded by the state; however, it was criticised as insufficient by the representatives of the Gypsies (Roma). It was reported that there were 155 minority organisations representing thirteen different groups. Hungarian Radio, 9 March 1993, BBC *Summary of World Broadcasts*, EE/1634 B2 (11 March 1993) and *ibid.*, 12 March 1993, *ibid.*, EE/1638 B/6 (16 March 1993).

[9] Quotations from Tömöry Ákos, Biztonságpolitika: Hadpárti mozgósítás', *Heti Világgazdaság*, 27 February 1993.

Hungary rejected all thought of changes in the country's frontiers by force. The entire political spectrum in parliament supported this new defence concept.

The country's difficulties did not end there, however. Hungary made it very evident that it wished to be integrated into NATO or at any rate receive some kind of Western security guarantee. The west, for its part, made it equally clear, repeatedly, that it had no intention of doing anything of the kind. This left Hungary with no alternative but to embark on a defence policy of its own, involving a modernisation and professionalisation of the armed forces and the frontier guard. Had Hungary existed in a vacuum, this might have had no repercussions, but in the overheated atmosphere of post-communism, those in the successor states who were in any case sceptical now grew more suspicious and could use Hungarian moves as a pretext for an armament programme of their own. There were certainly those in Hungary who wanted to construct a much stronger, much more nationalistically defined strategy, but for the time being the moderates held the line. Even so, some of the Hungarian opposition could be ranked among the sceptics and were concerned that the government could use its armed forces for domestic purposes, although there was no tradition of a politicised military in Hungary.

The aim of the new defence doctrine was to establish and armed force of around 100,000 men equipped with modern weapons and air defence system; many offensive weapons had already been scrapped under the CFE agreements and the process continued into 1992. Some units would be deployed as an airborne rapid reaction force, presumably under the impact of the war of Yugoslav succession, which alarmed the Hungarians because the country's southern frontier appeared completely open to incursions. The bombing of Barcs, a small town on the border, by the Yugoslav airforce in October 1991, and especially the admission by the pilot that this had been a deliberate act on his part (though he was not necessarily carrying out higher orders) exposed the weakness of the Hungarians for all to see. The problem was that the Soviet air defence system had been removed with the withdrawal of the Red Army in June 1991 and was not replaced until well into 1992.

The rearming that the Hungarian government launched in 1992 was certainly regarded as alarming in the successor states. However, given Hungary's military weakness in the face of a deteriorating

security situation (war of Yugoslav succession, division of Czechoslovakia, instability in Romania) and the lack of any evidence of
Western readiness to give Hungary military support should this
become necessary, Budapest argued that there was no alternative
to rearming.

Hungary and Serbia

The most serious situation was to the south, where the war in
Croatia in 1991 and the disintegration of Yugoslavia brought
Hungary a host of new problems, notably the presence of around
100,000 refugees (unofficial estimate). While the Hungarian
government was unequivocally more friendly towards Croatia (and
Slovenia) than towards Serbia, the bulk of the Hungarian minority
lived in the last of the post-Yugoslav states. Serbian policy towards
its Hungarian minority was one of impatience, but repression
was sporadic and in early 1993, many of the institutions established
by the minority still remained in being.

Budapest was deeply concerned at the potential spill-over from
the fighting. The waywardness and unpredictability of Serbia after
1991, the readiness of Serbian élites to use violence to gain territory
and the rise of an extremist Serbian messianism were highly alarming
for the Hungarians. This was made all the more acute by the
relative inactivity of the West, not just in its refusal to intervene
but by its general confusion about what to do in situations where
one ethno-national group was using force to change both frontiers
and the existing ethnic order by 'ethnic cleansing'. In addition,
there was a barely articulated concern that Western passivity in
the face of Serbian aggression was sending a message to nationalists
everywhere. The fear that ethnic cleansing could be applied against
the Hungarian minorities was a real one and Hungary felt helpless
to do anything about it other than through diplomacy.

Indeed, the success of ethnic cleansing in Bosnia-Hercegovina
undoubtedly created a precedent that was not lost on the Serbs
with respect to Vojvodina. From the perspective of extreme nation-
lists, the Hungarian-inhabited areas represented a useful space where
refugees from the south could be settled. Should ethnic cleansing
begin in earnest in the Vojvodina, it was hard to see how any
Hungarian government could stand aside, not least because Hungarian inactivity would create a precedent that would certainly
be exploited in Slovakia and Romania. The result would certainly

be hostilities, with the possibility of direct Serbian intervention in Hungary. The outcome of such a conflict was unclear. Belgrade gossip took the view tht the battle-hardened Serbian army could be in Budapest in two days; Hungarian military planners felt that the Serbian army was in such disarray that the Hungarians would have no trouble in throwing them back.

The Central European rumour mill was clearly busy on this question, indicating a good deal of unease in Hungary about Serbian intentions. Notably, it was suggested that in the event of a NATO intervention in former Yugoslavia, Serbian missiles would be fired at Hungary (Budapest was within range). In mid-February 1993 the Hungarian government felt forced to deny all knowledge of this scenario, but the implication was clear enough. Many in Hungary were quietly concerned whether the West would intervene should there be a Serbian attack on Hungarian territory. The precedent of Kuwait suggested that perhaps it might and the existence of sizeable Western investment in Hungary would also be a factor pushing in this direction. On the other hand, the West's inactivity in the war of Yugoslav succession implied that the West would not intervene actively in Hungary either.

The reality of the situation in the Vojvodina was very contradictory. The Hungarian minority had actually benefited from the collapse of the hardline regime in 1988, because for the first time since the end of the war, it was able to begin constructing its own institutions. Associations were set up, the press was free of restrictions, the black spots in history, like the post-1945 massacres of Hungarians by Serbian partisans, could be filled in and through the Democratic Alliance of the Hungarians in the Vojvodina (VMDK), the minority gained representation in the Serbian parliament. As against this, the atmosphere of uncertainty and fear was gaining rather than slackening as the overall situation in Serbian deteriorated. The Serbian paramilitaries, notably the ones owing allegiance to Vojislav Šešelj, repeatedly threatened the Hungarians with retaliation for alleged disloyalty; in reality, their very presence in Serbia was offensive in the eyes of extremists.

As in other post-communist countries, the ethnicisation of the state bore hard on the minority, in that virtually all legal, administrative and political instruments were in the hands of the majority, minority duties were strictly defined and exacted, but their rights were ignored and remedies were delayed. Military service by ethnic

Hungarians in the Yugoslav armed forces, later the Serbian army, was a case in point. Hungarians felt that the war in Croatia was absolutely no concern of theirs and from a political and cultural position they were reluctant to be involved. The Serbian authorities, on the other hand, interpreted the sitution solely from a legal perspective and insisted that, as citizens of Serbia, the ethnic Hungarians had the same obligations as everyone else. Hungarians complained that disproportionate numbers of them were called up (this could not be verified) and many of them deserted, going mostly to Hungary. Some Serbs deserted as well.

Somewhere of the order of 50,000 ethnic Hungarians had fled from former Yugoslavia to Hungary, but a considerable proportion of these came from the areas of Croatia occupied by Serbian paramilitaries in eastern Slavonia and Baranja. Around half were thought to be from the Vojvodina, many of them of military age and escaping Serbian conscription. The resettlement of Serbian refugees from Bosnia and Croatia exacerbated a tense situation as many of the latter were looking for somewhere to live and regarded the houses of the minorities as a useful solution. The authorities either stood by or actively encouraged these illegal seizures of property. It should be noted here, however, that the smaller minorities in the Vojvodina – Croats, Slovaks, Ruthenians – suffered far more than the Hungarians. Indeed, the Slovak minority was thought to have been effectively liquidated through emigration.[10]

The report by Tadeusz Mazowiecki, the rapporteur for the UN fact-finding mission, confirmed that the situation was very tense and the level of insecurity was high, but Mazowiecki, the respected former Polish prime minister, added that there had been no ethnic cleansing on the Bosnian model.[11] There were other pinpricks, like the Serbian law that only Serbian language place names be used on the territory of the state, thereby theoretically obliging Hungarian-speakers to pepper their conversation with Serbian terminology. Hungarian-language schooling was also reportedly under threat by the new law on education.

At the same time, the organisation for the Hungarians, the

[10] Hugh Poulton, 'Rising Ethnic Tension in the Vojvodina', *RFE/RL Research Report,* vol.1, no.50 (18 December 1992).

[11] Hungarian Radio, 27 January, BBC *Summary of World Broadcasts,* EE/1599 C1/7 (29 January 1993).

VMDK, was able to strengthen its position in the Vojvodina parliament, as well as in the Serbian and in the Yugoslav assemblies, gathering up to 85 per cent of the vote of the minority. This gave it a clear legitimacy to speak in the name of the Hungarian community in Serbia and its strategy was to demand territorial autonomy, presumably along the lines that the Serbs were demanding for the Krajina in Croatia.

What saved the situation was that Serbia was far more closely involved with Bosnia-Hercegovina and with Kosovo. As long as these two territorial objectives tied down Serbia's attention, the Hungarians could be reasonably secure that hostile measures against them would be sporadic rather than systematic. In this ambiguous situation, the presence of ECSC monitors was a small step in the right direction, but Western leverage over Serbia was minimal.

Hungary and Slovakia

With respect to Slovakia, it was hard to avoid the conclusion that until the very end of 1992 the Hungarian government completely failed to take the Slovaks seriously as a political factor and relied on its good relationship with the Czechoslovak government as its chief policy instrument. The fiasco over the Gabčkovo-Nagymaros Barrage (GNB) shows this most clearly. Some background to this increasingly complex issue would be useful at this point. In 1977 the Hungarian and Czechoslovak governments signed a treaty to harness the Danube as a source of hydroelectric power by building a system of barrages between Bratislava and the Danube bend. The Danube flows through purely Slovak (formerly Czechslovak) territory for a few kilometres around Bratislava and then constitutes the international boundary between the two states until it becomes Hungarian.

In Hungary the building of the GNB increasingly became a source of concern on environmental and cost grounds; successive Hungarian governments prevaricated over what to do and then it was finally decided to abrogate the 1977 treaty unilaterally. The Slovaks, on the other hand, grew more and more interested in the GNB project and it gradually became a symbol of national pride. They were prepared to ignore the environmental arguments, though some Hungarians suspected that the real reason behind this was that it would primarily be the Hungarian-inhabited areas of Slovakia, the Žitny Ostrov (Csallóköz), that would suffer. This was hard to prove, but what is clear beyond any doubt was that the Hungarian government did not understand that solid Slovak interests were behind the GNB. These interests were bureaucratic, like the water lobby, which favoured the project because it would be able to expand its budgets, patronage and bureaucratic control; and material interests like the constructon lobby, which saw the scheme as an excellent opportunity to make money and extend its power. These interests would not be deflected by environmental arguments and the Czechoslovak federal government lacked the leverage to stop the Slovaks, particularly after 1989, when the disposition of forces in the Czechoslovak parliament favoured the blocking minorities that the Slovaks were always able to put together. Crucially, the Hungarians failed to see that once construction was begun, the project would be irreversible.

The GNB scheme was, therefore, programmed to be a major burden on Slovak-Hungrian relations from the moment of Slovak independence. It involved both legal and political issues, as well as economic ones and the two sides tended to switch to whichever line of argument suited their position the best. This was the situation in the early part of 1993, by which time the West was becoming involved. There was growing recognition within the EC that poor Slovak-Hungarian relations would be a source of continuing instability in Central Europe and, under the impact of the war of Yugoslav succession, the West began to show a degree of concern that the GNB dispute should be settled through a compromise. There was pressure on both sides to achieve this.[12]

The question of the minority in Slovakia, while not an appendage of the GNB, became entangled in it, as the Slovak government relied increasingly on the rhetoric of nationalism to bolster its position. Vladimir Mečiar, the Slovak prime minister, categorically rejected any thought of collective rights for the minority and regarded cultural and/or territorial autonomy as the first step towards separatism. He repeatedly insisted that the deputies elected by the minority were not representative of minority opinion[13] and refused to meet them. The members of the minority were

[12] The GNB project is discussed in Karoly Okolicsanyi, 'Slovak-Hungarian Tension: Bratislava Diverts the Danube', *RFE/RL Research Report*, vol.1, no.49 (11 December 1992).

[13] The election coalition of Coexistence and the Hungarian Christian Democratic Movement together gained 76 per cent of the minority vote in the 1992 elections.

also uneasy that a number of symbolic steps had been taken, which appeared to downgrade their status in the new state, notably in the refusal of the Mečiar government to appoint an ethnic Hungarian as a deputy chairman of parliament, something that had been sanctioned by many years of post-war tradition.

The language law, which gave the minority the right to use Hungarian in settlements where they constituted over 20 per cent of the population, was also thought to be in danger. Minor pinpricks, like the decision of the Slovak government to remove bilingual road-signs in the heavily Hungarian-inhabited districts of the Žitny Ostrov, were regarded as harbingers of much worse things to come. This was exacerbated by the disingenuous explanations offered for this by Slovak officialdom, namely that bilingual road-signs would confuse tourists, a point made by the Slovak foreign minister, Milan Kňažko, among others. Equally, Slovaks argued that the fate of the Hungarian minority was linked with the treatment of the Slovak minority in Hungary and then pointed to the drop in the size of the latter. Quite apart from the intellectually dubious nature of this linkage – the stability of Slovakia depended essentially on the internal relationship between the majority and the minority and not on an external condition – the degree of integration of Slovaks of Hungary was historically much more thoroughgoing than of the Hungarians of Slovakia. At the same time, and this irked the Hungarians as well, Slovak spokesmen insisted that their minority was well treated and that the democratic state of Slovakia was doing everything to give the minority all the cultural rights that were appropriate.

The attitude of the minority itself was also relevant, because their values and actions influenced the Slovaks, above all by providing a pretext for Slovak extremists to call for anti-Hungarian measures. In essence, the attitude of the minority was that it had wanted to preserve the Czechoslovak framework, because it regarded Prague as the counterweight to the Slovaks; this made the Hungarians very suspect to Slovak nationalists, although they were doing no more than formulating their own interests. With the end of Czechoslovakia, the Hungarians were very apprehensive about their future as a community in the new state and made no bones about saying so. The leader of Coexistence, Miklós Duray, was in any event a deeply detested figure among Slovak nationalists because of his clear-cut defence of the minority in the communist as well as in the post-communist period. On the other hand, it should be clearly understood that there was no wish among the Hungarians of Slovakia to rejoin Hungary. They had lived in the same state as the Slovaks since 1918 – the interlude of 1938-45 only confirmed these attitudes – and had no wish to change. In a word, their commitment to the Slovak state was evident, but in exchange, they wanted that state to accept their political right to live as cultural Hungarians. This was the nub of the difficulty for Slovak nationalists. The proposition that Slovakia was simultaneously a state of Slovaks and Hungarians was completely unacceptable to them.

Other aspects of Slovak politics were a further source of anxiety, because they tended to show a high degree of intolerance for dissent on the part of the Mečiar government, which augured badly for the mind-set needed to reach compromise on the ethnic question. Thus the decision within days of independence to clamp down on the media and the fate of the new university at Trnava, though not linked in any way to the minority problem, were regarded as negative straws in the wind in that they affected the political atmosphere.

The Mečiar government, especially Mečiar himself, insisted that the media paint a 'truthful' picture of the country and took criticism very badly. It took control of the electronic media and also moved against some print journalists.[14] The story of Trnava university was highly complex, but the political essence of the crisis was that the Mečiar government saw the new university as a centre of opposition, as a place where the supporters of liberalism had found a hiding place and was, therefore, determined to prevent this, using legally dubious instruments where necessary.[15] In a broad sense, these concerns were certainly justified. The only stable, long-term prospect for the minority lay in the evolution of a Slovak civil society prepared to accept the pre-eminence of civic over ethnic values. A press free of state interference and the freedom of the academic sector were essential in this context.

The economic prospects for the new Slovak state were widely regarded as poor and the temptation for an economically embattled Mečiar government to use the minority as a means of deflecting

[14] Details in Jan Obrman, 'The Slovak Government versus the Media', *RFE/RL Research Report,* vol.2, no.6 (5 February 1993).

[15] See Adele Kalniczky, 'Academic Freedom in Slovakia: the Case of Trnava University', *RFE/RL Research Report,* vol.2, no.11 (12 March 1993).

popular dissatisfaction was evidently strong. In addition, there were doubts about the cohesiveness of the ruling Movement for a Democratic Slovakia and fear that in that event, Mečiar would use the Hungarian minority as a scapegoat for the ills of Slovakia and as a rallying call.

On the other hand, it is worth emphasising that although many of the atmospheric factors and, indeed, some of the structural ones too were unfavourable, the Hungarian-Slovak relationship was not hopeless. In particular, mediation between the two sides had distinct chances of easing the situation. This presumably helped to explain the remarkably high number of European organisations that were looking closely at the situation.

Fortuitously Slovakia was renegotiating its association agreement with the EC – the one signed with Czechoslovakia had evidently lapsed – and Brussels was insisting on the insertion of a clause protecting the rights of minorities. The Slovak government objected strongly to the insertion of such provisions, as well as stipulations on the environment and the arms trade. They argued that special minority provisions would be superfluous, because minority rights were already protected in the Slovak constitution. This argument was completely unacceptable to the minority and did not go down too well with the EC either.

Indeed, the Slovak government revealed its general distate for Western supervision in any form over its negotiations with the Council of Europe for admission as a separate member. During a visit to Strasbourg, the leader of the Hungarian Christian Democratic Movement Pál Csáky, submitted some documents outlining the Hungarian perspective on the situation. He was severely censured for this by the Morals and Ethics Committee of the Slovak parliament, on the grounds that Csáky had given a 'one-sided view' of the situation. In effect, the Slovak side was saying that there could be only one view, the Slovak one, a position that came very close to the mind-set of democratic centralism.

The Secretary-General of the Council of Europe, Cathérine Lalumière, made it absolutely clear that the solution of the minority question was a precondition for admission to the Council. In addition, interest was also taken by the newly appointed High Commissioner on National Minorities under the ECSC, who visited both Bratislava and Budapest in February 1993. Western interest in the issue was evidently prompted by fears of fall out and the impact of the Yugoslav situation, as well as a recognition that early intervention in the Slovak case would be far more effective than waiting for the problem to deteriorate.

There was one further point in the Slovak-Hungarian relationship that, while generic to post-communism, seemed particularly acute, though it was not viewed in these terms by either party. This was the sheer inexperience of the Slovaks, which led them to make mistakes in their handling of their foreign policy. Furthermore, the relative ease of the transfer of power in Hungary meant that a cadre of experienced officials could be retained, whereas Slovakia had a twofold burden to live with in this respect. The former communist officials were suspect and many of the Slovak foreign policy specialists opted to stay in Prague rather than go to Bratislava.

The Hungarian foreign minister, on the other hand, had had well over two years to learn how to conduct a non-communist foreign policy, one that was not structured by the Warsaw Pact and Soviet interest, whereas the Slovaks had barely started. The well-publicised disagreements between Mečiar and Kňažko illustrated this most vividly. In effect, Mečiar wanted to conduct his own foreign policy, but his foreign minister refused to accede to this during the early months of the Mečiar government. This made Slovakia an unreliable and unpredictable negotiating partner, something that all the other parties found disconcerting, if not actually irritating.

Hungary and Romania

The relationship between Hungary and Romania, though less tense in 1993 than before, was troubled. Hungarian opinion had welcomed the fall of Ceauşescu and expected a marked improvement in relations and in the treatment of the minority. These hopes were dashed with the attack on Hungarians in Tîrgu Mureş in March 1990. Since then, there has been an uneasy dialogue between the two governments, frequently punctuated by official and press polemics. On the other hand, in both states the military establishments have been careful to offer assurances that disputes would not be solved by force.

In particular, both the minority and opinion in Hungary were greatly perturbed by the avowedly anti-Hungarian attitudes and activities of the extreme nationalists in Vatra Romaneasca and the Greater Romania Party. The election of Gheorghe Funar as mayor of Cluj, where 20–25 per cent of the population is Hungarian, and his announcement that public notices in Hungarian would no longer be tolerated was emblematic of this state of affairs. However, it should be noted that the situation varied greatly from town to town in Transylvania and in Timişoara, for one, inter-ethnic relations were reasonably good. In the solidly Hungarian-inhabited Szekler countries, the situation was to some extent reversed, in that Romanians felt that they were in a minority and that their culture was neglected.

Until the 1992 elections, the minority was in a most uncomfortable position, in that it was the largest opposition party in parliament, something it neither wanted nor whose tasks could it discharge. However, as one of the components of the Democratic Convention, the main opposition grouping to the National Salvation Front, the Hungarians were returned to parliament in 1992, but were only one element in the opposition, which eased their exposed position somewhat.

The elections demonstrated both the light and shade in the Romanian situation. The fact that the Democratic Convention was able to gather a fifth of the votes indicated that the beginnings of a civil society in Romania, one that would be prepared to talk to the Hungarians, were discernible, indeed, the organisation of the Hungarians, the Hungarian Democratic Federation of Romania (HDFR), campaigned in an election coalition with the Convention. On the other hand, the elections also returned the Greater Romania Party (3.85 per cent) and the Party of Romanian National Unity (7.7 per cent), Gheorghe Funar's party, as well as the Socialist Labour party (3 per cent), the last being a chauvino-communist grouping. All three were strongly nationalist and anti-Hungarian; together they came to constitute a nationalist bloc in the parliament and Ilescu's Democratic National Salvation Front tended to rely on this bloc for support.[16]

Romanian attitudes towards the minority varied considerably. By and large, it was not a salient issue in the Regat, although any potential threat to the country's territorial integrity would be treated seriously. But in Transylvania, where the proportion of Romanians to Hungarians was 5:2, the question was paramount. Large sections of the Romanian population were genuinely con-

[16] Details of Michael Shafir, 'Romania's Elections: More Change than Meets the Eye', *RFE/RL Research Report*, vol.1, no.44 (6 November 1992).

vinced that the minority was a disaffected element working to dismember the province. The votes for the extreme nationalist parties reflected this.

Underlying this fear were a number of theoretical factors. The history of the Romanian national ideology was evidently one of these and the drive for the reunification, as the Romanians put it, of three Romanian lands was a very powerful motive in the nation's modern history. The establishment of Greater Romania in 1918 was more than just the acquisition of territory, it was also a deeply felt symbolic act. Consequently, the loss of northern Transylvania in 1940 was felt as a devastating blow. This helped to explain the high profile significance given to the territorial issue by all Romanian nationalists, moderates and extremists alike. The historical experience of the creation of Greater Romania and of its traumatising quality has already been mentioned; also relevant in this connection is the weakness in Romanian perceptions of the distinction between citizenship and nationhood. For many Romanians, the thought that some citizens of Romania may not be ethnic Romanians is strange or even scandalous, an anomaly that must be corrected.

Indeed, the sanctity of Romanian territory has acquired a near-obsessive quality and the merest whisper that something might be amiss in this department is enough to send many Romanians into a frenzy. This has important results for the way in which the minority is perceived. Virtually regardless of the content of minority demands, the Romanian response is inclined to be negative and to suspect the worst of the Hungarians.

This mindset was greatly exacerbated by the propaganda of the late Ceauşescu period, which liked to use the minority as a scapegoat for any shortcomings in the country and as a way of drumming up support. The underlying argument was that as outsiders, the ethnic Hungarians were never loyal to the Romanian nation-state and were looking for the first opportunity to dismember it yet again. Propaganda of this kind found fertile soil among the largely first generation ethnic Romanian working class that moved into Transylvanian towns from the 1960s onwards.

Their integration into urban modes encountered the immediate obstacle that the towns were heavily Hungarian for historical reasons, with the result that urbanisation came to be regarded as a kind of nationalist obstacle course, the aim of which was to defeat the Hungarians by excluding them from towns. The competition for jobs, status and power similarly came to be structured by ethnic considerations. This contest has made much of the newly urbanised Romanian population and the newly elevated intelligentsia in Transylvania highly sensitive to articulations of the Hungarian culture, which were felt to be deeply threatening, because their newly acquired urban Romanian identity was structured in a very homogenising fashion. This is the constituency to which the ultra-nationalist parties address their appeal. Furthermore, because this appeal resonates in the affective dimension of the Romanian consciousness, moderate Romanians find it difficult to adopt a more conciliatory position towards the minority for fear that they would be outflanked and dismissed as traitors to the nation. This last proposition makes the achievement of the Democratic Convention all the more remarkable.

To the above should be added the general lacunae of post-communist politics – the weakness of institutions, the lack of trust, the atomisation, the propensity to ideologise all interactions and the high level of suspicion in the competition for power. For a section of the Romanian élite, consequently, all Hungarians are by definition dubious elements imbued with the aim of undermining the Romanian state and defiling its otherwise innate purity. The anthropological perspective is clearly helpful in this context, in as much as the ethnic cleavage between the two groups has acquired very strong affective overtones and has made the crossing of these symbolic boundaries extremely difficult if not actually impossible. In simple terms, effective communication between the two communities is fraught with problems of deep level misunderstandings, which both sides tend to perceive as having been generated by ill-will. The demands of purity eliminate the potential for dialogue as the space where such a dialogue might take place has been filled.

For their part, the Hungarians were not interested in redrawing frontiers and were content to live in Romania, but not on the terms they were being offered by the Romanian majority. When translated into the perspectives of the minority, the terms of coexistence were rather poor – second class citizenship, being the permanent target of Romanians suspicions and resentments, being expected to shoulder the duties of citizenship but without any of the countervailing rights and, at the end of the day, being denied the right to self-reproduction as a collectivity. While the Romanian state and its spokesmen repeatedly denied that assimilation was the aim of Romanian policy towards the minority, the terms of coexistence could, in fact, be interpreted in this way.

The Romanian constitution was expressly unitaristic, drawing on a Jacobin tradition, with the Hungarians having been relegated to minority status rather narrowly defined. Added to this, it was often difficult to validate the rights that Hungarians thought they did have. The failure of the Bucharest government to intervene in Cluj after Funar had banned Hungarian-language material being displayed in public was a case in point. Another was the prevarication of the Romanian authorities over the setting up of a separate Hungarian-language university which was regarded as tantamount to rejection of this request, although on demographic grounds the approximately 2 million Hungarians could easily support such a tertiary level educational institution. The dismissal of the ethnic Hungarian prefects in the overwhelmingly Hungarian-inhabited Szeklerland, the counties of Covasna and Harghita, and their replacement by ethnic Romanians in July 1992 was immediately interpreted by Hungarians as a direct assault on their rights. The atmosphere of tension and suspicion generated a corresponding attitude on the part of the minority. The *c.*700,000 Hungarians of the Szeklerland were in any case in the different position to the Hungarians of other areas in that their contacts with the Romanian majority were far weaker, often to the extent of barely knowing Romanian. The ground for polarisation was consequently more fertile.

It should also be understood that the minority was not a compact, homogeneous bloc in political terms, but was divided into a variety of currents. The variety was not determined solely by attitudes to the majority, but by general philosophical convictions. This variety had been recognised and the HDFR formally accepted that different platforms could exist within it. At the same time, continuous tension had left its mark on the minority and there was distinct evidence of polarisation and radicalisation among some of their members. At the Congress of HDFR in January 1993 demands for territorial autonomy were made but not endorsed, indicating that the leadership remained in the hands of the moderates anxious to avoid all-out confrontation with the Romanians. All the same, the very word autonomy was like a red rag to a bull and fed the obsessions of the Romanian extremists who would not or could not see the distinction between territorial autonomy and cultural autonomy.[17] Indeed, President Iliescu quite explicitly stated on the 23 February 1993 that ethnic autonomy on a territorial basis was unconstitutional.

In broad terms, regardless of the more hardline statements of some Hungarians, notably Bishop László Tökés who spoke of 'ethnic cleansing' being carried out in Romania, the positions of the minority had undoubtedly improved since the fall of Ceauşescu. They were now able to establish their own institutions, like newspapers and associations; in the HDFR they had an organisation to protect their interests; and they could increase their economic power through opportunities provided by the economic reform.

Finally, in their attitudes to the Hungarian state the Hungarians of Romania were less than positive. They tended to distrust Hungary and sometimes actively to dislike it. Many of them felt strangers, indeed foreigners there and resented what they regarded as ignorant and clumsy intervention by Hungarian politicians in their affairs. Above all, they roundly condemned those like Csurka who as far as they were concerned were trying to use the minority problem for their own ends, to solve questions that had nothing to do with the minority itself, like the distribution of power in Hungary. Overall, the attitude of the minority towards the Romanian state was contradictory. The Hungarians accepted it and were fully prepared to live with it; they regarded Romania as their homeland. On the other hand, they wanted a Romania that did not as yet exist, one that was tolerant of their demands and made the distinction between citizenship and nationhood. The problem for the minority was that it was neither appropriate nor possible for the Hungarians to bring such a Romanian civil society into being; that was something that the Romanians themselves would have to do.

As far as the Hungarian state itself was concerned, officialdom in particular was very cautious towards Romania. The initial mistakes of 1990 – the constant harping on the minority question by the government – were fewer, though they had not disappeared entirely. The foreign policy establishment did what it could to find a *modus vivendi* with Romania, though not with any signal success. The bilateral treaty between the two states had not been signed by the spring of 1993, although it was about three quarters

---

[17] Michael Shafir, 'The HDFR Congress: Confrontations Postponed', *RFE/RL Research Report,* vol.2, no.9 (26 February 1993).

completed; the obstacles involved in the remaining quarter turned on issues of minority protection and the inviolability of the frontiers. Likewise, the Hungarian ministry of defence was very anxious to avoid confrontation with Romania, something that was reciprocated by its Romanian counterpart. On the whole, despite press polemics – there was special concern in Romania about Hungary's military doctrine and the rearmament programme – both sides understood that it was not in their interest to allow any escalation of tensions.

The west was nothing like as deeply involved in the Hungarian-Romanian relationship as it was with Slovakia. Nevertheless, the general principles deduced from the Yugoslav crisis, that minority problems could not be allowed to fester and that the West could and should take steps to preempt any deterioration, was applied to Romania as well. In their negotiations with the EC, the Romanians found themselves pressed to include a clause on the protection of minority rights and admission to the Council of Europe was made conditional on a satisfactory solution to the issue. However, the West's leverage in Romania was smaller than in Slovakia and the Romanians were unquestionably more sensitive on the issue. The existence of a sizeable section of the élite which was actively hostile to Europe made it easier to reject such demands and, conversely, harder for those who wanted a settlement for the minority problem.

There was a marked instability in the central Danubian area thanks to the unsettled relationship between Hungary and its neighbours, between the successor states and their Hungarian minorities and between these minorities and the Hungarian state. This instability was structural and would undoubtedly persist until genuine democracy took root in all the countries concerned and a civil society, ready to engage in dialogue with the minority, was rooted throughout the area. In the interim, given the existence of politically unsophisticated populations, many of them ready to accept simple, demagogic solutions, together with politicians ready to exploit nationalism as an easy resource, conflict would continue.

The West's passivity over Yugoslavia evidently encouraged nationalists and authoritarians elsewhere in the belief that their solutions by force would be condoned. In particular, the weak acceptance of ethnic cleansing by the West served as a precedent that others were studying with care. In this respect, a firmer line from the West and reiterated insistence that it would not recognise authoritarian solutions would unquestionably help to stiffen the resolve of democrats in the area and to deligitimate authoritarianism.

The steps taken by various Western organisations to involve themselves in the relationship between Hungary and Slovakia were undoubtedly initiatives in the right direction. Even if they failed to achieve all their stated objectives, they would demonstrate to all the parties concerned that the minorities' question was viewed through new spectacles in Europe, that a majority could not oppress a minority without this being noticed and that ethnic issues nowadays were recognised as having something of an international dimension. The problem was that what might work in the case of Hungary and Slovakia, and even that was not automatic, could in no sense be transferred in the same way to other relationships. The principles might be identical, but the modalities would differ.

The West also had a role vis-à-vis Hungary, both in offering reassurances and promoting the level of security in the region and, at the same time, in making it quite clear to the Hungarian government that the distinction between citizenship and ethnicity was a real one and must be adhered to when policies towards the Hungarians of the successor states were formulated. It would be too much to expect that the Hungarian state should abandon its role towards the ethnic Hungarians entirely – after all, Ireland plays such a role towards Ulster and Austria towards the South Tyrol – but the issue is far more sensitive. On the whole, the impression created was that official Hungarian policy was more cautious than the extremes of debate, but Western influence could be used to moderate these extremes.

All the actors in this situation had a role to play and their interactions could, and often did, complicate an already complex and politically charged scene. In particular, the vexed question of autonomy and its different definitions had considerable potential to envenom relations. Autonomy can be defined as existing at three levels – individual, cultural and territorial – and different distributions of power flow from whichever level one stresses. The majorities in the successor states tended to argue that individual autonomy, the rights of citizenship, were generally sufficient for minorities and that the state would act as the guarantor of these rights, but minorities responded that individual rights did nothing for the collective reproduction of communities, above all because they saw the state as having been ethnicised in favour of the majority. The lives of communities as communities could only be secured by legal and political instruments that the majority had to come to accept as the norm.

Both territorial and cultural autonomy raise serious problems in the eyes of the majorities in the successor states, because they see the very word autonomy as the first step towards secession. There are historical precedents that can be cited to justify this approach, but the true explanation certainly lies elsewhere, in the deep-level anxieties of post-communism, about the nature of power and the weakness of institutions that might frame this power. The result is often enough a reluctance to treat problems with even a minimum of goodwill and an approach that assumes the worst.

In fact, territorial autonomy is probably a concept that is increasingly outdated. In modern states, with high levels of social mobility, ring-fencing a particular territory for the security of the ethnic group that lives there is likely to be counterproductive because it diminishes the choices and life chances of members of the minority; it creates minorities within minorities; it leaves without protection those members of the minority who live outside the main area of settlement; and it intensifies majority suspicions. On the other hand, one can understand the fears of a minority that has long felt under pressure and feels that its rights will only be protected against an ethnicised state by this kind of territorial arrangement.

The ultimate solution lies in the development of citizenship in contradistinction to ethnicity. Currently, under post-communism, there is very strong propensity to regard all rights and duties within the state as deriving from the ethnic dimension of nationhood and to ignore or downgrade citizenship. This inevitably discriminates against those who are not members of the majority and will tend to promote friction, it will lower the value of citizenship in the eyes of the minority and could lead to far-reaching disaffection. But the shift from ethnicity to citizenship will not be an easy one, because the fears to the majority will first have to be dispelled and minority demands, however reasonable they may look from outside, have the contrary result.

Various devices, like repeated assurances from the minority, in the context of the Hungarians also from Hungary and above all from the West, will certainly be helpful. The inviolability of the territorial integrity of all the states involved is essential in promoting a favourable atmosphere. In this connection, the events in former Yugoslavia, with the threat of changing frontiers and ethnic cleansing, are a source of fear for all the parties, for majorities as well as minorities, precisely because the existing order is under threat. What can be imposed on the Muslims of Bosnia-Hercegovina, who did after all constitute the largest single ethno-national community in the republic, can also become the fate of any other nation, or so it is feared. The role of the West in providing reassurances in this respect is crucial, but an acceptable solution to the Bosnian crisis would be even better. Ultimately, only a stable democratic order in all the Danubian states will successfully guarantee long term stability.

26

INTER-ETHNIC RELATIONS
IN TRANSYLVANIA
RHETORIC AND REALITY

The Romanians

The centrality of inter-ethnic relations in Transylvania is beyond dispute. But the complexity of these relations is regularly clouded by politicians' rhetoric. The reality is that neither the Romanian majority nor the Hungarian minority is homogeneous and this factor influences attitudes, political responses and behaviour.

The total population of Transylvania is over 7 million and of these somewhere around 2 million are Hungarian. But the *c.*5 million Romanians are divided in their sociological make-up. The principal cleavage is between those who have lived in the region for generations and those who migrated there after the 1960s.

This cleavage is the classical one between old-established inhabitants versus incomers. Essentially, the traditional Romanian inhabitants of Transylvania have worked out a *modus vivendi* with the multi-ethnic character of the area. This does not particularly mean that they are particularly pro-Hungarian or even necessarily sympathetic to the minority, but they are generally prepared to accept that the Hungarian presence does not challenge their ideas of what is 'normal and natural'. They constitute both the absolute and relative majority of the region. There is at the same time a small minority of the old-established Romanians that remains strongly anti-Hungarian.

Broadly, they have learned to live with the multi-cultural, multi-lingual nature of Transylvania even when they do not speak Hungarian. For the elite, it is not unusual to send their children to German-language schools, partly because the teaching is good and because this gives them access to another language.

However, this Transylvanian Romanian elite has never been particularly influential in Bucharest and its political skills, including those of dealing with multi-ethnicity, have not been all that effective, given that their cultural norms differ from those of the Regatean majority. In this sense, there is a mild cultural boundary between them and the Romanians of the Regat. They are both Romanians, but understand this identity differently. On the other hand, they will certainly not make common cause with the Hungarians over issues like territorial autonomy, which the Hungarians have demanded from time to time, for fear that autonomy would lead to separation.

For the roughly 1 million migrants, who were drawn to Transylvania during the rapid industrial expansion of the 1970s and 1980s by offers of jobs and housing, the Hungarians are a near inexplicable and alien element. Sociologically, many of the migrants are from poor rural backgrounds and have had to cross several social and cultural boundaries, from village to town, from agricultural to industrial working, from the Regat to Transylvania.

Many of them, when they arrived there from the Regat, were shocked to discover that a significant section of the population was not only not Romanian, but insisted on speaking an alien language and had very alien ways of doing things. This exacerbated the alienation that all immigrants experience and gave it an anti-Hungarian focus. The anti-Magyar rhetoric of the Ceauşescu period found considerable resonance among them.

These migrants or, by now, former migrants have a particular burden to carry. Their existence in Transylvania depended on the centre and especially on the heavy subsidies that Bucharest paid to maintain the often uneconomic industries in which they worked. They were, to that extent, an unintegrated element, sufficiently numerous to continue with their own traditions, values and aspirations. Hence the old established Transylvanian Romanians have not been able to integrate them because of their dependence on the centre and their different sociological make-up.

The collapse of 1989 has been a severe blow to the migrants, their most dependable source of support – the communist state – has evaporated as the subsidies have dried up. They lack the skills to make their way in a market-oriented world. And crucially, they lack the links with the countryside which would allow them to add to their incomes and give them access to foodstuffs, given that their villages are in the distant Regat. Hence the return of the land to the peasantry has brought them few benefits.

There is a further disadvantage in their position. The ethnic Hungarians have evolved a strategy of working in the grey economy in Hungary and, given the much higher income levels there, can make enough from four months' construction work, say, to live more than adequately in Romania. This option is generally not open to Romanians, and especially not to the Regateans, for whom the idea of working in Hungary is foreign and threatening.

Since 1989, the top élite of Regatean managers and bureaucrats has either left to return to the Regat or they have the skills and know-how to make their way in the market economy, though their formerly privileged positions have been eroded. But that leaves the great bulk of Regatean migrants in a very exposed position. They are the constituency for nationalist mobilisation and for the anti-reform line associated with former President Iliescu, who was defeated in 1996. A minority is attracted to the much more virulent nationalism of Corneliu Vadim Tudor's Party of National Unity. Gheorghe Funar's Greater Romania Party receives its support from the anti-Hungarians among the old established Romanian population. The remainder, the greater majority, voted solidly for the coalition now in power.

The Hungarians

Just as the Romanians are divided by various cleavage lines, so the Hungarians have different attitudes and sociology. Broadly, they fall into three categories: those in the overwhelmingly Hungarian areas of the Szekler lands (*c.*700,000 people); those in the mixed areas of central Transylvania (around 500,000) for whom interaction with Romanians is an everyday experience; and those from the area closest to Hungary itself (again around 500,000). This last category is closer also in culture and values to those that are dominant in Hungary. These sociological cleavages are not translated into politics; Hungarians vote solidly for the Hungarian political party, the Democratic Union of Hungarians in Romania (UDMR).

It should be stressed at the outset that Hungarians of Romania are not necessarily well disposed towards Hungary. They have been known to refer to Hungary as 'the country where the cheese is artificially enriched with vitamin C', thereby implying a claim that their Hungarian identity is far more authentic than those of Hungary itself. The political fall-out of this is important. It means that there is next to no support for reunification with Hungary. When the Transylvanians go to Hungary, they are foreigners there.

In essence, their coexistence with the Romanians and their interaction with the Romanian state – even when that interaction has been hostile – have reshaped their identity and the gap between them and Hungary is growing, while their integration in Romania is an accomplished fact. Their attitudes to Hungary are further complicated by the divergence between Hungarian nationalist rhetoric, which regards the Transylvanians as the most authentic Hungarians of all, but which becomes incomprehension or discrimination when they make demands on the Hungarian state. The attitude of the Transylvanian Hungarians to the Romanians is very similar to how the long-established Romanians see them: they accept the majority, have learned to live with them but do not warm to them particularly. In this context, the threefold internal cleavage in the minority has some political relevance in attitudes towards the Romanian majority and the Romanian state.

In the Szekler lands, the Hungarian elite has more or less reestablished the dominant position it had before the Ceauşescu era industrialisation dislodged them. The Romanian top elite has largely gone, though the middle and lower level bureaucrats have remained. The area is fully bilingual in everyday practice as well as in theory; only the institutions of the Romanian state (police, military, railways) are monolingual. In the Szekler lands, low levels of competence in Romanian are widespread and at the lower end of the social scale, knowledge of Romanian is barely necessary. All this has the further consequence that in this region, the Romanians are the minority.

In Central and Western Transylvania and situation is quite different. Here the two populations are mixed and there is competition for both real and symbolic resources. Transylvania is changing rapidly. It is no exaggeration to say that it is undergoing a second modernisation, after the failed communist modernisation. This process is uneven and uncontrolled, with pulls in different directions. The impact of the Romanian state is comparatively weak, because its capacity (financial, administrative, coercive) is low. Yet at the same time, the matrix in which they live is created by Romanian rules and legislation.

There is also the economic pull of Hungary, not to mention its cultural prestige; for all the differential already noted above, Budapest is the pivotal pole of attraction. Even more significant here is the Hungarians' own set of aspirations, their skills and their determination to keep themselves in being as a cultural community, separate from both Hungary and the Romanians.

One of the paradoxes of the present situation is that the UDMR is a member of the government; without its votes, the coalition would fall. This is effectively the first time that the Hungarians are participating in a democratically elected Romanian government. Having acquired an attitude that regards the Romanian state and government as anti-Hungarian (the legacy of the Ceauşescu and Iliescu periods), the shift is not an easy one for many Hungarians to accept.

They see their party as their protector and it is hard for them to identify the Romanian state as being actively theirs. The legacy of suspicion is deeply engrained and, at the same time, their expectations of what they can gain from participating in the government are unrealistically high. Whereas in the Szekler lands, this problem is currently not acute, elsewhere it is and it could give rise to friction if these expectations of creating a fully-fledged Hungarian existence are not met. Given the vagueness of these expectations, it is unlikely that they can be. But the central significance of these demands on the Romanian state is that the Hungarian minority in Romania fully accepts it and constructs its political life around loyalty to that state and not to Hungary.

27

HUMAN RIGHTS AND THE
NATIONALITY QUESTION IN ROMANIA

The question of ethnic rights has unquestionably reached the agenda of human rights and plays a significant role in it. In this sense, ethnicity and the ways in which it is to be approached, argued and legitimated have become a part of the broader political debate which is to be found in any polity. This involves both the question of political power and the limitations on that power deriving from the intersecting claims of groups or individuals. These questions are complicated in the area of ethnicity, because ethnic groups are widely regarded as offering alternatives to the agenda of the majority of a very high level of intensity and, indeed, ones that the majority finds it hard to encompass within its own parameters. In simple terms, ethnic minority groups – as distinct from social or economic minorities – are difficult for the majority to accommodate, because the claims of the minority appear to impinge on too many interests that the majority regards as central to its own interest, perceptions of itself and crucially its self-definitions.

This need not mean that the classical nationalist argument, that every ethno-national group must strive to express its political identity in the form of an independent state, is necessarily valid. But it does imply that ethno-national issues can prove highly intractable and remain a source of continuous challenge to both the majority and the minority. The ways in which the actual terms of accommodation will be settled will depend on contingent factors, like the readiness of the two to find common ground, the historical, social, economic, anthropological etc. characteristics of the two groups and the immediate circumstances which necessitate the settlement in the first place.

In any situation, however, where the majority takes the view that minority claims threaten its own ethnic, moral, territorial or other vital interests as defined by itself, then settlement will be near impossible. In a word, the will to do so is absent and for the majority, the cost of accommodation is higher than continued conflict. An analogous proposition can be said to apply to the minority: it may pitch its demands too high, it may insist on a definition of its political identity that genuinely does threaten the interests of the majority, e.g. by demanding that it must be (re)united with its co-nationals in another state or by adopting a set of political values that the majority finds abhorrent. In such circumstances, conflict can continue and, indeed, assume the nature of settlement: a relatively low level of conflict may actually be the least unacceptable form of coexistence for both.

In Soviet-type systems, as contrasted with liberal democratic systems, ethnic relationships are further complicated by the legacy of the homogenising character of the original Marxist-Leninist ideology. These systems find it extremely difficult to come to terms with the complexity and multiple cleavages that are generated in modern societies and with the level of choice bred by them. Indeed, they operate on a set of tacit assumptions that complexity, differences and conflict are inherently undesirable and that the task of the political order is to eliminate these, rather than accommodate them.

Matters are exacerbated by the irreconcilable imperatives of the two ideologies. At the level of theory, Marxism and nationalism are directly contradictory. Marxism insists that the individual's transcendental political (and all other) identity is determined by his class: nationalists, by contract, claim that the national identity, which is derived from culture, transcends all others. The fact that in practice Marxists and nationalists have been able to find common ground and that, to quote Ignazio Silone, 'the first thing that socialists nationalise in socialism' does nothing to undermine this proposition.

The pact with the nationalist devil

What happens in these circumstances is that Marxists in power discover that the national identities of the people they rule survive the Marxist-Leninist revolution and persist thereafter. To be able to rule effectively, they must make some concessions to nationhood, even though this ineluctably undermines the class-derived internationalist aspects of their ideology. But it does have the consequence that ruling Marxist-Leninists have, in a way, made a pact with the nationalist devil, are prepared to let their authentic credentials erode, leaving themselves exposed to being outbid by true nationalists and having to make concessions to them. Hence, as this process goes on over time, ruling Marxist-Leninists may find that nationalist elements play an ever greater role in their underlying or even explicit assumptions. This, of course, makes accommodation with ethnic minorities far more difficult, because the ruling Marxist-Leninists cannot afford to make the concessions necessary for accommodation either in terms of their own ideology or of the nationalists'.

After the takeover, the communists opted to freeze existing nations. They pursued a two-pronged policy. They formally adopted the Leninist formula of 'national in form, socialist in content', thereby accepting at best that cultural differences would survive on the road to communism, but only in as much as these cultures would gradually and inexorably become permeated by socialist values. Second, under Stalin there was a far-reaching leveling down of East European national identities and the concept of socialist internationalism was for all practical purposes used to promote a kind of rather crude cultural Russification.

In this context, the new rulers of Eastern Europe accepted that existing nations would continue in being, but the proposition that the process of nation-formation might continue and that ethnic expressions might find some kind of outlet were firmly stamped upon. It was bad enough, from this standpoint, that nations – a form of false consciousness if ever there was one – survived, but the suggestion that others might yet arise was utterly preposterous. Ironically, by adopting this position, the new rulers of the area found common ground with the nationalists, who likewise had an interest in preventing the emergence of new ethno-national cleavages.

Finally, there is a methodological point to be made here. A good deal of the literature on sub-state nationalism and ethnic cleavages tends to view these from the standpoint of the minority. Studies of this kind are often useful in emphasising how differently two communities living in the same geographical space view identical phenomena and that shared ways of life do not lead automatically to the fading away of ethno-cultural distinctions, an assumption that tends to be made, consciously or otherwise, by both Marxists and post-Enlightenment liberals. The assumptions made here are that ethnicity constitutes a constant, rather than a dependent variable and that ethnicity in a multi-ethnic situation can be understood only against the continuous interplay of contact with other group(s). Hence while there is much to be said for assessing the history, grievances, auto-stereotypes of an ethnic minority, this approach can mislead by overlooking the wider context in which these operate. Thus it is the examination of the whole matrix, especially if some or much of the political, economic and institutional agenda is set by the majority, that can offer full illumination to the characteristics of the minority.

The Romanian matrix

These preliminary propositions should be taken as the background against which the position of ethno-national minorities in Romania – Hungarians, Germans, South Slavs and others – is to be analysed. Here, the emphasis will be on Romanian-Hungarian[1] relations, not least because the Hungarian minority numbering around 2 million constitutes a significant political problem regardless of the political system in Romania and because relations between the two cogently illustrates the difficulties in reaching ethnic accommodation in Soviet-type states.

The first problem lies in the definition of the matrix of ethnic politics: the salient features of Romanian and Hungarian political and other identities that determine mutual attitudes and behaviour. The questions that bear on this are how, in the framework of these identities, the communities perceive themselves, how they formulate definitions of homogeneity, what level of political pluralism they are prepared to tolerate, what value they place on conformity to collective norms, who is accepted as having the right to determine values and agendas, whether in real or rhetorical terms, and how they relate to other issues of politics, like accountability, representation, openness and, crucially, the distribution of power. Further, having assessed these issues of self-perception, what are the cultural markers by which the two communities differentiate themselves from each other, what is it that they regard as authentic in themselves and, consequently, false in the other. Analyses of these and related questions will, in effect,

---

[1] The term 'Hungarian', unless otherwise defined, will refer in this chapter solely to members of the Hungarian minority living in Romania. When Hungarians in Hungary are being discussed, this will be clearly indicated.

give answers to what is asked, sometimes despairingly, by member of the two communities. 'How can one be Romanian? How can one be Hungarian?'

There has been very little work done on these questions, indeed the literature of the anthropology of inter-ethnic relations is rather sparse. All the same, certain tentative propositions can be made, albeit on the strict understanding that what follows is to be regarded as a working hypothesis demanding further verification. Inevitably, some of the following will be seen by some as impressionistic and general; nevertheless, I would argue that it has some validity.

The gap between Romanian and Hungarian perceptions of political power, the legitimate uses of that power and, hence, the proper role of the state as against the individual are very different and near irreconcilable. In a nutshell, whereas the relationships between the Romanian state and the individual have been generally remote, exploitative and parasitical, the equivalent relationship in the Hungarian context has not been so antagonistic or one-sided. These contrasting attitudes towards power have inevitably produced different sets of expectations and demands. Both these collective mind-sets have long historical roots.

Discontinuities in the political tradition

The concept of the state in Romanian society, then, is relatively weak and any sense of reciprocity of rights correspondingly feeble. Romanian intellectuals of the influential traditionalist and neo-traditionalist currents regard it as an article of faith that Western concepts of rights and duties, of legality and institutional practices are alien to Romanian political culture and cannot be grafted on to it for that reason.[2] This distrust of procedures and the autonomy of spheres – central in the pattern of European development – can be seen to derive from the singularly fragmented and dependent pattern of Romanian historical development.

In its post-1500 history Romania has undergone three fundamental caesuras in its cultural models and suffered a corresponding

---

[2] Keith Hitchens, 'Gîndirea: Nationalism in a Spiritual Guise' in Kenneth Jowitt (ed.) *Social Change in Romania 1860-1940*, (Berkeley: University of California Press 1978), pp.140-73. On irrationalism see also Radu Florian, 'A román társadalom marxista vizsgálata Lucreţiu Patraşcanu müveiben' (The Marxist analysis of Romanian society in the works of Lucreţiu Patraşcanu), *Korunk*, vol.40, no.4, pp.250-5.

disorientation of values. As well as having important consequences for the cohesiveness of Romanian culture, these discontinuities affected its political integrity as well. The Romanian political élite was weak and dependent for most of its modern history. No native élite proved strong enough to construct anything resembling a strong state until after 1918. Rather, both élites and people experienced fragmentation, semi-foreign exploitation and the transformation of native political institutions into alien agencies of extraction. Strength in this connection refers primarily to internal cohesion and the organisational adequacy that allows the ruler to implement his will; external strength is a matter of keeping foreign influence to a level tolerable to the polity in question. It is worth noting that Romanian complaints have tended to focus on the latter and to ignore the former.

To make matters worse, the Romanian state was divided into two political units, Moldavia and Wallachia, and both of them were subordinated to the Ottoman Empire under a peculiar system of semi-autonomous vassalage. The relationship between the sublime Porte and the satellite rulers in the Danubian provinces was essentially tributary. This encouraged the Romanian elite to concentrate on the economic exploitation of the peasantry and thereby promoted the destruction of the preexisting bonds of loyalty between them. Transylvania, which was attached to the Porte in a similar fashion, was more remote from Constantinople, had a less atomised social system and was able to sustain a much more extensive autonomy. A large part of this depended on the accident of geography that Transylvania was at the outer edge of comfortable campaigning distance and was in any case better protected by its more rugged terrain.[3]

From the sixteenth century, the traditional nobility in the Danubian provinces, the boyars, was transformed by the weight of Ottoman power from landholders into *de facto* officeholders in the mediated service of the Sultan. Status came to be associated with office; office became a matter of purchase; and to hold onto it, its beneficiaries were obliged to expand the output of grain and to recoup their outlay by exploiting the peasants, their erstwhile followers and dependants. This brought about a major shift in the relationship between rulers and ruled. It weakened or destroyed

[3] William H. McNeill, *Europe's Steppe Frontier* (University of Chicago Press, 1964), pp.101-8.

the existing bonds of loyalty and gave rise to new, exploitative codes of conduct. Moral codes and values were transformed. As far as Romanian society was concerned, the political elite, the state which it controlled and political power itself came to be seen as alien, incomprehensible and parasitical. The political forms and rituals adopted in the same period by the élite intensified this alienation. In both the Provinces, but particularly in Moldavia, the rulers established a neo-Byzantine court, incorporating both Ottoman and Hellenic elements, as well as conscious archaisms and anachronisms. Their style of rule was more and more divorced from reality. Society responded by retreating into the more transparent world of the village and ignoring, where possible, the practice of politics as an unchangeable act of nature. [4]

Discontinuity also arose through the development of religion. Religion is generally a repository and guarantor of élite and popular values. In the Western cultural context, it played a central role in sustaining the principle of mutuality of obligations between rulers and ruled. In Orthodoxy this did not happen. The seventeenth century religious upheaval in the West did not leave the Danubian lands untouched, however, and Orthodoxy in Romania was influenced both by Roman Catholic Poland and Protestant Transylvania, as well as the reformist movements in Constantinople. When the conservative faction achieved dominance in Constantinople, the Romanians accepted that reform was off the agenda; the price was paid in intellectual stultification and the shift to empty ritual as opposed to content in the practice of religion. One consequence of this was to enhance passivity in politics through the spillover from religious to political codes of behaviour. External conformity, as distinct from integrated unity of belief and action, came to be regarded as sufficient in the practice of political behaviour.[5]

The chances of sustaining a unitary political tradition were further undermined by the relative independence of the élite from the ruler, underpinned as it was by the propriety of the grain trade. This enabled different boyar factions to look to different

---

[4] *Ibid.*, pp.108-10. See also Daniel Chirot, *Social Change in a Peripheral Society: the Creation of a Balkan Colony* (New York: Academic Press 1976).

[5] Czeslaw Milosz, *The Captive Mind* (London: Secker and Warburg, 1953), Chap.3, is the classic exposition, but see also Stavro Skendi, *Balkan Cultural Studies* (New York: Columbia University Press, 1980), pp.233-57).

foreign protectors, Poland, Transylvania, Vienna or Constantinople. Loyalties were unstable, offices were bought and sold, functions were exercised largely in the pursuit of money rather than for their ostensible purpose and, with the coming of Phanariot rule, the process culminated in the emergence of a system that was corrupt, inefficient, promoted backwardness and encouraged dependence on foreign power. The decline of the Ottoman empire in the eighteen century predictably affected the Danubian lands as well. The elite now had to look to new centres of power on which to depend, and this turned out to be France. This was almost automatically followed by the discarding of neo–Byzantine patterns and the wholesale adoption of Western, particularly French, styles. The aspirations of the Romanian political class thenceforward were a derivative of modernisation as perceived at one remove, distilled from the legacy of the Enlightenment and absolutism; it was this model that they sought to implant in the very different political soil of the Balkans. It is worth noting that no other European polity underwent two such major changes in its cultural aspirations in such a short period of time. Both the shifts were radical and contributed to the dislocations and discontinuities in Romania's political traditions.[6]

The impact of modernity

The period since the early nineteenth century has brought further changes, including a third radical cultural shift, the one derived from the imposition of Marxism-Leninism, but did little to foster a closer relationship between rulers and ruled. In effect, the Romanian élite relied heavily on the bonds of nationhood to create these links and to legitimate power. Other instruments, like social justice, political participation or economic development tended to be accorded a rather secondary role. In general, the Romanian state and the exercise of political power continued to be regarded by Romanian society as alien to the concerns of the majority. The peasantry remained subject to the exactions of a state that did very little for the great bulk of the population – a contention that is borne out by the fact that Romanian was the

[6] On the weakness of the Romanian state, see also Emmanuel Turczynski, 'The Background of Romanian Fascism' in Peter Sugar (ed.), *Native Fascism in the Successor States 1918-45* (Santa Barbara, CA: ABC-Clio, 1971), pp.101-11.

scene of the last *jacquerie* in Europe, 1907. The enlargement of the Romanian state after 1918 was largely of benefit to the élite and it was noteworthy that the Regatean élite was not altogether welcoming towards the Transylvanians with their rather different, legalistic, proceduralist political culture imbibed in Hungary. The interwar state did little to promote either social integration or national integration. The gap between the élite and the peasantry remained as substantial as ever in the political arena and attempts to bridge it through the pursuit of populist ideologies were not regarded with great favour. The three-tenths of the population that was ethnically non-Romanian was given little incentive to develop loyalty to the new state, which preferred to rest its legitimacy on highly homogenising images and propositions, grounded in abstract images of Romanian nationalism.

The communist takeover and its aftermath should be regarded as the third major cultural and political caesura, one which enforced far-reaching shifts in attitudes and values. They were accompanied by rapid and deep-seated change and accelerated transformation. These were perceived as having been imposed on Romania from outside by alien agencies. Inevitably the outcome has been dislocation and a near desperate attempt to cling on to what was familiar.[7] In these circumstances, it was hardly unexpected that interpretations of these seemingly inexplicable phenomena would give rise simultaneously to passivity, the minimalism that allows individuals to survive and to a propensity to pay heed to demonologies, to look kindly on irrational explanations and to cast outsiders in the role of hostile actors. The Hungarian minority was tailor-made for this role.

The post-1945 period has seen major improvements in the ability of the state to exercise its power in institutions, organisation and communication. Yet there is very little evidence that there has been any significant shift in the direction of closer links between rulers and ruled. This was as true of the Gheorghiu-Dej period as it has been of Ceauşescu's time in power. During the latter's rule, however, there has been a conscious and deliberate return

---

[7] Michael Shafir, *Romania: Politics, Economics and Society* (London: Pinter, 1985), esp. chap.9, has been influential in shaping my thinking on these issues. Steven Sampson, *National Integration through Socialist Planning: an Anthropological Study of a Romanian New Town* (New York: Columbia University Press, 1984) is highly persuasive on these processes.

to the strategy of promoting identification virtually exclusively through the rhetoric of nationalism, laced with elements of industrial development. In general, identification with the state, as distinct from party or nation, has tended to be weaker in Romania than in other East European countries. For many Romanians, the state has remained a parasitical body and for those in office, power is to be exercised for personal advantage. The sense of *civitas*, of a community in which there is a reciprocal relationship between rulers and ruled, is feeble.

Against this background of fractured historical development which has given rise to an unusually strong and deep-rooted perception of the state as parasitical, modern Romanian political relationships have been unable to evolve towards the more organic, consensual interactions found elsewhere. Instead of identification with the state as the primary focus of politics and the primary expression of political loyalties, Romanian political culture has sought solutions to the challenges of statehood and power in the construction of systems of myths, symbols and abstractions.

As a general proposition it may be argued that where the distribution of power is severely and persistently one-sided and no possibility of correcting this is perceived, those affected will look to alternatives. These can take two broad forms. They can either focus on alternative strategies of power maximisation through exploiting the gaps in the system (no system is perfect) or they can withhold performance, opt for passivity and seek avenues of self-satisfaction outside the existing range of options. Romanian society has resorted to both of these. In general, individuals tend to distrust the exercise of political power through its legal-rational form and will look for means of personalising it, by finding connections and friends within the system. Loyalties will be vested in the local community, in networks of individuals with shared experiences, on patron-client systems and analogous interactive relationships.

The alternative strategy of symbolic and mythopoeic response to power has a long and highly persistent tradition in Romania. In particular, explanations for the irrationality and intractability of political power and powerlessness have been sought in frameworks like 'the national soul' and 'the national specificity of the Romanian people'.[8] These concepts are put forward as

---

[8] George Schöpflin, 'The Ideology of Romanian Nationalism', *Survey,* vol.20, nos.2-3, pp.77-104.

axiomatic and as not open to empirical verification. These ideas are widely accepted by a society that has been consistently subjected to processes from top down and which has not been successful in developing its own autonomous systems of power. In this sense, mythicisation has been endowed with functions in Romanian political culture that are performed elsewhere by other interactions. It serves as compensation for the sense of discontinuity and dislocation and for the failure to construct an integrated polity. Every polity uses myths and metaphors to order the chaos and conflict of politics; where Romania differs is in the imbalance between abstract and concrete, between shadow and substance.

In this situation, the role accorded to the national and the weight which the national factor is expected to bear is markedly higher than in other polities. Every nation is to an extent a myth,[9] a surrogate for the personal community that is lost with the emergence of large polities, but usually there are other institutions, crucially those transmitting the reciprocal relations between rulers and ruled, which act as alternative load-bearers for the political system. The imperative of national homogeneity, therefore, has ineluctably emerged as the pivotal structure around which the Romanian polity has been constructed. This has been exacerbated by the Ceausescu experience, which has placed virtually all its eggs in the nationalist basket. The stresses of accelerated, coercive modernisation has eroded most other instruments of mediation between rulers and ruled and has left the rulers with a near unique concentration on nationalism.

The post-war period has seen repeated attempts by the leadership to effect a breakthrough[10] to modernity. To achieve this, it has relied on a very high degree of concentration of power, on a highly reductionist definition of modernity and it has tried to legitimise this in the name of a Marxian and/or modernist utopia. Not surprisingly, the response from society has been the more or less traditional one – passivity, adaptation, exploiting the gap between formal and real the personalisation of power. It was not that the high ideals of the alternative utopias were found not credible, but rather that they only marginally affected the individual

---

[9] Benedict Anderson, *Imagined Communities: Reflections on the Origin and Spread of Nationalism*, 2nd edn (London: Verso, 1983).

[10] Kenneth Jowitt, *Revolutionary Breakthroughs and National Development: the Case of Romania 1944-65* (Berkeley, University of California Press 1971).

in his attitude towards power, given the propensity to regard all these process as abstracted from everyday reality. Nationalism was another matter, at least for a while. The mobilisatory force of the nationalist idea was genuine, given that the experience of nationhood was authentic.

The values of the minority

To complete this equation, mention should be made of the particular modes and targets of nationalism chosen by Ceauşescu. These are, as might have been predicted, highly homogeneous and exclusive. Romanianness has been defined in a very restrictive sense and non-Romanians in Romania are for all practical purposes excluded from participation in the central mystery of nationhood – the religious terminology is not accidental – by the choice of categories and language employed. In current parlance, the term 'co-inhabiting nationalities' has been quietly dropped and been replaced by 'Romanians of Hungarian mother-tongue'.[11] If this referred to citizenship, it might be an acceptable formulation, but given the weakness of any concept of membership of the *civitas*, it embodies the agenda that all Romanians should have Romanian as their mother tongue. As long as some Romanians are deviant in this respect, the perfection of Romanianness is spoiled and, hence, the Hungarians are somehow to blame. The entire campaign to promote Daco-Roman continuity, by way of example, is centered on this for its crucial argument is that the Hungarians, as later entrants to Transylvania, cannot in any sense have the same rights there as the (real) Romanians.

The presence of the Hungarians in Transylvania is, therefore, a highly unwelcome obstacle to the achievement of this ideal of homogeneity. It brings Romanians face to face with the fact that their society is not as they imagine it should be. For there should be no misunderstanding of the depth and extent of the differences between Hungarians and Romanians in a wide variety of fields. Some analysts have argued that the two ethnic groups have much in common,[12] especially because their ways of life are similar, if

[11] See the interview with Károly Király, *East European Reporter,* vol.2, no.3 (1987).

[12] Hugh Seton–Watson argues this is *Eastern Europe between the Wars* (London: Archon, 1962), p.308, though not in materialist terms; he bases his argument

not actually identical. The trouble with materialist arguments of this kind is that they are reductionist and seek to arrive at a conclusion by considering only one sphere of human existence, the economic. Consequently, a wide range of other experiences, which are equally authentic to both groups, are ignored or subordinated to the economic or dismissed as 'irrational'.

The Hungarians, for their part, have undergone a very different set of political experiences and have emerged with a political culture that sets them apart from the Romanian majority in numerous significant ways. Most importantly, the Hungarian attitude towards political power is closer to the Western concept, albeit in its Central European variant. They have a long tradition of nobiliary, legalistic politicising, coupled with the memory of having held political power.[13] This memory does not, as such, attach to the Hungarian state, but to Transylvania itself and to the very particular institutions developed there, like religious toleration. It may be questioned to what extent this tradition remains in being, given the passage of time and the absence of educational institutions to transmit these traditions. Presumably, some transmission takes place through the usual informal agencies of socialisation. Later political experience, between the wars and after 1945, will have transformed these memories and most importantly have enhanced differentiation vis-à-vis the Hungarian state. This should not be taken to mean, however, any significant dilution of that separateness. The lesson that seems to be drawn from the Hungarians' political experience of Romania is that in order to remain Hungarian, one should persist with a Hungarian approach to politics, looking for institutional and legalistic action.

Thus the fragmentation that marks Romanian political culture is less salient among Hungarians. Institutions of power may be viewed as exploitative and parasitical, but on the whole they are not regarded as alien, hence the potential for establishing control and transparency over power is seen as real. A belief in the reciprocity of rights has led the Hungarians to harbour expectations of the state. From this it follows that the dominant response to powerlessness is not abstraction and mysticism, but is much more

---

primarily on shared cultural traits.

[13] See Katherine Verdery, 'The Unmaking of an Ethnic Collectivity: Transylvania's Germans', *American Ethnologist*, vol.12, no.1 (February 1985), pp.62-83.

participatory. This approach is underpinned by the Hungarians' religious tradition – Western Christianity – with its emphasis on internalisation and the integration of belief and action. Equally, having to an extent shared in the Enlightenment, Hungarians place greater value on the role of reason in politics and tend to dismiss the cult of irrationality with bewilderment.[14]

The differences do not, however, end with political culture, but affect a wide range of expectations in other spheres. Thus, by analogy, if the Romanians' expectation is that a system is unreal and inauthentic and exists to be exploited, the Hungarian approach is to assume that there will be at least enough correspondence between system and reality to make the former worth taking seriously. In this particular context, both parties to the transaction will emerge with diminished views of the other, for both will be deviant in terms of the social codes which are supposed to regulate such exchanges.

The agenda of late Ceauşescuism

The foregoing is the background against which late communism should be assessed. In the 1970s and 1980s, the fate of the Hungarians increasingly came to be perceived as a case of straightforward human rights oppression and discrimination. As suggested, the issue was more complex and more subtle and demanded understanding of the matrix of Romanian politics at greater depth. To start with, the very category of human rights involved and involves different perceptions by the two communities. Spokesman for the Hungarians, deriving their views from a Hungarian political context, have been inclined to argue that human rights constitute a universal cultural and political category and they seek to legitimate their demands accordingly. To the Romanians the situation looks different. The agenda of human rights in their perception tends to focus on formal rather than substantive issues. They preferred to insist that constitutional provisions give the minority ample rights: that Hungarians were adequately represented in Romanian institutions; that educational provision was fully appropriate to the needs of the minority, in as much as there are numerous

---

[14] The present author recognises that he is imposing a degree of homogeneity on the Hungarian community that it does not have in real life. This assumes that the general picture of Hungarianness as mediated by the Hungarian intelligentsia has found a broad general acceptance among the entire Hungarian community.

schools which are called 'Hungarian', and that Hungarian-language publishing was generous. Equally, the Romanian position placed great emphasis on legitimating the present in terms of the past. Daco-Roman continuity was put forward to support the argument that as first comers to the area, the Romanians notionally have full power to arrange the terms of the political and cultural agendas according to Romanian criteria. Second, Hungarian behaviour before 1918 and during the period of 1940-4 when the Hungarian state had reannexed Northern Transylvania was so evil that, implicitly, the Hungarians today should be grateful for the generosity shown to them by the Romanian state.[15] Hungarian counter-claims are mischievous, ill-intentioned, 'fascist' or open to any other labelling that seems suitably denigratory in the context.

What underlies these assertions is the sense that, in all these matters what the Hungarians are claiming is irrelevant, that formal provision is meaningless, that 'real life' lies elsewhere and that the state system is not a valid category where culture is concerned. Autonomy is not a concept that has much meaning in this connection. For the Hungarians to rely on formal legality or to demand political rights has limited reality in the Romanian matrix.

The Hungarian argument, therefore, can never actually match what the Romanians say, given that what has arisen is a classic dialogue of the deaf. Yet in all this there was and is a genuine political conflict that cannot find any simple solution. The Hungarian minority has become a focus of political power and that political power has been exercised for the most part without much control by them. In the Ceaușescu period, Romanian society, regardless of ethnicity, underwent a steady and inexorable loss of power even over its intimate environment as the state became ever more intrusive. It inevitably clung on to its national identity as a means of making sense of everyday reality and consequently the allusive 'anti-alien' propaganda of the state tended to fall on receptive ground. By the same token, the minority has sought

---

[15] Cornelia Bodea and Virgil Candea, *Transylvania in the History of the Romanians* (Boulder, CO: 1982) is an example of the former; Mihai Fatu and Mircea Musat (eds), *Horthy-Fascist Terror in Northwestern Romania, 1940-44* (Bucharest, 1986) falls into the latter category. Note that the title of this book avoids using term 'Transylvania' and prefers 'Northwestern Romania', presumably because the word 'Transylvania' conjures up an image of a multinational culture, while the latter implies homogeneity.

to deal with the impact of the state by maximising the resources it could muster through rallying around its ethnicity.

The agenda of the Ceauşescu period can be summarised in these terms. The Hungarian ethnic community, by reason of its differentness, was deviant and constituted an obstacle to the purported ideal of a modern, strong, respected Romania. Hence the fact that it found and finds itself used as a diversionary target by the leadership, an instrument for discharging the tensions that have accumulated, was perfectly appropriate. Allusive reference to the minority can and could be used to deflect criticism of leadership failures. Even if these are not fully credited by the Romanian ethnic community, they will be partially accepted as a component of the mythopoeia and demonology that fed what passed for political discourse in Ceauşescu's Romania. The Hungarians were also useful as a means of defining the Romanians' ethnic identity at a time when other markers, above all the Soviet Union, could not be used. The Hungarian presence, in this fashion, went a part of the way towards underpinning Ceauşescu's authority, which suffered a growing decline once he began to move towards greater compliance with the Soviet Union in the late 1970s and early 1980s and his strategy of rapid modernisation was seen to have failed. Similarly, the presence of the Hungarians allowed and allows the Romanian state to promote myths of conspiracy, again by allusion, to the effect that 'the aliens' were undermining the great Romanian project, essentially by their very presence. Thus the role and function of the Hungarian minority is that of a scapegoat.

At the same time, however, the Hungarians are, in an authentic, as distinct from a mythopoeic way, also a genuine alternative and constitute a danger for those who seek to define the Romanian agenda in the most restrictive fashion.[16] This alternative exists at several levels. At the simplest, it is the myth of the prosperity of the Hungarian state, with which, of course, the ethnic Hungarians are automatically associated (regardless of what their real loyalties might be). Given the four decades of privation suffered by Romanians under communism, the knowledge – probably exaggerated through rumour – that next door, under a similar political system, Hungary created a system that provided ample food was

---

[16] Ion Lăncrănjan, *Cuvint despre Transilvania* (Discourse on Transylvania), 1982, is a good example of this.

deeply unsettling. It was bound to lead to envy and resentment directed against the Romanian state and the minority. Second, the Hungarians are visibly and palpably different. When Regateans arrive in Transylvania they immediately notice this and respond to the relative alienness of the environment by attaching the blame to the Hungarians.

Third, for at least a section of the Romania intelligentsia, Hungary and the Hungarians played a contradictory role of being more Western, of being a channel through which Western ideas have reached Romania. There is a feeling, exaggerated no doubt, that at a time when Romania is suffering the miseries of late Ceauşescuism, Hungary has become a land of liberalism, openness and, in effect, a desirable myth-land. Again, the resentments that ensued impinged on the minority, which was regarded as the repository of the Hungariannes and the corporeal symbol of the Hungarian state in Romania.

Finally, in this broad area, the connection with Hungary did, in fact, have its impact on a section of the Romanian nation – the Romanians of Transylvania. There is an argument to be made that the Romanians of Transylvania constitute a suppressed and invisible minority. They were attached to the Romanian state after 1918, but had precious little impact on the form of state organisation and the political culture that evolved there. Indeed, it seems likely that since 1918, Transylvania has experienced a continuous net transfer of resources to the Regat, receiving very little in return. It may be that the Transylvanian Romanians are content with this, but there is no way in which this can be tested. Fragmentary and anecdotal evidence points in the opposite direction.[17] From the standpoint of the majority, however, the Hungarians can be blamed for the differentness of the Transylvanian Romanians, they can bear the responsibility for having diluted the integrity, homogeneity and unity of the Romanian nation.

The Hungarian dilemma

The state of affairs under Ceauşescu confronted the Hungarians with a major dilemma, on the other hand. Their possible agendas were stark. They could try to continue with sustaining a culturally

[17] The anonymous letter from an ethnic Romanian from Transylvania, in *East European Reporter*, vol.2, no.3 (1987), illustrates several of these points.

Hungarian way of life. This was increasingly regarded as impossible, except at the lowest level of the social scale. It was still feasible to live as a Hungarian, if one's demands on the state were kept to a minimum and contacts were scaled right down. Even then it was difficult to avoid the impact of the all-intrusive state, through the instruments of coercion, the state as sole employer, the state administration, the state as educator and as health care provider, as controller of the mass media and so on. In all these fields, the symbolic emphasis is against Hungarianness and in favour of individuals abandoning their ethnic distinctiveness. Centrally, the strategy of the Romanian system appeared to be directed at destroying what had hitherto been the natural and accepted process of upward mobility within the Hungarian community – this is feasible with a community the size that it is – and ensuring that upward mobility became equated with the adoption of Romanian culture. In this way, Hungarianness was accorded negative connotations by the system and numerous obstacles were placed in the way of sustaining it, let alone developing it. The blocking off of contact between the Hungarians of Romania and the Hungarian state, regarded as the most important generator of Hungarian cultural values, was an obvious move in this context. The fragmentation of the cohesiveness of the minority was another. To this end, Romanians were encouraged to settle in ethnically homogeneous Hungarian areas, whilst ethnic Hungarians who succeeded in acquiring tertiary qualifications were urged to settle outside the areas of Hungarian settlement.

The second possible strategy was assimilation. But this was not quite as straightforward as it might appear. The cost of assimilation for Hungarians was and is very high. It involved not merely learning Romanian, which most educated Hungarians have done anyway, but it meant abandoning one set of cultural codes in favour of another set, perceived as alien. What a Hungarian has to give up in order to become Romanian is, in the light of the foregoing, far-reaching, humiliating and affects deeply ingrained notions of ethos, world-view, and their sense of what is proper and improper, of what is culturally pure and impure. All this is further complicated by relatively hazy perceptions of whether or not the Romanian majority would countenance assimilation; what degree of loyalty it would demand from those who have assimilated; in all, what the terms of loyalty are. There is no question that ideas of two-tier ethnicity – Romanian for certain purposes, Hungarian for others – is absolutely unacceptable to the majority. For a Hungarian to be accepted as having assimilated, loyalty must be seen to be total; even speaking Hungarian can become a symbolic acting out of disloyalty in the eyes of Romanians.

The third option is emigration. This was a major issue, particularly for the minority intelligentsia for some time. Only in the mid-1980s did it begin to affect the mass of the population. Significant numbers of Romanian citizens emigrated through Yugoslavia and there was fragmentary evidence that the number of ethnic Hungarians among them is disproportionately high. They were looking to emigrate to Hungary or to the West. The Romanian authorities might have found this option acceptable, at any rate for intellectuals, but are less compliant with respect to other Hungarians, whose labour and skills they need. Besides, accepting that Hungarians could emigrate raises the deeper question of the acceptability of the Romanian state among ethnic Romanians. There have been stories of ethnic Romanians attempting to prove that they were Hungarian because they thought they might be able to emigrate as a result. Many of those who publicly supported Paul Goma in 1978 did so for this reason; the implication is that emigration was a desirable option for Romanians and Hungarians alike, which suggests that mass Hungarian emigration could have had a demonstration effect which would certainly have been unpopular with the state.

While the outlook for the Hungarians remained bleak as long as the overall political situation in Romanian was poor, in a word while Ceauşescu was alive, the longer outlook term perspective had two aspects. After Ceauşescu's demise, his successors inherited a demoralised, hostile, sullen and apathetic population, which regarded all political power with suspicion. In this situation of weakness, any post-Ceauşescu leadership had to neutralise hostility and look for support wherever it could be found. Here, abjuring the manifestations of Ceauşescuist absurdities in the promotion of nationalism might have been a relatively easy way of attracting tolerance from the Hungarians. This would have had the added benefit of gaining some goodwill from the Hungarian state. On the other hand, the underlying imperatives of Romanian-Hungarian relations as sketched in this paper – and it should be stressed again that many of the hypotheses advanced do require verification

– imply that inter-ethnic contact between the two will be fraught with difficulties for a long to come, until such a time, in fact, as the political, economic, legal and other cultural attributes of the two ethnic communities begin to find some form of mutual accommodation. In temporal terms, we are in the realm of the Greek kalends.

INDEX

Åbo Akademi, 235

Aden, 137

Åland Islands, 132, 228, 233, 284

Albania, Albanians: 67, 134, 239; Kosovo Albanians and the Serbs, 64, 250, 261, 268, 271, 286; and the myth of Kosovo, 92; in Macedonia, 126, 226, 268, 271; Greeks of, 262; under Yugoslvia, 360, 363-4

Alexander, King of Yugoslavia, 347-8

Alsace, 45

'*alter ego*', 269-70

American English, 225

Anglo-Saxon: thought-styles, world-view, 7-8, 10, 51, 228, 300, 305; 'universalism', 8; citizenship, 52; and commemoration, 74; and Protestant value system, 178-9; model of democracy, 184-5, 276

animals rights, 17

Antall, József: 371, 375, 377, 386-7; use of myths, 85

anti-democratic movements, 189-207

apartheid, 229

Apollinaire, Guillaume, 75

arbitration, 274

Arendt, Hannah, 100-2, 106, 112

assimilation: 19-27 *passim*, 272-3, 190-1; of rural populations, 19-22; and Third World migrants, 22-3; of European migrants, 23-4

Australia, 275

Austria: 206, 275; as kin state to South Tyrol, 239, 292, 407; Hungarians in, 371

Austria-Hungary: 44, 138, 140-1; disintegration of, 91, 137, 370

Austro-Marxism, 11-12

authoritarianism, rise of, 189-207

autonomy, 283-5

Azeris, and Iran, 140

Balkans, myth of military valour, 95

Baltic cities, ethnic diversity of, 237

Bangladesh, 265

Basque country, 13, 59, 132, 232, 329

Belarus, 22, 44, 183, 185

Belgium: 46, 59, 125, 132, 233, 275; empire, 137

Bohemia, Bohemianism: 120; and the Czech lands, 224

Bolsheviks, 148

Bosnia: 67, 72, 107, 134, 207, 232, 270, 275, 332, 342, 362, 392, 409; war in, 61, 62, 293; under Austria-Hungary, 139; Muslims myths and relations to the Serbs, 88; Muslims under Yugoslavia, 359-60

Bourdieu, Pierre, 6, 16

Bratislava: 160; ethnic composition, 251-2

'Brazauskas' effect, 199

Brezhnev, Leonid, 145

Britain: 5, 32-3, 51, 206, 267, 333; Scotland, 5, 19, 51; multicultural policies, 24-5; England, 44, 55, 311-323; Wales, 60; emphasis on tradition in 1950s and 1960s, 85; Commonwealth and Empire, 137, 140, 141

Brittany, 19

Brubaker, Rogers, 2

Bulgaria: 63, 69, 185, 344; and Turkish minority, 134, 226, 234, 262, 274; and Pomaks, 262

Canada, and Quebec, 65, 261, 307-8

Catalonia, 16, 19, 59, 132, 207, 231, 257, 284, 329

Catholicism: 345; in post-communist Central Europe, 105, 178, 193; Counter Reformation, 332

Ceauşescu, Nicolae, 124, 162, 246, 279; and Hungarian minority, 385-6, 400, 402, 411, 423-5, 430-3

Celtic mythology , 90